Part I. Win...

Chapter 1

Mellstock Lane

...dwellers in a wood, alm...
...has its voice... as well as its...
...of the breeze the fir-trees...
...ingly than they rock: the holl...
...itself; the ash hisses amid...
...its flat boughs rise...
which ...the bole of such tree...
does not destroy their individual tou...

ash

Historical Marginalia

THE A–Z OF GREAT WRITERS

TOM PAYNE

Colour
Library
Direct

Contents

Acknowledgments

This book would have been impossible without masses of help and support from a number of friends. These days few people, if any, can be said to carry around enough information in their heads to write such a work: I am certainly not one of them. I am therefore indebted to a number of heads for their wisdom, insight, and wide reading.

First of all I must thank my flatmates, Sarah-Jane Barton, Helen Brown and Laurence Howarth. They have answered awkward questions at all times of day and night, have shared with me their thoughts, notes, essays and libraries, and (most draining of all) have lived with the project from beginning to end. Their patience was vexed only when I tried to tell them how patient they all were. They made my task much easier than it might have been. In addition, the help of Murrough O'Brien has been unbelievable. I have had constant recourse to his astonishing range of knowledge and formidable memory: many of his thoughts have been so clearly formed that they appear here as little altered as possible.

Erik Gray and Matthew Hawkes have rescued me on several occasions, providing extensive help with a number of authors about whom they know more than any reference book. They head the list of people who have been ready with help and on-the-spot critiques of texts I must get around to reading. Without them, it reads, from A–Z: Roshini Aluwihare, Dr. Chris Ball, Poonam Brah, Judith Brierly, Sorcha Carey, José Charbit (the patron at Meaulnes Restaurant), Toby Clements, Dr. Geoffrey Day, Neil Day, James Elias, Matthew Fleggson, Tim Gordon, Simon Kirrane himself, Mark Latham, Mary Longden, Jonathan Mayor, Sara Owen, Martin and Petronel Payne (my parents), Charlie Raworth, Chris Waitt and Berni Zanzmer. To them all I owe large thanks and drinks. The responsibility for such gaffes and errors of judgement as this book might contain is mine, not theirs.

Simon Kirrane edited The A–Z of Great Writers with an extraordinary calm, keeping the whole project at once professional and fun. It's been quite a feat, and I am very grateful.

Introduction

Each entry in *The A–Z of Great Writers* has been an attempt to answer the question, "Why should I read this author?" The book's format aims to plead the writers' cases as appealingly as possible, by providing a list of their major works, a telling quotation whether it be by or about them, a brief survey of their careers and importance, and finally an illustration. The ensemble should make even the briefest flip through the book reveal the range of writers and work represented.

But a book can only have so many pages. Any restriction on the number of writers included risks raising charges of setting up a "canon" – a privileged group of scribblers whose work is prized to the exclusion of all others. Nothing could be further from the intention here, where voices from a wealth of traditions compete with those who reassess or even reject tradition itself. Yes, there are 389 writers, and they are all imaginative ones. Where a very few better known as philosophers (and one, Herodotus, as a historian) have appeared, it is for the character of their writings more than the doctrines they contain. And yes, there are cultures into which research has yet to make its fullest impact on an English language readership. Moreover, the attention on individual writers has meant less emphasis on the world's oral epics, collections of culture-defining verse or prose from the Bible to the Bhagavadgita.

Still, the list of names should introduce new and surprising figures, just as it did to the author. Omissions are always regrettable; but even the more controversial decisions and judgements made in these pages can only hope to provoke debate among book-lovers, rather than provide the last word on world literature. Ultimately, I hope that the sheer range of people, working in all literary genres, from all over the world, and from all ages from the undatable Homer to our own progressing times, will excite the reader into finding out more, and into making his or her own discoveries, even beyond the work discussed here. No book exists independently of other texts; one book leads to other books, and this one hopes to lead to many. If it encourages more people to read more, *The A–Z of Great Writers* will be doing its job – it already has for me.

Tom Payne.

TOM PAYNE
LONDON, 1997

Aeschylus

born Eleusis 524/5 BC; died Sicily 456 BC

Zeus directed mortals to believe in the law, to hold sacred: suffering teaches.

AGAMEMNON

THE LITTLE WE know of Greek tragedy before Aeschylus suggests that he transformed it completely. Previously, dramatic spectacles would consist of a character simply telling a story with a chorus commenting on it. Aeschylus introduced the possibility of a second character and defined the conventions of dialogue.

Despite these innovations, which were to prove so influential on a later generation of playwrights, **Sophocles** and **Euripides**, Aeschylus was viewed by them as a traditional figure. His pompous language comes in for some particularly irreverent treatment at the hands of **Aristophanes** in his play *Frogs* – although the younger playwright does at least allow Aeschylus the defence that his characters were noble enough to carry off such rhetoric.

Born in Athens when it was still ruled by tyrants, Aeschylus witnessed the gradual flourishing of democracy and remained a fierce patriot throughout his life. He fought against the Persians at Marathon in 490 BC and possibly at Salamis in 480 BC. The victory at the latter is described in a lengthy messenger speech in *The Persians* – a play in which the dramatist's natural sympathy for the underdog is tempered by austere warnings against the sin of pride.

This religious theme dominates Aeschylus' work, notably in his most famous series of plays, *The Oresteia*. This is the only complete trilogy to survive from Ancient Greece. It follows the moral contortions of Orestes, who must avenge his father by killing his mother. The climax, a court case in which Athena sits as judge and the Furies prosecute the hero, is a call for devotion both to civic and divine justice. It is believed that Aeschylus had been admitted into the religious "mysteries" of his native Eleusis and even revealed them in his plays, although no-one can agree on exactly where.

Although Aeschylus' verse is no longer what we expect from the theatre, it manages to sustain tension through simple plots and the gravity and grace of his language, in which the sublime can be balanced by pithy truths. For all this, his own epitaph fails to mention such literary achievements, recalling instead his patriotic service to the state in battle.

Akhmatova

ANNA

born Odessa 1888; died Moscow 1966

Will I melt away in an official hymn?

Don't bestow, don't bestow, don't

* bestow on me*

A diadem from some dead brow.

Soon I will need a lyre,

But that of Sophocles, not Shakespeare.

At the threshold stands – Destiny.

POEM WITHOUT A HERO,
TR. JUDITH HENSCHMEYER

LIKE MANY 20TH-CENTURY Russian writers, Anna Akhmatova's life and work is bound up with the political upheavals of her country. These events could not fail to touch her and their impact meant she produced consistently personal poetry. This won universal affection for her writing and many of her compatriots can recite her poems by heart. In her last long poem, *Requiem*, she justly declared herself the "voice of the Russians".

Yet this was true even before the 1917 Revolution. In 1910 she married the poet Nikolai Gumilev and became involved in the literary debates of the day. In a bid to break away from symbolism and to describe real experience, the two of them formed the Acmeist group with **Mandelshtam**. But it wasn't until *Evening*, Akhmatova's first mature collection, that she found her own voice and verse form. These often tragic reflections on love are delivered in a direct and unclichéd language. It sold out instantly.

Despite attempts to remain neutral to the new Soviet order, she could not remain indifferent for long. Her by then ex-husband was shot as a counter-revolutionary in 1921 and because of her association with him she was unable to publish anything between 1923 and 1940. In 1946 Stalin's culture minister, Zhdanov, denounced her as "both a nun and a whore who combines harlotry with prayer". From then until Stalin's death in 1953, she was officially silenced. She tried to secure the release of her son, who had been arrested in 1949, by writing in praise of Stalin. But this was to no avail until 1956, when Khrushchev was in power.

During this time she worked on *Requiem*, a lament for Stalin's victims, and *Poem Without a Hero*, which occupied her for the rest of her life. The latter reflects the era's complexities, beginning with a poets' love-triangle, moving with a frustrated longing toward its ending, a vision of camps in Siberia.

By the time of her death, she was honoured throughout Europe, and had inspired a new generation of Russian poets, outliving many of those who had persecuted or loved her.

Alain-Fournier

HENRI-ALBAN born La Chapelle d'Angillon 1886; died Les Éparges 1914

As the day draws to a close, while I long for it to end, there are men who have invested in it all their hopes, all their love, the last ounce of their strength. There are men at the point of death, and men facing an overdue note, who are praying that tomorrow may never come. Others know they will wake up with a feeling of guilt. Some are so tired that this night will never be long enough to give them the rest they need. And by what right do I, who have wasted this day, make claims on tomorrow?

LE GRAND MEAULNES, TR. FRANK DAVISON

ALAIN-FOURNIER was the pseudonym of the French prose writer Henri-Alban Fournier, whose death during the battle for the Meuse in 1914 robbed the literary world of an especially lyrical and poignant storyteller.

During his short life he worked as a literary journalist, in Paris and briefly in London. By the time of his death, at 27, he had accumulated a only a slight *oeuvre*, comprising a few short stories, letters, which have been published in four volumes, and a novel, *Le Grand Meaulnes*, which made his name.

Alain-Fournier shares many traits with the novel's narrator, François Seurel. Both are sons of schoolmasters; both come from the same area (the Cher *département*); and both became passionately devoted to a girl named Yvonne.

The tale is remarkable for the mystery it instils in ordinary things and for the secrecy with which the characters conduct their lives. A strong sense of place illuminates its happenings, as do the changing seasons, which provide the *mise en scène* for this story of French boyhood and young love. All these have ensured the book's wide appeal, not just to adolescents, but to generations of readers in France and beyond. The hero's name has even been taken by a Paris restaurant.

Alain-Fournier's poems and short stories were collected under the title *Les Miracles* in 1924. His correspondence has also appeared posthumously.

Alcott

LOUISA MAY   born Germanstown, Philadelphia 1832; died Boston 1888

"My lady," as her friends called her, sincerely desired to be a genuine lady, and was so at heart, but had yet to learn that money cannot buy refinement of nature, that rank does not always confer nobility, and that true breeding makes itself felt in spite of external drawbacks.

GOOD WIVES

LOUISA MAY ALCOTT is still chiefly remembered as a charming writer for children. She was born in Germanstown, Philadelphia, USA, and educated at home by her father Bronson, who belonged to a radical, vegetarian group of philosophers known as the Transcendentalists, and counted **Emerson** and **Thoreau** among his closest friends. For all this, Alcott wrote as a practical matter, about the things that happened around her.

Like **Whitman**, she worked helping the wounded in the American Civil War, on which experience she based *Hospital Sketches*. She returned to a hungry brood of sisters and began writing to support them. This became considerably easier after the success of *Little Women*, published in 1868. The book centres on the four daughters of Dr March, and their mother's difficulties raising them in the absence of a father. Alcott casts herself as the gamine Jo, and much of this and subsequent books reflect incidents in her life: the joy of first appearing in print; the family amateur dramatics; and the loss of a sister (in literature as in life she was called Beth). The family's history unfolds beyond this account of girls becoming women, to bring us to a time when Jo, herself, has children.

Her work has been an inspiration to female writers ever since, including **Joyce Carol Oates**, and she was an indefatigable campaigner for women's rights and universal suffrage. Recently, interest in her range has taken a turn, after the publication in 1995 of *The Chase*, a steamier tale of love and cruelty, subtitled *A Long and Fatal Love Chase*.

Amis

KINGSLEY

born London 1922; died London 1995

His mouth had been used as a latrine by some small creature of the night, and then as its mausoleum. During the night, too, he'd somehow been on a cross-country run and then been expertly beaten up by secret police. He felt bad.

LUCKY JIM

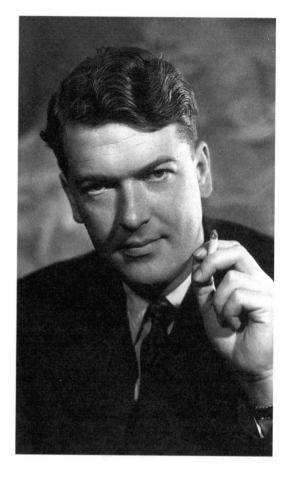

KINGSLEY AMIS BEGAN his literary career as a poet. His use of metre and rhyme resemble that of his great college friend Philip Larkin, with less forceful content. He published four volumes and continued to write verse throughout his life; but it was his novels that caught the public's attention.

His first book remains, for many, the best. *Lucky Jim* is dedicated to Larkin, and has spawned many subsequent campus novels by the likes of **David Lodge** and Malcolm Bradbury. It follows a young lecturer, Jim Dixon, who is anything but lucky in formative encounters with faculty politics and girls. The narrative pokes fun at the foibles and pretensions of academics and their minions, while exploring the different things love means to men and women. It is cherished for its knockabout humour and sustained prose, blending **Wodehouse** situations with a realism characteristic of the immediate post-war period. (Amis fought in the Second World War, and held university posts at Swansea, Princeton and Cambridge).

The put-upon, hapless hero reappears again and again in Amis' stories, sometimes retaining the name Jim, as in *That Uncertain Feeling* and *I Like it Here*. Although primarily comic, his writing began tackling more controversial themes (religion, impotence and madness among them) and his work increasingly divided his reading public, especially after the publication of his misanthropic diaries.

For all his flamboyance and avowed fondness for alcohol, Amis was a disciplined writer, setting himself to produce 500 words a day. Early in his career he was counted with the Angry Young Men, and as an old one maintained a political conviction untempered by political correctness, which was warmly satirised by Stephen Fry in *The Hippopotamus* (1994).

Andersen

HANS CHRISTIAN

born Odense 1805; died Copenhagen 1875

To bright-eyed children row on row

Enraptured by your fancies you

Are all the magic they need know

To make a story wonder-true

ELIAS LIEBERMAN,
STORY-TELLER'S MEMORIAL, ON THE
STATUE OF HANS CHRISTIAN ANDERSEN IN
NEW YORK'S CENTRAL PARK

ANDERSEN WROTE PROLIFICALLY in almost every genre, but his immortality derives from the 168 fairy tales he wrote for children. These have been translated into more than 100 languages.

The stories were most often Andersen's own, although some came from history, and others he had heard in the oral tradition that flourished during his Danish boyhood. His tellings and retellings were aimed as much at adults as at younger readers (or listeners), and all come with instructive morals. Often the point of a story is that we should look to the little things: the steadfast toy soldier whose bravery comes from knowing his place and still standing his ground; the ugly duckling from whose scruffy smallness a swan grows; the frog who successfully courts the princess; or the child who is the only one in his land with the temerity to point out that the emperor is utterly naked.

The stories appeal to children with their simple style, free use of conversation and occasional infantile diction. Andersen considered them to be of two types: *eventyr*, in which magic would sway a tale's outcome, and *historier*, where events would be more controllable. Even then, there would be a fair representation of talking animals.

In his time, Andersen was almost as well-known as a travel writer and he began composing the *Fairy Tales Told for Children* while in Italy, which also provided the setting for his novel, *The Improvisatore*. He felt comfortable travelling throughout Europe, visiting almost every country in it, and stayed with **Dickens** for five weeks on a trip to England. It was only towards his death, however, that his fellow Danes recognised his talent for storytelling and came to love him as their national author.

Andrić

IVO   **born Travnik, Bosnia 1892; died Belgrade 1975**

With these stories about what might have been, but never was, which was often lovelier than all that has been, he sheltered, as it were, from the everyday "reality" around him. Thus he avoided living, and tricked his fate. Now he has been lying in the graveyard on Alifakovac nearly 50 years; but he still lives on from time to time, here and there, as a story.

A STORY, TR. CELIA HAWKESWORTH

IVO ANDRIĆ WAS A MEMBER of the Young Bosnia Movement, implicated in the assassination of Archduke Franz Ferdinand in 1914. His subsequent three years in prison convinced him that fanatical causes were futile and his writing life was spent reconciling the disparate elements of East and West, as well as the religious divisions of his country.

He did this in short stories and novels, which read more like series of connected incidents or characters than well-made plots. *The Bridge on the Drina* examines the people living near or dying on the bridge at Visegrad and won him the Nobel Prize in 1961 – the only time it has been awarded to a Yugoslav writer. *The Days of the Consuls*, a trilogy chronicling his native Travnik under the Turkish occupation during the 1890s, also appeared in 1945.

All his work is distinguished by attention to characterisation. He relies on a number of cameos – such as hearty Bosnian Catholic priests, or the Westerner stranded in the East – which are representative of the ambiguities throughout his prose. As someone who constantly kept a copy of **Goethe**'s *The Sorrows of Young Werther* by his bedside, he was clearly well-versed in the Western philosophical tradition – something that is particularly evident in his characters' psychology. As a storyteller, however, his work belongs firmly in the Eastern tradition, especially because of his suspicions of what is taken to be "real life". Consequently, his writing is imbued with a sense of doom and sublime-sounding truths are fleetingly spoken by his moribund or decadent characters.

Angelou

MAYA

born St. Louis, Missouri 1928

My crime is "heroes, dead and gone,"

dead Vesey, Turner, Gabriel,

dead Malcolm, Marcus, Martin King.

They fought too hard, they fought

  too well.

My crime is I'm alive to tell.

AND STILL I RISE

MAYA ANGELOU'S WRITING speaks for a generation of black Americans, but has reached far beyond. Her four collections of poetry and five-volume account of her life document a pride borne through suffering that touches a universal readership.

Throughout her memoirs, she recounts the unpredictable events of her past at a brisk pace. We follow her story from her parents' break-up, through the trauma of rape by her mother's lover, to a successful career in show business. This led her to Europe and ultimately Africa in search of her roots. But in Mali and Ghana she encountered a lifestyle startlingly different to the American one of her youth.

Over the years she took on many diverse jobs and her confidence helped her succeed at them despite little or no previous experience. She trained as a dancer, but she worked as a cook, was involved in a brothel and managed a restaurant. Her attempt to join the US Army failed, on the grounds that the dancing school she had attended was a Communist institution.

Although this may sound as if her autobiography could contain any number of different lives, a consistent personality nevertheless emerges: one that is dignified, strong and loving, with a refusal to accept a society riddled with racial and sexual strictures and prejudices. In her encounters with white people, she shows a superior intelligence that turns to defiance when necessary.

Her poetry, like her prose, is shot through with refrains from Blues culture and often displays a song-like quality. In her collections, private love-lyrics and elegies to black freedom campaigners sit side by side.

In tribute to her unifying spirit, she was commissioned to write and perform a poem for the inauguration of President Clinton in 1993, which she called *On the Pulse of Morning*. She has a lifetime appointment as Reynolds Professor of American Studies at Wake Forest University in North Carolina.

MAJOR WORKS

I Know Why the Caged Bird Sings (1970)

Gather Together In My Name (1974)

Singin' and Swingin' and Gettin' Merry Like Christmas (1976)

All God's Children Need Traveling Shoes (1986)

Wouldn't Take Nothing for My Journey Now (1994)

Collected Poems (1995)

Anouilh

JEAN

born Bordeaux 1910; died 1987

In a tragedy, nothing is in doubt and everyone's destiny is known. That makes for tranquillity. There is a sort of fellow-feeling among characters in a tragedy: he who kills is as innocent as he who gets killed: it's all a matter of what part you are playing.

ANTIGONE, TR. LEWIS GALANTIÈRE

JEAN ANOUILH WAS a versatile and internationally acclaimed playwright. He wrote some 40 dramas, dividing them into different categories, such as "Dark plays", "Pink plays", "Bright plays", "Costume plays", "Grating plays" and "New grating plays".

In his early career, Anouilh wrote jokes for films scripts and worked as an advertising copywriter. Although he was influenced by the dramatist Giraudoux, who was busily trying to revive the classical themes and verse forms of such masters as **Corneille** and **Molière**, this experience as a commercial writer gave Anouilh a unique insight into how modern audiences respond to words.

Consequently, Anouilh's fame rests on plays that take seemingly elevated or aloof themes and make them accessible without impairing their nobility. He adapted the plots of **Euripides** in *Médée* and of **Sophocles** in *Antigone*. In the latter, he tries to place his audience in the Ancient Greek situation of knowing the story before seeing it represented, and uses the device of the chorus to comment on the action and the process of tragedy. Like **Cocteau**, he used innovative techniques to tell mythical stories with a human angle. His writing is full of digressions and cameos, while preserving that unity of time and space in action so admired by Aristotle.

It is a reflection of his dramatic objectivity that *Antigone* appeared in Paris in 1942 without offending the French or the occupying Nazis. The heroine embodies a youthful faith in ideals, while the king merely obeys orders. This duality informs plays dealing with more religious subjects, such as *Becket, or, The Honour of God* and *The Lark*, about Joan of Arc. Both centre on characters embarking upon spiritual crusades in an equally compelling material world.

Apollinaire

GUILLAUME

born Rome 1880; died Paris 1918

I leave to the future the story of

  Guillaume Apollinaire

Who was at war and knew how to be

  everywhere

In the happy towns behind the lines

In the whole rest of the universe

THE MARVELS OF WAR

IN HIS SHORT LIFETIME, Apollinaire was at the forefront of every artistic movement pulsing through *fin-de-siècle* Paris. In writing about the Eiffel Tower he was the prophet of modernism: "Here, even the cars look like they're ancient." In writing about art, he was cubism's leading apologist. Writing about his own artistic impulses, he coined the term "surrealist". He found beauty in everything. He wrote plays, stories and art criticism; but the true medium for his all-embracing personality was poetry.

In this he was a ceaseless experimenter. In *Alcools* (1913), he abandoned punctuation. This didn't prevent his verse from making musical or syntactical sense. Many of his poems have become songs, and Poulenc wrote a score for his play *The Breasts of Tiresias* – the first performance of which caused a riot in 1917. His faultlessly lyrical ear bent towards end-stopped lines with rocking internal rhymes, which allowed the content of his stanzas to go wherever it wanted. This let his daring vocabulary loose to unconscious operations through the principle of "automatic" writing. In *Calligrammes* he presented his poetry in pictorial form, so that the reader's eye lands on a cannon or star-shaped poem, with various choices of where to begin. Here he slipped in the comment, "I'm also a painter."

He never made these innovations at the expense of sincerity or soul. His capacity for love and vastly generous friendship shines through, such that one can see why he led Paris' artistic community from Montmartre to Montparnasse, and how, when his burial coincided with the Armistice celebrations, his mourners believed the Tricoleurs were draped for him. As a performer, prisoner (falsely accused of stealing the *Mona Lisa*), soldier and socialite, he was all things to an enormous circle of artists.

Aragon

LOUIS

All's hushed in shade the enemy reposes
Somebody told us Paris fell tonight
I'll not forget the lilacs nor the roses
Never nor two loves that have taken
flight.

LILACS AND ROSES

LOUIS ARAGON LEFT a large literary legacy in many genres. Critical attention can move from his voluminous fiction to his polemical essays, or from his Surrealist experiments to his love poetry. His enduring achievement is the fusion of all these throughout a life filled with public convictions and private love.

He saw action in both World Wars. During the first, as an near-qualified doctor, he served in the Medical Corps. There he met **André Breton**, with whom he later edited the Surrealist journal *Littérature*, whose content owed much to **Apollinaire**.

He was a more convincing advocate of surrealism than exponent of it – although he tried to shock, he seemed unable to repress his more romantic instincts. Throughout World War Two, he helped organise Resistance movements and lent his poetic voice to the cause. His skill at composing formal French verse and at drawing on a rich tradition of national songs and old legends, proved especially useful, both as marching songs and tracts that seemed familiar enough to escape the Vichy government's censors.

Beyond his wartime activities, his political sympathies were Communist, marked by his friendship with the Russian poet **Mayakovsky**. Through him Aragon met his lifelong love, the writer Elsa Triolet, and this partnership was intrinsic to everything he thought good for the state. For some, his love poems remain his finest accomplishment, composed in classical French metres with lilting refrains.

He stopped endorsing Soviet policies in 1968 because of the invasion of Czechoslovakia, increasing evidence of human rights abuse and the state censorship that he had encountered in his own country.

Aragon (centre) with (from right) Picasso and Jean Cocteau.

Aristophanes

born Aegina? 457–445 BC; died Aegina? Before 385 BC

Do not begrudge me in the audience
if I, though poor, tell the Athenians
about the state, making a comedy.
The thing is, comedies know what is true,
and what I have to say is weird but true.

ACHARNIANS

ONLY 11 PLAYS survive from the comic dramatist Aristophanes, but his lines and jokes were so often quoted and studied throughout antiquity that we are left with a thousand fragments culled from other sources. Apart from being funny, his writing is an indispensable guide to the political and social scene of late 5th-century Athens.

Nothing was sacred to him. He satirised statesmen, the great tragic playwrights and even the gods. He managed it with a balance that still has scholars divided on where he stood on any given issue. Many think he mocked democracy, when he lampooned Kreon for paying people to make up juries, as in *The Wasps*, or when he presented gods making off-beam proposals in the assembly. Others think he was more motivated by personal grudges than by big ideas. In *Clouds*, for example, a chorus member steps forward to complain that the last Aristophanes comedy failed to win first prize at the last drama festival. The same play also portrays Socrates as a wheedling sophist – a depiction **Plato** later blamed for Socrates' arrest and execution.

Aristophanes' gift, however, was for savage parody – especially of **Euripides**, whom he dresses as a woman in *Ladies' Day*, so eager is the tragedian to witness ceremonies prohibited to men; and **Aeschylus**, whose overblown rhetoric he ridicules in *Frogs*. But his truly comic skill is in turning the world as he knew it upside down. In *Lysistrata*, Athenians were shown the unthinkable: that women could govern men by denying them sex, thus ending war, while in *Birds*, two Athenian citizens use birds to set up a celestial court to rival the gods.

As with all Ancient Greek drama, and much comedy, these techniques strived more to identify the limits of normality than to flout them. Consequently, it is possible to see Aristophanes as an establishment figure, albeit one with a fruity sense of chaos.

Asimov

ISAAC

There was a time when humanity faced the universe alone and without a friend. Now he has creatures to help him; stronger creatures than himself, more faithful, more useful, and absolutely devoted to him. Mankind is no longer alone. Have you ever thought of it that way?

I ROBOT

ISAAC ASIMOV WROTE PROLIFICALLY throughout his life on a vast range of subjects. He was a polymath, and compiled encyclopedias, wrote extensive history books, a commentary on the Bible and detective novels. For a long time, he balanced his frenetic literary activity with a post as Chemistry Professor at Boston University Medical School, USA, before devoting himself completely to writing books.

By far the best known of these are his science fiction novels. As a researcher he had studied the properties of DNA and his work frequently considers the problems of personality, predetermination and survival. In his most famous stories, published gradually under the collective title of *Foundation*, a scientist posits a mathematical system for using statistics to predict the future. His subsequent attempts to anticipate what he thinks is the imminent destruction of the galactic empire are thwarted by random events he couldn't foresee, making for numerous twists in the tale.

Asimov explored the possibilities of machines adopting human personalities in his series of short stories, *I Robot*. These are variations on a theme, concerning the constraints humans would have to impose upon automata if they were to serve mankind without going out of control. Each piece provides a virtuosic investigation into what might happen when these rules conflict and as Asimov demonstrates, the consequences can be worrying.

For his vision, Asimov won acclaim as a kind of prophet. He coined the term "robotics", and was the first writer to incorporate the possibilities of lasers and nuclear power into his work. As his texts age, his forebodings emerge grounded or groundless in almost equal measure, leaving readers as impressed by his gifts as an imaginative storyteller as by his powers as a seer.

Atwood

MARGARET

born Ottawa 1939

"Or maybe I'll make it a short course this time," David said. "For the businessmen how to open Playboy centrefold with the left hand only, keeping the right free for action, for the housewives how to switch on the T.V. and switch off their heads, that's all they need to know, then we can go home."

SURFACING

MANY CONSIDER Margaret Atwood to be a feminist writer. While her protagonists tend to be women who find ways to survive suffering, her target is as often the mechanisms of Western society as male intolerance.

She uses a range of techniques. A recurring theme in her novels is memory, and her characters use their deeply personal recollections to deal with history as a whole. In *Cat's Eye*, the representation of Canadian life from the '50s through to the '80s reflects her experiences. But elsewhere the perspective can be futuristic, as in *The Handmaid's Tale*, or historical. Tony is a history lecturer in *The Robber Bride* and Atwood's latest novel, *Alias Grace*, is based on the life of 19th-century Canadian murderer Grace Marks. She has been known to take her narratives as far back as prehistory, as in *Life Before Men* and her most critically acclaimed novel, *Surfacing*.

Atwood also uses satire to strike at Western mores by seizing upon the smallest, most familiar things around us. In her hands, the simplest tasks, such as ironing, can assume a mystical importance while cooking is a *leitmotif*. Food references pepper her *oeuvre* – most obviously in her debut novel, *The Edible Woman*, in which a market researcher responds to a consumer society by eating her own effigy in cake form. She has even gone so far as to publish a volume of recipes called *CanLit Foodbook*.

She has also written a non-culinary study of Canadian literature, *Survival*, which aroused controversy with its perceived discrimination in favour of women, as well as short stories and 14 collections of poetry. She has been nominated for the Booker Prize three times, and the 1997 Orange Award for fiction.

Auden

W.H.   **born York 1907; died Kirchstetten, Austria 1973**

Our apparatniks will continue making the usual squalid mess called History: all we can pray for is that artists, chefs and saints may still appear to blithe it.

MOON LANDING (AUGUST 1969)

AUDEN WAS PERHAPS England's finest poet of the 20th century. He emerged as a precocious left-wing voice in the 30s, in Alan Bennett's words, "like a student into digs". He was the foremost writer of a coterie that included Cecil Day-Lewis, Stephen Spender and **Christopher Isherwood** – collaborating with the latter on several plays, most notably *The Ascent of F6*.

In his youth, his work and life were overtly political: he witnessed the Spanish Civil War and married **Thomas Mann**'s daughter Erika in 1935 to get her out of Nazi Germany.

The publication of *September 1, 1939* marked the outbreak of war and an important development in Auden's career. By then he was already settled in the United States and was fast turning away from political solutions to the crisis. He later repudiated the poem's most quoted line, "We must love one another or die", as illogical; but it stands as a plea for the most personal kind of understanding.

Much of Auden's work dealt with this kind of love, sometimes with a **Proust**-like search for an explanation, sometimes with a refreshing flippancy. Other motifs include the harshness of time, the abuses of history and the power of music. He collaborated with composers, most notably Britten and Stravinsky, to produce some of the best libretti in opera.

His verse, meanwhile, never lost its own musicality. He would write ballads, sonnets, or in strict metrical patterns of his own devising and was as at home with Anglo-Saxon schemes as with the cadences of **Horace**. He was able to adopt the forms of **Pope** or **Byron** without losing his unique diction, distinguished by compassion and devastating understatement.

He became a US citizen in 1945 and Professor of Poetry at Oxford in 1956. Unlike **Eliot**, his first publisher, he seemed at ease with his public role, and even into his old age was ready with apt or trenchant lines in response to global events. He died in 1973, and is commemorated in Westminster Abbey.

Austen

JANE   **born Steventon Hants, 1775; died Winchester, Hants 1817**

Where people wish to attach, they should always be ignorant. To come with a well-informed mind, is to come with an inability of administering to the vanity of others, which a sensible person would wish to avoid. A woman especially, if she should have the misfortune of knowing anything, should conceal it as well as she can.

PERSUASION

THERE IS NO MENTION of Jane Austen's literary achievements on her tomb in Winchester Cathedral, as only four of her novels appeared during her lifetime. This is partly because of the extensive rewriting all her work underwent before reaching the state that many of her readers consider perfection.

She began early, with parody. At 14, she had **Richardson** in her sights: *Love and Friendship* is a skit on his correspondence novels. Another early book, *Northanger Abbey*, plays with the Gothic genre. This accounts not only for her command of style, and her humorous touch, but also the feeling that her books present a world of their own, with rules and characters peculiar to it.

It is a world where practical considerations preside over passionate ones. In *Sense and Sensibility*, for example, Marianne makes an impulsive choice, and errs; while in *Pride and Prejudice*, the independent-minded Elizabeth refuses to marry for convenience, before slowly coming to love Mr Darcy – that he's a wealthy London gentleman helps. It is a world in which all characters, major or minor, are key components, each tipping one way or the other the balance between social acceptability and unfettered self-expression.

Her prose is noted for its understatement and irony, although it is gentle enough to prevent the light treatment of the social types portrayed from descending into ridicule. Even so, some read Austen's work as a sustained satire on her age's conventions. Others more pryingly look for private causes for this view of life, citing her permanently single status (although she was once engaged for a night). Whichever way one reads Austen, one will be aware of a supremely delicate manner rendering a complex kind of living into the subtlest kind of art.

Auster

PAUL

born Newark, New Jersey 1947

The question is the story itself, and whether or not it means something is not for the story to tell.

CITY OF GLASS,
FROM THE NEW YORK TRILOGY

PAUL AUSTER HAS BROUGHT complex theories of language and meaning to a large audience with his beguiling novels.

After leaving Columbia University, he spent four years in France. He has translated books from French and his writing seems to owe much to recent European literary developments. His preoccupation with deferral and series of signs pointing to other signs that ultimately lead nowhere, is in the same tradition as **Calvino** and **Perec**. He is an avowed admirer of the latter, of whom he has written that a reader might enjoy his books without following every linguistic trick – the same is true of Auster.

In *The New York Trilogy*, the narrative conducts its search for elusive truths through detective stories. These immediately involve the author, who has yet to understand why he has begun searching for clues, let alone what the clues portend. The enquiry techniques of previous literary sleuths can be detected, beginning with a **Chandler**-like attention to physical detail, through to Father Brown's more spiritual methods. The closing novel sets a man to search out a friend, who is searching for the roots of language, by keeping someone devoid of human contact since birth, who is also searching....

In *The Music of Chance*, this pursuit is more cyclical, with the end reflecting the novel's beginning. In between, characters bet, lose a wager, and must redeem the debt by building a gratuitous wall. This meaninglessness engrosses them utterly. The professional gambler Pozzi is named after the *Waiting for Godot* character Pozzo, as if in homage to **Beckett**, whose representation of intense human activity in the face of nullity is also Auster's aesthetic project. He has adapted the book for the screen.

Bábel

ISAÁK EMMANUÍLOVICH   born Odessa 1894; died Siberia 1941?

Bloodstained tracks marked that way of ours, and singing flew above it. So it was in the Kuban, and when we fought the Green Guerrillas. So it was in the Urals and the foothills of the Caucasus, and so it is to this day. Those songs are indispensable to us. No-one can see an end to this war, and Sandy the Christ, our squadron singer, is not yet ripe for death.

THE SONG

ISAÁK BÁBEL'S WRITINGS are few. His stories are often very short, much like his life, but both have accommodated extremes.

He was born in a ghetto in Odessa, where, as a Jew, he had personal experience of the anti-Semitism of the Cossacks, which was tolerated by the authorities. During the pogroms, he saw his family's shop destroyed, while his father was forced to pay homage to a Cossack raider. Despite this, his patriotism led him to join a Red Army regiment in the Soviet campaign against Poland during the revolution, where he was a supply officer in a Cossack regiment.

His writing is full of stark contrasts he experienced. He had studied the Talmud, and was a devotee of French literature, which set him apart from his more impulsive comrades during his military service. His short stories often reflect their violence, while his characters envy or emulate it. He reports it in terse tales that, whether written in natural and repetitive dialect or in more poetic diction, always retain their economy. In *Red Cavalry*, his first book, this kind of understatement shocks. In the later *Odessa Tales*, he introduces a host of ghetto gangster characters whose Yiddish wit and indifference to the consequences of their actions produce a similar effect.

In 1934, Bábel spoke at the Soviet Union's First Writer's Conference. A man of few words, he declared himself "the master of a new literary genre: the genre of silence". In Stalin's Russia, this was dangerous. Although the exact reason for his arrest is unknown, his speech could scarcely have been ignored. He was imprisoned in 1939, shortly after finishing a film script, *Old Square, No. 4*, whose domestic characters were caricatures of leading revolutionary figures, most prominently Stalin. He died in a gulag, sometime between then and 1941.

Baldwin

JAMES   **born Harlem 1924; died St. Paul, France 1987**

Now, this country is going to be transformed. It will not be transformed by an act of God, but by all of us, by you and me. I don't believe any longer that we can afford to say that it is entirely out of our hands. We made the world we're living in and we have to make it over.

NOTES FOR A HYPOTHETICAL NOVEL
IN NOBODY KNOWS MY NAME

JAMES BALDWIN WAS A WRITER of great integrity and courage. His novels began appearing in the racially torn America of the '50s. While his essays, and some characters in his stories, fully express the anger he felt at black oppression, he often sought the solutions to ghettoisation and injustice in spiritual as much as political remedies.

His first novel, set in the Harlem of his childhood, which would recur throughout his work, was *Go Tell It on the Mountain*. It is the story of a preacher who blocks his son's search for God by demanding that the boy submit to him first. Just as the hero, Jimmy Grimes, overcomes this, so Baldwin used the novel to exorcise his rage at his father. He followed this with *Giovanni's Room*, whose subjects of race and homosexuality prevented it finding a publisher in the United States, although the book was published in Britain in 1956.

Baldwin feared that from then on his work would be judged simply as that of a black, gay writer. Although *Another Country* returned to a sexual relationship between two men, the cruelty they experience is less explicit than before, with the hero Vivaldo fighting a fear of his proclivities to accept a more universal love. Baldwin further eluded pigeonholing with a picture of intimate family life, *If Beale Street Could Talk*, whose narrator is a pregnant teenager, with a lover in prison and a supportive mother.

His prose is often a vivid evocation of life in New York's projects and his dialogue contains prophetic insights in the vernacular used there. This is also true of his plays. In his essays, he comes across as a fearless but compassionate thinker.

Ballard

J.G.

So there came into being the new Europe, a visionary realm that would miraculously fuse the spirits of Charlemagne and the smart card, Michelangelo and the Club Med, St. Augustine and St-Laurent.

THE LARGEST THEME PARK
IN THE WORLD, FROM WAR FEVER

JAMES GRAHAM BALLARD looms large on the literary landscape for his daring imagination and consistent ability to provoke controversy. But this is at the expense of his reputation as an experimenter in form as well as content.

He was born in Shanghai in 1930 and interned in a Japanese camp during the Second World War. The experience engendered his acclaimed autobiographical novel *Empire of the Sun*, which was nominated for the Booker Prize and won the James Tait Black Memorial Prize in 1985. The sequel, *The Kindness of Women*, follows the hero Jim to his new life in Britain.

Apart from these books, his work deals with the fantastical. For two years he trained as a doctor, and a knowledge of science pervades his early tales of foreboding global destruction. But they are never just science fiction. Throughout his first three novels and two subsequent collections of short stories, Ballard goes beyond the chemistry of crises to explore their psychological consequences.

He took human responses to modern disasters further still in his next two novels, *The Atrocity Exhibition* and *Crash*. He described the latter as "the first pornographic novel based on technology" and its treatment of the erotic potential of road accidents retains its ability to shock (Westminster and Lanarkshire councils have banned screenings of the film version, released 1997).

Ever topical, Ballard's latest collection of stories, *War Fever*, takes news headlines to unpredictable conclusions, while pursuing playful exercises in style. One episode comprises an 18-word sentence, filled out with a footnote examining each word. The concluding piece is an index purporting to suffix the biography of a man apparently in the midst of the century's key events, but of whom no other trace exists.

His latest novel, *Rushing to Paradise*, is a satire on French nuclear testing in the South Pacific. In his portrayal of the pro-environment, pro-euthanasia heroine, Ballard shows characteristic fearlessness in espousing unfashionable attitudes.

MAJOR WORKS

NOVELS
The Drowned World (1962)

The Drought (1965)

The Crystal World (1966)

The Atrocity Exhibition (1970)

Crash (1973)

Empire of the Sun (1984)

The Day of Creation (1985)

SHORT STORIES
The Four-Dimensional Nightmare (1963)

The Terminal Beach (1964)

Vermilion Sands (1973)

War Fever (1990)

Balzac

HONORÉ DE

In Balzac, even the door-keepers have genius. All his minds are weapons loaded to the muzzle with will. Just like Balzac himself.

BAUDELAIRE, TR. GRAHAM ROBB

SUSTAINED BY AN UNSHAKABLE belief in his own powers and a staggering 50 cups of coffee a day, Balzac spent the last 20 years of his life writing the 90 novels that comprise *La Comédie Humaine*. His title

suggests a work to complement **Dante's** *Divine Comedy* and Balzac succeeded in thoroughly realising the world he presented. The books are divided into groups, such as 'Philosophical Studies', 'Scenes of Private Life', 'Parisian Scenes' and 'Provincial Scenes', with their characters capable of appearing in several of the fictions, or of knowing the cast of another of them.

For such an extraordinary figure, who filled his work with personality and commentary on surrounding detail, one might suggest **Sterne** as a model, but Balzac's unique writing apprenticeship is more informative. At 20, he tried writing tragedies: his novels are about ordinary people, rather than heroes, who fall prey to destructive obsessions, which they play out as if on stage. By 25, he was writing thrillers anonymously: the *Comédie* is full of pacy political intrigues and plotting. It was only after 1829, and a series of disastrous forays into the printing industry and Sardinian silver-mining, that Balzac started writing under his own name and it wasn't until 1842 that he began publishing his books under their collective title.

His literary penchants are completely of their time: he can immerse a reader in a psychological enquiry concentrating on the shape of characters' heads, before an exhaustive account of what their clothing signifies. His descriptions of architecture and landscape digress into revealing historical curios. This kind of concern extends to the issues of his age, especially money-making and changing ideas of family. His work stands as a comprehensive account of his world and it is hard to imagine what novels would have been like since, without his great influence.

Barrie

J.M.

born Kirriemuir 1860; died London 1937

Every time a child says "I don't believe in fairies" there is a little fairy somewhere that falls down dead.

PETER PAN

SIR JAMES MATTHEW BARRIE'S literary reputation has not worn well since his death and he appears to have fallen from fashion because of the spiritual, unreal quality of his plays and stories that distinguished him from the naturalism of the late 19th century.

Then, he was best known for novels and sketches in which he wrote of his native Kirriemuir in Scotland and that he gave the fictional name of Thrums. These sentimental stories often display his skill as a journalist, which gave him particular insight into giving the public what it wanted – he wrote specifically of his experience in newspapers in *When a Man's Single* (1888).

Today, however Barrie is remembered primarily for his plays, particularly *Peter Pan*. Still widely performed and adapted, it is the story of a little boy who wouldn't grow up and so retained his ability to fly. Barrie's contemporary, the English novelist Max Beerbohm, thought this a reflection of Barrie, whom he felt had maintained a childish innocence, "…but all this while, bless his little heart, he was suffering".

Beerbohm was referring to Barrie being forced to deal with the practical world of the theatre, although he enjoyed a string of West End successes. Many of these showed an acute awareness of the fragility of social systems and niceties. In *The Admirable Crichton*, for example, Barrie has a bungling Earl stranded on a

desert island with his family and unerring butler. The glimpse, in isolation, of class structures in all their absurdity struck many as fine satire in the tradition of **Oscar Wilde**, while some saw it almost as a call to revolution.

In further plays, he shows behavioural strictures governing all classes with humour and poignancy. But throughout his writing, he questions these givens and, in *The Legend of Leonara*, goes so far as to argue that the tags society has given us are not enough to ensure that we act accordingly – in this he anticipates the work of **Luigi Pirandello**.

Bataille

GEORGES

born Billom 1897; died Paris 1962

I was not even satisfied with the usual debauchery, because the only thing it dirties is debauchery itself, while, in some way or other, anything sublime and perfectly pure is left intact by it. My kind of debauchery soils not only my body but also anything I may conceive in its course, that is to say, the vast starry universe which serves as a backdrop.

THE STORY OF THE EYE

NEXT TO HIS PHILOSOPHICAL writings, Georges Bataille's corpus of fiction seems slight; but in it he puts the extremity of his theory into pure practice.

Bataille teases his reader by annotating texts with biographical detail, as if to explain why he writes the way he does. He describes his hatred of his syphilitic father dying in horrific agony. Although based on fact, these passages serve less to document a life than to frame his discussions of youthful depravity and unrestrained sexual adventure.

Such texts embody Bataille's account of how energy works. He ascribed pleasure to its expenditure. The more reckless this burning of energy, the purer the pleasure. He finds expression for this in most bodily functions and in the very fact that he writes about them. In his novel *L'Abbé C*, the story of a debauched twin's attempts to corrupt his saintly brother is presented by an editor who has a nervous breakdown just from reading it. For the editor, as for Bataille, telling the story has the same value as the events it describes.

This is how his most discussed novel, *The Story of the Eye*, operates. Throughout the narrative, an adolescent couple surpass themselves with increasingly outrageous moral transgressions. They finish by forcing a priest to violate all that is sacred to him while they commit his murder. Here, the structure of the narrative, as well as its symbolic content, reflects the unstoppable effusion of accumulated impulses.

As a writer, he began with religious inclinations, but flouted them after 1920. He aligned himself with surrealist writers, but was disowned from the movement by **André Breton** because of his interest in faeces and the works of the Marquis de Sade. In his handling of all these themes, his research was meticulous, and his scholarship as profound as when he was writing about palaeography or antique coins.

Baudelaire

CHARLES PIERRE

born Paris 1821; died Paris 1867

My cat, seeking a bed upon the tiles,

Restlessly shakes its thin and

*   scabby frame.*

An old poet's spirit wanders

*   in the gutters*

With the sad voice of a shivering

*   phantom.*

SPLEEN

WHEN DISCUSSING Baudelaire's poetry, critics can agree on hardly anything except its massive impact. Some have found his writings immoral, while others see an irrepressible Catholicism in them. In fact, Baudelaire's remarks on his work express the same confusion. He said that he put all his religion and all his hate into his lifetime's collection of verse, *Les Fleurs du Mal.* "I shall write the opposite," he concluded, "…and I'll be lying like a dentist."

Baudelaire was a brilliant schoolboy, but was expelled at 18. He squandered what he thought would be his inheritance in Paris and soon became destitute. An absorption in the city's squalor persists throughout his poems, but these are seldom without a sense of beauty and wonder. In fact, the remarkable thing about Baudelaire is the way he maintains a poet's poise and diction throughout strictly formal verse, while regarding the repellent. This is especially true of a poem such as *Une Charogne*, which delicately details a fetid corpse, while rhapsodising over it elegantly as though it were another of nature's miracles.

His poems stand as formidable towering technical accomplishments, but they are more than that. They often describe what it means to be a poet and this accounts for their massive influence ever since. For Baudelaire, a poet is an exile, a lonely figure – someone with insights beyond good and evil, who can express them in an aesthetic form that might bring a kind of redemption. For this he has often won comparisons to **Dante**.

His fame rests on *Les Fleurs du Mal*, which appeared in 1857, the same year as **Flaubert**'s *Madame Bovary*. Like that book, it was tried for obscenity, and parts of it were banned for years. He added more poems to the work in subsequent editions, most notably in 1862, giving the impression that his writing is a single artistic statement. It is this that seems to have confused commentators, except **T.S. Eliot**, on whom Baudelaire was a huge influence.

MAJOR WORKS

La Fanfarlo (1847)

Les fleurs du mal
  (1857, republished with
  additions, 1861)

Artificial Paradises (1860)

Little Poems in Prose (1869)

Beaumarchais

PIERRE AUGUSTIN CARON DE **born Paris 1732; died Paris 1799**

In the end, the urge to tell someone, "I love you," becomes so pressing that I say it on my own, running in the park, to your mistress, to you, to the trees, the clouds, to the wind that carries them along with my lost words...

THE MARRIAGE OF FIGARO

IN SPITE OF HIS REPUTATION as one of France's greatest comic dramatists, Beaumarchais' first audience was for his autobiography. He published it from 1774 to 1778, and presented himself as the social underdog in an ongoing inheritance dispute. The public loved it.

His writing for the stage has been called "more journalism than art". If this is true, Beaumarchais was an excellent journalist. Just as his memoirs caught the public mood, so his *Marriage of Figaro* (portraying a household in which a Count pretends to concede his right to sleep with a bride-to-be under his jurisdiction, only to be exposed) showed an unerring sense of where power was going in pre-Revolutionary France. On the one hand, Beaumarchais' vision of a household in which the servants know more than the master seems to come from **Plautus**, and to be harmless enough; on the other, da Ponte's attempts to turn the play into an opera libretto in Vienna a year after its publication met with censorship. The text was considered dangerous.

But this does not diminish Beaumarchais' achievement as an artist. Through all the playful antics of *The Barber of Seville,* just as in the more involved intrigues of *The Marriage of Figaro,* he took immense care over staging details, costumes and characterisation. The successes were immediate and far-reaching. Translations of each play appeared in England within a year of their first French performance; Mozart's and da Ponte's *Figaro* was performed the year after that.

The drama, *Eugénie,* set in London, didn't enjoy the same success and Beaumarchais' fortune declined with the revolution. He was accused of arming counter-revolutionaries and he fled to Holland. He later returned to his native Paris, where he died in a fine house on the boulevard that now bears his name.

Beauvoir

SIMONE DE

born Paris 1908; died Paris 1986

I feel at one with women who have assumed responsibility for their lives and who struggle to succeed. However, this does not prevent me from being interested in that part of failure which is inherent in every life.

INTRODUCTION TO THE BROKEN WOMAN

SIMONE DE BEAUVOIR'S novels and memoirs chronicle the shifts in her thinking throughout her life. For some readers, her first three novels are too obviously the work of a philosopher; for others, her fourth, *The Mandarins*, lacks the clarity and reasoning of those that preceded it.

Despite this, she successfully used the novel to explore and express her philosophy of existentialism. This demands, among other things, that people make "authentic" personal choices and through storytelling de Beauvoir illustrated both circumstances and consequences of this type of thinking. In *All Men are Mortal*, for example, the narrative closely follows the thoughts of a hero in his response to the prospect of death. As in her previous book, *The Blood of Others*, the need for action against authority (in this case, the struggle against the Nazis in France) when one's conscience demands it, finds an expression that goes beyond the theorising that existentialism renders redundant.

In this she followed **Sartre**, whom she met at the École Normale Supérieure and who became her lifelong companion. She seemed so much to rehearse his views that she was dubbed "La Grande Sartreuse", but in her stance on feminism, her own thinking became more clearly distinguished, particularly with the publication of *The Second Sex* in 1949, which made her name. Again, philosophical argument is sustained by personal conviction. In this case the belief that in society the idea of "woman" is a male myth and that male codes force women to adopt fixed roles as mothers and lovers. Her later novels explore these myths (notably in the advertising world of *The Beautiful Images*) and how female characters respond to them.

The fluid nature of her belief system meant that she could reassess her opinion that socialism was necessary for women's equality, and that individuals could act independently of society. Her autobiographical books examine how and when these changes occurred.

MAJOR WORKS

She Came To Stay (1943)

The Blood of Others (1944)

All Men Are Mortal (1947)

The Second Sex (1949)

The Mandarins (1954)

Should Sade Burn? (1955)

The Beautiful Images (1966)

Memoirs of a Dutiful Daughter (Autobiography, 1958)

The Prime of Life (1960)

The Force of Circumstance (1965)

Beckett

SAMUEL

born Dublin 1906; died Paris 1989

I know those little phrases that seem so innocuous... they rise up out of the pit and know no rest until they drag you down into its dark.

MALONE DIES

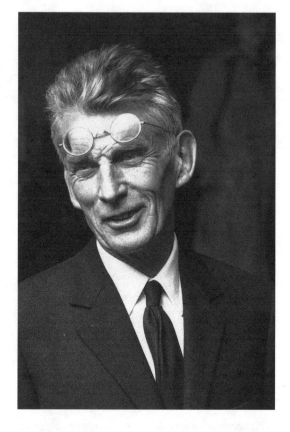

IN HIS EXTRAORDINARY novels, Beckett began finding ways to express the human need to find something to say when faced with an eternity of silence – a theme that dominated the plays that brought him fame.

These first books, like all his writing afterwards, show the influences of his compatriot and friend **Joyce**'s experimentation and of Descartes' philosophy, which had asked how we know we exist.

Beckett's work explores how people deal with the possibility of non-existence. In the last novel of his trilogy, *The Unnameable*, the persona adopts the Joycean technique of interior monologue. But rather than using it merely to examine a character's state of mind, Beckett portrays an individual talking to himself, as if talking is an urgent necessity.

The double act in Beckett's most famous play, *Waiting for Godot* has a similar need. Without knowing why, Vladimir and Estragon await someone who never arrives. Sometimes hopeful, sometimes despairing, they spend the play diverting one another, and the audience, with knock-about comedy, seizing on one another's phrases to spin them out into word games. Although either member of the duo can snap the action into a different pace, the dialogue – which is always rhythmical – always ends with a dying fall.

Although this dramatic project seems strictly theoretical, Beckett was always aware of the practical possibilities of theatre. He pushed these to their limits, working within the same constraints that govern the novels. Often these are physical: characters find themselves in dustbins, or clay pots, or, as in *Happy Days*, buried, first up to the waist, then up to the neck.

Here, as elsewhere, the protagonist, Winnie, tries to keep herself stable by piecing together half-remembered tags and shards of language. In all these situations, Beckett's writing becomes our diversion too, and, like the characters in *Endgame*, in which time itself is drawing to a conclusion, we shift between wanting it, and wanting it never, to stop.

Behan

BRENDAN

born Dublin 1923; died Dublin 1964

If I was you

And you were me,

On the way from Les Halles

With this load of cognac

Full of grub and booze and glee

You'd write a verse or two in praise of me.

THANKS TO JOYCE

BRENDAN BEHAN WAS a well-loved and short-lived Irish playwright, whose work, for all its political content and macabre plots, is much better known for ribald wit and warm personality.

He educated himself in prison. He had joined the IRA when he was 14 and from 16 spent three years in borstal for trying to blow up a naval base in Liverpool. On his release he was deported to Ireland and in 1942 was again gaoled for his part in the shooting of a policeman. He spent the following four years in various prisons with other IRA convicts. These experiences formed the basis of his writing.

In 1956, his first play was produced. Set in gaol, *The Quare Fellow* brims with banter and profane jokes exchanged the night before an inmate is to be hanged for murdering his brother. He followed this in 1958 with *Borstal Boy* – a record of the time he spent as a young detainee in England.

With success came a change in lifestyle. His public adored him and sudden wealth enabled him to fund a steadily worsening drink problem. He still found time to write (just) and wrote his next play in 12 days. Originally written in Irish, *The Hostage* shows the frenzy of its composition. It flows with his

customary merry wit in an expansive structure, accommodating references to himself as playwright and sections aimed straight at the audience. The themes remain sinister, made more so by their jocund treatment: two IRA officers have captured a British soldier and will execute him if one of their own is hanged in Belfast. (Behan was sentenced to death by the IRA for dissension after he wrote to them asking if, since he was tried in his absence, he might be executed in his absence, too.)

Throughout his life he retained his patriotism, and is known in his country as much as an Irish-language poet as a playwright. He grew disaffected with dogma and cultivated the persona of an extravagant *bon viveur*, frequently appearing on television drunk. He died of alcohol abuse at 41.

Behn

APHRA

born Wye, Kent 1640; died London 1689

HERE LIES A PROOF THAT WIT CAN NEVER BE DEFENCE ENOUGH AGAINST MORTALITY.

ON HER TOMB

AMONG APHRA BEHN'S fictional works, some commentators have included her autobiography, *The Life and Memoirs of Mrs Behn, Written by One of the Fair Sex*. It tells of a youthful expedition to Surinam and a career spying on the Dutch navy and Commonwealth refugees. There she married a merchant and incurred enough debt to land her in prison on her return to England. She used the Surinam part of her life in *Oroonoko*, to display attitudes to race and slavery that were well ahead of her time. An earlier romance, *The Court of the King of Bantam*, meanwhile, shows her great personal knowledge of theatre.

It was her plays that made her famous. She was a great innovator of the Restoration stage, especially with use of music, and collaborated with **Dryden**. Her subject matter singled her out from her contemporaries: a key target of her satire was the arranged marriage. Her scenes brazenly enacting adultery and cuckoldry might seem in keeping with Carolingian tastes, but sometimes she could go too far even for them: *The Lucky Chance, or, An Alderman's Bargain* was censored for indecency.

Although she was loyal to the Stuarts, and consistently Tory (she lampooned the Whig Leader, the Earl of Shaftesbury, in 1682), her onstage antics landed her in more off-stage trouble – when the Duke of Monmouth, the King's illegitimate son, became the subject of her acerbic wit she found herself in prison for a second spell.

Such a controversial woman was bound to turn heads in society and she attracted sneering comments from her male peers. The poet Robert Gould persistently referred to her as "chaste **Sappho**", without actually naming her, and some of the sniping has continued long since her death.

Apart from her plays, of which 17 authentic examples survive, she was a prominent poet, composing Pindaric odes to prominent persons of the day, and an important translator, especially from French. She was, according to **Virginia Woolf**, the first woman in England to make a living out of writing and she was the first woman to be buried in Westminster Abbey in her own right.

Belloc

HILAIRE

born Saint-Cloud, France 1870; died Sussex 1953

*WHEN I AM DEAD, I HOPE IT MAY BE
SAID: "HIS SINS WERE SCARLET, BUT HIS
BOOKS WERE READ."*

EPITAPH

BELLOC WROTE PROLIFICALLY in every genre except drama. His work leaves the image of a man at once profound and silly, compassionate and careless.

His eccentric views find few advocates now. Throughout his work he argues for a return to a Europe united by Catholicism, while rejecting capitalism, socialism and Protestantism. The latter he associated with Prussia – he could never call the country Germany, scarred as he was by the ravages of the Franco-Prussian War, which forced him to leave his native France in the year he was born. He was able to admire Mussolini and the Roman Empire that he thought *Il Duce* embodied, while detesting Hitler, whose atrocities against the Jews in Germany he predicted as early as 1922. Although the Holocaust shocked him deeply, his writings were often anti-semitic.

Denied a History fellowship at Oxford because he was a Catholic, Belloc persisted in bookish analyses of social ills, on which he worked with G.K. Chesterton. **Shaw** dubbed them "the Chesterbelloc", but they called themselves "Distributists", united in a vision of domestic self-sufficiency in which everyone would own three acres and a cow. Belloc even entered politics in 1906 as the Liberal MP for South Salford, only to denounce Parliament as a sham four years later, when he and Chesterton exposed the Liberal government's involvement in shares scandals.

The joy of Belloc lies in his awareness of his own eccentricity. He used his establishment education to knock the establishment. He never achieved this quite so well as in his verse for children, which warns against the consequences of madcap transgressions, as in the poem *Algernon, Who Played with a Loaded Gun, and, on Missing his Sister, was Reprimanded by his Father*. With such antics, he united such disparate figures as **Auden** and **Evelyn Waugh** in admiration. When he died, the Requiem Mass at Westminster Cathedral was attended by a vast range of mourners, demonstrating that he commanded affection well beyond the confines of his bizarre world.

Bellow

SAUL

born Lachine, Canada 1915

University presses sent manuscripts for his professional judgment. They lay in bundles, unopened. The sun grew hot, the soil was damp and black, and Herzog looked with despair on the thriving luxuriant life of the plants.

HERZOG

SAUL BELLOW'S WRITINGS aim to retrieve the element of the spiritual that the urban climate of the 20th century often seems to have destroyed. His tales of angst are set against the chaos of the metropolis (usually Chicago) and he strives to pick out the individual from the increasingly blurred crowd.

Throughout his novel-writing career, he has tackled this with a wealth of techniques. His first two novels, *Dangling Man* and *The Victim*, were strictly structured and doggedly realistic. His first big critical success, however, took a very different approach. *The Adventures of Augie March* is a picaresque ramble through the life of its hero, set in '50s America, the style is more relaxed and the work full of wildly contrasting episodes and locations.

Bellow's most celebrated look at a man trying to find peace in a clamorous world is *Herzog*. A middle-aged academic in the Berkshire mountains writes letters to anyone, including dead philosophers and God. His crazed attempts to kill his ex-wife, however, lead him out of his seclusion and his failure to do the deed finally frees him from the need to keep corresponding with the void around him. It is only then that he achieves some sort of peace.

Bellow's most complete examination of the old, refined man contemplating the agonies of his age is perhaps embodied in the hero of *Mr Sammler's Planet*, who has inside knowledge of the Bloomsbury set and of Auschwitz. As well as the individual conscience, the values of an entire culture seem in peril.

Bellow's hope is often placed in preserving memory, which in turn lends purpose to the activity of writing. In *Something to Remember Me By*, his reminiscing persona concludes: "Well, they're all gone now, and I have made my preparations. I haven't left a large estate and this is why I have written this memoir, as a sort of addition to your legacy."

Bennett

ARNOLD

born Hanley, Staffordshire 1867; died London 1931

Down below is Burslem... If it were an old Flemish town, beautiful in detail and antiquely interesting, one would say its situation was ideal. It is not beautiful in detail, but the smoke transforms its ugliness into a beauty transcending the work of architects and of time.

THE MAN FROM THE NORTH

ARNOLD BENNETT'S WRITING owes much to the legacy of **Balzac**, especially his treatment of provincial settings. Most of the action in Bennett's books takes place in his native Five Towns, the area in Staffordshire famous for pottery.

The upsurge of capitalism documented by Balzac was fully developed in industrial Britain by Bennett's time. He wrote of it intimately, taking the reader from individual, thoroughly realised streets, to views of the towns around from neighbouring hills. Throughout, we witness progress and its impact on the landscape and humanity.

He was particularly remarkable for his sympathetic treatment of female characters. He was made assistant editor of *Woman* magazine in 1893, for which he wrote advice columns, and in 1918 he contributed to Marie Stopes' pioneering pamphlet on birth control. These contributions to women's issues were perhaps the reason that his depiction of women was less clouded by romanticism than in the work of most of his male contemporaries.

He was one of the leading exponents of realism in England. George Moore was a mentor, but his technique owes as much to the theory and practice of **Emile Zola**, which he encountered during time in Paris from 1902 to 1912. His narrative and characters share a practical attitude toward the real world. The dialogue in his books is often curt and written in dialect, and comment on the action can be similarly understated.

Bennett's working methods reflected the industrial climate in which he lived. In his journals he occasionally speaks of "producing" novels or even "manufacturing" characters. His apparent lack of themes disappointed **Henry James**, but he found a great admirer in Max Beerbohm.

Betjeman

JOHN   born Highgate, London 1906; died Trebretherick, Cornwall 1984

We should not giggle as we like

At his appearance on his bike;

It's something to become a bore,

And more than that, at twenty-four.

THE WYKEHAMIST

FOR MANY CRITICS, the amiable figure of Sir John Betjeman, rambling round old churches and pleasing a huge public with hymn-like verses, has been easy to dismiss as irrelevant to the concerns of serious poetry. The problem is that he managed to address deeply felt convictions in poetry that often seems frivolous.

This is what made him such a fine satirist. His ringing and accessible lines reveal an amazing ear for musicality and cadence and for the way people speak. When characters emerge from a poem, it is hard to tell whether Betjeman's lines pity or mock them. Often his sensitivity is most felt when he holds back, or gives a piece a throwaway ending.

In poetry and prose, as well as on television, he became famous for deploring desecrations of architecture and lapses of taste. His education was traditional and aesthetic: he became friends with **Auden** and MacNeice at Oxford, but left without a degree, drifting into teaching and architecture criticism. Volumes of his poetry began to appear in 1931 and he was always a stickler for the way they were presented. His verses and descriptions, often set in the home counties, sometimes epigrammatic, sometimes elegiac, won greater readerships with passing books. His *Collected Poems* was an instant bestseller in 1958.

Blake

WILLIAM

born London 1757; died London 1827

I must Create a System or be enslaved by another Man's.

THE BOOK OF LOS

BLAKE WAS A SELF-STYLED voice "crying out in the wilderness" – a prophet very few heard during his lifetime. Even if subsequent generations, including the Romantics, have thought him mad, still, they could not ignore his vision.

A facet of his genius was to look deeply into the events of his own age, while seeing beyond them. His writings followed the American Revolution and coincided with the French Revolution and he was a friend of Tom Paine, the pamphleteer who was passionately involved in both. He railed against all the constraints of his era – political, sexual and religious. In *Visions of the Daughters of Albion* he portrays women's sexual freedom. As for religion, his response to the Bible was ecstatic rather than doctrinal.

In all these beliefs, Blake held that understanding could only come about by perceiving the cosmos' most childlike delights alongside its horrors. Thus his *Songs of Innocence* is balanced by the *Songs of Experience*, where the lamb is balanced by the tiger, and simplicity by poverty. Likewise, in *The Marriage of Heaven and Hell*, knowledge of Christ is impossible without acknowledging the satanic.

Normal verse-forms could not accommodate these revelations: Blake began with beguilingly simple lyrics, before working with longer lines, then exploding into aphorisms in his later work. Similarly, words were never enough to him either, and he'd often painstakingly make his own books, uniting the texts with his own engravings and sewing the whole together by hand.

Throughout his work the message remains the same: that we see truths by means other than our eyes. In this he agreed with **Plato**, who also believed in the notion that the soul can comprehend intangible forms. Again like Plato, he accounted for the universe by devising his own myths, with forces such as Urizen representing order and Orc chaos.

But he could not accept Plato's view that poets say things that they don't understand. His accounts of his vision are as detailed as its expression is pure. There have been plenty of poets since, each with a private understanding of his meaning, and a public hankering after his pronouncements. To liberate them, there was only one William Blake.

Blixen

KAREN

born, Rungsted, Denmark 1885; died, Rungsted 1962

When I handed him the paper [on which I had written his story], he took it reverently and greedily... He could not afford to lose it, for his soul was in it, and it was part of his existence.

OUT OF AFRICA

KAREN BLIXEN CUT a remarkable figure in Denmark, where she often struck her readers as aristocratic or completely out of keeping with prevalent literary trends. Her stories and memoirs won immediate acclaim in Britain and the United States, but took longer to achieve the same popularity in her own country.

She was bilingual and wrote *Seven Gothic Tales* (1934) in English, before translating them into Danish. As this first book's title suggests, these stories were written very much in the European Romantic tradition and are full of the kind of magic and witchcraft that had become deeply unfashionable in an age that had wholeheartedly embraced realism. Her characters' actions are governed by forces they do not instantly recognise or understand. They wander through a decadent, aristocratic world tinged with shades of sadism and incest in search of their true identities. Their quest, however, often leads them to discover that they've been powerless all along and must yield to a divine order.

She wrote much of the book during the 20-year period she spent in Kenya running a coffee plantation. Her recollections of that time first appeared in Denmark under the title *Out of Africa*, which was welcomed for being more realistic. Some readers, however, find her endowing the new, distinctly European world around her with the same mysterious qualities that characterised her earlier tales. The book was written entirely on her return to Europe, and tells of her marital problems, her love of the country and its people, and of the financial difficulties that forced her to leave.

She then published two further collections of short stories, including similarly supernatural psychology, but fewer historical trimmings. In 1944, her only novel, *Angelic Avengers*, appeared. It is a pastiche on English romantic novels, set in England, and with an opening that closely resembles that of **Charlotte Brontë**'s *Jane Eyre*. Although few found this up to the standard of her shorter work, the posthumous publication of two volumes of her letters has enhanced her reputation as a markedly individual and open-minded European figure.

Blunden

EDMUND **born London 1896; died Long Melford, Suffolk 1974**

War might make his worst grimace

And still my mind in armour good

Turned aside in every place

And saw bright day through the

black wood.

THE SHEPHERD

EDMUND BLUNDEN IS PERHAPS better known for the work he has done as a teacher and editor of poetry than for his own emphatically English verse. But the energies he devoted to the writing of others, even in his youth, explain much about his own style.

He published the poetry of **John Clare** and collected the poems of **Wilfred Owen** and Ivor Gurney. These two strands of Romantic and War poetry were ever present in his own work, and often interwoven in his life.

Unlike Gurney and Owen, he survived the First World War, despite repeated exposure to gas attacks and the battle known as "Third Ypres", which became the title of one of his most famous poems. Although he is remembered as a war poet, even on this subject his writing is in the pastoral vein of the 18th and 19th centuries.

Here, in F.R. Leavis' words, he was "creating a world in which to find refuge". This world was similar to that of **Keats**, whose choice monosyllables and richly rural diction Blunden imitated, although sometimes taking it all too far. In his first two collections, a handful of poems deal with the war, but it wasn't until 10 years after the Armistice that he could confront his traumatic experiences. He did this in *Undertones of War*, written while he was a professor at Tokyo University. If distance from Europe helped him see events more objectively, nothing could prepare him for the next great war. He returned to Japan in 1948 and recorded his impressions in *After the Bombing*.

He had withdrawn from Oxford University in 1919, feeling alienated by his incommunicable insights into war. In 1966 he became Professor of Poetry there, by which time his attempts to describe his experiences and his dedication to other poets' accounts of the trenches had won him praise and thanks.

MAJOR WORKS

Pastorals (1916)

The Waggoner and Other Poems (1920)

The Shepherd (1922)

English Poems (1925)

Undertones of War (1928)

Collected Poems (1930)

Poems 1930-1940 (1940)

After the Bombing (1948)

Poems of Many Years (1957)

43

Boccaccio

GIOVANNI

born Florence? Certaldo? 1313?; died Certaldo 1375

A corrupt mind never made clean sense of a word: and just as noble words don't impress such a mind, so words that aren't so noble cannot contaminate a well-disposed mind, just as mud cannot affect the sun's rays, nor brute earth the beauties of heaven.

THE DECAMERON

EVEN IF BOCCACCIO WERE to have written only poems, his influence on Western literature would still be strongly felt. But it is for *The Decameron*, his collection of 100 stories, that we remember him most – stories that reappear in the works of **Chaucer**, through to the plots of **Shakespeare** and beyond.

In its immediate historical context, it seems an extraordinary project. **Dante** had written his *Divine Comedy* 50 years earlier, when writing in Italian, rather than Latin, seemed vulgar. But Dante's verse ennobled the language and, like **Petrarch**, Boccaccio followed his example, but in prose. However, he had the advantage of a thorough grounding in rhetoric, especially through his studies of canon law, in which – along with literature – he had immersed himself at King Robert of Anjou's cosmopolitan court at Naples.

The Decameron drew on traditional sources: folk tales that had circulated for generations, the seasoned speech-maker's mock modesty, the classical framing of a story within another story. But the origins of this bundling together of tales also stretch as far back as the *Thousand and One Nights* and even to Sanskrit texts.

Boccaccio's scheme places 10 narrators in a garden, to escape the plague that hit Florence in 1347. Over 10 days (*Dek'hemera* in Greek, hence the book's title) each must tell a story a day. Everyone has a turn at dictating a theme for the day, but this must be on an aspect of love. Some stories are courtly, some tragic, and plenty are bawdy – Boccaccio's range of language did not preclude the double entendre. The characters are united by a faith in telling stories to make things better, to comfort, or to distract in a time of sorrow.

Later in life Boccaccio almost abandoned literature to take holy orders, but Petrarch dissuaded him and Boccaccio ended his days writing a commentary on Dante's *Inferno*.

Böll

HEINRICH

born Cologne 1917; died near Bonn 1985

It seems that I have been singled out to ensure that the chain of black sheep is not broken in my generation. Somebody has to be the black sheep, and it happens to be me.

BLACK SHEEP, TR. LEILA VENNEWITZ

HEINRICH BÖLL HAS BEEN called "the voice of Germany's post-war conscience". As a teenager, he resisted pressure to join the Hitler Youth, but was conscripted for service during World War Two. During the war we was wounded three times and later captured. After his release in 1947, he settled in Cologne.

There he began writing novels. The first dealt exclusively with war and its utter futility. *The Train was on Time* is about a man's premonition of his death on the Eastern Front. It hit home with its first-hand realism and sense of doom. His first great international success was *Acquainted with the Night*, whose protagonist returns from a POW camp to his family, all sharing a small single room in an urban wilderness. His feeling that no-one can understand his experience manifests itself in domestic violence. There are, however, signs of Böll's hope for reconciliation. It also set the scene for his later representation of gutted cities, fragmented families and the human cost, not just of the war, but of Germany's economic recovery from it. This is especially true of *Tomorrow and Yesterday*.

Often his work is cast in simple language, eschewing high German in favour of a more direct style that owes much to **Hemingway**. His characters avoid intellectualising their plight, often stopping short of trying to express their emotions, finding it, perhaps, as difficult as the author did. Later, Böll wrote love stories, long and short, providing the strongest strain of optimism in his work. He was also able to couch his thoughts in satire: perhaps his most famous tale, *Dr Murke's Collected Silences*, has a radio engineer collecting recorded pauses. It is a triumphant response to the problem of how to speak when words seem useless. He won the Nobel Prize in 1972.

MAJOR WORKS

The Train was on Time (1949)

Adam, Where Art Thou? (1951)

Acquainted with the Night (1953)

Tomorrow and Yesterday (1954)

The Clown (1963)

Group Portrait with Lady (1971)

The Safety Net (1982)

Borges

JORGE LUIS

born Buenos Aires 1899; died Buenos Aires 1986

Time is the substance I am made of. Time is a river that carries me away, but I am the river; it is a tiger that mangles me, but I am the tiger; it is a fire that consumes me, but I am the fire. The world, alas, is real; I, alas, am Borges.

A NEW REFUTATION OF TIME

BORGES WAS A completely bookish writer. It would be wrong to say that for him books were the only reality, but to a mind that mistrusted any belief system, and a man trying to avoid political tides, they were more than a source of comfort.

He spent much of his life in libraries, including eight years working in a Buenos Aires branch library. One of his few political gestures – forthright criticism of Perón's regime – led the dictator to dismiss Borges from his post and appoint him inspector of chickens and rabbits at Cordóba Street market. He was later Professor of English Literature at Buenos Aires University and the head of the Argentine National Library.

Although he seemed to withdraw into academia as an ordered haven from the chaotic world, he still did not think books were safe. Undoubtedly he found the library and its cataloguing system a fine image of order when creating imaginary universes, but he also conceived *The Library of Babel*, a place containing all possible books made up from every conceivable combination of letters, the patterns of which may or may not even constitute languages. Once he had envisaged this kind of cosmos, anything seemed possible: in later pieces we find him mixing real scholarship with fictitious texts, creating new authors for old books, or fabricating passages of books as real as Pliny's *Natural History*.

Like the earlier great librarian **Callimachus**, he found, "the composition of vast books is a laborious and impoverishing extravagance. I have preferred to write notes upon imaginary books." It is true that his stories are concise and often read like essays – a device that makes the title of his first collection, *Fictions*, all the more significant: the pieces are not there to discuss real things.

With encroaching blindness and the need to compose by dictation, Borges tended toward the shorter form, the parable. Public recognition came late, with the 1961 Formentor Prize, and recently a surprising cottage industry has emerged in biographies of this least lifelike of writers.

Bowen

ELIZABETH

born County Cork 1899; died London 1973

However rash it might be to speak at all, Sarah wished she knew how to speak more clearly. The obscurity and loneliness of her trouble was not to be borne. How could she tell the others the feeling of dislocation, the formless dread that had been with her since she found herself in the drawing-room?

THE HAPPY AUTUMN FIELDS

ELIZABETH BOWEN'S NOVELS and short stories have been compared to the work of **Virginia Woolf**. This is partly due to her concentration on characters' inner feelings, which her narratives tap into at will. There is also a fastidious, Woolf-like attention to detail and an exploration of the intense emotions that proceed from them.

She was raised in Dublin, but settled in England after her marriage in 1923. Thus her work is often set on either side of the Irish Sea. Many of her early stories are set in London. But during the Blitz, which destroyed her house, she wrote more about Ireland, as if to escape from the horror around her. *The Heat of the Day* recalls the bombing and the plot introduces politics and espionage – although here, as elsewhere in her work, personal concerns prevail over public events.

Another London tale, *The Demon Lover*, is about the capital after the Blitz, depicting a city peopled with ghosts, which are made convincingly real. Her short stories often glimpse the supernatural, but never become too fantastic.

She famously declared the novel to be a "non-poetic statement of poetic truth". This truth often strikes out from her dense descriptions and the especially domestic, familial settings of her work, to announce the agonising temporality of life and that everything around us is either infinitely precious or vulnerable. Both World Wars represent moments of great change and loss in her work, as does the Treaty that separated Ireland in 1922, which forms the backdrop for *The Last September*.

Boyd

WILLIAM

born Ghana 1952

My first act on entering this world was to kill my mother.

THE NEW CONFESSIONS

WILLIAM BOYD BELONGS to the normally comic tradition of "The Englishman Abroad", except that he's Scottish. He was born in Ghana, West Africa, and his novels are often set in similar countries that sometimes remain nameless The first, *A Good Man in Africa*, about a low-ranking, low-life British diplomat, placed Boyd in **Evelyn Waugh** territory. A subsequent book moved to East Africa, and used a wide range of narrative voices to document the immediate effects of World War One on a remote town.

America is another of Boyd's locales. he continues to document clashing cultures in *Stars and Bars*, in which a young art expert finds himself in New York. As if the glitterati were not bewildering enough for the hero, he is then sent to make an important purchase from a typical Southern family. This book, together with *On Yankee Station*, won praise on both sides of the Atlantic. The author was astute enough to make his naïve British hero every bit as ridiculous as his hosts appear to him.

In his writing, Boyd has experimented with different techniques, angles and models. In *The New Confessions*, the precedent is **Rousseau**, and the thoughts of the narrator wander. For *Brazzaville Beach*, he chooses a woman narrator. Hope Clearwater's story is set in Africa, where she is observing the behaviour of chimpanzees. Digressions and flashbacks describe the circumstances that brought her there: she has left Britain and a failed relationship. She learns from her field study and sudden rootlessness to accept the flux of her life, rather than to strive to find permanence. The book won the James Tait Black Memorial Prize in 1991.

Bradbury

RAY

born Waukegan, Illinois 1920

Man, in his immense tidal motion, is about to flow out toward far new worlds; but man must conquer the seed of his own destruction.

THE MARTIAN CHRONICLES

RAY BRADBURY HAS a special place among science fiction writers. He is admired as much for the poetry and humanity of his work as for its visionary qualities.

In all his work Bradbury is concerned that human values and ethics survive in a society that is becoming increasingly impersonal and technological. *The Martian Chronicles* and *Fahrenheit 451* are early expressions of this and, for many readers, his best books.

In the former, a vision of colonists settling on Mars provided a setting in which the author could address the problems of 50s America. On the new planet, the issues of racism, nuclear power and Cold War politics appear throughout a series of related stories. By treating such themes in isolation, in fable form, Bradbury made his own values more strongly felt.

Even in pessimistic narratives, Bradbury demonstrates hope for the future and faith in literature. This is clearest in his most famous book, *Fahrenheit 451*. It is named after the temperature at which paper burns. Bradbury took his confidence to the limit by envisaging a society that completely bans the written word. The nightmare regime condemns all books to be burned and we meet the man whose job it is to throw them on the fire. The narrative then follows his subversion as he falls in love with a dissident. Although the work belongs in the "dystopian" tradition of *Brave New World* and *1984*, Bradbury provides a way out.

He remains a prolific and extremely versatile writer. Besides short stories and novels, he has written plays, poems, detective stories and, in 1956, the screenplay for *Moby Dick*. *Fahrenheit 451* has been adapted as an opera. Critical response to his work has varied. Today, new generations of readers are discovering his passionate prose, after a period in which he lapsed in favour, but his earlier work was read avidly by **Graham Greene**, **Christopher Isherwood** and Bertrand Russell. Although his writing has never been confined to science fiction, he is most at home there, writing in the genre he calls "the history of ideas, the history of our civilisation birthing itself".

Brecht

BERTOLT   **born Augsburg, Germany 1898; died Berlin 1956**

Food is the first thing: morals follow on.

THE THREEPENNY OPERA

BRECHT'S MOST REMARKABLE achievements were as a playwright. From early in his career he sought to transform theatre. He never wanted his audiences to be so moved or convinced by a play that they stopped thinking for themselves. To this end, he strove constantly to remind them that they were in a theatre.

He did this by deflating moments of pathos, either with a cabaret-style song or a choral figure commenting on the action in doggerel, or by introducing written signs indicating historical allusions or aspects of the pastiche. His plays snatched elements of many influences: Medieval mystery plays, where representations of the devil could beguile the spectators before the actor would destroy the illusion; **Shakespeare**'s intrusions of the banal; expressionist plays, with their short, immediate scenes; and cabaret. His musical collaboration with Kurt Weill, a patchwork of borrowings from musical history, makes this last device particularly unforgettable.

These techniques, often grouped under the term *Verfremdung*, or alienation, served Brecht's political purpose. They challenged Aristotle's comfortable notion that theatre was merely the imitation of an action. Instead they tended towards forthright, Communist-based social criticism. This became urgent with the accession of Nazism, which drove Brecht out of Germany from 1933 to 1947.

But Brecht was no propagandist. He was a completely practical writer, insisting that his work was "education first, entertainment second". The target audience for his drama, as for his poems, was the working class. While his early work delivered, with shows put on in cafés, his first great success, *The Threepenny Opera,* was a huge hit with the privileged socialites who were the butt of his satire and rage.

The pragmatism of his stagecraft reflected the ideas it strove to convey, in particular the Marxist principle that the end should justify the means to ensure progress and survival. His most famous characters, such as Mother Courage and Galileo, face agonising personal decisions and often choose what an audience may consider the less honourable option. Brecht's theatre succeeds when it defies our expectation that drama should deal foremost with noble themes and fine actions.

Breton

ANDRÉ

born Tinchebray, France 1896; died Paris 1966

Poetry happens in a bed as with love

Its unmade sheets are the dawn of things

Poetry happens in the woods

It has the space it needs

ON THE ROAD TO SAN ROMANO

ANDRÉ BRETON IS KNOWN chiefly as the poet who gave a voice to surrealism. He was a key organiser of the Surrealist group – the first to fully articulate its theory and to put it into literary practice. He was more responsible than anyone for the contents of the Surrealist manifesto, and for

introducing the group's members to one another.

In 1916, he joined the Dadaists, a group founded by Tristan Tzara, which created works of art by cutting up shapes and letting them fall haphazardly. Poems were made from randomly dispersed newspaper-snippings. In 1919, he co-founded the journal *Littérature*, in which he published "automatic" writing. This exercise was indebted to the recently departed **Apollinaire**, whose unpunctuated poetry, and technique of changing subject matter according to where the sounds of words took him, gave way to the free association of words and images that was the definitive model for Breton's verse.

Breton did much to cultivate the state of mind required by such writing. He had met Freud and was fascinated by the sub-conscious. If its workings could be tapped into and exposed, a different, dream-like reality would emerge – one that would hardly be compatible with the way our waking brains organise the evidence of the senses. For this reason, it was essential that writings produced in this way were not revised later, when the trance was over. **Allen Ginsberg** described this as, "first thought, best thought" and, along with **William Burroughs**, he was chief among later explorers of these poetic techniques.

This research generated writing with a highly sexual content. Breton's idea of love was brimming with fantasy and idealisation of the beloved, often in the figure of a child bride. This is best documented in his novel, *Nadja*. Another consequence was a greater role for the reader, who could witness the sparks given off by the "violent clash of images" in his or her head, where a whole new chain of subliminal associations could begin.

Brontë

ANNE **born Haworth, Yorkshire 1820; died Scarborough 1849**

I am at a loss to conceive how a man should permit himself to write anything that would be really disgraceful to a woman, or why a woman should be censured for writing anything that could be proper and becoming for a man.

PREFACE TO THE SECOND EDITION
OF THE TENANT OF WILDFELL HALL

ANNE WAS THE YOUNGEST of the Brontës and perhaps the one whose career suffered most from the vagaries of the brother Branwell. Each of the sisters took teaching work to fund the boy's possible literary success. When this failed and Branwell turned increasingly to alcohol and opium, Anne arranged for him to join her in teaching at Thorpe Green Hall. His romantic indiscretion with the mother of the house ruined the arrangement for both of them.

Charlotte Brontë's biographical note mentions her sister contemplating "at first hand… the terrible effect of talents misused and faculties abused", and finds this borne out in Anne's novel, *The Tenant of Wildfell Hall*. The book shares features of structure and atmosphere with **Emily Brontë's** *Wuthering Heights*, published the year before, and provides in the heroine's husband an account of something similar to Branwell's decadence.

Much of Anne's earlier life finds expression in her only other novel, *Agnes Grey*. Like her sisters, Anne worked as a governess and her charges were as problematic as the Bloomfields in the story. The narrative, seen largely through the eyes of its heroine, is shot through with personal responses to nature, which seems in turn to respond to the action: the images of doves and the sea have an especially important bearing on Agnes' emotional state.

The book contains discussion of poetry and incorporates a sample that Anne wrote elsewhere. Her verse is characteristically in the same lyric form used by her sisters. The earlier poems are naïve in tone (especially compared with Emily's), but yield to a gloomier mood towards the end of her short life. In *Agnes Grey*, poetry is seen as a musical effusion that witnesses and solaces less musical moods; and it is hard not to read Anne's stanzas without seeing an expression of the despair her patient, Christian persona struggled to exclude from her daily life.

Brontë

CHARLOTTE

born Haworth, Yorkshire 1818; died Haworth 1848

I am not talking to you now through the medium of custom, conventionalities, nor even of mortal flesh: it is my spirit that addresses your spirit; just as if both had passed through the grave, and we stood at God's feet, equal – as we are!

JANE EYRE

THE THREE NOVELS Charlotte Brontë published in her lifetime approach their subject matter in very different ways, although the last, *Villette*, borrows many elements of plot from her first, then unpublished effort, *The Professor*. But that subject remains the position of women, and all her heroines seek to love men, on equal terms with men – and to be allowed to express that love.

Jane Eyre tackles this in the fullest vein of Romanticism. It is cast as an autobiography and our narrator impresses upon us the depth and individuality of her feelings, in an age when women were not supposed to express any emotion. It is she who professes her love to Mr Rochester, not the other way round, and the early parts of the novel explain how her childhood made her so wilful. Throughout, there are sinister elements of the Gothic novel, the intervention of the supernatural and the overbearing presence of nature to compound the heroine's lonely plight. At one point she tells us, "I have no relative but the universal mother, Nature."

The protagonist of Brontë's next book, *Shirley*, is no less independent. Charlotte described Shirley elsewhere as a picture of her sister **Emily**, as she might have been had she survived. But the setting is in stark contrast, incorporating social and historical accuracy into its appeal for greater equality between the sexes.

Villette draws on the author's experiences of teaching in Brussels, where she fell in love with a fellow teacher. In the novel the parity between the couple is established gradually, through a series of tests, while the real-life romance had a less happy ending.

Charlotte was the eldest of the surviving Brontë siblings and she outlived them all. She was the only one who pursued the eventually successful courtship that each sister described in their novels, but when she did marry, she died while pregnant.

Brontë

EMILY

born Haworth, Yorkshire 1818; died Haworth 1848

No coward soul is mine,

No trembler in the world's storm-

troubled sphere:

I see Heaven's glories shine,

And faith shines equal, arming me

from fear.

LAST LINES

EMILY REMAINS the most enigmatic of the Brontës, an impression deepened by the intimations of mystery and madness that pervade her work.

She was not known to have any good friends; instead she maintained a kind of twinship with her younger sister **Anne**, with whom she invented the kingdom of Gondal as a setting for their stories and poems. It was a while before **Charlotte** discovered that Emily had been writing poems, then suggesting the three of them should publish their verse together. A month after publication, only two copies had been sold, but Emily's work stood out from the rest of the volume.

Her only novel, *Wuthering Heights*, appeared in the same year as her sister Charlotte's *Jane Eyre*, but enjoyed nothing like the same success. Readers were unprepared for either for the levels of violence, the forthright language, or the sheer technical brilliance of the book. The story is narrated by Nellie Dean to our own narrator. Her story has a remarkable balance between passionate engagement and mute witnessing. The result is a drama full of inherent ironies and repeated histories: but that is for the reader, not the teller. For Nellie, the speech

and action of her subjects is all. The approach draws on many of the effects that Aristotle divined in Greek tragedy.

The action centres on Heathcliffe, a gypsy orphan who is rescued by Mr Earnshaw from the streets of Liverpool. The "strange bond" between him and his foster-sister is never fulfilled and after her death he spends his days in savage jealousy and vengeful bitterness. The immense power of these emotions is sustained by the force of his rhetoric and the atmosphere of the moors, all the way to a more hopeful conclusion.

Long after Emily's untimely death *Wuthering Heights* finally gained recognition as one of the finest English novels ever written.

Browning

ELIZABETH BARRETT born County Durham 1806; died Florence 1861

...But poets should

Exert a double vision; should have eyes

To see near things as comprehensively

As if afar they took their point of sight,

And distant things as infinitely deep

As if they touched them.

AURORA LEIGH

IN HER LIFETIME, Elizabeth Barrett Browning was more famous than her husband **Robert Browning** and in 1850 she was tipped to succeed **Wordsworth** as Poet Laureate. Her complete grasp and free handling of metre, together with the depth and immediacy of the ideas her poetry expresses, secure her place among the best of English poets.

She was educated at home and showed precocious literary talent. She was reading Homer in Greek at age 10 and had written her first epic poem (on the battle of Marathon) by the time she was 19. Her father watched this promising career protectively, paying for the publication of her *Essay on Mind* and translation of **Aeschylus**' *Prometheus Bound*. But he kept her at home and would not allow his children to marry. The situation worsened after ELizabeth's brother drowned, a blow from which she never recovered.

Her elopement with Browning in 1846 left her father unforgiving. The couple fled to Italy, where they championed the cause of Italian unity and independence. In this, as well as poems on social reform and the role of women, especially in literature, her verse was often overtly political.

Although this never diminished the quality of her work, it did lead to a decline in public favour.

Her love-lyrics remain her most popular compositions, above all *Sonnets from the Portuguese*. These are not translations, but love poems to her husband, who dubbed her "the Portuguese". In them she adheres to the rigours of sonnet form without allowing it to cramp her style or constrict her syntax. The same combination of poetic strictures and freedom of expression is evident in her chief work, *Aurora Leigh*, which reads as much like a novel as a blank verse epic. Indeed, the narrator digresses to suggest that contemporary themes are riper for poetic treatment than the dustier myths that, say, **Tennyson** was expounding. She died four years after its publication, a literary celebrity, and her *Last Poems* appeared posthumously, in 1862.

Browning

ROBERT
born Camberwell, London 1812; died London 1889

"But try," you urge, "the trying shall

suffice;

The aim, if reached or not, makes

great the life:

Try to be Shakespeare, leave the rest

to fate!"

BISHOP BLOUGRAM'S APOLOGY

BROWNING'S POETRY took a long time to find public admiration, and ever since has proved easy to lampoon. He wrote verse voluminously and at great speed. Refined diction and flawless lyrics were never his – he was too spontaneous, too daring an experimenter for that. His real achievement was to fill his poems with a wide range of characters and to use the rhythms of natural speech fully to explore the psychology and motivation of the poetic *personae* he presents.

It was not always to be that way. His earliest influence was **Shelley**, and Browning's first published poem *Pauline* imitated his confessional approach. The ridicule this received was not his last public disappointment. In 1837, his play *Strafford* ran for just five nights at Covent Garden, although it was a clearer sign of his true talent. His book *Dramatic Lyrics* was a collection of dramatic monologues – a form he made his own.

But he had no success with that either, although he was by then moving in the same circles as **Wordsworth**, **Tennyson** and **Dickens.** In 1845 he began corresponding with the acclaimed poet **Elizabeth Barrett** and married her the following year. He lived in the shadow of her fame until she died in 1861, when he moved back to England from Italy, which they had chosen as their home. His books gained increasing recognition and the vast poem *The Ring and the Book* secured his fame. Written in 12 volumes, it examines a real murder case in 17th-century Rome from a wide range of dramatic perspectives.

Although Browning the poet was celebrated for finding the voices of Italian painters, vain or uncertain bishops, grammarians, musicians, freedom-fighters or travellers, his admirers listened in vain for the voice of Browning the man. While he maintained a high profile, he would never discuss his work in public. But the public honoured it with degrees and Browning societies dedicated to his legacy, which have enabled new generations of poets to explore the vast range of rhythmical, dramatic, emotional and spiritual possibilities he created.

Buck

PEARL   **born Hillsboro, Virginia 1892; died Danby, Vermont 1973**

"It is for your sake, old Buddha, that the rain comes down, the fortunate rain, blessing us all because of you."

IMPERIAL WOMAN

IN 1938 PEARL BUCK was the first American woman to win the Nobel Prize. The award came as a big surprise to everyone, including her, and few commentators discuss her without questioning this decision. But it can be justified by the Swedish Academy's commitment to promoting peace and idealism, whatever the merits of Buck's prose.

Throughout her life she strove hard to improve Sino-American relations through her work as a missionary and teacher in China, where she lived for 40 years. She began thinking in Chinese and said that when she wrote in English she was translating as she went. Thus American and Chinese strands of storytelling are fused in her work. In a lecture she pointed out that novels were not considered to be literature in China. When she is literary in the Chinese manner, Western readers have often criticised her work for being overly didactic and her language almost biblical. Still, her most accomplished novel, *The Good Earth*, although set in China, is recognised as a story with peculiarly American qualities.

Her treatment of the land as part of the people who till it belongs in the tradition of **Willa Cather** and **John Steinbeck.** As in the latter's *The Grapes of Wrath*, a family of subsistence farmers seeks a way to survive in the city – in this case because of crop failure. Although the reader is told how impossible staying alive in the city would be, Wang Lung, the head of the family, is spared from finding this out when a raid on a palace secures him enough money to buy his own land. Despite the setting, it is still possible to read this as an American tale of a household's advancement in society and a realisation of the American Dream.

The Good Earth was the first of a trilogy and Buck followed it with many more novels about Chinese peasant life, as well as a biography of her parents, who had also worked as missionaries in China.

Bulgakov

MIKHAIL

born Kiev 1891; died Moscow 1940

Everything passes away – suffering, pain, blood, hunger and pestilence... but the stars will remain... Why, then, will we not turn our eyes to the stars? Why?

WHITE GUARD

MIKHAIL BULGAKOV balanced fantasy and realism in plays, stories and novels that served a subversive, satirical turn in the Russia of his day and beyond. In spite of this, together with political indifference and a belief in God, he remained a great favourite of Stalin, who was shocked at the news of the writer's early death.

Bulgakov worked as a doctor – for a while on the front line during World War One and subsequently in a country practice. He abandoned medicine in 1919 and wrote *A Country Doctor's Notebook* about his experiences. The book shows the compassion that was to characterise his work, however fanciful it became.

During his lifetime, his real successes were in the theatre. The best loved of these was *Day of the Turbins*, which he adapted from his novel. In Soviet Russia it aroused controversy because of the sympathy it showed towards officers of the defeated White Army. But Stalin saw the play 15 times and thought the characters' great bravery made the Bolsheviks, who vanquished them, seem all the more invincible. When it seemed Bulgakov's stage career was over, he threatened to leave the country, but Stalin intervened and secured him the job of producer at Stanislavsky's Moscow Arts Theatre. Rows with the director over a play about Bulgakov's hero **Molière** led him to resign in 1936.

By then he was already working on the novel he knew would be his finest work. *The Master and Margarita* takes the story of a writer in love to the pitch of **Goethe**'s *Faust*. The Devil arrives as a society sophisticate in Moscow. The city becomes a fantastical place, with cats running a bureaucracy taken to unnatural extremes. The author balances this action with a meticulously researched account of Christ's trial and crucifixion in a very real Jerusalem. Although the narrative never stabilises, it leaves the reader in a world that, through all its gyrations, has a very definite moral core.

Bunyan

JOHN

**born Elstow, Bedfordshire 1628;
died on the way from Reading to London 1688**

*Though with great difficulty I am got
hither, yet now do I not repent me of all
the trouble I have been at to arrive where I
am. My sword, I shall give to him that
shall succeed me in my pilgrimage, and my
courage and skill to him that can get it.*

MR VALIANT-FOR-TRUTH,
THE PILGRIM'S PROGRESS

JOHN BUNYAN EXPRESSED his devout Puritan beliefs in simple but profoundly affecting prose. He was an inspired preacher and communicator, who knew how to make complex theological ideas comprehensible through storytelling and allegory.

His convictions led him to fight on Cromwell's side during the English Civil War from 1644 to 1646 and he became deeply involved in the religious debates that followed, espousing the creeds of such non-conformist sects as the Ranters, with whom he shared the idea that the individual conscience is above the law. In 1660 he was arrested for preaching without a bishop's licence and spent most of the next 12 years in Bedford gaol.

There he wrote a number of pamphlets and explanations of his faith. When serving a subsequent sentence in 1675, he began work on *The Pilgrim's Progress*. It remains his most important and widely read book. In it Bunyan addresses the evangelical question, "How may I be saved?" It takes the form of a dream narrative, drawing on the influence of William Langland and the anonymous *Dream of the Rood*. The author shares his vision of Christian, a journeyer through life, whose city is about to be destroyed.

Christian comes upon various people and places, which either represent aspects of the soul or provide a glimpse of the age's spiritual scene. As well as meeting Misters Valiant-for-Truth, Hopeful and Faithful, he encounters Mr Worldly Wiseman, an embodiment of the Church of England. He also confronts the Giant Despair, is daunted by the Mountain of Law and is diverted by Vanity Fair – an emporium of all that might distract a soul, where the Catholic church has a particularly large stall and the Pope appears as a caged ogre.

Here, as elsewhere in his spiritual mission, Bunyan refashioned old literary genres into an accessible, modern idiom. A plain man, he wrote for ordinary people, in the hope that as many readers as possible could read *The Pilgrim's Progress*. He also hoped that they might undertake the pilgrimage it advocates.

MAJOR WORKS

Gospel Truths Opened (1656)

A Vindication (1657)

The Holy City, or The New Jerusalem (1665)

Grace Abounding to the Chief of Sinners: or, A Brief and Faithful Relation of the Exceeding Mercy of God in Christ to his Poor Servant, John Bunyan (1666)

A Confession of my Faith, and a Reason of my Practice (1672)

The Pilgrim's Progress from This World, To That Which Is to Come; Delivered under the Similitude of a Dream. Wherein is Discovered, the Manner of His Setting Out, His Dangerous Journey, And Safe Arrival at the Desired Country (1678-1684)

The Life and Death of Mr. Badman (1680)

The Holy War, or The Losing and Taking Again of the Town of Mansoul (1682)

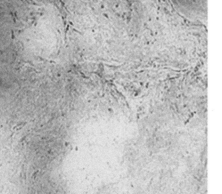

Burgess

ANTHONY

born Manchester 1917; died Monaco 1993

*Well, the gumbrils are humming. The
birds ingest rumbling, crumbling blunder.
Yet a thumbril is lovely, a warm start.
Loud crowd the lies, lies loud for the
crowd, the crowds lie loud...*

MOZART AND THE WOLF GANG
(VERBALISING MOZART'S 40TH
SYMPHONY, K551, LAST MOVEMENT)

IN 1958, ANTHONY BURGESS was told he had 12 months to live. Over the next year, he wrote five-and-a-half novels – fewer than he'd hoped. The news was a false alarm, but it set this writer of incredible intellect (he had just been translating **T.S. Eliot's** *The Waste Land* for his Malaysian pupils) on his apparently unstoppable literary career.

His work was preoccupied with the relationship between literature, language and music. But this did not stop him addressing social concerns; instead, it helped him. In his most controversial book, *A Clockwork Orange*, violent youths in a future age adopt their own slang formed from Russian and Cockney (nadsat) and are inspired to crime by listening to Beethoven. The composer also provides the theme of a later book, *Napoleon Symphony*, which George Steiner compared to a Beethoven score. Burgess was also a prolific composer and strove to imitate music with his words.

Joyce, whose texts Burgess worked to make more widely accessible, was his exemplar for this. His literary scholarship is everywhere, especially in the novels based on poets' lives (*Nothing Like The Sun*, on **Shakespeare**; *ABBA ABBA* on **Keats**; and *A Dead Man in Deptford*, on **Marlowe**). His novels gloss other texts: *1985* continues from **Orwell's** *1984* and the aging man of letters in *Earthly Powers* includes the likes of **Somerset Maugham** in his copious literary reminiscences.

Despite his erudition, such books abound with humour and humanity and the fact that he embodied these qualities made the obituary notices of 1993 especially poignant. He wrote as though every year might have been his last.

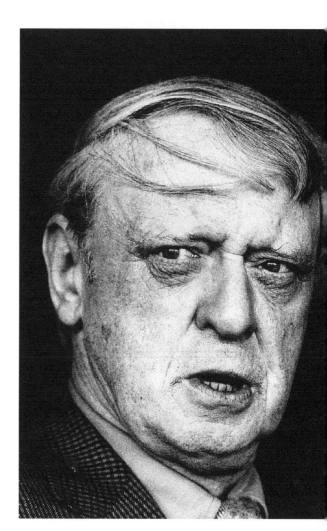

Burns

ROBERT

born Ayrshire 1759; died Dumfries 1796

O Lord! Yestreen, thou knows, wi' Meg,

Thy pardon I sincerely beg;

O! may't ne'er be a livin plague

To my dishonour,

An' I'll ne'er lift a lawless leg

Again upon her.

HOLY WILLY'S PRAYER

MAJOR WORKS

Poems, chiefly in the Scottish Dialect (1786)

Collected Works in Poems and Songs, ed. J Kinsley (3 vols, 1968)

SCOTLAND'S BEST-LOVED POET, Robert Burns was especially popular in his homeland because he wrote in such a rich strain of Scots. This has given his life and work a kind of mythic status. His biographers have either disapproved of his hard drinking and apparent immorality, or else lionised him unquestioningly.

He was born in Scotland, at a time when its culture and traditions had been brutally repressed by the English after the defeat of Bonnie Prince Charlie at the Battle of Culloden in 1746. The country's agricultural heritage was also waning in the dawn of the Industrial Revolution. Burns was a farmer's son and had worked as a ploughman. This gave him a real insight into the hardships of country life, which sets him apart from the Romantic poets of the era, who rhapsodised the simple charms of rustic life.

Burns' father was determined to give his son an education – he studied **Shakespeare** and The Bible, as well as learning French. Perhaps his most immediate influence was **Alexander Pope**, whose metrical precision and deft rhyming Burns' ear was well-equipped to emulate. But it was native Scottish poets such as Hamilton and Fergusson who demonstrated just how expressive his own dialect could be.

As his poems circulated, they won the widespread admiration of his compatriots – except the Scottish clergy, who deplored his *Holy Willy's Prayer*: the stanza above is one of the least blasphemous. As well as this kind of elegant satire, he proved his skill in narrative poetry with *Tam O'Shanter*, with elegy and mock elegy, with ballads and songs. In many of these there is excellent humour. Their structures, often typical of 18th century stanza or couplet forms, provide the framework for a rich and fresh language of their own, which is as full of such textbook devices as alliteration and assonance as of the slang and easy rhythms of everyday speech.

This has made him accessible and well-loved beyond his native Scotland. His vocal enthusiasm for the French Revolution ensured his songs were as popular among the British Chartists of the 19th century as with the Russian revolutionaries of the 20th century. Burns night is celebrated in Moscow each year with something of the fervour that Scots display on every January 25th – the poet's birthday.

Burroughs

EDGAR RICE

born Chicago 1875; died 1950

Hundreds of thousands of years ago our ancestors of the dim and distant past faced the same problem, which we must face, possibly in these same primeval forests. That we are here today evidences their victory. What did they do that we may not do?

TARZAN OF THE APES

EDGAR RICE BURROUGHS wrote a lot of adventure and science fiction novels at extraordinary speed. Each one was part of an on-going series. He worked on four of these simultaneously: one was set on Mars, one on Venus, and one in the centre of Earth. But the best known of the four is the series beginning with *Tarzan of the Apes*.

As a child, Burroughs had been an excellent student. When he left home, he developed a taste for adventure, which he nurtured on his brother's ranch in Idaho, US, and at the military academy in Massachusetts. After a number of occupations, including selling pencil sharpeners, he wrote *Under the Moons of Mars*, in which John Carter leaves Arizona to explore the red planet, known to its inhabitants as Barsoom. These people are the fragmented social groups of a once-united, mighty civilisation.

Tarzan shared the wanderlust of Burroughs' other characters, but it is our world that seems like another planet to the self-taught child of the jungle. To Burroughs, the earth must have appeared quite small, peopled as it was by definable types. But through Tarzan's gaze its wonder is expanded. There were hints of this vision in earlier works, particularly *Under the Moons of Mars*. John Carter's last look at Arizona, before heading off for the planet, evokes the American landscape with awe, as though it is already other-worldly.

Despite its pulp status, Burroughs' work demonstrates a fine sense for rhetoric and structure, such as the frame device with which the Tarzan cycle begins. The profits, including radio and cartoon rights, meant the author could become Edgar Rice Burroughs Inc in 1923.

Burroughs

WILLIAM   **born St. Louis, Missouri 1914**

---

*I decided to lop him off if it meant a
smother party. (This is a rural English
custom designed to eliminate aged and
bedfast dependents. A family so afflicted
throws a "smother party" where the
guests pile mattresses on the old liability,
climb on top of the mattresses and lush
themselves out.)*

THE NAKED LUNCH

WILLIAM BURROUGHS' WORK has its theoretical
roots in Dadaism and automatic writing. In practice
it articulates the author's relationship with hard
drugs. The sustained states of mind which he
explored could hardly have been anticipated by his
surrealist forebears and Burroughs has struggled to
find literary form to express them – just as he
struggled with addiction.

After graduating from Harvard with an English
degree, Burroughs worked as an anthropologist, a
private detective and in advertising. Throughout the
40s and 50s, he roamed the globe in search of
narcotics havens, eventually settling in Morocco in
1953. The same year, he published the mock-
confessional *Junkie: Confessions of an Unredeemed
Drug Addict*, under the pen name of William Lee, the
persona that featured in all his later books.

His experiments with structure and style in *Junkie*
paved the way for *The Naked Lunch*, his most famous
book. This combines a babel of dictions – refined,
underground, authoritarian – and a host of genres

in its attempt to contain the hallucinations, violence
and sado-masochistic gay sex which Burroughs
tried to describe.

It was initially banned for obscenity, but the ruling
was overturned, although the debate continued to
rage over whether it actively promoted drug use, or
sustained a powerful argument against it. In fact, he
only managed to complete the book after finding a
cure for his addiction in England. The left-over
material filled three subsequent books, in which
Burroughs explored the theme of escape from
control. In them his advocation of complete personal
freedom suggests that drug dependency is an
obstacle to liberation, with each addiction leading to
a need for something else.

Byron

GEORGE GORDON, LORD   born London 1788; died Missolonghi 1824

The fire that on my bosom preys

Is lone as some volcanic isle;

No torch is kindled at its blaze –

A funeral pile.

ON THIS DAY I COMPLETE MY
THIRTY-SIXTH YEAR.
MISSOLONGHI, JANUARY 22, 1824

FOR MANY, Byron was the spirit of the Romantic age. Born shortly before the French Revolution, he made liberal speeches in the House of Lords, wrote lethal anti-Tory satire and finally died for the cause of Greek freedom.

This made him a hero to poets such as **Goethe** and **Pushkin**, composers such as Beethoven and Tchaikovsky, and painters such as Delacroix. But it is possible to see him more as a throwback to the 18th century – an establishment-educated nobleman with voracious reading habits and a strong work ethic, whose output aligned him more with **Pope** than his contemporaries. Indeed, he saved his most savage lines for the likes of **Wordsworth** and **Keats**.

His first published work was *Hours of Idleness*, while his second, *English Bards and Scotch Reviewers*, was an attack on the critics who dismissed the first. But it was the appearance of *Childe Harold's Pilgrimage* in 1812 that drew the literary world to throng him. The verse travelogue reflects the author's roving, while his hero shares his feeling of discomfort with his age. Byron later added two cantos to the work to incorporate Belgium, Italy and Napoleon.

If poetry brought him fame, his looks and lovers preserved it. His beauty was often painted and his romances were a constant source of scandal. Meanwhile, his writing continued to betray his preferences for the near-east over Britain and showed his exhaustive knowledge of the area's history. He even compiled an Armenian dictionary.

Towards the end of his life, he was able to combine the satire of *A Vision of Judgement* with his interest in writing about fate-buffeted young men (such as *Mazeppa*) to produce his masterpiece, *Don Juan*. The stanza form incorporates masterful comic rhymes, sustained side-swipes at Wellington and Southey (then Poet Laureate), as well as shipwreck and domestic tragedy. The joy of it is in its bathos and constant digression: one imagines it could have ended anywhere. Before he could complete the vast project, Byron died at Missolonghi, Greece, where he remains a national hero.

Calderón de la Barca

PEDRO   **born Madrid 1600; died Madrid 1681**

Who's calling me, such that, from the

hard core

of this round earth, concealing me

within,

you see the wings that soar?

Who shows me to myself?

GOD, IN THE MIGRANT LAMB,
TR. BERNI ZANZMER

CALDERÓN WAS THE LAST surviving playwright from that great age of Spanish comedy associated chiefly with **Lope de Vega**. Of all the dramatists of his generation, he was the one who commanded the most respect from audiences, patrons and, perhaps most importantly, the church. In a period when the censor's job was to check the soundness of the theological argument in a play, Calderón's work encountered the fewest problems. His orthodox beliefs and noble poetic diction made him by far the most established (and establishment) author in late 17th-century Spain.

He was poet at the courts of Philip IV and Charles II, where he regularly produced comedies that often dealt with the theme of love. He would frequently present Love and Hate as allegorical figures, involved in intrigues and counter-intrigues. Calderón brought these figures further to life with his very active use of staging. Unlike **Shakespeare**, his production and stage directions are indispensable to the action, calling for vivid sets and intricate hiding places. Although the characters were Classical or Old Testament in origin, they pointed to strictly Christian

morals and dramatised debates about atonement or transubstantiation.

Calderón had a monopoly on the *autos sacramentales* (sacred pieces) that were staged in Madrid from 1648 until his death in 1681. This involved writing two plays a year to be performed on carts (sometimes needing as many as four to accommodate all his theatrical devices). The most famous of these is *Life's a Dream*, which is still in the

Spanish repertoire. It is his fullest discussion of the difference between appearance and reality, in which the hero is unsure whether he is awake or asleep. Ultimately, he comes to realise the superiority of eternal truths over ephemeral ones and, along with Calderón's other protagonists (including a Faustian figure), he learns that in this life his only hope is Christ.

65

Callimachus

born Cyrene c. 305 BC; died Alexandria c. 240 BC

Whatever subtle golden balms I'd place upon my head with garlands fine to smell turned into breathless flesh. Whatever fell to my base belly when I stuffed my face was gone the next day; but whatever strain I heard, I kept: those things alone remain.

CAUSES

WE KNOW CALLIMACHUS was one of the most read and admired of the Greek poets, for **Catullus**, **Horace**, **Virgil**, **Propertius** and **Ovid** are forever paying tribute to him, either with outright praise or studied imitation.

He lived and worked in the Greek colony of Alexandria in Egypt and his work is known as "Alexandrian" – a term embracing any classical poetry that was economical, densely worked and demonstrating wit through arcane allusions. Callimachus could scarcely avoid using such techniques. He worked in his home town's almost legendary library, for which he compiled a catalogue of 120 volumes. This incredible reading list enabled him to write treatises on language, sport, traditions, birds, nymphs, winds, and how months or places got their names. In an age before computers, he was able to identify words that appeared only once in the whole of Greek literature.

His poetry is full of this kind of information. He writes furiously against bards who churn out long heroic epics, especially (and most personally) Apollonius of Rhodes, chronicler of Jason and the Argonauts, and his own motto is best translated as "big book, big bad" and he reckoned it better to "keep the Muse trim". Although we know he composed at length, he crammed in his material and often strayed from large to small themes. When he attempts to describe Hercules killing the Nemean lion, he prefers to dwell on the peasant Molorchus, his problems with rodents and the mythic history of the mousetrap.

This episode appears in his *Aitia* (*Causes*), a work of which – like his hymns, epigrams and scholarly texts – little survives. Much of it was burned when Western crusaders ravaged Constantinople in 1204. But whole poems appear in the work of subsequent Latin poets, which, if not always direct translations, are loving homages and exercises in the kind of scholarly composition he made an aesthetic principle.

Calvino

ITALO

born Santiago de las Vegas, Cuba 1923; died Rome 1985

Lovers' reading of each other's bodies... differs from the reading of written pages ... It starts at any point, skips, repeats itself, goes backward, insists, ramifies in simultaneous and divergent messages, converges again, has moments of irritation, turns the page, finds its place, gets lost.

IF ON A WINTER'S NIGHT A TRAVELLER,
TR. WILLIAM WEAVER

THE ITALIAN NOVELIST, short-story writer and essayist Italo Calvino filled much of his work with an enquiry into what is possible. Throughout his career, he raised this question with a flamboyant intellect, which he deployed with an enormous sense of fun. His learning and ease with the language of research pervades most of his fiction and is most effective when it seems least appropriate.

His first novel, *The Path to a Nest of Spiders*, deals with his experiences in the Italian resistance during World War Two. This, and his subsequent collection of short stories, counted him among the new wave of realist writers appearing in Italy.

He blended this with an historical attention to reality in his trilogy, *Our Ancestors*, such that the impossible, fairy-tale characters seem all the more likely. He shares with **Borges** an interest in probability and alternative worlds and explores it scientifically in several stories, assessing the chances of unusual deaths witha clinical detachment..

He indulged his penchant for mathematics in OuLiPo, a polymaths' literary circle that included **Queneau** and **Perec**. A tale by the latter inspired Calvino's loveliest examination of fiction's possibilities, *If On A Winter's Night A Traveller*. The story becomes a romance between two of its readers, who hunt the book we turn out to be holding. Its mesh of skits and responses show how wildly texts and readers can play with each other.

Camus

ALBERT

born Mondovi, Algeria 1913; died Villeblevin 1960

All those folk are saying, "It was plague. We've had the plague here." You'd almost think they expected to be given medals for it. But what does that mean – "plague"? Just life, no more than that.

THE PLAGUE, TR. STUART GILBERT

ALBERT CAMUS WAS a French novelist, playwright and essayist, whose work was concerned with the crises of his age.

Born in Algeria, for whose football team he kept goal, the country provided the setting of his first novel, *The Outsider*, in which a young man is tried and executed for shooting an Arab.

The narrator and protagonist of the book, Meursault, is unable to recognise guilt, emotion, or any truths beyond immediately perceptible ones. In this study of the human condition Camus aligned

himself with the existential philosophy of his friend **Jean-Paul Sartre**. Although Camus was the less original thinker, Sartre maintained his admiration for his literary brilliance and looks.

Events before and during the World War Two encouraged Camus to explore tragedy in its fullest, classical sense, and to take it further. In his play *Caligula* he portrays the depraved Roman emperor as another existential protagonist who, feeling power thrust upon him, wonders quizzically how to exert it, before indulging his most brutal instincts on recognition that, from his bad eminence, human life is worthless. This seemed to mirror the actions of Hitler, whose subsequent occupation of France is symbolised by Oran, the afflicted town in *The Plague*. Camus' clear and unflinching prose style leads the reader through events that acquire a tragic inevitability; but unlike even tragedy, the story cannot admit any divine intervention: "All they knew was that they had called on God, and God had not answered them."

Camus fought with the French Resistance. His personal campaign against a brutal regime made him consider the nature of innocence in a world so weighed down by guilt. This is the theme of his long essay, *The Rebel*. *The Fall* is a richly artistic exploration of what follows from our action or inaction. The increasingly psychological nature of his work seemed to presage a change in beliefs and some thought his stance was becoming almost religious. After his early death in a car-crash (he'd hitched a ride with a stranger), his note-books appeared and an edition of a novel on which he had been working has recently been published as *The First Man*.

Capote

TRUMAN

born New Orleans 1924; died New York 1984

If I were free to choose from anyone alive, just snap my fingers and say "come here you", I wouldn't pick José. Nehru, he's nearer the mark. Wendell Willkie. I'd settle for Garbo any day. Why not?... Love should be allowed. I'm all for it.

BREAKFAST AT TIFFANY'S

TRUMAN CAPOTE CREATED outstandingly polished prose, both in fiction and non-fiction. He was born in New Orleans and began writing at an early age. By 22 he had won the O. Henry Memorial with his debut novel, *Other Voices, Other Rooms*. The book reflects Capote's southern childhood and his acceptance of his homosexuality – a theme that could scarcely have attracted more attention than the winsome cover photograph of the author.

The controversy over the book began a career of brilliant self-publicity. Capote was never out of the gossip columns. He travelled widely and moved among the celebrities of his day, many of whom he'd gripe about in later life. His own real taste of stardom came with *Breakfast at Tiffany's* – fuelled by the film and his fee. As in much of his work, it portrays a character with a unique way of doing everything, someone who doesn't quite fit in. Few readers have resisted the charms of Holly Golightly, or the elegance with which her tale is told.

Capote had written non-fiction (most notably *The Muses are Heard*, about a musical tour of Leningrad) before he produced *In Cold Blood*. His idea was to create a non-fiction novel. He followed a murder case, from the moment the crime was reported until the culprits' execution. Carefully recalled contributions from those involved in the events seem to create an even-handedness as the author's voice is submerged in the polyphony. But on long-awaited publication, critics accused Capote either of feeling too natural a sympathy for the killers, or of doing too little to save them (if his reporting could provide evidence for their insanity). The work displays the author's skill in handling narrative and his tremendous ear for convincing, powerful speech. It is more often cited as an argument against, than for, capital punishment. He published little during the rest of his life, leaving the novel *Answered Prayers* unfinished.

Carroll

LEWIS

"Contrariwise," continued Tweedledee, *"if it was so, it might be; and if it were so, it would be: but as it isn't, it ain't. That's logic."*

THROUGH THE LOOKING-GLASS

LEWIS CARROLL WAS the pseudonym of Charles Lutwidge Dodgson, a shy and lonely lecturer in mathematics at Oxford University. He was born in Daresbury in Cheshire, the third of 11 precocious children, with whom he devised endless word-games, board-games and mathematical puzzles.

These inclinations and his academic training, along with a childlike joy in the absurd, explain his ability to tell stories that contort the logical procedures he had mastered. The first was the inspired fantasy *Alice's Adventures in Wonderland.* This has been read as an extemporised story recounted to Alice Liddell, whose father Henry was co-author of the still-definitive Greek dictionary, Dean of Carroll's college, and the subject of **Hardy**'s funniest poem.

Although apparently a nonsense tale for children, some read into it a kind of logic, hidden beneath the seemingly random array of now immortal characters – Tweedledum and Tweedledee, the Mad Hatter and his circle…. Recent research has begun to explore the extent to which these figures were based on public persons and movements of the day, or are caricatures of Carroll's friends and colleagues.

The fantasy continued with *Through the Looking-Glass,* which contained the same blend of apparent lunacy with fine skits on contemporary poets (especially **Browning**). Carroll's ear for comic verse has been the envy of literary figures as diverse as **Auden** and **Belloc** and, in *The Hunting of the Snark,* Carroll so impressed Queen Victoria that she asked the author for a copy of his next work. Three years later she received his treatise on geometry, *Euclid and his Modern Rivals.*

Later work for children, mostly in verse, tried to incorporate Christian teaching – Carroll was ordained in 1861. But these seemed to miss what one reviewer thought was the key ingredient of his popularity with children – his ability to keep their attention while seeming not to teach them anything. After all, "What is the use of a book without pictures or conversations?" John Tenniel's illustrations to Carroll's books have come to be loved as much as the texts they illuminate.

Carver

RAYMOND   born Clatskanie, Oregon 1938; died Washington 1988

Breathing evenly and steadily once more, we'll collect ourselves, writers and readers alike, get up, "created of warm blood and nerves", as a Chekhov character puts it, and go onto the next thing: Life. Always life.

INTRODUCTION TO
WHERE I'M CALLING FROM

'ERRAND' IS PERHAPS the least typical of Raymond Carver's short stories. It has fine restaurants, champagne, history and the occasional digression. It was to be his last and concerns the death of **Chekhov**. But from this apparent lushness, the narrative closes in on tiny details and leaves the reader to gauge their emotional charge. It is the truest tribute the American writer could pay to the author who inspired him most.

Carver began by writing poems and found the experience of writing short stories similar. His first story collection, *Will You Please Be Quiet, Please?*, appeared in 1976, towards the end of his long struggle with alcoholism, a problem that affects some of his characters. As he had, they are always struggling for a living, in stories whose words and images are assembled with a care and economy that makes the prosaic poetical.

More books brought acclaim, awards and funding, enabling him to write full-time. Although his stories retained their grittiness, they became longer over the years. His characters became more inclined to hope for change, rather than wait for something else. One of his most praised pieces, 'A Small, Good Thing', has a baker atone in an instant for the menacing calls he has made to a dying boy's mother. Carver's work had often focused on the smaller consequences of life-or-death situations, but this kind of resolution was to come much later.

Towards the end of his short life, Carver came to terms with his imminent death. He made a selection of his best stories and wrote farewell poems to his wife Tess Gallagher, before concluding with his description of Chekhov's passing, which presaged his own. By then the comparison had become commonplace.

Cather

WILLA

born Winchester, Virginia 1873; died 1947

The land was open range and there was almost no fencing. As we drove further out into the country I felt a good deal as if we had come to the end of everything – it was a kind of erasure of personality.

FROM AN INTERVIEW

WILLA CATHER'S NOVELS reflect her insights into the lives of the pioneers and settlers of the American West. Her examination of life on the frontiers takes in the spiritual element of survival, the struggle of coming to terms with change and the troubled recognition of an individual's talents (as in *Lucy Gayheart*, whose heroine aspires to be a singer). She witnessed this when she moved from Winchester, Virginia, to Nebraska at the age of eight. It was at the university there that she received her education, going on to teach and write.

Her first volume, *April Twilights*, was a collection of poems. She lived in New York from 1906 to 1912, where she worked as managing editor of *Maclure's* magazine, and a resulting novel, *Alexander's Bridge*, is a rare glimpse of an urban setting in her work.

Otherwise, her artistic home is the soil. A telling moment is when Jim Burden, the narrator of *My Ántonia*, is found reading **Virgil**'s *Georgics* – Willa Cather undoubtedly shares the poet's conviction that the land is as much a living entity as those who work on it, as well as the observation that such work must be unremitting. Her strong and individual characters are attuned to the seasons and nature seems to respond to the action (as when cattle balk at

entering the barn where a suicide has taken place).

Her writing was often set in the past and later dealt with real events: *Death Comes for the Archbishop* tells the story of French Catholic missionaries in the south-west. In this description of an attempt to spiritualise the land, Cather's religious convictions become clearer. They also pervade *Shadows on the Rock*, considered by many to be her finest book. It is set in Quebec at the end of the seventeenth century, where a family has newly arrived from France. Euclid, the father, feels the pain of exile, while his daughter responds much more warmly to the harsh environment. The book won the Prix Femina Americaine in 1933.

Catullus

GAIUS VALERIUS

born Verona 84 BC; died Rome 54 BC

Licinus, yesterday, luxury day,

we dabbled masses in my jotter books

and both agreed our work was

*   marvellous:*

severally scribbling each our little lines

each toyed with now this metre, now

*   with that,*

trading them back and forth in wine

*   and wit.*

SONGS, 50

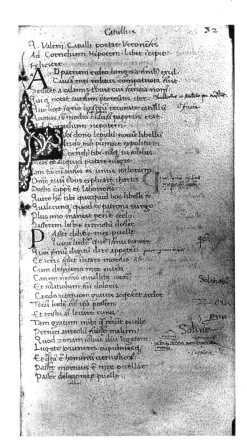

CATULLUS WAS THE MOST startlingly original poet in Latin. He came from northern Italy to settle in Rome, to whose *demi-monde* of sophistication and slack morals his poetry responds in kind.

Many have tried to chronicle his love affair with a girl named Lesbia based on evidence in these poems. This is bootless. His 116 poems are arranged more according to style than content and are prey to the violent mood swings the writer seemed to cultivate: a poem in which he tries to be strong in the face of rejection dissolves into splenetic railing. The dominant theme is the fickle nature of his lover, whom he accuses of outrageous exploits.

In all this, Catullus is notable for his passion, irony and rich rudeness. In his own day, critics were more inclined to take him to task for his scholarship. He wove translations of **Sappho** and **Callimachus** into his work and, like the latter, deplored the literary bombast that generals were urging his peers to produce. Although Cicero branded his output "newfangled", we often find Catullus harking back to a lost age. This might have been an age before the death of his brother, an age of innocence, which he equates with the fall of Troy.

Throughout, Catullus never becomes sentimental. He avoids this with his grim sense of humour and ensures that his work, although dominated by the past, will always remain vital. He freed Latin verse of its earlier, staid character; experimented with Greek metres in a way that **Horace** could perfect; he was the earliest master of elegy in his language and, although **Ovid** and **Propertius** wrote more elegant verse in that genre, neither could bring off his kind of spontaneity. Today, he is perhaps the most eagerly translated of all Latin poets.

Cavafy

CONSTANTINE

born Alexandria, Egypt 1863; died Alexandria 1933

When you undertake your journey to Ithaca,

pray that the course be long...

and if you find her poor, Ithaca has not mocked you:

you have become so wise, experienced so much

that you've already grasped what all these Ithacas mean.

ITHACA

CAVAFY SEEMS AN UNLIKELY father of modern poetry in Greek. He barely visited Greece – except, most notably, for the award of the Phoenix and for an operation in 1932. He stood emphatically outside the Greek tradition and while his contemporaries Kostis Palamas and the New Greek School were invoking the epic past, Cavafy was finding a voice that was completely his own.

He lived most of his life in Alexandria, where he worked as a civil servant for the water board. His first language was English and he even spent five years in Liverpool. His earliest influences were **Browning,** from whom he learned the dramatic technique of focusing on characters caught up in moments of historical change, and **Baudelaire,** whose model he used to portray the city around him. Many of his poems also share the latter's preoccupation with lost beauty and decline.

His work was born quietly into the world. Only 21 poems appeared in book form during his life, although his brother helped him circulate about another 200. However, they did not go so unnoticed that their open discussion of homosexuality allowed him to walk the streets trouble-free. **E.M. Forster** introduced Cavafy's work to English readers in 1919. But in his day, he was better known as an historian than a poet.

His themes are often historical: never documenting the great moments of Greece's imperial past, but rather those of defeat and decadence. The ambiguous impact of Christianity on the Byzantine Empire and that civilisation's dealings with the outside world provide the ideal setting for all that his characters express. Often, they are coming to terms with regret, guilt, or fleeting sensual pleasures and are unnerved by the presence of anything more spiritual. Cavafy captures this in poems that are almost always short. But they are rounded by echoes and resigned cadences, which, though they seem ironic and understated, go as far as words can to express loss, and then leave off.

Celan

PAUL

born Czernowitz, Bukovina 1920; died Paris 1970

You vary the key, you vary the word

that is free to drift with the flakes.

What snowball will form round the

* word*

depends on the wind that

* rebuffs you.*

WITH A VARIABLE KEY,
IN FROM THRESHOLD TO THRESHOLD,
TR. MICHAEL HAMBURGER

AS WELL AS HIS NATIVE Romanian tongue, Paul Celan was fluent in French, English and Russian. He translated poetry from all these into German, the language he used for his verse. His cultural range, which won him a lectureship at Paris' most prestigious university, is spread throughout his *oeuvre*, often imperceptibly. After his parents were deported in 1942, both of whom died in Nazi death camps, he unceasingly addressed the problem summarised by Adorno: "There can be no poetry after Auschwitz."

In his attempts to express the unspeakable, he bent words into a form of music. His first collection contained the much-anthologised *Death Fugue*, whose rhythms force out what might never have been said without them. But he came to resent this poem – it was too direct.

Celan's later books became more obscure. The surreal images and focus on sight in the earlier works yield to a greater concern with language itself. He increasingly broke up the syntax and words of his poems, sometimes in the interests of lyricism, but more often to create new possibilities in German. It was a source of surprise that, after the Holocaust, he chose that language; and it was a sign of healing that most of the honours he was awarded came from Germany.

But healing proved impossible. His work became more concerned with darkness and nothingness. He wrote much-admired love lyrics, but even these seem to come from the shadow of death. George Steiner wrote, "**Dante** and Celan are the great familiars of love's ways in hellishness." In one of his last poems, Celan wrote, "I hear that they call life/our only refuge." It was a refuge he denied himself: he committed suicide in the Seine.

Cervantes

MIGUEL DE   **born Alcalá de Henares 1547; died Madrid 1616**

He's a muddle-headed fool, with frequent lucid intervals.

DON QUIXOTE

IT SEEMS ONLY NATURAL that someone with Cervantes' history should have created *Don Quixote*. Like his hero, he was pummelled by fate. He fought at the battle of Lepanto (an event he works into his masterpiece), where his left hand was maimed. On his return he was captured by pirates and was sold as a slave to a Greek in Algiers. As a public servant, he was imprisoned for failing as a tax-collector and, as supplies officer for the Spanish Armada, inadvertently took corn belonging to the church, for which he was excommunicated. As well as sharing his novel's structure, his life shared its theme – consistent failure. As a playwright he was overshadowed by his contemporaries. He abandoned his attempt at a pastoral novel, *Galatea*, and his poetry was not as accomplished as his prose.

But *Don Quixote* was a success in Cervantes' lifetime. Its open and rambling format took in most of the genres he had attempted elsewhere: the dramatic plots of his *Exemplary Novels,* one of which resurfaces in its entirety; the verse of popular ballads; and extensive scenes of the rustic idyll. But all these are hung around the exploits of Don Quixote, who has none of his creator's sense of perspective. On next to no income, he strives to emulate the chivalrous deeds recorded in the knights' histories to which he has become dangerously addicted. He enlists a local peasant as a squire, and chooses a mistress without consulting her (she is a local girl distinguished by a light moustache). He randomly attacks people who bear him no hostile intentions, including pilgrims, and devises fantasies based on everyone around him. Some are eager to cure him of his delusions, while others indulge them for a savage laugh or a quick profit. The work sets out to attack tales of chivalry, but even when its hero is cured, we wonder if his new-found lucidity is much of an improvement. Ultimately, this knight with the pasted-up helmet and a long-suffering donkey is fighting a battle with the real world, but he doesn't yet know it.

Chandler

RAYMOND   **born Chicago 1888; died Southern California 1959**

*You're not human tonight, Marlowe.
Maybe I never was or ever will be.
Maybe I'm an ectoplasm with a private
licence. Maybe we all get like this in the
cold half-lit world where all the wrong
things happen and never the right.*

THE LITTLE SISTER

RAYMOND CHANDLER'S writing has reached a readership beyond those who have become understandably addicted to his compelling detective stories. They have unique qualities of style, plot and even philosophical enquiry that make him at once accessible and profound.

The style is immediately appealing, but also ground-breaking. Chandler pumps his prose through his beleaguered hero, Philip Marlowe, with a masterly control. As the detective stops to review information he has assembled, or as he assesses new situations, the narrative assumes his attention to detail, but never at the expense of character. The narrator is jaded, always in danger, never sure of what will happen next (for all his skill, he is often prey to intricately organised scams), and hilarious in his descriptions: "'Yes,' he said, in a voice that sounded like Orson Welles with a mouthful of crackers."

Chandler's plots are always elaborate. He wrote some 20 short stories for *Black Mask* magazine between 1933 and 1939, before tackling his first full-length novel, *The Big Sleep*. His work won him a contract to write in Hollywood, where he died an alcoholic, planning a return to England.

The stories often have an improvised feel and conclude with loose ends left dangling from webs of intrigue and counter-intrigue. He said that when he became stuck, he found it useful to bring in a man with a gun. The themes and characters that mark Chandler's work show his debt to **Dashiel Hammett**, but the sense of the moral vacuum that is Marlowe's lonely Los Angeles is his own.

In this milieu, Chandler readers begin on what even the narrator believes will be a whodunit. But each truth Marlowe uncovers leads to some deeper mystery, until no guilt can be apportioned and we are all staring at a collective culpability that led **Auden** to call these books "extremely depressing," while praising them "not as escape literature, but as works of art."

Chateaubriand

FRANÇOIS-RENÉ DE

born St. Malo 1768; died Paris 1848

M. Chateaubriand was not intended by Nature for a statesman. He has too much of the generosity, prodigality, and recklessness of genius.

STENDHAL

CHATEAUBRIAND'S PROSE is the most widely admired in French. He was **Hugo**'s inspiration and **Proust**'s hero – the latter's character Swann was always more interested in a work of art if Chateaubriand had written about it.

Chateaubriand's *oeuvre* cannot be called Classical or Romantic. His forms are strictly the former: much of his output is scholarly, *belle-lettriste* or traditional. He wrote mostly prose, but thought the poet above all other human beings. But for all his reactionary tendencies, demonstrated in his fight against the French Revolution in 1791, and more gradually in his exegesis of Catholicism, his spirit belonged to the Romantic age. He emphasised his personal experiences as an adventurer and as a participant in the epoch's great events.

He left France in 1791 and sailed to America, a land whose desert was the scene of his great novel, *Atala*. Subtitled *The Loves of Two Indians in the Wilds of America*, it takes the avowed view that *les sauvages* are not as noble as **Rousseau** thinks them. Still, Chateaubriand tells their tale as though it were an elevated Greek one, citing **Sophocles** as a model.

After his return to Europe, involvement with the *emigré* army and flight to England, Chateaubriand resettled in France in 1800. His tract *The Genius of Christianity* was vast and impassioned, incorporating fiction as well as theology. Napoleon made him an ambassador to the Vatican, but Chateaubriand resigned when the Emperor had the Duc d'Enghien executed. In 1814 he wrote a pamphlet arguing for the legitimacy of Bourbon rule against the Bonapartes, and Louis XVIII was glad to have him at his side during the regime that followed. When that too was overthrown in 1830, Chateaubriand withdrew from public life to devote himself completely to literature. He translated *Paradise Lost* into French and wrote his extraordinary autobiography, *Memoirs From Beyond the Grave*.

Chaucer

GEOFFREY

born London, c. 1340; died London 1400

Sin I fro Love escaped am so fat,

I never thenk to ben in his prison lene;

Sin I am free, I counte him not a bene.

MERCILES BEAUTE

CHAUCER WAS THE FIRST poet in the strain of English that would come to dominate the British Isles: he remains one of the very best.

Throughout his life he worked as a public servant and was frequently at court. His missions abroad, to France and Italy, account for two distinct styles evident in his early work. During the first trip, he encountered French Romance literature, prompting him to translate *Romaunt of the Rose*. From this period also dates *The Book of the Duchess*, incorporating a French-style dream sequence, (as would his later *House of Fame*) and the poet's own self-deprecating persona, which reappears in *The Canterbury Tales*. In Italy, he quite possibly met **Petrarch** and even **Boccaccio**, many of whose stories Chaucer adapted in his own masterpiece.

The eventual fusion of these styles brought about Chaucer's third phase: the English, which he made his own. Into it he translated Boethius and a treatise on the astrolabe. Such wide reading accounts in part for the diversity of *The Canterbury Tales*; but Chaucer's range of stories recounted in a dramatically coherent sequence by a hotchpotch bunch of pilgrims to the shrine of Thomas à Becket would have been unimaginable without the author's gift for character and satire. The company he presents is more than a cross-section of late medieval society. In the work's general prologue we read of characters we might easily meet tomorrow.

On the journey to Canterbury and back, each pilgrim would tell two stories on the way and two on the way back. Chaucer never realised this massive conception, but in the wild swings in tone, such as from the Knight's Tale of chivalry to the Miller's searingly ribald account of a cuckold's revenge, the author accommodates extremes of behaviour and language, with most of humanity in between.

MAJOR WORKS

The Book of the Duchess
(1369)

*The Parliament of Fowls;
The House of Fame;
Troilus and Criseyde*
(all 1369–1387)

Anelida and Arcite (c. 1380)

Palamon (1380–1386)

The Canterbury Tales
(1386 onwards)

Treatise on the Astrolabe
(1391, 1392)

Cheever

JOHN

born Massachusetts 1912; died New York State 1982

All my work deals with confinement in one shape or another, and the struggle toward freedom... a sense of boundlessness, the possibility of rejoicing!

INTERVIEW WITH JOHN FRITH

JOHN CHEEVER'S STORIES almost exclusively take place in American suburbia. But the apparent normality of this atmosphere highlights extremes of behaviour and emotion that seem to seep out from the cracks in the tasteful wallpaper.

His heroes are usually male, often with good jobs and well-kept gardens; their journeys to and from these places take them through an America whose countryside is dying under the weight of freeways and supermarkets. But Cheever's questioning of their lifestyle goes much deeper than simply to ask, "Are they happy?" These characters can begin this enquiry themselves, typically by looking beyond their marriages for love, and then buckling under the guilt of even considering it. In this way the most ordinary problems become crises. But the world Cheever creates can bring forth still bigger monsters.

In *A Vision of the World*, a man finds a strange object while digging up his flower-bed. This sets off a hallucinatory narrative, culminating in the subject's inability to hear anything but a gibberish mantra. It is not made explicit here that suburbia can have this effect, but it is in the later work *Bullet Park*, when an express desire to shock a community leads a man to attempt the crucifixion of his neighbour.

Cheever's world is not exclusively macabre or surreal. He is concerned with the boundaries of what is acceptable, an interest that was born when he was expelled from preparatory school for smoking. What finished his education began his career: *Expelled* was a startling debut story for an 18-year-old.

Subsequent collections compounded his fame, especially the *The Enormous Radio* and *The Swimmer*, in which an aging athlete sets out to swim in every pool in Westchester County. The actions of Cheever's characters can be heroic as well as manic and motivated by fairly conventional psychology. In later work, most notably *Falconer*, themes of earthly love and spiritual redemption dominate.

Chekhov

ANTON

born Taganrog 1860; died Badenweiler, Germany 1904

If I give you a professor's ideas, you must not look for Chekhov's ideas in them. If I give you wine, do you try to taste beer?

LETTER TO ALEXEI SUVORIN

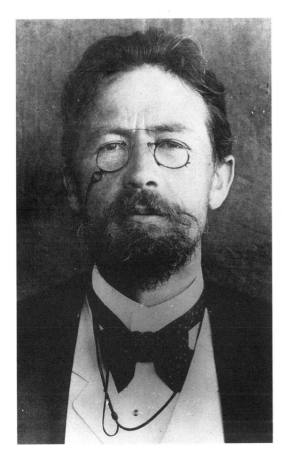

CHEKHOV WROTE MORE than 300 short stories besides his five plays. In all these, he strove for a kind of realism but, through an even-handed representation of his characters, and supreme control of his forms, he did something more, managing to engage passionate concern for every event that he shows us.

He practised as a doctor and found time to write many stories, although the journal publishing them could only accommodate very short ones. He was soon allowed more space, however, to expand his treatments of every kind of character. Men and women from all classes and professions people his tales. Although he was much influenced by **Tolstoy**, and especially *Anna Karenina*, his characters were less aristocratic and his treatment of those struggling, less sentimental. Chekhov could not share Tolstoy's spiritualism either.

In the plays, people living apparently tedious lives often wonder what will become of them after death. The end of *Uncle Vanya* has Sonya telling her despairing uncle that "we will see the angels" – but others, like Dr Astrov, or Vershinin in *The Three Sisters*, are more concerned with earth than heaven, speculating on the prospects of happiness in a distant future.

The world he portrays is often one of wasted life with folk doing little to stave off indolence. Boredom menaces the characters, although Chekhov claimed he never found anyone boring, nor created boring people. It is hard to be happy after a Chekhov play or story, but few episodes pass without a joke, and few characters remain unredeemed in the readers' or audience's eyes.

He began his career writing comic tales, and ended it with *The Cherry Orchard*, which he tried calling a farce. It is resonant with his musical dialogue but so full of unreleasable domestic tensions that one could neither call it tragic or comic. Like Beethoven, Chekhov had such unfailing artistic instinct that he created a body of work which eludes categorisation while remaining perfect on its own, unique terms.

MAJOR WORKS

STORIES

Motley Stories (1886)

Ivanov (1887)

Sleepy (1888)

A Boring Story (1889)

A Marriage Proposal (1889)

Saghalien Island (1891)

PLAYS

Ivanov (1887)

The Bear; A Marriage Proposal (both 1889, in one act)

The Wood Demon (1889)

The Seagull (1896)

Uncle Vanya (1896)

The Lady with the Dog (1899)

The Three Sisters (1901)

The Cherry Orchard (1904)

Christie

AGATHA

born Torquay 1890; died Wallingford, Oxon 1976

The big houses have been sold, and the cottages have been changed and converted. And people just come – and all you know about them is what they say of themselves.

A MURDER IS ANNOUNCED

AGATHA CHRISTIE WAS a poet and authoress of children's books. To posterity, she would have remained so, had her sister not expressed a belief that the writer, nearing 30, could not handle the rules governing the detective mystery. The result was *The Mysterious Affair at Styles*, and some 30 subsequent intrigues followed, involving the Belgian sleuth Hercule Poirot as their unraveller.

A hugely international audience has devoured her novels ever since, with sales especially good overseas. To many, there seems to be much that is absolutely English. There are murders in vicarages involving well-to-do and perfectly polite characters and, with the exception of Poirot, her detectives fit in with this appealing framework, too: Miss Marple is the little old lady from Middleton, Middleshire, who has an unfailing eye, while Tommy and Tuppence Beresford are good-natured amateurs who stumble across clues more by serendipity than deduction. Laws are broken often, but taboos seldom

She took her literary success to the stage, with the excellent *Witness for the Prosecution* and most famously with *The Mousetrap*. The latter has become the longest-running play ever in London's West End theatre district, and its audiences are entreated not to divulge the culprit's identity.

This is the key element of her popularity. Although the murder mystery is a genre which demands strict adherence to convention – a factor which led Christie to describe herself in her autobiography as a "literary sausage-maker" – she is a story-teller *par excellence*. Her increasingly-familiar world of reappearing characters may make seasoned readers think they can crack the whodunit before the end of the story, but Christie's ability to keep the outcome a mystery, by subtly blending in new ingredients, usually keeps them guessing to the end.

Churchill

CARYL

born London 1938

> *We've come a long way. To our courage and the way we've changed our lives and our extraordinary achievements.*
>
> MARLENE'S TOAST IN TOP GIRLS

CARYL CHURCHILL'S ingenious and experimental plays use innovative theatrical techniques to explore political and sexual themes.

She takes on history to examine the moral climate of post-war Britain. Her first major success, *Light Shining in Buckinghamshire*, is set in Cromwell's England, and shows his former supporters rising against him as they feel dispossessed. Subsequent plays bring the past closer to the present: the first half of *Cloud Nine* portrays sexually-repressed Victorian colonists in Africa, while the second brings the same characters (only 25 years older) 90 years forward into the future. Throughout, male characters are played by women, old by young, black by white, and so on. This adds kink to the confusion of a farce-like script, and made Churchill's name. Her next work, *Top Girls*, which used a similar time device, had notable female characters from art, literature and history exchange their survival stories before transforming into businesswomen. Churchill looks at the human cost of female success (especially when achieved by adopting male values) and, in the character of Marlene, points to the rise of Mrs Thatcher.

In *Serious Money*, the past again illuminates the present: the author pays homage to the satirical writings of 17th century playwright Thomas Shadwell in a verse account of the Thatcher-driven 'Big Bang' – London's business transformation. The play was a box-office success, if not a critical one.

Churchill's plays usually rely on invention either in casting or in language. Her latest play, *The Skriker*, takes the verbal tricks of *Serious Money* into a contemporary fairy tale: a woman can transform not only herself but also, by word association, the meaning of what is being said. As elsewhere in her work, the audience is never allowed to become too familiar with what is happening on stage. In all this, Churchill has worked in close collaboration with progressive acting companies and was the first female writer-in-residence at the London's Royal Court Theatre.

MAJOR WORKS

Objections to Sex and Violence (1975)

Light Shining in Buckinghamshire (1976)

Cloud Nine (1979)

Top Girls (1982)

Fen (1983)

The Skriker (1994)

Clare

JOHN

born Helpstone 1793; died Northampton 1841

I love the verse that mild and bland

Breathes of green fields and open sky

I love the muse that in her hand

Bears wreaths of native poesy

Who walks nor skips the pasture brook

In scorn – but by the drinking horse

Leans o'er its little brig to look

How far the sallows lean across

THE FLITTING

IT IS STILL VERY difficult to separate the work of John Clare from the image his contemporaries would project of him. Their view of a barely literate peasant, too sickly to work but touched with genius, sold his first published volume of poems, and made the author the toast of London for a while. The construction remains attractive; but later consideration of Clare's work has been better able to concentrate on the treasures in his subsequent books. By then, his London audience had already grown disenchanted with the novelty.

Still, his first book contained much of the nature poetry valued in the age of **Heaney** and Hughes even more than in his own, for its spontaneity, and its preference for showing rather than telling. But later work impresses still more with its glimpses of his rural England (Northamptonshire) vanishing like Eden: he was to lose his happy seat to the seasons and increasing industrialisation, but his patrons' wish to install him in a larger home unsettled him more. The Paradise of love was to leave him too: of the many women in his life, he was to miss the first most. Even when Mary Joyce was dead, Clare believed she was his wife. But by now, he was in lunatic asylums. He was allowed to walk in the woods, and continued to capture the fragility of nature and feel himself at one with it – but he had begun developing other selves. He explained how he had written certain **Burns** poems, and his attempts to be **Byron** led to some very unfortunate verse. Still, his pathological sensitivity could manifest itself in his writings as before, and he never lost his ear for song-like stanzas, nor the force of argument that could cohere through unpunctuated sonnets.

Cocteau

JEAN   **born Maisons-Lafitte, nr. Paris 1889; died Paris 1963**

So get it into your head that these victims, which so moved the young girl you took, are nothing but noughts wiped off a blackboard, even if one of those noughts was an open mouth crying for help.

THE INFERNAL MACHINE

APART FROM BEING A POET, novelist and dramatist, Cocteau acted in his own plays, designed the sets (although he collaborated with Raoul Dufy and Picasso on such projects), organised the composers (he is responsible for the grouping of "Les Six", and composed music himself), invented ballet scenarios, executed lively line drawings and directed the films he scripted.

Whether he was guided by classical aesthetics or Dadaist innovation, he showed excellent taste and sardonic wit. As a writer with knowledge of so many other fields, he was always aware of where words stopped and actions began; *The Human Voice* and *Le Bel Indifferent* (written for Edith Piaf) both have women bawling into nothing but silence. In the film *Orphée*, a poet envies a rival who is lionised for producing a book with no writing in it; later, his own poetry reaches him from the underworld through a car radio.

Like **Apollinaire**, Cocteau saw machines as conduits of inspiration: the aeroplane in his poem *The Cape of Good Hope* transports the traveller beyond the world of things, while his view of fate as "The Infernal Machine" gave his great play its title. This latter shows how Cocteau could bend myth to fit the concerns of his age. By favouring low-key dialogue to the extremes of Giraudoux, he lost no intensity, and prepared the way for **Anouilh.** The drama presents Oedipus on the brink of his terrible discovery as a type of "cursed poet" – a wanderer with strange insights; a figure which had already appeared in Cocteau's novels. Privately, he seems to have led a similar existence; in his public work, its expression gains force to the author's panache and sardonic wit.

Coetzee

J.M.

born Cape Town, South Africa 1940

We have all tumbled over the lip into the cauldron of history: only you, following your idiot light, biding your time in an orphanage (who would have thought of that as a hiding place?), evading the peace and the war, skulking in the open where no-one dreamed of looking, have managed to live in the old way, drifting through time, observing the seasons, no more trying to change the course of history than a grain of sand does.

THE LIFE AND TIMES OF MICHAEL K

J.M. COETZEE'S WORK strives to give a voice to the voiceless, and to find words for the disenfranchised or oppressed. He does this in short, sparing novels which are at once compassionate and unsentimental as they present the horrors of war and human evil. They are all the more undaunted in their accounts for being sustained by hope.

He was born in Cape Town and though educated in England and America is now a Professor of English in his homeland. His first book, *Dusklands*, expressed his rage at Imperialism, comparing American activities in Vietnam to the Boers' control over South Africa from the earliest days of colonisation; while a later book has a British magistrate in an unnamed African country yielding to pity for the regime subjects and recognising their inevitable freedom. Its title, *Waiting for the Barbarians*, comes from a poem by **Cavafy**, and Coetzee shares that poet's vision of bureaucracy dwindling into irrelevance. His latest book, *The Master of Petersburg*, set in **Dostoyevsky**'s Russia, shows another search for human values in a collapsing society. Its hero tries to track down a relative who has disappeared in a Kafkaesque city.

Coetzee's treatment of this theme comes out strongest in *The Life and Times of Michael K*, although the author denies that his central character's name has any connection with Joseph K from Kafka's *The Trial*. It is the story of a simple man trying to take his mother across a war zone to her birthplace. His loyalty, and attachment to the earth that responds to him, transcends the causes and campaigns that rage around him. He is retarded, and unfathomable to those around him, but as he rests on his journey, discovers a magical gift for making things grow.

Cohen

LEONARD

born Montreal 1934

Keep looking at that belly-button,

Leonard Cohen. It got angel dust in it.

GEORGE BOWERING,

IN CANADIAN LITERATURE, NO. 33

We are ugly, but we have the music.

CHELSEA HOTEL

OUTSIDE HIS NATIVE CANADA, Leonard Cohen is better known for his songs than the earlier poetry and novels. These are as good an introduction as any, since they combine his lyrical gift with the sensuality and soul that shows throughout; but such a limited look means one misses the rich variety of his work, as well as his humour.

His poetry can swing from controlled rhyme to free-falling satire. In the former, he is metaphysical, using words as icons: his rose is not a rose. In the latter, he is as trenchant as **Ginsberg**, but more concise. His refrain-led verse is less a mantra against government policy than a vision of mad freedom. Seemingly trivial concerns become timeless (the lines on loss, 'Is there anything emptier/ than the drawer where/ you used to store your opium?' are worthy of **Catullus** on towels), while his treatment of Jewish persecution is more harrowing for being balanced with the more ephemeral trappings of love. He expresses his Judaism within the context of Christian and Greek cultures in his first book, *Let Us Compare Mythologies*, and later, in *Flowers for Hitler*, with statements of universal guilt.

His novels continue to explore sexual discovery and spiritual awakening often in a verse-like form. *The Favourite Game* follows a poet in his youthful progress around Montreal. *Beautiful Losers*, meanwhile, reads at once as confession and lament; a scholar pours out his fantasies, invoking both his late wife and the canonised Iroquois martyr, Catherine Tekakwitha. The narrative shifts from internal monologue, to epistolary novel, to third person account; but Cohen executes each with the same spirit and freedom.

He might appear to us now as a cousin to the Beats, once removed; an alternative voice for '50s Canada and '60s London; but even in music, so bound with these temporal links, he transcends the dictates of fashion, sharing his vision with a quiet, unshaking voice.

Coleridge

SAMUEL TAYLOR
born Devon 1772; died Highgate, London 1834

O pure of heart! thou need'st not ask of me

What this strong music in the soul may be!

What, and wherein it doth exist,

This light, this glory, this fair luminous mist,

This beautiful and beauty-making power.

DEJECTION: AN ODE

BOTH IN THEORY AND in practice, Coleridge expresses best in English what a Romantic poet is. His early years were troubled – he fled, disillusioned, from Cambridge and joined the army, only to flee back; then, inspired by the French Revolution, joined in an aborted scheme to establish an egalitarian society in America, which in itself led him to an unhappy marriage.

Coleridge's idea of poetic genius was to feel ideas and shape them within the soul. The feeling most evident in his own early verse is an obsessive guilt. His creation, the Ancient Mariner, has since become the very archetype of remorse. A sailor kills an albatross and must atone for it. His contrition is endless and he is doomed to recount his actions to those he makes listen.

He published this and four other poems with **Wordsworth**'s work in their vital collection, *Lyrical Ballads*. Their friendship affected each other's work and thought enormously, visiting Germany together, where Coleridge began his study of Kant's philosophy. In 1810, however, the two fell out – a blow which came on top of Coleridge's marital problems, unrequited love and increasing addiction to the opium he had been taking medicinally.

His Romantic cast of mind had always rendered his output unpredictable – *Christabel* remains unfinished and a visit from 'a man from Porlock' caused him to abandon the ecstatic *Kubla Kahn* – but from 1810 onwards his work became increasingly fragmentary. He lived with Dr and Mrs. Gillman in Highgate, who helped but never healed his condition. It was here that he began his critical masterpiece, *Biographia Literaria*. Much of it uses Wordsworth to explain the idea of individual genius as opposed to talent. In this book, Coleridge argues that, 'No man was ever yet a great poet, without being at the same time a profound philosopher', a notion supported by his own greatness.

Colette

born Saint-Sauveur-en-Puisaye 1873; died Paris 1954

These women who had been dispossessed of their rightful childhoods and who, as girls, had been more than orphans, were now in maturity the fond instructors of a younger generation. They never looked ridiculous to me. Yet some of them wore a monocle, a white carnation in the buttonhole, took the name of God in vain, and discussed horses competently.

THE PURE AND THE IMPURE,
TR. HERMA BRIFFAULT

COLETTE REVEALS HERSELF throughout her stories and novels which correspond to different times of her life and draw on people around her. Throughout, her writing seeks a kind of self-knowledge, but the one truth her works reveal as really worth knowing – and which transcends any rules of behaviour – is love.

The task of knowing Colette is complicated by the problem of her early work. For a long time, she was renowned chiefly for the *Claudine* novels. These she wrote at the behest of her pornographer husband, who insisted that she record episodes from her school days. He made sure she incorporated shades of domination and sensuality among women. In *Claudine en Ménage*, Colette described more emotional relationships and began to find her own voice – although she still used her husband's pen-name, Willy, yielding the praise to him. She left him in 1906,

proved she was the real author, became a dancer and began writing under her own name.

Her life onstage and new-found freedom prompted more psychological work. *The Vagabond* fictionalises the marriage break-up, as the later memoir *My Apprenticeship* recalls it.

Her style is distinguished by its elegance and compression – like her sensual description, it is the more successful for being sparing. Although she was a deeply personal writer, as prized now for her letters and *Sido*, a reminiscence of her mother, she could express sympathy for all her characters, men as much as women, animals as much as humans. Both are civilised, but only the humans are corrupted by the process. She was the first woman to become President of the Académie Goncourt; she was also a member of the Académie Royale Belge and received a state funeral when she died.

Compton-Burnett

IVY

born London 1892; died London 1969

Families can seldom be explained, and they make better gossip without any explanation. To know all is to forgive all, and that would spoil everything.

DAUGHTERS AND SONS

IVY COMPTON-BURNETT'S NOVELS are all set in the last decade of the 19th Century, and are concerned with large families in old homes. If they are ostensibly well-off, they are nonetheless in a state of decline, morally as in their surroundings. The drama of these books derives from the secrets they keep from one another, and the tensions that emerge between relatives.

In this, she is often compared to the Greek tragedians: her father was eager for her to learn Latin and Greek, and she studied Classics at London University. If the atmosphere of her tales differs from these models, the themes are similar. Strong patriarchs or matriarchs preside, and the characters' actions take ethics to the limit: fraud, murder, theft, suicide and incest are among the subjects they try not to mention at meal time.

But still they talk about them. Compton-Burnett's books are made mostly of dialogue. Her technique is much like **Oscar Wilde**'s, in so much that she takes a cliché and finds an edge to it. Although she can also bring off a similar wit and polish, the effect is more sinister, as the speakers search for handy phrases to fill the silence.

Hilary Spurling's biography tells of Compton-Burnett's own childhood and finds an explanation for the gloom and strangeness that pervades the stories. Bereavement of siblings marked her youth and she always wore black, as though constantly in mourning. The harshest loss was that of her brother Guy at the Battle of the Somme in 1916. Not only did she never speak of the war, but also worked only in an imaginative world that existed before it. Although her style recalls the novels of that period, her irony is one born of hindsight and the knowledge her generation has of the steady fall of the old order into horror and destruction.

Congreve

WILLIAM

born Bardsey, nr. Leeds 1670; died London 1729

Madmen show themselves most by pretending to a sound understanding, as drunken men do by over-acting sobriety.

LOVE FOR LOVE

CONGREVE WAS THE MOST successful playwright in the London of his day but the influence of his intellect was far reaching. He attended both school and Trinity College, Dublin, with **Swift**, helped **Dryden** in his translation of **Juvenal** and in his own early prose work, *Incognita*, consciously attempted to establish a working definition of the novel.

He was, however, careful not to direct his intelligence merely at his educated friends and the luminaries of William III's court. His comedies enjoyed long runs at Covent Garden (when two weeks on stage constituted a hit), and after a Congreve play, the acting company could afford to rest for the season. So it is all the more surprising that he only wrote four comedies. These are all long and make great demands of the performers. The writing in them shows that he knew his actors' capabilities well, and gave them bizarre characters. These would often be monomanic types, labouring under some delusion, be it that their love is requited, that they are rich, mad or married, or that they can tell the future. Sometimes these figures are cured by the wit Congreve spreads among all his creations, and sometimes not. But their compulsions impel fiendish plots, where rejection in love can lead to schemes of revenge, which themselves can lead to more delusions…

Where the characters seem predictable (Congreve's world is one where most women are of easy virtue, for example), the pace of the dialogue animates them. They are rich in idiolects, with verbal tics or leanings towards certain types of metaphor. Ben in *Love for Love*, for example, can barely open his mouth without a torrent of sea images bursting out.

Besides the comedies, he wrote one tragedy, *The Mournful Bride*, and much verse – including a lament for Queen Mary. He wrote words for the greatest composers of his day too, including Handel, and his *Judgment of Paris* became a text for three composers to set for a competition.

He was highly honoured before his death: **Voltaire** visited him and **Pope** dedicated his translation of the *The Iliad*, and when he did die he was buried in Westminster Abbey.

Conrad

JOSEPH

born Berdichev, Ukraine 1857; died Ashford, Kent 1924

To him the meaning of an episode was not inside like a kernel but outside, enveloping the tale which brought it out only as a glow brings out a haze, in the likeness of one of these misty halos that sometimes are made visible by the spectral illumination of moonshine.

HEART OF DARKNESS

PERHAPS WE SHOULD BE less surprised that one of English prose's finest exponents was Polish and spoke no English until he was 20. For Joseph Conrad brought to his adopted language and country a sense of life's strangeness that was lacking in the Victorian tradition.

He left Poland in 1874, after experience of Russian oppression, and joined a ship at Marseilles. Adventures like those that fill his stories led him to England, where he found a precarious kind of stability; the darkness of cosmopolitan London, seething with political tensions, was as close as he could find to a home.

It was here that he wrote his tales of honour and betrayal, focusing on the behaviour of crews in crises. Although tales of sailors' bravado feature in his work (especially *Youth*), he uses the sea as a setting for an enquiry into the effects of extreme stress on his characters' behaviour. He takes recognisable European personalities, like the quixotic Lord Jim or the refined Kurtz of *Heart of Darkness*, and follows them to the limits of morality.

He is concerned with the soul and seldom finds unalloyed goodness there. His sense of the abstract pervades his language, which eschews concrete nouns and tends to describe phenomena negatively. The newspaper report that summarises the happenings of perhaps his finest novel, *The Secret Agent,* concludes, 'An impenetrable mystery will hang forever over this act of madness and despair.' That book is rare in Conrad's corpus for its irony, its glimpses of corruption at all political levels and the tragedy the story reaches through the grimmest farce. Its action centres on the corpulent figure of Mr. Verloc, and his part in a plot to blow up Greenwich Observatory, London's most powerful symbol of global order. Its theme, the fear and love of anarchy, is one the author frequently explored and as with all his themes, he strove to render it timeless.

Cooper

JAMES FENIMORE   born **New Jersey 1789; died New York State 1851**

The whole party moved swiftly through the narrow path, towards the north, leaving the healing waters to mingle unheeded with the adjacent brook, and the bodies of the dead to fester on the neighbouring mount, without the rites of sepulture – a fate but too common to the warriors of the woods to excite either commiseration or comment.

THE LAST OF THE MOHICANS

WITH HIS STORIES of early American pioneers, Cooper pioneered the American novel.

He was educated at, and expelled from, Yale before exploring his country and the sea, and his later books are full of the latter. He wrote his first novel when challenged by his wife to produce something better than the book they were reading. *Precaution* is in the style of **Jane Austen**, and was a failure. His next, however, *The Spy*, was a bestseller. Its inclusion of General Washington as a character marks the beginning of Cooper's bid to render American history into epic form.

This is the achievement of the 'Leatherstocking' series of novels. They introduce the woodsman, Natty Bumppo, whose popularity obliged Cooper to feature him in a further five books. Bumppo's appeal is that he is alone among the pioneers portrayed as a representative of innocence and simplicity. The only other bearers of such noble attributes are the

native Americans and their plight as pawns between the warring factions of white invaders dominates *The Last of the Mohicans*. It is an action-packed escape narrative whose climax, a funeral ceremony, aims at the dignity of *The Iliad*. If Cooper's dialogue should fail to convince, we should bear in mind his epic model.

The success of such books led him to Europe, where he busied himself with democratic movements and became an apologist for the American way of government. But on returning home, his increasingly elitist views, which found their way into the *Littlepage Trilogy*, led to a decline in his popularity. It is as well that he is remembered for his more compassionate works.

Corneille

PIERRE

born Rouen 1606; died Paris 1684

... the theatre

is at so high a point, all worship it ...

And those whose splendid statesmanship

preserves

By its illustrious measures all the world

Find in the sweetness of so fine a sight

Means to unbend from such exacting

tasks.

THE THEATRICAL ILLUSION,
TR. JOHN CAIRNCROSS

PIERRE CORNEILLE WAS the first great French dramatist. He was the first to pen the ennobling tragedies in rhymed pairs of Alexandrines so associated with *le grand siécle*, and which gave Racine such a precedent.

With only his second work, *The Cid*, he broke barely established rules of tragedy. The play's exposition wastes no time in establishing the dilemmas that will bedevil its characters for the ensuing five acts, and all that follows complicates them with subplots, another innovation. The play's vigour thrilled audiences, but divided the French Academy, whose tastes were as up to date as Aristotle's and whose pronouncements were Cardinal Richelieu's.

He was shaken by this disapproval and turned to plays on Roman themes. These better caught the mood of change Richelieu was bringing over France. By setting his action in Rome's periods of transition (the early Republic of **Horace**, or the early Empire

of Cinna), Corneille deftly mirrored shifts in French power, and the increasing onus on kingship.

These pieces brought him a steady income, as well as **Racine**'s opprobrium and **Moliére**'s ridicule. Still, Corneille's earliest and possibly finest achievements were as a comic playwright, where his gift for agonising situations found expression in the tricky spots of farce. This work remains the best known. *The Theatrical Illusion* is a play within a play: a magician allows a man to watch the son he had feared was dead. The usual Cornelian clash between love and duty troubles the characters in the vision, but just as the loose ends are tied, the father watches his son and new wife die a violent death. He is to be comforted, as is the audience, by the knowledge that the characters have become actors and are themselves performing in a play: everyone survives after all. It demonstrates Corneille's feel for the power of theatre, and his own genius for wielding that power.

Crane

HART   born Garretsville, Ohio 1899; died at sea in the Caribbean 1932

The imaged Word, it is, that holds

Hushed willows anchored in its glow.

It is the unbetrayable reply

Whose accent no farewell can know.

VOYAGES

THE TRAGEDY OF Hart Crane's early death has long precluded a balanced assessment of his work. Throughout his short life he was an outsider – poor, homosexual and alcoholic – and he ended it all with suicide at the age of 33 when he jumped off a boat while at sea in the Caribbean. Consequently, he left behind a small volume of work, including the beginnings of an epic, *The Bridge*.

In the history of American poetry, *The Bridge* stands out as an example of what might have been. The task of writing a national poem, which so beset Joel Barlow, **Whitman**, **Pound**, **Williams**, **Ginsberg** and **Charles Olson**, seemed to have fallen to one of the best. Hart Crane's vision of his country starts on Brooklyn Bridge, and looks seaward, invoking the memories of **Melville** and Christopher Columbus. His work in shipyards sated his love of water for a while, as well as his passion for machinery and this adds the modernist edge to his work.

But what is most extraordinary about Crane is his language. His diction is extremely ornate and rather arcane. Words run away with him, and he apostrophises irrepressibly. He will often begin a poem with a clear stanza form, and then transform it as the subject matter takes over. The discipline of his approach seems to come from a reading of **Donne**

and **Herbert**; but his rapturous tone shows, perhaps, the most forceful impact **Rimbaud** has had on literature in English.

And indeed, Crane has much in common with the French Symbolist: the alarming precocity, the restless experimentation and the sudden end of a writing career. This has led to his reputation becoming mythical and makes his poetry sound prophetic. It is true that his descriptions never shrink from the sublime, but his verse is frequently forced enough that we are witnessing something very human. His effort and pyrotechnics – his failure even – show the mechanics of rendering the ineffable. In Crane's hands, it is as high an achievement as bringing it off.

MAJOR WORKS

White Buildings (1926)

The Bridge (1930)

Collected Poems (ed. Waldo Frank, 1933)

Complete Poems and Selected Letters and Prose (ed. Brom Weber, 1966)

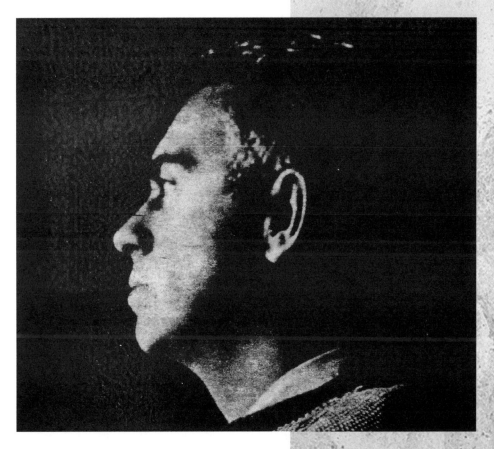

cummings

e.e.

born Boston, Massachusetts 1894; died New Hampshire 1962

and may myself do nothing usefully

and love yourself so more than truly

there's never been quite such a fool who

*   could fail*

pulling all the sky over him with one

*   smile*

SPRING

THOSE LITTLE LETTERS MIGHT have done for cummings' reputation. They are the first thing his readers notice, and even quite sensible critics cite typographical innovation as his principal achievement. **Apollinaire** used it, but it never proved quite the same distraction.

Still, it is integral to cummings' work. He was a painter, but his visual daring helps the hearer of poetry as much as the reader. A poem like *ygUDuh* only hits you when you've cracked it. Elsewhere, the poet's emphasis on seemingly random syllables lifts a verse to the pitch of singing. Often, his words hardly need the help. For cummings, capital letters and spaces are obstacles, as are distinctions between parts of speech. This is not to say his poems avoid syntax, rather that his supreme control over it allows him to explore it more acutely. He uses verbs as nouns, finding more life in them ("Scorning the pomp of must and shall/ my father moved through dooms of feel"); and sets advertising slogans beside national songs and natural speech – something which make his satirical poems so catchy. In this, his vocabulary may be conventional, but his words breathe.

This is why it is so hard to find rivals to his love poetry. His theme is traditional enough. The more unpredictable his combination of images, the more we imagine we've seen it before. One can attribute this to a mixture of his Cubist instincts in painting (he exhibited in Paris) and his New England Transcendentalist background (his father was a preacher, and made his son read **Emerson**). But there is a romantic singularity in cummings' achievement. He found a distinct mode of self-expression and, unlike the Cubists, never exhausted it.

Dante

ALIGHIERI

born Florence 1265; died Ravenna 1321

How I became so frozen and so faint,

reader, don't ask: I cannot write it down,

because no utterance comes near to it.

I didn't die, and didn't stay alive.

INFERNO

IN *THE DIVINE COMEDY*, Dante gives a complete and self-contained view of the universe. It is a spiritual vision, founded on the cosmography and philosophy of his day. The poet is taken by the poet **Virgil** on a tour of Hell. His path is strewn with obstacles and prevaricators – Satan's kingdom is full of political rivals, abusers of papal power, usurers and people born too early to have received the Gospel.

In keeping with the contemporary theology, the ascent to Heaven is via Purgatory, a vast spiralling mountain. Dante's guide here describes the structure of the cosmos and the workings of love. The presentation of these derives from Aristotle, whom, we learn, only Christians have interpreted correctly. The principle of Divine Love as Aristotle's Prime Mover of all things is developed further in the heavenly journey around the planets to the realm of the angels. Here the poet's difficulties in facing the Inferno are mirrored by his senses' inability to comprehend, save by degrees, the blinding light of God's glory.

Dante's extraordinary achievement is to make this vision utterly possible. He does this by working even chaos into a coherent system. Moreover, he does it in the execution: he is a master poet, whose very psychology fits in as well with modern views of appetitive love as with Aristotle's; and whose imagery carries this by making the most surprising, and yet the most exact, mental connections since **Homer**. While the rhetorical patterns owe much to his epic antecedents, his own verse-style is a three-line rhyming stanza whose order is a microcosm of the tripartite universe.

Here Dante is the self-aware poet, especially in knowing where words become powerless and truths too fantastic to unfold. His other works discuss the pioneering work he did in making poetry Italian. The finest, *The New Life*, is a treatise incorporating lyric verse on the love he first felt for that same Beatrice who guided him through Paradise. Only **Proust** since has really rivalled the Florentine for approaching love with an academic rigour that never robs it of its mystery.

MAJOR WORKS

The Divine Comedy
Inferno
Purgatory
Paradise (begun 1307; Vision traditionally dated 1300)

The New Life (1292)

Convivio

On Common Eloquence (both between 1304 and 1307)

On Monarchy

Davies

ROBERTSON

born Thamesville, Ontario 1913; died Ontario 1995

Drug addiction is horrible, addiction to drink is pitiable, but to be a slave of the salted-nut habit is to be lost indeed.

THE DIARY OF SAMUEL MARCHBANKS

ROBERTSON DAVIES' BOOKS exude refinement. From small-town Canada to unchanging Oxbridge, his characters are restrained in speech, usually cultured, putting on *The Tempest* or *St. Matthew's Passion* and often willing to tell you what they're reading at the time.

It is an alluring world and one which leads critics to consider Davies a natural conservative. But he is not without a sense of perspective. Early on in his career, he produced a newspaper column using the persona of Samuel Marchbanks, a Dr. Johnson for the 20th Century, with blusterous opinions on just about everything. In giving him to the world, Davies seems capable of self-parody and so keeps even his innate control under control. In this, his writings show a constant awareness of the literary world's machinations: his disdain for them led him to comment once that "critics are like eunuchs who complain about other people's children."

His writings were the first to have brought Canadian literature to international attention. His stories often begin in his native Ontario, where his home town of Kingston became fictionalised as Salterton in the eponymous trilogy – and his characters can fetch up in the England he knew as a student and actor. In a large body of work, to which he was still adding to in spry old age, he explores guilt, memory and "the isolation of the human spirit". He brings it off with a delicacy of touch which has earned him respect as a humourist. In his hands, seemingly small events can have epic, even tragic consequences, such as a mix-up over a wedding announcement, or a fatefully misdirected snowball. In the latter, when the intended target realises what has happened, his 10-year-old thoughts are already on **Dante**.

Defoe

DANIEL

born London 1660; died London 1731

Wherever God erects a house of prayer,

The devil always builds a chapel there;

And 'twill be found, upon examination,

The latter has the largest congregation.

THE TRUE-BORN ENGLISHMAN

IF DEFOE'S MOST FAMOUS works cannot properly be called novels, it is because he wrote all of them as factual accounts and with an apparent purpose beyond the desire to divert his readers. To do this, he had to invest his prose with absolute accuracy where possible and minutely-imagined detail where not. Moreover, he had to immerse himself in the personality of his narrators, using all the psychological research of his day. As if for further authenticity, he eschewed the well-made plot. Finally, he always concealed his identity.

Although this was common practice in his day, Defoe had special reason to worry. He had worked as a spy and a spin-doctor both for Tories and Whigs. He had been pilloried (literally) and imprisoned for a pro-Dissenter pamphlet and for libel. As a journalist and confidant of William III, he had been active in the making of policy and, as a former merchant who had travelled Europe extensively, he had gone bankrupt.

Given such a life, Defoe's works had much to teach. *Robinson Crusoe* and *Moll Flanders* both tell the stories of tenacious survivors. The former is a fictionalised account of the sailor Alexander Selkirk's real experiences; the latter tells of a girl's life as a whore and robber in London until her repentance, as recounted to our anonymous author in Newgate Prison. As so often in Defoe's writing, the protagonists here need to be saved, either physically or spiritually. Elsewhere in his massive *oeuvre*, we find heroes with sensational lives turning penitent: only for *Roxana, The Fortunate Mistress*, was it too late.

These books sit beside his real histories, but even then Defoe embellishes and pretends to be a witness. In his *Journal of the Plague Year*, he invites speculation that the writer might have been his uncle (Defoe would have been five during the plague). All his works are full of information, which in themselves would justify their appearance; but in prefaces he would insist, even as he titillated, that it was for the reader to find a moral for him or herself.

DeLillo

DON

born New York 1936

MAJOR WORKS

Americana (1971)

End Zone (1972)

Great Jones Street (1973)

Ratner's Star (1976)

Players (1977)

Running Dog (1978)

The Names (1982)

White Noise (1985)

Libra (1988)

Mao II (1991)

He is commenting on the documentary footage even as it is being shot. Then he himself is shot, and shot, and shot, and the look becomes another kind of knowledge. But he has made us part of his dying.

LIBRA

LIKE MANY RECENT American writers, especially **Saul Bellow**, Don DeLillo is concerned with the individual's loss of identity in contemporary society.

But his approach goes to the roots of the problem and he analyses not just the malaise but his medium for exploring it: like **Paul Auster**, his most fundamental concern is with language itself.

His first novel, *Americana*, takes an advertising executive across the country in search of himself. His rôle as someone who wields words to influence group behaviour is one that subsequent DeLillo characters play. In the next novel, *End Zone*, we meet a victim of this rhetoric, a footballer obsessed with the language of nuclear Armageddon, which he finds reflective of his own sporting ambition.

DeLillo sees this as a uniquely American phenomenon, wrought by the social controls at the disposal of mass media. In *White Noise*, the characters' dialogue echoes the verbiage that pours out of radios, until the two become indistinguishable. Its hero must wade through it all in his professional capacity as Professor of Hitler Studies. That the author is as interested in the phenomenon of information, and how we receive it, as in the contents of that information itself, shows in his next novel, *Libra*. Through disjointed dialogue, associative puns, and pure imagination, the narrative strives to find reasons for the assassination of Kennedy between the lines of the Warren Report.

The study of how linguistic manipulation can sway crowds continues in *Mao II*, with its focus on the mass marriage of Moonies and the terror of the Hillsborough football disaster. As ever, DeLillo is as inventive in plot, in which writers find themselves as victims of mistaken identity, as he is in language. Here he shows the daring imagination and fecundity of ideas that begins to explain why he is as comfortable writing science fiction.

100

Desai

ANITA

born Mussoorie, Uttar Pradesh, India 1937

Was it not India's way of revealing the world that lay on the other side of the mirror?... if you refused to look into it, if you insisted on walking around to the back, then India stood aside, admitting you where you had not thought you could go, India was two worlds, or ten.

BAUMGARTNER'S BOMBAY

ANITA DESAI WAS BORN in India to a Bengali father and a German mother. She writes books for children, short stories and novels, two of which have been nominated for the Booker Prize.

Her work concentrates on the post-war, post-Partition Indian experience. In the novels, it is an urban one and she writes of the city's allure. In *Voices of the City*, three young people move from Bombay to Calcutta to become a part of its inexorable human chaos. In the later *Baumgartner's Bombay*, a displaced German Jew finishes up in a similarly frightening Bombay. In one vignette, he escapes from a ranting restaurateur to reflect, "Escape – a funny word to use of the Colaba streets…"

Indian immigrants in the London of *Bye-Bye, Blackbird* find the metropolis no less daunting. But in the noise of the traffic, the smoke of Battersea Power Station and the machinery of the Underground, the protagonist finds a spirituality that replaces his original terror. In England, the foreigner must induce this sense of a town's inner life. In India, it abounds already. Desai's gift for describing natural phenomena and wildlife and using them as symbolic reflections of her characters' plights, has no shortage of material in Calcutta, Bombay or Delhi, where pigs, cattle, monkeys and even the flora and fauna contribute to the action.

Ultimately, however, Desai's cityscapes present a harsh, unforgiving country which has been compared to the realm of **Ruth Prawer Jhabvala**'s works. Where Bombay and Calcutta bustle, Delhi stagnates; but it is no less severe in its degradation of the once-lauded Urdu poet who survives there throughout *In Custody*. But even in this account the author articulates her often hellish vision in purely-formed novels and prose which engages the senses immediately.

MAJOR WORKS

Cry, the Peacock (1963)

Voices of the City (1965)

Bye-Bye, Blackbird (1971)

Where Shall We Go This Summer? (1975)

Fire on the Mountain (1977)

The Clear Light of Day (1980)

In Custody (1984)

Baumgartner's Bombay (1988)

Dickens

CHARLES

born Portsmouth 1812; died London 1870

Such was the pleasant little family circle now assembled in Mr Pecksniff's best parlour, agreeably prepared to fall foul of Mr Pecksniff or anybody else who might venture to say anything whatever upon any subject.

MARTIN CHUZZLEWIT

DICKENS' NOVELS ARE many things to many readers. They can be read for their rhetorical flourish or for their extraordinary caricatures; as page-turners, or as rich historical documents; savoured for their unpredictable dialogue, or revered for their social concern.

Their author left school when he was 15, taught himself short-hand and became a court reporter. In the meantime, he became well-acquainted with the streets of London and the terrifying plight of the capital's poor. As his newspaper columns grew ever larger, he campaigned against the Corn Laws and child-labour. When his journalism evolved into fiction he was still fighting for legal reform.

Most of Dickens' work was initially published in serial-form in the popular newspapers of the day. A great populist writer, Dickens knew how to please his audience as well as escalate sales with devices such as the now well-established cliff-hanger.

In his depiction of children, Dickens found, perhaps, his most effective register for engineering change. Today, his treatment of childhood may strikes us as mawkish, but his dark fascination with the criminal underworld, captured so brilliantly in his work, often provides a perfect counterbalance and his work is shot through with brutal murders. If Dickens had a weakness for crime, however, he was tough on its causes, which he identified strongly with institutionalised poverty.

His characters, some enchanting, many more disgusting, enact these themes through ad-libbed plots. Their wild range of idiolects draws on the author's marvellous ear, and his passion for amateur dramatics. The scenic form of the novels betrays their sketch-like origins. Often stories within a novel appear as self-contained episodes. . The first book, *The Pickwick Papers*, grew out of individual observations by the Pickwick Club. In later works, narrators and their juxtaposition would give the stories a more controlled shape. Phiz's illustrations enhance the whole throughout, brimming with caricatures and set pieces; speedily drawn, they cap the entertainments and enhance with detail… as if the story-teller needed help.

Dickinson

EMILY **born Amherst, Massachusetts 1830; died Amherst 1886**

I'm Nobody! Who are you?

Are you – Nobody – too?

Then there's a pair of us!

Don't tell! they'd advertise – you know!

How dreary – to be – Somebody!

How public – like a Frog –

To tell one's name – the livelong June –

To an admiring Bog!

NO. 288

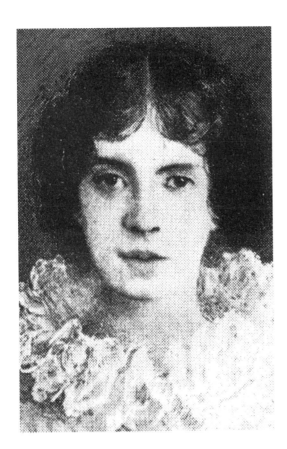

"PHOSPHORESCENCE... that's the genius behind poetry." These words are attributed to Dickinson in a play, and indeed her poems are full of light: the poet craves for summer, and admires bees, "the Buccaneers of buzz" as she calls them; while her language wanders into hot places, "This January Day/ Jamaicas of Remembrance stir". These visions stream into the wintery world of a reclusive writer, who never visited such spots but whose imagination reaches for them, selects them for their random connotations and their euphony, and makes them real for a reader.

Dickinson's poems seem uncontrollable. Some readers hear popular tunes jingling along with the words, and the rhymes feel hymn-like, but within these ad-hoc metres, words can pause, and dashes supply much of the punctuation, as though language breaks off. And Dickinson takes it as far as it can go. She jumbles the senses – "Inebriate of Air – am I/ And Debauchee of Dew –" and reaches a satiety of synaesthesia – "I could not see to see", compressing near-ungraspable states of mind into tiny stanzas and short lines. Often one feels as though one has stumbled on a moment of revelation half-way through.

Much has been made of Dickinson's unhappy life – she harboured literary ambitions, but published only seven out of some 1,800 poems in her lifetime; and many have speculated on the identity of the beloved who caused the pain in her verse. But "Death is the supple suitor/ That wins at last" and her work is all the more extraordinary for lacking any thought that it might itself be immortal. The poetry's fullness of life and absorption with death seems all the truer for having such little self-regard, as much as for the unforgettable rightness of its phrases.

Donne

JOHN

born London c. 1572; died London 1631

Divorce mee, untie, or breake

that knot againe,

Take mee to you, imprison mee, for I

Except you'enthrall mee,

never shall be free,

Nor ever chast, except you ravish mee.

HOLY SONNET

DONNE'S POETRY is commonly called "metaphysical". **Dryden** and **Johnson** styled it so after his death, but one can see how it stuck. Donne's poetry includes frank recognitions of the physical, especially in his lush and smutty elegies, after **Ovid**; but in other lyrics, particularly those where the poet finds himself alone with a girl, the emphasis is on what lies beyond that – the "Vertue attir'd in woman". He describes a kind of lovemaking between souls and, in his poem *The Ecstacie*, works language to make that sensual, too.

Often such effects look too much like verbal tricks. Mercilessly intellectual, he can make us accept an image and then twist it into some new proposition: because a flea has bitten a girl as well as the poet, she has nothing to lose by yielding to him. Thus women become ruled provinces, and tears globes. He puns on his own name, in the *Hymn to God the Father*, so that he embodies the sins for which the poem atones. One prays for him, but shudders at the application of so fine a legal mind to the art of seduction.

But Donne's true greatness emerges when his thoughts are simplest. His wonderful sense of closure comes from an orator's ear for modulating complex arguments into a perfect cadence. His *Valediction: Forbidding Mourning* must be his best example, where the last line encapsulates the whole. Here the poet strives to console rather than cajole, and we are more likely to trust him.

It is this which makes him so fine a religious poet. After his ordination in 1615, his subject matter, though not exclusively Christian, still demanded subtlety to commend leaps of faith. It is this quality which has made his sermons, many delivered when he was the Dean of St. Paul's Cathedral, so durable. He attains his customary beauty with rhetoric rather than rhyme, and the courtly sophist gives way at last to the mystic divine: "all severall soules containe/ Mixture of things, they know not what."

Dos Passos

JOHN

born Chicago 1896; died Baltimore 1970

He talked about spies and British intrigue and pan-Slavism and the Socialist revolution and laughed all the time and said everything was well on its way to ballyhack.

THE 42ND PARALLEL FROM U.S.A.

JOHN DOS PASSOS' OUTPUT is a mixture of fact and fiction, told in a mélange of styles, ranging from the poetical to reportage: his extensive work owes as much to experimental novels as it does to his personal experience of history.

He began writing at Harvard, although the novel he began there, *Streets of Night*, appeared in 1923, six years after he graduated. This began his enquiry into the theme of urban fragmentation which found its fullest expression in *Manhattan Transfer*. This work was to pioneer the techniques he employed throughout the vast trilogy for which he is most famous, *U.S.A.*

It is a sprawling, polyphonic opus. It balances verbalisations of newsreel footage with random shots from a roving camera. These latter read like imagist poetry, while the biographies of the narrative's principal characters themselves burst into free verse. The aim is to analyse the actions of key figures from their very roots, as people whose development we sympathetically follow from their childhood at the beginning of the century, as they face one another from opposite ends of the political spectrum. The reader is left uncertain as to whether public events triggered private responses, or vice versa, while the powerful play of American life itself goes on.

Dos Passos continued his attempt to render history at its most complete in accounts of the nation's conception in *The Head and Heart of Thomas Jefferson*. The further this project took him, however, the further from his original left-wing sympathies he drifted. He never abandoned his own past, however, and continued to explore his Latin-American roots, in *Brazil on the Move* and *The Portugal Story*, as well as his friendships with **Hemingway**, **cummings** and **Hart Crane** in *The Best Times*.

Dostoyevsky

FYODOR

born Moscow 1821; died St. Petersburg 1881

If, when you tell a lie, you skilfully put in something not quite ordinary – something eccentric, I mean, something, you know, that very rarely or even never happens – it sounds much more plausible.

THE IDIOT, TR. DAVID MAGARSHACK

DOSTOYEVSKY'S TALENT was barely controllable. It remains barely surpassable.

He abandoned a career as a military engineer to write. His first novel, *Poor Folk*, was well-received, especially in progressive quarters, but his next, *The Double*, failed to match such success. In 1849, he drifted into radical politics, was rounded up with the Petrashevsky circle, sentenced to a mock execution and then sent to Siberia where he served as prisoner and then soldier for eight years. The experience left him epileptic and prone to compulsive gambling.

The House of the Dead is an account of his prison years, while *Crime and Punishment* is filled with his insights into criminal psychology. Dostoyevsky's feel for the extremities of personality, and his ability to write through them without wasting a word, make this novel an extraordinary experience. Here the author's preoccupations appear in their simplest form – the vanity of violent action and redemption through Christ.

Later, these ideas appear within the context of Dostoyevsky's virulent pan-Slavic religiosity, which dominates his public diaries and often gives way to anti-semitism. But it never disfigures his novels.

The Idiot sets a Christ-like, epileptic prince into a world of rogues, radicals and frustrated aristocrats, to leave us nearly as bewildered as the hero. *The Brothers Karamazov*, meanwhile, gives Dostoyevsky's beliefs their most compelling expression: but the narrative's energy seems torn between Father Zossima's preachings and their atheistic counter.

The artist's hectic soul is bound up in this. Dostoyevsky complained that he could never write a perfect novel like those of **Tolstoy** or **Turgenev**, given the circumstances under which he worked. Still, each of his novels went through several drafts, however rapid they were, and were full of babbling lovers, repentant sinners, and people in whom mercy and brutality contend with each other. Though they often come from newspaper stories and speak with voices that we think we hear every day, they go to the limits of what is human and take us with them in the process.

Doyle

SIR ARTHUR CONAN

born Edinburgh 1859; died Sussex 1930

As Cuvier could correctly describe a whole animal by the contemplation of a single bone, so the observer who has thoroughly understood one link in a series of incidents, should be able accurately to state all the other ones, both before and after.

THE FIVE ORANGE PIPS

SIR ARTHUR CONAN DOYLE was internationally renowned, even in his own time, as the creator of Sherlock Holmes.

Holmes' methods derived from Doyle's teacher of medicine at Edinburgh University, Dr Joseph Bell. They involve a rigorous use of deduction. A Sherlock Holmes story is always told by the detective's companion, Dr Watson. He is the perfect foil: a medic, like the author, he is drawn into the mystery so deeply he can't regard the facts of the story with his friend's dispassion but he can recount it with real verve. His own attempts to emulate his live-in hero may lead the reader down false trails, but always succeed in communicating real atmosphere as he takes special pains to illuminate a very murky London.

Early on in the tales, Doyle was careful to introduce the possibility that Holmes might be fallible. While his arch-rival was always the nefarious Moriarty, his most impressive adversary must remain 'the woman,' Irene Adler.

Despite their enormous popularity, Doyle grew bored of writing Sherlock Holmes stories by 1893, and plunged Holmes and Moriarty to their deaths in the Reichenbach Falls in what was supposed to be the last story about the Baker Street sleuth, *The Final Problem*. His readership, however, clamoured for more and, after an eight-year gap *The Hound of the Baskervilles* finally appeared, with the hero miraculously saved. Still, Doyle was happy to divert his considerable energies to causes about which he was more passionate, including his defence of Britain's conduct up to and during the Boer War, in which he served as a physician. He also worked as a missionary and his interest in the spiritual grew after the First World War in which he lost his son. Besides the Sherlock Holmes stories, he left behind the adventures of the scientist Professor Challenger, who would have been well at home in Jurassic Park, and a six-volume history of the Western Front from 1916–1919.

Dryden

JOHN   **born Aldwinkle All Saints, Northamptonshire 1631; died London 1700**

Death in itself is nothing; but we fear

To be we know not what, we know not

where.

AURUNG-ZEBE

DRYDEN WAS THE MOST versatile and influential man of letters in 17th-century England. His output covers an immense range – some 30 dramatic works, including operas and a masque (he and Purcell had the luck to be collaborators and on the latter's death, Dryden wrote a lament of singular grace); sustained satirical poems; translations from Latin and **Chaucer**; as well as literary criticism.

His fortunes were bound up with the times. He was born a Puritan and along with **Milton** and **Marvell**, was a civil servant in the Protectorate. He continued as an administrator during the Restoration, writing an elegy on the death of Cromwell and verses welcoming Charles II. His poetry was always topical; *Annus Mirabilis* commemorates the events of 1666, dwelling on naval victory over the Dutch of that year, while *Absalom and Achitophel* puts the leading figures of the Court at the time of the Popish plot into a Biblical setting. So it is appropriate that before becoming Poet Laureate, he was appointed Historiographer Royal, in 1669.

His forthright lampoons, particularly of Shadwell and Rochester, left him prone to literary and even physical attack (he was mugged at Covent Garden by Rochester's hired heavies). Although he was a fashionable figure, even when being mocked, he did not join in the public rejoicing with the accession of William and Mary, choosing to retain his new Catholic faith. It cost him his court position and he was banned from commenting on public affairs

This left him translating **Virgil**, **Ovid**, **Juvenal** and **Lucretius**, with no obvious allegorical intent. For a man who had frequently adapted other works (producing an operatic version of *Paradise Lost* and basing his play *All for Love* on *Antony and Cleopatra*), it is fitting that he should have spent his final years in bringing his own pellucid verse as close as English has yet come to the elegance of his originals. In this, as in all else, he enriched the language amply and made the way plain for **Pope**.

Dumas

ALEXANDRE THE ELDER   **born Villers-Cotteràts 1802; died Dieppe 1870**

ALEXANDRE THE YOUNGER   **born Paris 1824; died 1895**

The resemblance between heroes and the earthly is too great, the analogy too close; the spectator who follows the development of a passion in the actor will want to check it just at the point where it would be checked in himself.

DUMAS THE ELDER, ANTONY

Theatre is as unpitying as arithmetic.

DUMAS THE YOUNGER,
PREFACE TO A PRODIGAL FATHER

DUMAS THE ELDER ONLY admitted to being the father of Dumas the Younger when the was seven years old – and the latter struggled with his illegitimacy throughout his life. They were both compulsive womanisers, however, and both found it possible to examine the consequences of private indiscretion in their public work.

The elder Dumas' play *Antony* not only contains discussion of what theatre goers expect from tales of heroism: it also portrays a man who kills his mistress to avoid scandal. The audience recognises this as abnormal behaviour and yet, 42 years later, the younger Dumas presents an equally shocking story in a much more realistic setting: *Claude's Wife* has Claude killing his spouse as moral retribution for her infidelity. (The author had himself fathered a child with a married Russian countess.)

Both managed to titillate the Paris of their day with their treatment of scandal, from the orgies and bloodbaths of the Elder's *La Tour de Nesle* – with its glimpses of a former aristocracy that were sure to offend the new Royalist régime – to the Younger's *Camille*, which mobilised the censor for having a courtisan as its heroine (the play is the basis of Verdi's *La Traviata*).

The Elder's more enduring popularity rests on his novels, especially *The Three Musketeers* and *The Count of Monte-Cristo*. In these he continued with his brand of historical romance à la **Victor Hugo**, but with a lightness of touch which charmed his public enough to save him from financial ruin. His son kept the crowds coming to his increasingly moralising plays by guaranteeing quality of structure and an excellent ear for how dialogue works on stage. Together the two Alexandres Dumas dominated French letters for most of the 19th Century.

du Maurier

DAPHNE

born London 1907; died Cornwall 1989

> *We are all ghosts of yesterday, and the phantom of tomorrow awaits us alike in the sunshine or in shadow, dimly perceived at times, never entirely lost.*
>
> GROWING PAINS (PUBLISHED IN THE USA AS MYSELF WHEN YOUNG)

DAPHNE DU MAURIER wrote numerous short stories, memoirs, histories and a notable biography of Branwell Brontë (see under **Anne Brontë**). Two of her short stories have been famously filmed: Alfred Hitchcock's *The Birds* and Nicholas Roeg's *Don't Look Now*. Both stand as chilling realisations of her power as a suspense writer.

Her best-loved accomplishments in this field are her six historical romances, on widely varying themes. The first four of them hark back to the Cornwall she first saw when was 20. She was born into an artistic family: her father was George Du Maurier, the theatrical manager and creator of the rôle Bulldog Drummond, She received a cosmopolitan education, growing up in Hampstead and going to school in Paris. But she stayed in Cornwall and her writing would constantly return to the West Country. Eventually she lived in Menabilly, the 70-room mansion which became the Manderley of *Rebecca*, which remains her most popular work.

It is as Gothic as the novel, which owes some of its plot to *Jane Eyre*, as a young wife wonders what happened to her predecessor, the first Mrs de Winter (who dies in the beginning). The heroine of *Rebecca* is typical of the central character in a du Maurier story: she has an innocence and trust, together with a natural curiosity, which echoes the plight of Mary Yellan arriving among smugglers on the Cornish coast in *Jamaica Inn*, and anticipates the abandon of Dora St. Columb, as she finds liberation in the piracy of *Frenchman's Creek*.

Much of the suspense draws on the uncovering of evil, and the over-bearing sense of guilt which haunts even the most benign characters as if forever. The three mentioned above have all been filmed, as was her next work, *My Cousin Rachel*. On the page, the rhythm of du Maurier's prose can attain great elegance: The opening paragraph of *Rebecca* is the most famous example.

Duras

MARGUERITE

born Indochina 1914

If the very fact of being alive means that we can do harm, however much we don't want to, just by choosing or making mistakes ... why then, I too will go through with it.

THE SQUARE,
TR. SONIA PITT-RIVERS AND IRINA
MORDUCH

MARGUERITE DURAS' WORK explores the problem of love and the world that impedes it. Over her long career, she used widely different novelistic techniques to discuss this, as well as producing a large number of screenplays.

She began to write shortly after the outbreak of the Second World War. A memoir of those times appeared in 1985. Called *Pain*, it tells how her husband, Robert Antelme, was deported to Germany for being a Communist and contains her reflections on the genocide as it became revealed. She concludes that the guilt of these crimes is so enormous that it must be shared by us all. Her most famous writing, the screenplay *Hiroshima, Mon Amour*, focuses on two parallel relationships as a way to confront the horror.

After the war, she divorced Antelme. She had already published two realist novels, and a third would follow in 1951, *The Sea Wall*. Here women struggle with their environment and wonder to what extent their lives might be different. Her next two books took a more ironic look at the search for love, represented in *The Sailor of Gibraltar* by the heroine Anna scouring the Mediterranean for her lover, and

in *The Little Horses of Tarquinia* by a situation that results in perpetual bickering.

Later, her treatment of such love becomes more stylised, notably in *The Square*, which is almost exclusively dialogue between a young maid and a travelling salesman, who meet one another by chance. Their immediate ease with one another allows them not only to discuss the unvarying quality of their lives in a probing, theoretical way, but also to find in each other some hope.

In her latest novels, she began to rework earlier plots, and twice portrayed men paying women to help establish their ideal of love.

Durrell

LAWRENCE

born Julundur, India 1912; died Avignon 1990

Journeys, like artists, are born and not made. A thousand differing circumstances contribute to them, few of them willed or determined by the will - whatever we may think.

BITTER LEMONS

LAWRENCE DURRELL'S WRITING stands self-consciously outside the British literary tradition. The author found England uncongenial – he was born in India and persuaded his parents to move from Kent to Corfu – and lived around the Mediterranean for most of his life. It is here that his series of novels are set.

These show a sympathy for the thinking of Freud and Einstein, and the influence of **Joyce**'s technique in fictionalising their ideas of identity and time. Durrell takes the former's account of sexuality as something that defines the personality and uses eroticism as a means of exploring his characters. He was encouraged in his sensual expression of this theme by his correspondence with **Henry Miller**. Einstein's theory that time is relative is echoed in the books' structures with the author hardly ever telling a story in chronological order – although this very much depends on which author is telling the story.

The first novel of The Alexandria Quartet, *Justine*, for example, is the product of a novelist within the whole opus, while *Balthazar*, the subsequent volume, throws it into a completely different perspective. Throughout the tetralogy, Durrell plays with different points of view on the same episodes and builds up ironies as characters act in ignorance of what the reader understands has already happened.

He writes with a travel writer's sense of place and his locations shape the characters as much as events do, even declaring at one point in his work that "We are the children of our landscape". His settings show all the signs of decay from their mythical past. The Alexandria he describes is the city of **Cavafy**, whose poetry and presence hovers over his books. The same sensual and complex prose characterises the later Avignon Quincunx. Durrell also made a name for himself as a poet and his verse reads as a luxuriant response to the work of **T.S. Eliot.**

Eco

UMBERTO

born Alessandria, Italy 1932

Scratch the heresy and you will find the leper. Every battle against heresy wants only this: to keep the leper as he is. As for the lepers, what can you ask of them? That they distinguish in the Trinitarian dogma or in the definition of the Eucharist how much is correct and how much is wrong?

THE NAME OF THE ROSE

UMBERTO ECO IS AN academic with a staggering range of interests and reference. His professional field is semiotics – the interpretation of signs – and he finds them everywhere. He produces linguistic

texts of unsurpassed rigour and newspaper columns scrutinising current trends with a jolly scholar's eye. But his finest, most durable offering so far must be the novel, *The Name of the Rose*.

It is a murder mystery set in a medieval monastery. Brother William of Baskerville's Holmes-like hunt for clues leads the narrator, a young monk, to ponder signs and their meanings. In an intellectual climate founded on faith and reason, the things signified point, however logically, towards an irrational core: although the killer is unmasked, the quest for knowledge appears to lead nowhere.

Still, Eco's own knowledge makes the journey to chaos sublime. From his research into Aquinas' aesthetics and his inexhaustible supply of information on 14th-century heresy, botany, illumination and witchcraft, he has constructed a tale for our own times. While some think of it as a whodunit with some literary theory on top, the whole – however ironic its intention, and however parodic its execution – unites form and meaning to pose the most fundamental questions about human existence.

The scepticism of empirical systems to understand the world is akin to that of **Borges**, who is represented by the manic master of a labyrinthian library in the novel. This stance is similar in Eco's next novel, *Foucault's Pendulum*, where three dodgy publishers start investigating a document which describes a secret energy source known only to a league of Medieval knights. Their findings lead to a complete re-interpretation of history, with much satire on the way. The scientific erudition explored here here takes over in his latest offering, *The Island of the Day Before Tomorrow*, which explores our arbitrary ways of measuring and defining time.

MAJOR WORKS

The Name of the Rose
  (1980)

Foucault's Pendulum (1989)

*The Island of the Day
  Before Tomorrow* (1996)

Eliot

GEORGE

born Warwickshire 1819; died London 1880

We see no white-winged angels now. But yet men are led away from threatening destructions; a hand is put into theirs, which leads them forth gently towards a calm and bright land, so that they look no more backward; and the hand may be a little child's.

SILAS MARNER

GEORGE ELIOT WROTE NOVELS of great stature. Queen Victoria devoured them, and while Eliot captured her age, she never pandered to its strictures.

She keenly observed the effects of the Industrial Revolution and the sudden transferences of wealth in her novels become, not so much the plot motivations that we find in **Jane Austen**, as an element that colours human relations more subtly. For Eliot, psychology and motivation take precedence. *Adam Bede* contains the line, "Our deeds determine us, as much as we determine our deeds," and much of her books' interest comes from the response of her characters to crises.

In *Silas Marner*, this idea is played out in comparative miniature: a miser loses his horde and it is replaced, as if by a miracle, by a golden-haired foundling. The moral is obvious; subtler is the way his affection is transferred, almost as if his want of an object precipitated the child's arrival.

Here, as elsewhere, Eliot's skill relies on her telling stories in a recognisable form, but allowing readers to form their own conclusions about the structure of life. In *Middlemarch*, widely held as her finest work, the process is likened to the scratches on a table which only seem to form a pattern when a candle is held over them. This illuminates *Middlemarch* itself, which sets two men off in their contrasting bids to make complete sense of the world as they see it. Here the work relies on both writer and reader to construe its meaning. Eliot performed her part by drawing on her sensitivity, especially in the equitable treatment of men and women in her fiction. Ultimately, her work was a plea for progress, that set out to expose hypocrisy, champion the poor over the rich and the individual over gossiping communities – urgencies she very much felt in her own life, living in sin on the Strand.

Eliot

T.S.   **born St. Louis, Missouri 1888; died London 1965**

The progress of an artist is a continual self-sacrifice, a continual extinction of the personality.

TRADITION AND THE INDIVIDUAL TALENT

AT HARVARD, Eliot aspired to be a philosopher. But his vast reading of religion and anthropology as well as Elizabethan poets and the latest French imagists, left him writing a completely new kind of English verse.

Although technically 'free verse,' it never sounds liberated. Although crammed with allusions and tongues, it never feels fussy. Eliot handled *personae*: his most famous poem, *The Waste Land*, was originally titled *He Do the Police in Different Voices*, and while still a young man, he found the voice of a timid, middle-aged, middle-class American called J. Alfred Prufrock.

The technique gains its effect from the verse's immense musicality. Although he was helped in this by **Pound**'s fine ear (and new research is discovering just how much), Eliot's own instincts were to hear a rhythm and only then supply the words. Indeed, he explained that his *Four Quartets* were an attempt to capture the melancholy of Beethoven's last string quartets.

All this enabled him to keep his poetry objective, rather than let words topple out. For Eliot, it was a key to disengaging his own personality, so great a step after the Romantic obsession with that aspect of the poet. It made him a dazzling critic too, more willing to argue about empirical criteria for good writing than good or bad taste. This meant that, though his conclusions could be as arbitrary as anyone's, he could argue them forcibly – qualities which helped him as a playwright (nominally as a verse one) and allowed him to steer his characters away from Shavian ranting.

Much of this, however, articulated a particular world-view – that of the English establishment, albeit an Anglo-Catholic one. Subsequently, his noblest theme is atonement; although he makes this a clearer goal for Celia in *The Cocktail Party* at the end of his career than for any of the lost voices that speak his words throughout it, it is nevertheless a hope in all his writing. He was awarded the Nobel Prize for Literature in 1948.

Ellison

RALPH WALDO

born Oklahoma 1914; died Oklahoma City 1994

The question of how the sociology of his existence presses upon a Negro writer's work depends on how much of his life the individual writer is able to transform into art. What moves a writer to eloquence is less meaningful than what he makes of it.

THE WORLD AND THE JUG

APART FROM A COLLECTION of essays, Ralph Ellison published little except the novel that made him famous: *The Invisible Man.* It is narrated by an unnamed black man in 1952, from a room underground in Harlem. He talks of his own search for identity – one which takes him all over the United States, and through the diverse strands of opinion represented by the Civil Rights movement. His "invisibility" lies in his being treated as a number only, not just by white society, but also by black political extremists.

It was the latter which brought the book so much controversy. He was fiercely opposed to segregation between the races: this led him to the conclusion that black separatism was also wrong. But if he seemed overly eager to compromise and co-operate with white society, it was because he had a multi-cultural vision of America.

It was as a student of history and literature that he found ways to express himself. **Joyce** was a key influence; and his project has much in common with Stephen Dedalus's mission (in *Ulysses*) to forge a national identity. But perhaps his musical training provided the real impetus to write *The Invisible Man.* For Ellison, jazz was a uniquely American art form that black people had given to America, and even famously declared that one Fats Waller lyric posed the central problem of race for the entire continent: "What did I do/ To be so black and blue?"

His own childhood was spent in Oklahoma, in a house where white and black people mixed freely. His writing would plead for such tolerance everywhere. He developed this stance in subsequent essays. The bulk of a second novel was destroyed in a fire: he never really recovered from the loss.

Emerson

RALPH WALDO   born Boston, Mass. 1803; died Concord, Mass. 1882

'Tis the good reader that makes the good book; in every book he finds passages which seem confidences or asides hidden from all else and unmistakably meant for his ear.

SUCCESS

RALPH WALDO EMERSON'S spiritualism and his effusive expressions of it, are key to an understanding of American Romantic writing.

His faith in the soul was formal at first. He was born into a long line of preachers and was himself ordained as a Unitarian pastor in 1829. However, his wide reading and questioning mind led him to doubt the sacraments, a scepticism he shared with his congregation before leaving it. A fusion of Swedenborg's philosophy, the poetry of **Coleridge** and **Wordsworth**, and a fair smattering of German and Hindu thought poured into Emerson's own Pantheistic view of the universe.

Although he is chiefly considered to be a philosopher and essayist, his response to this all-pervading soul is profoundly that of an artist. He wrote some poems, but considered all his writing to be poetry. He found a poetic language in Creation's coherence, and a metaphysical counterpart to every physical law. In response to this, the poet must become one transparent eye.

He was disappointed by his travels to Europe, however, where these notions of beauty seemed to him repressed. On meeting Wordsworth, he found him reactionary and rambling. While his reflections on England provide excellent satire, his visit to Paris' Jardin des Plantes proved epiphanic.

In these stances he was ever the American – Oliver Wendell Holmes called his lecture, *The American Scholar*, an intellectual Declaration of Independence – and he was the mentor to a whole school of American poets. His home in Concord, Massachusetts, was the centre of Transcendentalist philosophy, from where he'd correspond with other writers or else set out from to lecture all around the country. While his own work became less coherent as he approached old age, the help and encouragement he gave to the likes of **Walt Whitman** rendered literature an inestimable service.

MAJOR WORKS

Essay on Nature (1836)

The American Scholar (1837)

Essays (1841, 1844)

Poems (1847)

Representative Men (1850)

English Traits (1856)

Conduct of Life (1860)

Society and Solitude (1870)

Letters and Social Aims (1876)

Erasmus

DESIDERIUS

born Gouda 1466; died Basle 1536

If anyone is shocked at this being more frivolous than theology should be, or more trenchant than befits a Christian, then I didn't say it – Democritus did.

IN PRAISE OF FOLLY

ERASMUS OF ROTTERDAM was a Renaissance scholar and theologian, who was probably born in Gouda. As a philosopher and literary giant, his chief attributes were his intimate grasp of Greek thought,

at a time when Western Europeans were only just re-learning how to read it in the original, his independence of mind and a wit that was as merry as it was subtle. The first two inform all his voluminous writings, while the last is especially evident in his satire, *In Praise of Folly*, which is still widely read today.

He wrote it while he was staying with Thomas More. Together they had studied Greek and translated Lucian, the satirist who began his account of lunar exploration saying, 'Everything here is a lie.' *In Praise of Folly* employs the same technique. Folly speaks throughout, reminding us that we shouldn't take her too seriously. Her gender is significant; while the voice the author gives her is dizzy, the choice of speaker becomes more interesting as she concludes that fools can often make sense, too. She ends by explaining **Platonic** theories of love, which Socrates acquires from a woman in *The Symposium*. It is one of many moments when the author wrong-foots the reader, and allows us to be convinced by the literal interpretation of a discourse we had taken for pure irony. Even what looks like manifest chauvinism might admit an alternative slant.

In this way, Erasmus finds the perfect medium for his views on love (at once scholarly and mystical), and on society, particularly ecclesiastical. These were humanist: he was unashamed about bringing all classical literature to the service of theology, not just **Plato** and Aristotle. He had a liberal view of salvation, which extended to those who had not heard the gospel but were still redeemable. His satire is at the church's expense, and particularly Pope Julius II's, and his books were later burnt. He anticipated the Reformation but was innately ecumenical, and opposed a split.

Euripides

born Phyla? c. 485 BC; died Macedonia c. 406 BC

I want to be under high hiding-places

so that God might make me fly upon a

   bird's wing

with the fluttering flocks elsewhere

HIPPOLYTUS

GREEK TRAGEDY was an art form which played to all sections of the (male) Athenian community, however drunk the audience was. Of the three great tragedians, Euripides understood this best, and delivered plays of the highest quality.

He won the tragedy prize six times only (on 23 known attempts); but public familiarity with his work is evident in the laughs **Aristophanes** expected from mocking it.

Euripides would write for ordinary characters: the deferential nurse, or the farmer living as Electra's husband, who boasts that he never laid a hand on her. He uses simpler language than his predecessors used. Most of his audience would have sat as jurors, so his use of legal oratory, with characters "contesting" a point, made his drama still more accessible. In this way, he could explore motivation more fully, and try to explain the most extreme actions.

These included matricide, infanticide, and incest: in testing the limits of morality, he bent the rules of theatre too. His chorus became increasingly engaged in the action; in *Hippolytus* he used two choruses and possibly a fourth actor. His musical settings stretched words: even without singing, we can hear that the energy and pulse of his lyric episodes are stunning.

Although he could present scarily sexist

characters, his championing of women set him at the opposite extreme to **Aeschylus** and unlike **Sophocles**, he preferred the thorough exploration of psychological crises to architectural plots. So he explored passion fully, especially female; and in the *Bacchae*, gives us a temptation scene held out over a lengthy, metrically-controlled exchange. When the curious party breaks down, so does the metre. Although his verbal tricks make him difficult to render into theatrically-viable English (for in spite of his comic skill, we risk finding him unintentionally funny or pedantic) moments like this abound, when we can appreciate Euripides' amazing facility, both as dramatist and poet, for finding the right stroke at the right moment.

Faulkner

WILLIAM **born New Albany, Mississippi 1897; died Oxford, Mississippi 1962**

Poor man. Poor mankind.

LIGHT IN AUGUST

...there is only one me to try to tell them and how can I ever tell them, and make them understand? How can I?

UNCLE WILLY

WILLIAM FAULKNER WAS a story-teller of startling originality and power. His early ambition was to be a poet, but his first published efforts were derivative. He took odd jobs (*As I Lay Dying* was composed on night-shifts when he was watching a dam)`and began to write purely for himself.

He followed the advice of Sherwood Anderson, to write about the area he knew best. He made his native Mississippi the backdrop for a compassionate and vast study of human failure, the Yoknapatawpha novels. The Compson family features throughout, and little by little we learn of the small but overpowering moments of their tragic past. These are explored in instants, which Faulkner's prose extends to whole volumes: his characters articulate different notions of time passing, with Quentin saying, "Only when the clock stops does time come to life."

He found ways to express them in their most elemental forms. His stories present an emotional landscape as much as a physical one, seen from many viewpoints: *As I Lay Dying* is composed of 59 separate internal monologues, some running for pages of vast sentences, some of only few words and one of just one. Faulkner first used this technique in *The Sound and the Fury*, which opens with the free thoughts of a mute with a mental age of three; he is unloved by all in his family save his sister. The novel concludes when the family's black maid risks taking the boy to her segregated church, where she affirms a Christian form of love that transcends doctrines and divisions.

Faulkner managed to completely immerse himself in the characters of the South and this made him seem racist to some readers; in fact, racism is the worst sin he finds in his blinkered homeland. His descriptions of lynchings, segregation and the cruelty of men who would advance themselves at whatever human cost stand as attempts to right these wrongs. His vital and all-seeing method of achieving it in art was rewarded when he won the Nobel Prize in 1950.

Ferber

EDNA　　　**born Kalamazoo, Michigan 1887; died New York City 1968**

In their eyes was that distrust of Emma which lurks in the eyes of a woman as she looks at another woman of her own age and doesn't show it.

SISTERS UNDER THE SKIN

EDNA FERBER'S STORIES of strong women with emotional needs captured, and described, large sections of the United States. But any consistency in her themes belies the great variety and versatility of her writing.

From the beginning, she was a professional writer; but her experience at the *Milwaukee Journal* must have made her look beyond that – it was during this period that she suffered a kind of breakdown. This all figures in her first novel, *Dawn O'Hara*; otherwise Ferber seldom sneaked autobiography into her fictions, with the exception of *Fanny Herself* (1917).

She attained something approaching public rapture by creating the character Emma McChesney, a forward-thinking woman working for a skirt company who faces her daily dilemmas and gradual loss of youth with practicality, wise-cracks with a new kind of frankness. This at once caught the tone of the *New Yorker* circle in which she was moving, and gave readers a sense that they knew Emma intimately (several critics proving eager to marry her). After a trilogy of such novels, *Cosmopolitan* sent her a blank cheque to keep her turning them out. Ferber did the right thing, and moved on while she was ahead.

Her subsequent novels explore vast tracts of American land, from the Oklahoma of *Cimarron* to Alaska's bid for statehood in *Ice Palace*. Although Texans disliked her treatment of them in *Giant*, whose subject-matter anticipates that of the TV show *Dallas*, even there she shared her characters' faith in the pioneering spirit which created her country. This made her patriotic style especially effective in war-time. But perhaps the most enduring of all her tales is the most diverting: it is the idyllic *Show Boat*, which follows the Cotton Blossom Floating Palace Theatre along the Mississippi and Ohio rivers; simply entertaining, in which three generations of an acting family feel the tug of the past.

Fielding

HENRY   born nr. Glastonbury, Somerset 1707; died Lisbon 1754

The first care I always take is of a boy's morals; I had rather he should be a blockhead than an atheist or a Presbyterian.

JOSEPH ANDREWS

FIELDING'S WRITINGS were often about literature itself. But if his work only seemed to exist as glosses in the margins of other books, his own sprawled out of them to be some of the greatest in English.

His youthful plays dealt with the theatre and scholars and he enjoyed great success. **Swift** recalls that he laughed for only the second time in his life during *Tom Thumb*, a spoof of revenge tragedies, which ran for 40 nights. Fielding's last play, *The Historical Register*, was about drama critics, and caused Walpole to introduce severe censorship into the London stage.

He continued his campaign against Walpole, as a journalist in *The Champion*. Then he took an approach similar to Gay's *Beggar's Opera*, and in *Jonathan Wild* likened Walpole to the man who had monopolised London's organised crime by turning informer: in later life Fielding, as a magistrate and early advocate of a police force, was to play a great part in the breaking up of criminal gangs.

But Fielding's greatest target was **Richardson**, whose epistolary tale *Pamela* captivated the reading public in 1740. *Shamela* appeared soon after, treating the earlier book's moral tone as hypocritical. Fielding never denied authorship and Richardson never forgave him. *Joseph Andrews* followed, again using Richardson's characters, but along a wandering story line conceived more in homage to **Cervantes**. The author, however, styled the book in a new genre, which he called the 'comic epic in prose.' It was a form he would make his own.

When Richardson's *Clarissa* appeared, Fielding hailed it as a masterpiece and just had time to pay tribute to it in his own greatest triumph, *Tom Jones*, which was published soon after. It is a huge work, chronicling its foundling hero's seemingly random amorous progress in spite of his remaining in love with the heroine Sophia. Fielding never quite found the same form, although his last book, *Amelia*, sold out instantly. He died in Lisbon three years later, trying to relieve his chronic gout.

Fitzgerald

F. SCOTT

born St. Paul, Minnesota 1896; died Hollywood 1940

'Fixed the World's Series?' I repeated.
It never occurred to me that one man
could start to play with the faith of fifty
million people – with the single-
mindedness of a burglar blowing a safe.

THE GREAT GATSBY

F. SCOTT FITZGERALD's elegiac novels chronicled the hedonism of booming America. He continued to do so when the boom had disappeared and this accounted for a decline in his popularity; but the causes of the era's passing are clear in *The Great Gatsby*, a book published at the height of the Jazz Age.

For many, Fitzgerald embodied the glamour of those times, just as his great fictitious creation, Jay Gatsby, represented its tragic flaws. He shared his extravagant lifestyle with his wife Zelda, gave lavish parties and paid large bills by writing for glossy magazines. His friend **Ernest Hemingway** strongly disapproved of this, considering him a fine and serious writer, and certainly Fitzgerald had the turn of mind to see the superficiality of much around him.

The perfect form and symbolism of *The Great Gatsby* makes it a timeless tale, but it has singular importance in the history of literature on "The American Dream". Like **Henry James**'s novels on the 'international situation', it portrayed a national temperament ill-fitted to gratuitous sophistication and, like subsequent writers, Fitzgerald showed how impossible it would be to realise that dream and maintain the sense of innocence on which it depended.

This kind of disillusionment marks all his work, from *The Beautiful and the Damned* through to *The Last Tycoon*. This latter was left unfinished on his death. It tells the story of a movie executive who has moved from rags in New York to riches in Los Angeles; the megalomania that has driven him there leads him to contemplate murder. On the posthumous publication of what Fitzgerald wrote (drafts and an entire plot summary), critics felt that at last the author was finding the form of his greatest work, and through the reworked drafts could witness the level of perfectionism that he demanded before he could consider a book finished. He was mourned as the writer of one of America's greatest novels.

Flaubert

GUSTAVE

born Rouen 1821; died Croisset 1880

Human language is like a cracked kettle on which we beat out time for bears to dance to, while all the time we are longing to move the stars to pity.

MADAME BOVARY

FLAUBERT PUBLISHED RELATIVELY few works in his lifetime. His more voluminous letters (published posthumously) explain why. Although he wrote unceasingly, many hours a day, he agonised for long periods of time over the choice of each word. This commended him highly to 19th-century champions of stylised prose.

Flaubert's own style was naturalistic. Much of his work on novels was taken up with research, so that the details of the action should be as accurate as possible. For his *Sentimental Education* he devoured literature on the 1848 uprising in Paris; he spent months in Tunisia to make his novel *Salammbô*, set in Carthage, come to life. In the former case, he worried that the details were overtaking the narrative in importance; in the latter, archaeologists were quick to fault his finds. Even when he knows his setting intimately, like the small-town Normandy of *Madame Bovary*, he compresses a meticulously realised atmosphere into his paragraphs.

But other factors accounted for the success of his books. *Madame Bovary* was a bestseller after an unsuccessful attempt to ban it for obscenity: the heroine's adultery becomes progressively more casual throughout the book and the sensuality unmissable. *Salammbô* followed in its wake and started a Carthaginian craze in Paris. Flaubert found himself famous for the wrong reasons: he hated the theme of *Madame Bovary* and resented the text's existence. When a book of his failed, as did *Sentimental Education*, he shrugged it off publicly, and nursed his bitterness.

His last finished work, *Three Tales*, contained the story *A Simple Heart*; it was a bid to prove that he was not so bitter after all. It tells of a maid with a passionate attachment to everything and provides the most perfect example of how Flaubert's own immersion in a narrative's actual things could generate its own kind of beauty.

Ford

FORD MADOX born Merton, Surrey 1873; died Deauville, France 1939

After 45 years of mixing with one's kind, one ought to have acquired the habit of being able to know something about one's fellow beings. But one doesn't.

THE GOOD SOLDIER

FORD'S OUTPUT NUMBERS some 80 books, alongside 400 articles and essays. He wrote elegant criticism and honest memoirs, but the sheer variety of his work can be felt in his novels alone. These range from historical romances to magnificent skits. The former include the *Fifth Queen* trilogy, and *Young Lovell*. Of the latter, we have *The Simple Life Limited*, which ribs those who espoused the fashionable causes of the time in a way that sometimes makes Tom Sharpe read like social realism. Its observations owe much to Ford's own feelings about his family connections with the Pre-Raphaelite Brotherhood. (Ford's original name was Ford Hermann Hueffer: he changed it in homage to his grandfather, Ford Madox Brown.)

His own thoughts and instincts, however, were progressive. He was a tireless supporter of the campaign for Women's Suffrage and he did much to promote what he found best in *avant-garde* writing. He published and supported **Joyce** and **Pound**, and could claim to have discovered **Jean Rhys** and **D.H. Lawrence**. He collaborated extensively with **Joseph Conrad** and contributed to most of the latter's great novels. For himself, he was modest about his work, but recognised *The Good Soldier* as his best, "a great auk's egg" as he called it. Here Ford's knack with detail adorns his fondness for anecdotes, as the narrator rambles through his account of his wife's infidelity. For all that is discursive in its style, nothing irrelevant is included and the elegance with which the digressions rejoin this "saddest story" is a marvel. His other masterpiece is the tetralogy, *Parade's End*, which applies his techniques of beginning a story at a point which is more natural to the teller than the reader; and of relating observations rather than feelings to construe a narrative about the First World War, its roots, and its impact on private lives. **Auden** wrote of the whole, "There are not many English novels which deserve to be called great but *Parade's End* is one of them".

Forster

E.M.

born London 1879; died Cambridge 1970

I hate the idea of causes, and if I had to choose between betraying my friend and betraying my country, I hope I should have the guts to betray my country.

TWO CHEERS FOR DEMOCRACY

Ronny had repressed his mother when she enquired after his viola; a viola was almost a demerit, and certainly not the sort of instrument one mentioned in public.

A PASSAGE TO INDIA

E.M. FORSTER WROTE short stories, essays and biographies, as well as five novels – the last in 1924. All these are touched with an instinctive compassion.

Forster spent his school days in misery and this left him timid. He was always modest about his literary achievement, and shy in company: though he was intimate with members of the Bloomsbury set, he was closer to the edge than the centre of that circle.

He wrote especially well of outsiders, many of them victims of a peculiarly English way of life. *The Longest Journey* tells the apparently personal tale of a would-be writer still traumatised by bullying at school. Forster's own first published tale, *The Story of a Panic*, places English picnickers in Italy under the spell of Pan and explores English discomfort with other cultures – a theme which resurfaces throughout Forster's work: the spontaneity of the Italians unsettles travellers in *Where Angels Fear to Tread* and again in *A Room With a View* in which a girl's awakening to aesthetic forces seem almost indecent to those around her.

A Passage to India is Forster's most complex investigation of these themes. It sets English people against the oppressive background of the Raj, whose strict racial taboos they flout in a quest either for 'the real India' or uncomplicated friendship. They go in too deep: unlike Italy, the subcontinent remains beyond their grasp, not least because of the country's own rigorous social stratifications. The author's frequent plea, that we should connect more with our true feelings and with nature, finds its frustration here, where the very land seems hostile. But even when anticipating the problems of Indian Independence and partition, for many inconceivable at the time of publication, still nowhere does Forster relinquish his faith in people over principles.

Fowles

JOHN

born Leigh-on-Sea 1926

When they were nearer land he said, 'I wish you hadn't told me the sordid facts. That's the trouble with provincial life. Everyone knows everyone and there is no mystery. No romance.'

She teased him then: the scientist, the despiser of novels.

THE FRENCH LIEUTENANT'S WOMAN

JOHN FOWLES' NOVELS and stories have consistently evoked a rich aesthetic world to explore the themes of personal freedom and self-knowledge.

As a result, he produces very aware texts: aware of their own status as art, and aware of their authorial source. There is the writerly self-analysis of *Daniel Martin*; but *The French Lieutenant's Woman* is perhaps the best example of this process, and certainly his most famous work. The novel is set in Victorian Dorset, and nods towards conventional 19th-century plotting and narrative; but it is full of authorial comment, and manipulates the unnatural constraints of the past by forcing events to a conclusion more likely in the present. Or rather, two conclusions. The book belongs more to the writer than the reader. Fowles admitted that he had to let the lovers part, but couldn't, and so gave the work two endings, giving the reader the choice – although even this recalls the previous century and **Charlotte Brontë's** *Villette*.

The book's hero and heroine are echoed elsewhere in the Fowles corpus. Sarah is an idealised, elusive woman – the author has said as much – and for her, Charles suffers almost sadistic trials, while the *ingénu* schoolmaster in *The Magus* is plagued still further by his own "master" in a struggle for control of what Fowles calls "the godgame." Control, over people and art simultaneously, was his earliest theme. *The Collector* kidnaps an art student, kills her and analyses her as an object, beginning a soulless aesthetic project. The story involves class differences, as does the next: *The Aristos* argue over élite and popular views of culture. In *A Maggot*, Fowles finds support for the latter, arguing that we learn more about the 18th century from its mediocre writers than we do from **Pope** or **Dr Johnson.**

MAJOR WORKS

The Collector (1958)

The Aristos (1965)

The Magus (1966)

The French Lieutenant's Woman (1969)

The Ebony Tower (1974)

Daniel Martin (1977)

Mantissa (1982)

A Maggot (1985)

The Tree (1992)

Tessera (1993)

Frost

ROBERT

born San Francisco 1874; died Amherst 1963

That day she put our heads together,

Fate had her imagination about her,

Your head so much concerned with outer,

Mine with inner, weather.

TREE AT MY WINDOW

IT HAS BECOME AXIOMATIC to say that Robert Frost was something like America's Poet Laureate. He was an unusually public writer. Although he left Dartmouth College and Harvard without a degree, he had 44 conferred upon him subsequently; he won four Pulitzer prizes; the Senate formally congratulated him on his 75th and 85th birthdays; his visits to Russia and Israel assumed a diplomatic significance; and he read at President Kennedy's inauguration.

But if anything, Frost's reputation has suffered from this prominence. His achievements, and his pride in them, have led critics to attack him for being too popular or low-brow. To the world, Frost presented himself as a simple farmer (he had run a farm in Massachusetts for five years); with his literary peers he could display his erudition.

This has a curious effect on Frost's poetry, such that it is better read when one forgets the hype. It is at once simple and formal: his great trick is to incorporate speech rhythms into blank verse, and to keep each line at once controlled and relaxed. The result is a kind of home-spun wisdom delivered with lyrical grace, as though the poet were less a seer than a good neighbour. His insights often came from nature, and he had a closer affinity with the English poets of the Georgian school than with his American contemporaries (though he was much admired by **Pound**). He observes, and reports; but he has an ear for the one-line dictum. These are characteristically stoical, and lend themselves readily to quotation. His most famous poems, like "Out, Out", are even more celebrated for their grimness. But generally Frost uses his craft to put us in a resigned frame of mind in the way he tells his story, so that his own conclusions don't alarm us.

Gaddis

WILLIAM

born New York 1922

– No but here's a pin. For where your coat's torn. You shouldn't be upset about this appointment, she went on, pulling the tear together, – but I'm glad it's so important to you. There, she straightened the pocket flap and sat away, – but I wish it were a novel.

– Why would you say that, he muttered.

– The way you look, she said not looking.

– Like a novelist? Only problem is a novelist has to understand women.

J R

WILLIAM GADDIS IS THE author of three novels, each of them highly experimental, each using a highly stylised brand of satire to assess the plight of the soul in post-war America.

At the root of his work is a hope in salvation; but to establish a viable means of achieving it, when contemporary life offers such a babble of temptations and alternative theories, takes the narrative hundreds of pages. Gaddis' technique strives to mimic this kind of chaos, with plot conveyed mostly in dialogue in which only verbal tics can tell us who's talking, and leads some to find his texts unreadable. Still, he uses his own artistry, not only to posit art as a redeeming force, but also to question even that while he is doing it. His first novel, *The Recognitions*, has a hero who,

like Gaddis himself, is the son of a preacher and has artistic ambitions. But he discovers that even artistic endeavour can be flawed, as forgery and commercialism dog his progress around the international art scene.

The book's guiding principle is contained in the palindrome, "trade ye no mere moneyed art", which was to inform the long-awaited second novel, *J R*. Its protagonist is an eleven-year-old masterminding a business empire from payphones around his school. But his mission is set against that of a composer, who suffers as he avoids selling out. This sounds a note of hope, which was to echo in Gaddis' most recent book, *Carpenter's Gothic*, about a misunderstood Vietnam veteran who works for a preacher.

Galsworthy

JOHN   **born Coombe, Surrey 1867; died Hampstead 1933**

Thank Heaven she had not that maddening British conscientiousness which refused happiness for the sake of refusing!

IN CHANCERY

JOHN GALSWORTHY WROTE well-made plays and technically-assured novels, the most famous of which constitute the series *The Forsyte Saga*.

His early training was as a lawyer, and he was called to the bar in 1890. He also worked in his father's business, which enabled him to travel widely. Although a knowledge of the law provides much material for the second *Forsyte* novel, *In Chancery*, Galsworthy practised only briefly. In fact, his play *Justice* aimed at the inequalities of the law and its plea against solitary confinement is believed to have pushed Winston Churchill, then Home Secretary, into long-awaited prison reform. Other dramas draw sharp contrasts between the rich and the poor, notably *The Silver Box*, which argues that if an MP steals from a prostitute, no-one will care, but if a servant steals from an MP, then the retribution is harsh.

The negative effects of money and position are the premise for *The Forsyte Saga*, whose first volume deals with Soames Forsyte's inability to see the good in anything save the acquisition of money and property: his priorities poison his marriage, and the consequences fill the subsequent two novels. He is a violent husband, almost immune to the love of others, unless it is likely to deliver him a necessarily male heir. The whole is filled with remarkable detail – such as physical descriptions in the tradition of **Balzac** and the compassionate rendering of his heroine Irene's inner thoughts. Soames himself attained such stature during his time in print that his death made news headlines.

Galsworthy's writing was widely admired in his time, and praised by the likes of Sassoon and **Conrad**. Galsworthy met Conrad when the latter was the first mate of a ship on which Galsworthy was travelling, and at work on his own first novel. The two struck up a lifelong friendship, and Conrad's encouragement helped the younger novelist considerably. He won the Nobel Prize in 1932, a measure as much of his social concerns as his ability to bring them to a wide audience.

Gaskell

ELIZABETH

born Chelsea 1810; died Hampshire 1865

I see men here going about in the streets who look ground down by some pinching sorrow or care – who are not only sufferers but haters.

NORTH AND SOUTH

ELIZABETH GASKELL'S STORIES, five finished novels, and other literary work, deal with the divided Britain of the Victorian age.

She saw it at first hand. She was born in Chelsea, but lived with an aunt in Knutsford, near Manchester, throughout her childhood. The town provided the setting for her most celebrated novel, *Cranford*. She married the Reverend William Gaskell there in 1832, and joined him in his work with the poor, distributing food and clothes at Cross Street Chapel. It was a time of great political agitation, with Manchester a centre of Chartist activity. Gaskell observed these tensions intimately. *Ruth* is the story of a woman who has an illegitimate child by a reactionary Member of Parliament, and it dramatises the hypocrisy Gaskell saw.

She wrote *Mary Barton*, her first novel, to distract herself from the grief of losing a son in infancy. It is her first story involving industrial relations, brought to such a state of disrepair that employees draw lots to choose someone to murder the mill-owner's son. As elsewhere in Gaskell's work, moral and romantic dilemmas cloud what at first seemed like political actions. With its tight plot and social realism, it attracted the attention of **Dickens**, who published her work in *Household Words* thereafter. They had a difficult working relationship, but shared many artistic concerns, as is evident in the independently-reached similarities between *Hard Times* and Gaskell's *North and South*.

She was consistently progressive in her style and subject matter, and braved the opprobrium of her husband's parishioners for her depictions of prostitution and illegitimacy. She challenged traditional views of women's rôle in society throughout her work, and in her biography of her friend **Charlotte Brontë** did so with particular directness. This work upset contemporary ideas of what people wanted to know about a life and several passages had to be removed for seeming libellous.

Gay

JOHN

born Barnstaple 1685; died London 1732

One may know by your kiss, that your gin is excellent.

THE BEGGAR'S OPERA

LIFE IS A JEST; AND ALL THINGS SHOW IT, I THOUGHT SO ONCE; BUT NOW I KNOW IT.

HIS EPITAPH

JOHN GAY HAD A LONG WAIT for the literary success he deserved. He was a second son, and so denied the education his middle-class parents lavished on his elder brother. Still, he dedicated himself to poetry. He arrived in London, and waited for court preferment. After a series of secretarial posts, he was offered the post of gentleman usher to a two-year-old princess.

If this was the best the court could offer, he had to consider himself lucky to have fallen in with the Scriblerus Club, forming around **Pope**, **Swift** and Arbuthnot, although Pope and Swift zealously guarded Gay's output, deciding what he should and should not publish. When his own verse did emerge, it was as polished as any of his Augustan contemporaries, and he could transform the Latin pastoral to hymn or mock his surroundings with a rare facility.

Even on the stage, he was under his peers' aegis, collaborating with Pope and Arbuthnot on a learned comedy called *Three Hours After Marriage*. But he was the only one with any feel for what the public wanted, and what the times required; his own *The Beggar's Opera* fulfilled these needs with something approaching genius. It was a ballad opera, an entirely original genre which enabled Gay to take side-swipes at the contrivances of Italian opera so cultivated by his friend and collaborator Handel. He did this by writing new words for traditional songs. But its real satire is political and social: even then, it remains timeless. Peachum, the thief-taker, embodies at once Jonathan Wild, who would live off criminals before sending them to the gallows in exchange for rewards, and the Prime Minister Walpole, whose nepotistic government allowed such organised racketeering to flourish. The piece finds these faults in human nature as much as in individuals, and lent itself ideally to **Brecht**'s concerns when he and Kurt Weill turned it into *The Threepenny Opera*.

Genet

JEAN

Acts must be carried through to their completion. Whatever their point of departure, the end will be beautiful.

A THIEF'S JOURNAL

JEAN GENET USES the rich language of fantasy to illumine a world of inverted morals; where crime has its own sanctity, can be assessed aesthetically, and can culminate in the criminal's martyrdom.

The fantasies are extremely intimate ones, and leap out of dramatic situations, in novels and plays. In his first novel, *Our Lady of Flowers*, much of the internal monologue comes from a state of masturbatory rapture; in the later *Funeral Rites*, most of the action takes place in the protagonist's head, as he mourns his French Resistance lover by matching the man's degradation with his own sexual surrender to the Nazis.

Such writing draws as much from the life of the mind as from life itself: in both, Genet had plenty of material. He was abandoned by his mother (she was a prostitute), and spent most of his life between the ages of 10 and 38 on the run or in custody. As homosexual and prisoner, he found the concept of rôle-play, and the contrast between submissive and dominant, particularly appealing.

Theatre was the perfect medium for communicating this. His characters spend more time in their imaginary lives than their stage ones, until the performers stop being performers. In *The Maids*, two girls become so involved in imitating one another imitating their Madame, that the murder they fail to inflict upon her takes place among themselves instead. In keeping with Genet's avowed taste for theatre with men playing women's rôles, this three-hander often has an all-male cast. The challenge to an actor here is to maintain the purity of the exercise, without being tempted by camp. *The Blacks* takes this to a racial level, where black people mimic not only the extremes of white behaviour, but also perceived notions of blackness: the result is a bloodbath.

The characters follow their fantasies through to the finish to bring off a tragic inevitability. The unstoppable language takes them there, lending squalor a roseate lushness, and romanticising the prison as a medieval fortress. Once they have embraced this order their deeds become more than a parody of conventional desires and hold the value of aesthetic necessity.

George

STEFAN   **born Büdesheim 1868; died Minusio, Switzerland 1933**

Now the dream, highest pride, upward

springs,

Boldly quells then the god who lent

wings...

Till a cry to the depths thrusts us all,

We so bare, face with death, we so small!

DREAM OF DEATH, TR. CAROL NORTH VALHOPE AND ERNST MORWITZ

STEFAN GEORGE EMBRACED the idea of a higher reality beyond the tangible world. His work seems to aspire for a greater purity still: he thought wine and women were both deleterious to the poet's song, and surrounded himself with male aesthetes whom he could persuade of the same. This circle was called the Georgekreis, within which he was the autocrat.

As a German, he wanted his nation to attain a similar refinement. He was frustrated by what he considered the crudeness of those around him, and by a language too ornate to articulate his ideals. He craved the abstractions of **Nietzsche**, and echoed the philosopher's praise of strength. George expressed this patriotically. His verse would speak of a new Reich, and a Führer, which the incipient Nazi movement found extremely useful. This appalled him. He was too much the poet to care for their politics, and had no sympathy with their anti-semitism. In 1933, he rejected Goebbel's offer of high honours in the new régime and left for Switzerland, where he died later that year.

If his verse had nationalistic leanings, it was in the name of beauty. He combined the two in his view of the youth of Maximilian Kronberger, whom he mythologised as a boy emperor, dead at 16. His earlier work was more decadent and espoused the aestheticism of **Oscar Wilde**; then his model of the young despot was the debauched Heliogabalus. Even then, his verse remained pure. He would execute it under rigorous constraints and avoided repeating any rhyme. His determination to blend form with content meant that he had to express his meaning with whatever vocabulary his rules left him, accounting in part for his distinct style.

Gide

ANDRÉ

born Paris 1869; died Paris 1951

"Put as little order into your story as you please," said Jammes. ...

"Then you must allow me to talk a great deal about myself."

"Which of us ever does anything else?" was Jammes' rejoinder.

ISABELLE, TR. DOROTHY BUSSY

ANDRÉ GIDE'S STYLISH and sometimes exotic handling of prose touched on many concerns sure to arouse controversy. He was a forthright critic of French imperialism and, after his visits to Chad and the Congo, became a Communist for a while. **E.M. Forster** considered him the perfect humanist, particularly for the way Gide's love of mankind balanced a natural curiosity. The latter attracted more attention.

In moral matters, he anticipated the work of **Sartre** and **Genet**, and in *The Immoralist*, wondered how far people are constrained by their environments: can they reinvent themselves? But Gide's exploration was more guided by the battle between the sensual and the spiritual than by the needs of the hour. In *Strait is the Gate*, the spirit seems to prevail; but this is partly because of pride militating against freedom, and the sensuality of religion itself.

His fictional treatments complement what appear to be his more atobiographical works. He was a bisexual wanderer married to his devout cousin, and during that time strove to explain his soul's struggle to her in writing. But even his memoirs show the artistry of his story-telling. In his largest, most complex work, *The Counterfeiters*, a novelist is writing the novel *The Counterfeiters*, sharing Gide's own dependence on structure and frame devices to make sense of the vaguely connected plots occurring around him. Here the real author shows his admiration for **Dostoyevsky**, borrowing stories from newspapers, snipping from them at moments of crisis. But, as elsewhere, he retains a love of beauty, and in writing of forgery, asks the question that rises throughout his *oeuvre*: how successfully could the form and elegance of his art render the truths of his life?

Ginsberg

ALLEN

born Newark, New Jersey 1926; died New York 1997

Poets be fools of their own desire – O Anacreon and angelic Shelley! Guide these new-nippled generations on space ships to Mars' next universe

WHO BE KIND TO

ALLEN GINSBERG WAS THE POET of the Beat generation. Although his work exists beyond that time, we know it comes from a survivor of that hazardous age who handed it down in all its detail.

His poetry is a rich mix. His method, as he describes it, is a form of meditation, using the mantra "Om": while the altered state of consciousness this produces would seem to generate "automatic writing", Ginsberg juggles a range of sources and allusions. He cites many precedents for *Howl*, the poem which made him famous, including other poems with refrains, such as Christopher Smart's mad *Jubilate Agno*. For all his verse's abundant freedom, however, Ginsberg spent a long time mastering classical metres, translating **Catullus**, or working with Elizabethan models.

A Ginsberg poem, however, could not be mistaken for any of these. His writing is confessional and often vast. It takes on folklore and mysticism, sensuality and religion (especially Buddhist and Jewish: his most harrowing poem is *Kaddish*, a Hebrew-styled lament for his mother). Whatever it takes to combat his enemies – the CIA, sexual repression, the atom bomb, colour TV – he prosecutes his cause with anything from ballads to harangues.

His graphic and unflinching accounts of gay sex, his forthright language, and openly drug-induced streams of consciousness, have led him to be censored and arrested. This alone would give him authority as a leading counter-cultural figure but he is more than just this. He has given the cause a poetry which can reach **Whitman**'s expanses and attain **William Carlos Williams**' delicacy of cadence. He has acknowledged both these as influences and the latter helped his early career considerably.

Nevertheless, he stamps his own name, and those of his friends, all over his volumes, filling them with unpunctuated anecdotes which sometimes make the reader feel he or she just had to be there. All this might seem like vanity, but in being the first to own up to it (Ginsberg frequently complained about his deteriorating looks) his candour seems more generous than self-seeking.

Goethe

JOHANN WOLFGANG VON born Frankfurt 1749; died Weimar 1832

Now slants the fiery god toward the west,

Hasting away, but seeking in his round

New life afar: I long to join his quest,

On tireless wings uplifted from the

ground.

FAUST, PART ONE, TR. PHILIP WAYNE

GOETHE MIGHT STAND as Germany's finest poet, yet he embraced all Europe. His juvenilia includes work in English and French; he broke off government work to explore Italy, and entered a classical period of writing, translating Latin authors and imitating their metres. At the end of his life, he was a huge fan of **Byron**'s *Don Juan*, and wished his own language capable of such comic rhyme. But he did more than any of his compatriots to extend the range and power of German, stretching its natural capacity for new words, taking on its folk poetry and its song rhythms, as much as its philosophical diction.

His career spanned the end of Classicism, and the beginning of Romanticism. But for all his involvement with the German 'storm and stress' movement, he had more faith in controlled poetics and an ordered world view than in spontaneous outpourings of emotion. Not that he was incapable of these. He could write poetry anywhere and all Europe was caught up in its passion. His prose work, *The Sorrows of Young Werther*, for example, was supposed to have men on the wrong corners of love-triangles reaching for their guns. Goethe's concerns went beyond the individual's emotions, however: as a polymath, with interests including all branches of science as well as the arts of painting, music and theatre, he formulated theories of evolution and light in which he saw a unity in creation, and a kind of Pantheism.

This is especially strong in the mighty *Faust*, his life's work. Taking the 16th-century legend of a man tempted by a pact with the Devil, he portrayed a scholar wracked by his vision of the world's beauties (which Goethe incomparably glossed, even marrying Faust to Helen of Troy), and in doing so reflected his own quest for knowledge and faith in salvation.

Gogol

NIKOLAI

born Sorochintsy 1809; died Moscow 1852

This world is full of the most outrageous nonsense. Sometimes things happen which you would hardly think possible: that very same nose, which had paraded itself as a state councillor and created such an uproar in the city, suddenly turned up, as if nothing had happened, plonk where it had been before, i.e. right between Major Kovalyov's two cheeks.

THE NOSE

GOGOL'S CHARACTERS BEGIN with all-too human delusions, which usually escalate into madness. Readers are tempted to see Gogol's own obsessions and literary ambitions (not to mention sexual hang-ups) as an explanation for this, as well as for his own bizarre end; but his literary and historical sources, together with his own magnificent comic style, are vital.

Literary aspirations took him to St Petersburg, where he worked as a public official and even as Professor of History at the university. The crazed types who people his stories are often frustrated civil servants who lose it completely, or dignitaries undone by embarrassment (like that of losing one's nose at the barber's). These figures waver between fear of humiliation (having too shabby an overcoat) and hope for unattainable social rank (becoming the King of Spain, in *The Diary of a Madman*, for example). These conflicts generally precede lunacy.

They are first-person narratives: Gogol's use of speech, random thought patterns and even typography at once pay homage to his model **Sterne** and go to the roots of personality. This explains why his one play is the constant joy of Russian theatre. *The Government Inspector* blends his old theme of provincial pettiness with an identity mix-up, leading a nobody to believe that he really is the inspector that a corrupt community holds in such dread. While nobody survives this satire, the piece's importance is more than social; where public honesty is at stake, so is honesty to oneself.

Gogol craved a moral element in his work and a holy man talked him into burning much of his largest work, *Dead Souls,* for failing to achieve it. What **Pushkin** read of it had a profound effect on him: the extant text gives us the clearest glimpse of his talent for sheer poetry, with its apostrophes on the progress both of Russia and the human spirit.

Golding

WILLIAM

**born St Columb Minor, Cornwall 1911;
died Newquay, Cornwall 1993**

I have hung all systems on the wall like a row of useless hats. They do not fit. They have come in from outside, they are suggested patterns, some dull and some of great beauty. But I have lived enough of my life to require a pattern that fits over everything; and where shall I find that?

FREE FALL

WILLIAM GOLDING'S NOVELS characteristically approach the battle good and evil fight over human beings, by setting it in isolation. The first, and the most famous, is *The Lord of the Flies*. It follows a group of boys stranded on an island, whose attempts to establish order descend into anarchy and murder. It presents a view of morality the author could not escape after the Second World War, during which he served in the Navy; but the means of expressing it came from his dislike, both of Ballantyne's insular idyll, *The Coral Island*, and of having taught school-children in Salisbury.

The sea brings the worst out of people in his other novels; in *Pincher Martin*, a naval officer struggles to survive the elements once he is washed up on a rock – but at length we come to realise that it is nothing less than his salvation at stake. In a late trilogy, Golding sends a group off from 19th-century England to settle in Australia. The trip takes the Victorian image of life itself being a journey, while the peculiarly English make-up of the crew, with its attitudes on class and religion, make the vessel in *Rites of Passage* a ship of state.

The sin inherent in Golding's tales is ineluctable. Mankind has fallen already. Rather than go back to Genesis, he returns to the dawn of *homo sapiens*. From *The Inheritors*, we emerge as an innately aggressive, cunning species. A religious reading of the problems we have reconciling morality with our flawed nature occurs in *The Spire*; it tells of a medieval churchman's architectural plea for redemption, in which his human frailties have their counterpart in the building's own structural faults. The very title of *Darkness Visible* recalls **Milton**, and his own poem of the atonement.

Golding was awarded the Nobel Prize for Literature In 1983.

Goldsmith

OLIVER

born Co. Longford, Ireland c. 1730; died London 1774

But me, not destined such

   delights to share,

My prime of life in wandering

   spent and care;

Impelled, with steps unceasing, to pursue

Some fleeting good, that mocks me

   with the view...

My fortune leads to traverse

   realms alone,

And find no spot of all the

   world my own.

THE TRAVELLER

THROUGHOUT HIS SHORT LIFE, Oliver Goldsmith embraced a wide range of experience, and explained to his brother, "I had learn'd from books to love virtue, before I was taught from experience the necessity of being selfish." His youthful travels rendered him penniless, and must have showed him how to survive – he got by as a busker, an apothecary's assistant and an usher at a school in Peckham – and yet his dealings in practical matters show naivety. When threatened with the debtor's prison, it was **Dr Johnson** who sold Goldsmith's *The Vicar of Wakefield* for the necessary £60.

That book was criticised for its lack of insight into human behaviour, but praised for its morality – the opposite of what his brother might have expected. His characters seemed too romantic, even his vicar too virtuous. The qualities it displayed resembled those his theoretical writings disparaged: he preferred harder, realer truths to the more inflated sentiments of **Richardson**; but Goldsmith's work shows a family prevailing over disasters by the dozen – a contingency real enough to the author.

The events of his best-known play, *She Stoops to Conquer*, appear still more implausible, in which a young suitor mistakes the home of his prospective bride's parents for a pub, and behaves accordingly. Still, we could regard this as portraying each setting more faithfully through comparison with the other, even were it not likely that Goldsmith had made a similar error in his own youth. In the piece, he continued his assault on all that he considered trite in contemporary writing. He sustained it with great distinction as a poet, using an epigrammatic, even bitchy kind of wit to repudiate the fault of taking the world too much at face value.

Goll

YVAN

born St. Dié, Vosges 1891; died Paris 1950

And this single dusk

When even the gods are jealous

Of a kiss made of honey and electricity

Is worth more than the centuries of

    centuries.

DO NOT CALL DEATH!

YVAN GOLL WAS A Jewish poet born in Alsace-Lorraine, an area which has repeatedly swung from French to German control. His background already gave him a rich cultural mixture – he was fluent in both French and German, and wrote poetry in both languages. He tried writing in English, and produced a German translation of *Ulysses*. His linguistic journeys bespeak the kind of rootlessness that would be his most dominant theme, most notably in the poems of a wondering Everyman, *John Without Land*, whose peregrinations follow Goll's, with no more hope of settling anywhere. This enables the poet to embrace the whole of human experience, as did **Whitman**; but he does it in remarkably controlled, rhyming quatrains, and with epigrammatic elegance: "I buy Manhattan with a single smile/ I sell it back for immortality."

He resembled that other polyglot **Paul Celan** in his range of influences: he spent the First World War in Switzerland writing Expressionist poetry, and in France would champion Surrealism. The two poets were working with such similar subject matter and resources that Goll's wife Claire accused Celan of plagiarism, upsetting the latter deeply.

But it was Claire, a fellow poet, who would inspire Goll most, and give him his best hope of happiness. Many poems show him finding a refuge in his love that saves him from the world's otherwise overwhelming horrors. His work is more approachable than Celan's in this respect, especially when Goll is being lyrical: "When you cry, the sun is eclipsed/ But when you smile, new stars are born."

After the war, he wrote very little in German, until the very end of his life, when he began work on *Traumkraut*. It was published after his death from leukaemia.

Gorky

MAXIM

born Nizhniy-Novgorod 1868; died Moscow 1936

I sought the friendship of those who were foreigners even in their own country.

MY UNIVERSITIES

GORKY'S WRITING is notable for introducing the technique called "socialist realism", which became the prescribed approach for writers working in the Soviet Union. He began his career with the short stories that brought him widespread attention: that of **Chekhov** welcome, that of the authorities less so. The former encouraged him in letters which read like a masterclass; he praised whatever in Gorky was sparing, and advised him against words which swung the narrative too much, and against rhetoric. However, Gorky was to be a political writer and the traits some have regarded negatively, for their want of refinement, were to become Gorky's tools.

Although he is now read chiefly for his memoirs, and his reminiscences of **Tolstoy**, his reputation was sustained by in his novels and plays. His most political play was *The Lower Depths*, which expressed much of Gorky's philosophy and the punishing life he'd led as a labourer even before he was orphaned at the age of 10. His two most famous novels are *Foma Godeiev*, in which a father embodies the insurgent capitalism at the expense of his sensitive son, and *Mother*, about Bolshevik activity in an industrial town. He was indispensable to the Bolsheviks, both before and after the Revolution, trying to collect funds in America in 1905, and controlling the crowds in the excesses of the October Revolution in 1917.

He was a key link between the intellectual and popular movements, but he was regarded with suspicion by both. Although his death invites conspiracy theories from either side, there can be no doubt that Stalin must have been a little comforted by the health concerns that kept the nation's gadfly in Capri for much of his later life. From there, Gorky continued to encourage and advise young writers. His home town of Nizhniy-Novgorod adopted his name as its own. His pen-name at least: for Alexei Mikhailovitch Peshkov changed his name too, to the Russian for "bitter".

Grass

GÜNTHER

born Danzig 1927

And so from this Yorrick came no citizen, but rather a Hamlet, a fool.

THE TIN DRUM

GRASS IS A HIGHLY cultured writer who remains extremely critical of his country. Germany's history has made a profound personal impact on him, and he has been bound up with its public events during the war and beyond.

His most famous and daring response to this has been the Danzig Trilogy, particularly its first book, *The Tin Drum*. Throughout, the narrator, who has refused to grow physically since the age of three, languishes in an asylum for a murder he didn't commit. He emerges as a brilliant outsider, a *faux naif* and the best hope his delirious nation has of being restored to humanity. His drum beats steadily through the age's hysteria, while his gift for screaming can wreck Nazi rallies. Grass's own book can be read as a similarly alarming shriek aiming to awaken Germany's conscience.

The allure of Hitler reaches deeper into the trilogy's other two books. *Cat and Mouse* depicts a man impelled to join the Nazis by another physical peculiarity (this time a huge Adam's Apple). *Dog Years* follows the rage of a character who embraces and then rejects Nazism, driven to beat his half-Jewish friend, before plaguing his former military colleagues with sexual diseases.

Grass himself joined Hitler Youth, and was drafted into the air force during the war. His experimental and allusive work offers a first-hand, hideously real account of National Socialism's power, using often unreal plots and authorial comment to drive his point further home. He has continued this as a playwright, poet and political thinker. In the last rôle, he has written speeches for Willy Brandt (stung by the personal assaults Chancellor Adenauer launched against his friend), persistently scrutinised public life in open letters, and produced essays arguing against German reunification. His versatility extends to music and the plastic arts, influencing respectively the inner content of his books and their outer design.

143

Graves

ROBERT

born London 1895; died Majorca 1985

Gone are the drab monosyllabic days

When 'agricultural labour' was still tilth;

And '100% approbation', praise;

And 'pornographic modernism' filth;

Yet still I stand by tilth and filth and

praise.

TILTH

BEFORE ONE OF THE LECTURES Robert Graves delivered as Professor of Poetry at Oxford, an undergraduate was heard to remark that his value lay in the fact that he was "wrong about everything". Indeed Graves tended to avoid agreeing with people.

For sure, he wrote fiction unashamedly for money, in order to sustain his true passion for poetry, and in so doing disciplined himself to write economically and in accordance with public taste, but even his novels were aimed to cause upset. *King Jesus* for example, showed a Christ who had not died on the cross. Other projects and sentiments, meanwhile, showed breath-taking hubris. He modernised **Shakespeare**, and re-translated *The Rubáiyát of 'Omar Khayyám* with his usual freedoms, only to contest that he was using a better manuscript. His poetry, however, is conventional, and while his lyrics are lovely, his premise, "Man Does, Woman Is" has become outmoded and his views on fellow poets such as **Eliot** and **Auden** frankly laughable.

That said, Graves' knowledge was vast. His scholarship did not stop with the classics. His control of mythological sources was enormous, and his ability to communicate it unmatched. Indeed, his novels have popularised Ancient Rome nearly as much as Asterix has. A polyglot and a polymath who gleaned his knowledge as much from life as from books, he was as complex as he was clever. There's no doubt he knew the horror of war – having read his own obituary after mistakenly being reported dead at the age of 21 – and yet he spoke out against poets like Auden and **Virgil** who never saw military action. Through all these contradictions, however, emerges a kind of incomprehensible bravery that make Robert Graves' convictions as bold as his insights.

Greene

GRAHAM

born Berkhamsted 1904; died Antibes 1991

If I love or if I hate, let me love or hate as an individual. I will not be 59200/5 in anyone's global war.

OUR MAN IN HAVANA

GRAHAM GREENE'S NOVELS can be read just as he styled many of them – as entertainments – but with his wit and control of tension comes perhaps the most profound examination of morality in 20th-century English fiction.

A constant theme with Greene is betrayal. His work in intelligence, notably under the double agent Kim Philby, informs his treatment of espionage; but for all the 'thriller' content of his books, he is most acute on human motivations rather than political ones.

This shows in his earliest 'romances', and their historical settings; and in the years before the war, his exploration of the international situation focused on individuals acting out of private malaise rather than public feeling. If Greene's characters act politically, it is out of personal anxiety, like their espousal of Communism in *It's a Battlefield* and *The Confidential Agent*.

With Greene's conversion to Catholicism, these themes emerge in a religious context, and with greater vehemence after 1938, when the Church sent him to Mexico to report on state persecution of Christianity. Greene felt that a sense of religion enriched the novel (impoverished, for him, since the death of **Henry James**), and he expressed it in plots handling the most agonising dilemmas. Priests frequently appear either to instil meaning into a moral void, as in *Brighton Rock*, or to articulate their own doubts. This latter alarmed many in the Catholic Church, especially with the frankness of the "whisky priest" in *The Power and the Glory*.

Later work described turbulent landscapes like Cuba and Haiti; the Anglo-Saxon characters caught in these spots try to face pressures while maintaining their integrity. They are in life-or-death situations: in West Africa, as in Brighton, Greene realises the full dramatic potential of the troubled conscience facing impossible decisions.

MAJOR WORKS

England Made Me (1935)

Brighton Rock (1938)

The Power and the Glory (1940)

The Heart of the Matter (1948)

Our Man in Havana (1958)

The Comedians (1966)

The Human Factor (1978)

Grimm

JAKOB LUDWIG KARL
WILHELM KARL

born Hanau 1785; died Berlin 1863
born Hanau 1786; died Berlin 1859

There's a fine of three marks for anyone who doesn't believe this story.

THE CLEVER LITTLE TAILOR,
TR. DAVID LUKE.

THE WORK OF the Brothers Grimm fits comfortably into a history of a national German identity throughout the 19th century and beyond; but their achievement was quieter and less intimidating than those of many of their compatriots, attributes which have helped make them more durable. The Brothers' response to their country was not to wish it were Greece, nor to find those around them boorish and bourgeois or unworthy of a heroic age. Rather they pioneered a study of their own language and mythology, looking to German legends and folk tales, and recording stories that had been circulating for ages.

The results included Jakob's treatise on *German Grammar* and formulation of Grimm's Law, accounting for his language's phonetic shifts; they collaborated on the *Deutsches Wörtebuch* project which has since been established as the definitive continuing work on German vocabulary and its etymology. Wilhelm edited Jakob's works, as well as medieval texts (most notably *The Song of Roland*). He also published critical appraisals of many national legends.

But the most famous accomplishment of their combined careers was the collection known in English as *Grimm's Fairy Tales*. It is the fruit of two years' work spent travelling around their country and transcribing stories which had been transmitted orally for generations. The task yielded some of the best-known children's tales, and was warmly welcomed on its appearance. Over the years, people have questioned the nature of the exercise, asking how faithfully the two philologists can have rendered the spoken qualities of the stories. The act of writing can freeze an oral tradition forever (witness **Homer**) and in the Grimms' case, more orthodox versions of tales like *The Sleeping Beauty* have prevailed over less seemly ones, for example the variation of that story where the slumbering heroine awakes to discover that she is pregnant. Still, even this information would be lost to the general ear without the Brothers' labours, and their imaginative world can retain its capacity to frighten as well as enchant.

Gunn

THOM

born Gravesend 1929

separate words return to their roots

lover and mother melt into

one figure that covers its face

nameless and inescapable

BRINGING TO LIGHT

THOM GUNN PUBLISHED his first poetry while still an undergraduate at Cambridge, and the first volume, *Fighting Terms*, appeared just after he left. In it his control of strict verse is evident, as is the influence of Metaphysical poets (he imitates one of **Herbert**'s trickiest forms in *The Last Man*); but Gunn uses a similar subtlety of argument to express something more dispiriting. A common trick of his is to investigate a word's meaning by threatening the quality that defines it: *The Nihilification of Nothing* devotes a whole poem to the process, and it occurs in chiasmatic lines like, "longing so hard to make/ inclusions that the longing/ has become in memory/ an inclusion". This kind of thinking cancels itself out, leaving a void, and Gunn manages it everywhere with **Donne**-like economy.

In his poetry, as in his life, he took less for granted and greater freedoms. He left for the US in 1954, where he became interested in drugs and bikers, but still described them with formal grace. His poetry takes greater liberties too and, by *Jack Straw's Castle*, he was writing increasingly free verse. In 1982, *The Passages of Joy* gave the world his first openly homoerotic pieces, and the thrill of this verse "coming out" makes the collection less bleak than any of his previ-

ous ones. We can still recognise Gunn, however, narrating gay sex in the loo of a Mcdonald's with his natty five-line rhymed pentameter stanzas.

Since then, some of his friends have died of AIDS. *The Man With Night Sweats* laments them in its closing sequence, in language that reminds us of the earlier nullity. Lines like "Abandoned incomplete, shape of a shape," recall his earlier method, and lines like, "Their deaths have left me less defined," show just what he has lost since those happier times. But even this collection ends on a note of hope: a chance meeting with a gay man and his adopted son.

Hammett

DASHIELL

**born St. Mary's County, Maryland
1894; died New York City 1961**

What disturbed him was the discovery that in sensibly ordering his affairs he had got out of step, and not into step, with life.

THE MALTESE FALCON

DASHIELL HAMMETT revolutionised crime writing. He had worked in the Pinkerton Detective Agency, and his grittier view of the gum-shoe sleuth began appearing in *Black Mask* magazine throughout the 1920s. In 1929 he published his first novel, *Red Harvest*, which introduced the Continental Operative. He was not the last Hammett hero to find brutal ways of making the city a safer place in which to live, but critics have seemed particularly eager to come up with the book's final body-count: there are some 30 deaths, ranging from the painful to the perfunctory.

Here there is already evidence of Hammett's political radicalism (he was later to serve six months in prison during the McCarthy witch-hunts): in his novels, the ends always justify the means, and his protagonists prosecutes those ends with a thoroughness that anticipates **Genet**. This kind of detective stretches morality in a way barely known hitherto, and his lifestyle won him the epithet "hard-boiled".

In this, as well as in literary style, Hammett was a great influence on **Raymond Chandler**. His writings introduce dream sequences (especially in his second book, *The Dain Curse*, which tends toward the supernatural), and the reflections of a drugged detective, later to occur in Chandler's *The Little Sister*. Later still, **Umberto Eco** would find a use for Hammett's device of killing someone by poisoning the pages of a book

Hammett's two most significant novels are *The Maltese Falcon* and *The Glass Key*, which both show people looking for justice, but necessarily compromising themselves to achieve it. The former is considered his finest plot, and the latter stands as an acute examination into moral ambiguity: the story of a political racketeer accused of murder, and his friend's mission to clear him, brings out the theme of human loyalty under pressure. Other work has been published posthumously by his wife, Lillian Hellman.

Hamsun

KNUT

born Lom, Oppland 1859; died Grimstad 1952

Happy creatures! To be almost nothing is also something.

WAYFARERS, TR. JAMES MCFARLANE

HAMSUN IS CONSIDERED THE best Norwegian writer since **Ibsen**; but it is important to remember not only how unlike Ibsen his work is – indeed, the stance he takes is often in reaction to Ibsen – but also how his literary achievements anticipated those of much more celebrated authors. His open enthusiasm for Hitler was an enormous blow to his reputation. But in 1943, the Führer met the ageing author, was asked, "What will Norway's rôle be?" and said afterwards, "I never want to meet that man again."

Much of Hamsun's work celebrates the strong and moral; but it avoids preaching. When he began his career, Norway was full of social realists, whose methods Hamsun found inadequate for conveying psychological truths. His early work reacted strongly against this and the contemporary Scandinavian interest in French Romantic poetry. Hamsun's own poetry remains widely admired and informs the sweep of his prose work. His first and most famous novel, *Hunger*, takes place in the narrator's head, as the starving writer wanders around the capital recounting his subjective impressions. A lonely hero fetches up again in *Mysteries*, in a coastal village. Nagel sets himself up as a fraud, only to reveal that everything about him is actually true. He strives to make people feel better only to disappear again after a few weeks.

Hamsun's heroes are often writers, and in *Victoria*

the protagonist takes Hamsun's original name. In the later *The Growth of the Soil*, however, Hamsun's model of single-mindedness and self-sufficiency is a farmer miles from anyone except his wife. The hero sets himself up as the count of his land, reflecting Hamsun's absorption with nobility (other characters find countesses singularly beautiful). Here as, as elsewhere, Hamsun presents a kind of strength that can appear brutal, and while the novel shocked, it contained enough idealism to secure the Nobel Prize. This has been seen as calculated (his later work is much less optimistic); but by 1920, with his finest work already done, his talent was due for international recognition.

Hardy

THOMAS   **born Upper Bockhampton, Dorset 1840; died Dorchester 1928**

Yonder a maid and her wight

Come whispering by:

War's annals will cloud into night

Ere their story die.

IN TIME OF "THE BREAKING OF NATIONS"

HARDY'S THIRD NOVEL finds a young, self-taught scholar restoring a Cornish church, and falling in love with Elfrida Swancourt, the daughter of a disapproving priest. *A Pair of Blue Eyes* holds many clues to the author's life and work: he trained as an architect, and his plots stand as structural wholes, each action leading logically to the next, and supported by the rhythm of the seasons. Often, the result is finely-wrought tragedy; this novel features the independent but doomed heroine that would recur in Hardy's books, to be represented most ruthlessly in his penultimate novel, *Tess of the D'Urbervilles*. The end of that novel invokes the pitiless progress of tragedy in its quotation of **Aeschylus**.

He was born in Dorset, where he played the fiddle at weddings and was later engaged to disinter bodies making way for a road. Nearly all his stories take place in Wessex. He gives real locations fictional names; but visitors find that what they read is real enough. Like the poet Richard Jeffries, he portrayed the dignity and suffering of the rural poor, in the face of such obstacles as industry, new wealth, and uncomprehending idealism. But more than that, they contend with the universe's injustice and, from *The Return of the Native* onwards, they never win.

His work was increasingly attacked for its atheism and supposed immorality. He revised his novels right until his death, often toning down his earlier, sensual instincts; but with the outrage that greeted *Jude the Obscure*, he abandoned novel-writing and began publishing his poems. Throughout 900 of them, he never used the same verse form twice. These brought him the fame we now associate with his prose (his most admired verse then was an epic, *The Dynasts*, now largely ignored). They compress the theme of an unsympathetic world into song-like stanzas, whose cadences are as irresistible as the fate they describe.

Hardy died in Dorset, at Max Gate; he designed the house himself.

Harrison

TONY   **born Leeds 1937**

Hindu/Sikh, soul/body, heart v. mind,
East/West, male/female, and the ground
these fixtures are fought out on Man,
*   resigned*
to hope from his future what his past
*   never found.*

                                                    v

MAJOR WORKS

The Loiners (1972)

The Oresteia (1981)

v (1984)

The Trackers of
*   Oxyrhynchus* (1990)

IN CONTEMPORARY BRITAIN, Tony Harrison is a poet of rare social importance and technical accomplishment. His poems address a divided nation, and hit home.

He does this in clear language, whose frankness offends some. As well as being an astounding handler of form, he is also a polyglot; he mastered Latin and Greek before his teens and has translated opera libretti from Czech. His verse includes snippets of other languages, including the endangered Cornish.

Harrison himself is from Leeds. His stated poetic goal is to write poetry his father would understand. His sonnet sequence, *The School of Eloquence*, articulates this with unerring pathos. Rather than parade his learning in front of the reader, he draws attention to the difference between his classical education and much of his audience's experience. But his use of the classics is invaluable to today's problems. As well as rendering **Aeschylus** with a rare immediacy, he has written an extraordinary verse play, *The Trackers of Oxyrhynchus*, which follows the Greek scholars Grenfell and Hunt on their trail for lost tragedies. All they turn up are a **Sophocles** satyr play full of the plum lewdness that genre requires, and appeals from the homeless. The analogy between their priorities and ours becomes stark.

Harrison's poetry reaches an unusually large public, through his drama (he has written adaptations of medieval mystery plays) and television. He continues to address urgent social concerns, like Alzheimer's Disease, the Gulf War, and the controversy over Rushdie's *The Satanic Verses*. The earliest remains the best. *v* addresses all the opposing factions of society, in a response which begins with rage at the graffiti on his family graves and works towards an understanding of its deeper causes.

Throughout, he maintains a poet's self-consciousness, leading him to find much guilt in himself: for Harrison, poetry is *The Heartless Art*, and his work strives as much to heal itself as those around him.

Hartley

L.P.

born Peterborough 1895; died London 1972

*The life of facts proved no bad substitute
for the facts of life.*

THE GO-BETWEEN

L.P. HARTLEY'S NOVELS and short stories examine the roots of personality. His characters strive for self-knowledge and the quest often begins in childhood. His world is one of lost innocence and just as children are robbed of their illusions, so is Hartley's age. The Victorian values of the well-to-do figures who people his work disappear in the social change for which he accounts so subtlely.

The lush background of his tales can betray his own origins: action frequently takes place in the countryside of East Anglia, and can wander into the fashionable sets of Oxford and Venice. But Hartley undermines the formality and expectations of such locales with his own prose style. His sentences are finely balanced, and his structure rigorously controlled, all the while depicting an old order of strained elegance in decay.

Hartley can offer some comfort to people who feel they have wasted their lives for ignorance of themselves. Eustace emerges from the *Eustace and Hilda* trilogy, which follows its hero's emotional development from childhood to his death bed, less in the shadow of his sister, and at last capable of love, however long this has taken. The narrator of Hartley's most famous book, *The Go-Between*, has less to console him. He recalls a hot, hot summer holiday spent in Norfolk, and how events showed him, not only what sex was, but also how tragic its consequences could be when transgressing social niceties. Leo Coulston is now a bitter, solitary man, caught in the past until the final page; but his recollections are childhood ones. What he doesn't understand literally is conveyed with an exact symbolism: the thermometer that measures the rising tension; the dreamed-up magic spells that assume lives of their own; the green bicycle that compounds at once the boy's innocence and how he loses it – by taking messages between lovers divided by class. As elsewhere, Hartley's exquisite articulation of his themes owes much to **Henry James**; but the tragic effect he achieves is rare indeed.

Hašek

JAROSLAV

born Prague 1883; died Lipnice 1923

I am very fond of the good soldier Schweik, and in presenting an account of his adventures during the World War, I am convinced that you will sympathise with this modest, unrecognised hero. He did not set fire to the temple of the goddess at Ephesus, like that fool of a Herostratus, merely in order to get his name into the newspapers and the school reading books.

And that, in itself, is enough.

THE GOOD SOLDIER SCHWEIK,
TR. PAUL SELVER

The Good Soldier Schweik
(1923)

JAROSLAV HAŠEK WAS a prankster and short-story writer who was well-known and liked in Prague, where he lived in the years before the First World War. During the conflict he fought first for the Austro-Hungarian Empire, which ruled Czech-oslovakia, before deserting to join the cause of Czech independence. When the war ended, he joined the Russian Communist party.

In 1921, he began work on his one novel, *The Good Soldier Schweik*. In its meandering, episodic form, it resembles **Cervantes'** *Don Quixote*, and shares that work's use of a character whose incomplete but charming personality sets him at odds with the world around him.

But Schweik is different. He is a little man who has no idea that he is anything else. He is a dog breeder caught up in the Great War. His weakness is that he craves the quiet life in a time of chaos, and yet his docility leads him into the kind of situations where his cheery co-operation with absolutely everyone looks like stoicism. His guilelessness is worthy of a **Shakespearean** fool, and his insights consequently as profound. By sheer accident, he finds himself at the hub of global events, and a part-time national hero.

Hašek's prose collaborates with this notion of the heroic. All the corrupt officials Schweik encounters in his picaresque rise through an army he barely even joined are presented with a kind of nobility of purpose; the writing does nearly as much as Schweik does to expose their shallowness and hypocrisy. The work's own rambling and unfinished character is worthy of its protagonist, and is almost too charming for the mordant satire it conveys.

Havel

VÁCLAV

born Prague 1936

What is your favourite tunnel? Are you fond of musical instruments? How many times a year do you air the square? Where did you bury the dog? Why didn't you pass it on? When did you lose the claim? Wherein lies the nucleus? Do you know where you're going and do you know who's going with you? Do you piss in public, or just now and then?

THE INCREASED DIFFICULTY
OF CONCENTRATION

HAVEL'S WORK, and his great courage in standing by it in the face of state oppression, have been so intimately linked with the cause of freedom and democracy in what was Czechoslovakia that his presidency of the Czech Republic now seems like an extension of it.

His way into the theatre was as a factotum; by 1960 he had become the writer-in-residence at the Theatre on the Balustrade. Here he became known for his plays satirising mind-boggling bureaucracy, which showed the influence of Absurdist theatre. Although his work was regarded as subversive, the increasing liberalism of the '60s meant that his plays were performed until the Russian invasion of 1968.

Thereafter, Havel was repeatedly arrested for his artistic and political activities. The former consisted of three plays about a writer called Vanek: in one, his rich friends try to entice him to the current political dogma; in another, the writer has a job interview at a brewery, but the brewer is more interested in the actresses Vanek might know. The plays show Havel's distinctive style, where dialogue loops round and round. At first, the device exacts nervous laughter, but with each repetition the inevitability of a character's predetermined remarks becomes all too real. Havel took the title rôle when these plays were performed in private houses, writing the last, *Protest*, in 1978, the year he founded the pro-democracy movement Charter 77. This political act led to the longest term he spent in prison, 1979–1982.

Subsequent plays emerged outside his country: *Largo Desolato* shows a philosopher under pressure both to recant and reaffirm his writings. *Temptation* takes the Faust myth to reflect a state offering personal advancement in exchange for the soul. His continued commitment to democracy brought him public support from **Stoppard**, **Beckett** and **Pinter**. He has less time to write nowadays.

Hawthorne

NATHANIEL   born Salem, Massachusetts 1804; died Concord 1864

That blue-eyed darling Nathaniel knew disagreeable things in his inner soul. He was careful to send them out in disguise.

D.H. LAWRENCE

NATHANIEL HAWTHORNE occupies a solitary place in the history of American letters. Although he lived in Concord, Massachusetts (in the Old Manse), the traditional home of the Transcendentalists, he did not share their euphoric view of the soul, and read their magazine, *The Dial*, only when he felt like dropping off. And although he was perhaps the finest and earliest to explore the idea of sin in the New World and, in *The Marble Faun*, set it in the European *milieu* that would be so important to **Henry James**, still he stands apart from that tradition. He believed more in original sin than the seeping corruption from seedier cultures.

For sure, he was quite capable of linking this to the Old World influences that formed America. *The House of the Seven Gables* tells the story of a home which was cursed by a wizard facing persecution at the hands of English settlers in Hawthorne's native Salem. But this kind of sin is innate rather than imported. Indeed, Hawthorne's stories often begin with a sin analogous to the Fall of Man. This introspective kind of guilt never precludes redemption, however: in *The Scarlet Letter* the culpable party confesses when it is not quite too late, while in *The Marble Faun*, a murderer comes to accept responsibility for his actions.

Hawthorne knew Europe well – he had been American Consul in Liverpool, whence he moved to London before following the American tourist trail through France to Italy – and the notebooks from his time there produced much of the material for his stories. But he saw his achievement as an American one, and as something to rival work from across the Atlantic. His friend, admirer and neighbour **Melville** concurred, comparing his tragic creations to those of **Shakespeare**.

HD

born Bethlehem, Pennsylvania 1886; died Lake Geneva 1961

I saw it now

as men must see it ever afterwards;

no poet could write again

'the red lily,

a girl's laugh caught in a kiss'

it was his to pour into the vat

from which all poets dip and quaff,

for poets are brothers in this

HELIODORA

THE STYLE OF THE NAME is **Ezra Pound's** fault. He published Hilda Doolittle's work under the sobriquet "HD, Imagiste", and the name stuck. She considered herself at once "discovered" and "dubbed" by this man who – according to **William Carlos Williams** – was in love with her, and to whom she was engaged in 1907. In 1913, however, she married Richard Aldington, whom she succeeded as editor of *The Egoist* while he was way during the war, and who defended her Modernist poetry.

In many respects, however, she was an unlikely Modernist. Her poetry was taken up by Pound in his gathering of poetry tending away from Romantic lyrics towards sparing, *haiku*-like 'images', and these remain her most anthologised pieces. Her work was certainly experimental, however, and her husband declared her to be one of the first writing *vers libre* in English, while her prose work drew on **Joyce's** techniques of interior monologues and contrasting styles. But throughout she maintained a refinement and tone that is markedly personal and confessional. Her novels are heavily biographical, with *Bid Me to Live*, her most accomplished novel, following the poet to London and Cornwall.

Her prose drew on her poetic ear and reveals her reliance on the classics to reflect her own experiences. She wrote the verse drama *Hippolytus Temporizes*, and the great poem *Helen in Egypt* published posthumously. She knew her Latin and Greek much better than Pound did, but displayed it more modestly, having narrators seeming to forget their Classics even when it would prove most handy to them. Her poem *Heliodora* provides a superb gloss on a fragment to raise questions about originality and possession of literature. Here, she recognises problems that were hers: her work has taken a long time to be assessed fully and in its own right.

Heaney

SEAMUS

born Castledawson, County Derry, Northern Ireland 1939

And we lifted our eyes to the nouns.

Altar-stone was dawn and monstrance

noon,

the word rubric itself a bloodshot sunset.

IN ILLO TEMPORE

HEANEY HAS AN ACUTE consciousness of what writing is, and what it must do. It is rare that a reader can be given so strong a sense that words are things in themselves, and that language is a tool for putting them together.

The poem *Digging* came at the beginning of his career. He describes his forefathers' farm-work, and concludes, "Between my finger and my thumb/ the squat pen rests./ I'll dig with it." Later, *The Haw Lantern* has a poem, *Alphabets*, in which the very letters become objects. Heaney often begins a poem with a sequence of nouns, broken up by full stops. Things become whole sentences; a recent collection is called *Seeing Things*.

What he makes us see most is rural Ireland. Violence drove him to leave Ulster for the Republic in 1972. His verse has little room for causes and, if politics enters his work, it is drawn from more tangible phenomena. It is hard to ignore a feeling of group brutality in his description of a bog woman unearthed and found garrotted; while the sexual imagery in *Act of Union* tells us more about sex than the Irish situation. *Casualty*, though clearly from a Catholic, is more a human response to the Troubles than an ideological one.

But his poems have work to do for society as well. *The Haw Lantern* contains more poems on the writer's rôle as a conscience, guarding justice. He addresses public concerns, like human rights, in work set in imaginary states (more states of mind than nation states) owing much to **Czeslaw Milosz**. He has recently spoken of Ireland's need to recognise its dual nationality as the only way to approach peace. People in his verse always strive for contact and understanding, nowhere more movingly than in *Clearances*, the sonnet sequence in memory of his mother. Peeling potatoes, they are, "never closer the whole rest of [their] lives". What brings a community together in another poem is a *Mud Vision*. The Swedish Academy spoke of his "ethical depth" when awarding him the Nobel Prize in 1996 (he was rambling around Greece when it was announced); and he got deep by digging up things.

Heine

HEINRICH

born Düsseldorf 1797; died Paris 1856

The story is an old one,

but stays forever new;

and when it falls to someone,

it breaks his heart in two.

BOOK OF SONGS

SCHUMANN'S SETTINGS of poems in Heine's first collection, *The Book of Songs*, provide an alluring introduction to this lyricist's strange world. They mix tenderness with the macabre, and the natural with the supernatural (when a lover's paranoia leads him to think the flowers are talking about him); in doing so, the work is always harmonious *per se*, but marked by violent swings of mood. Schumann's piano postludes fill the silence which must confound a reader who has just put down one of Heine's terse epigrammatic poems. For in the verse, so much makes musical sense, but fails to cohere. Why should requited love occasion weeping?

Heine's bitter irony – sometimes even sarcasm – is meant to leave us restless. He was that way himself. He was born to Jewish parents in Düsseldorf, converted to Christianity out of what seems like pragmatism, and moved to Paris in 1831. In this last, he continued to embrace foreignness, writing about the French for German readers, and essaying introductions to German thought to the French. His poetry represents his cultural range, as he hymns Greek gods, Jewish food, Cologne Cathedral, and further, more imagined locations.

In these, as elsewhere, Heine expresses himself with a beguiling simplicity. He takes a straightforward story-telling style into a fairy-tale atmosphere, and keeps the consequences inexplicable. Joyous examples open what some consider his finest book, *Romanzero* – Rhampsenit shows us a kingdom full of laughter, whose monarch stops a thief by offering his daughter's hand and, ultimately, the throne. Heine extends these fantasies in his longer poetry, especially the mock-epic *Atta Troll*, in which a dancing bear on the loose in the mountains lectures on themes related to contemporary German life. Here he combines the satire and symbolism which collude to bewitch readers throughout his corpus.

Heller

JOSEPH   **born Brooklyn 1923**

But that girl who wants to play the accordion for you today is old enough to be a mother. How would you feel if your own mother travelled over three thousand miles to play the accordion for some troops that didn't want to watch her? How is the kid, whose mother that accordion player is old enough to be, going to feel when he grows up and learns about it? We all know the answer to that one.

CATCH-22

JOSEPH HELLER IS GLOBALLY famous for his first novel, *Catch-22*. It is a vast satire which draws on all the tiniest aspects of military life, as seen during the campaign in Italy during the Second World War. Almost every episode is structured as a self-sustaining feedback loop, whose inevitability helps to carry the work's main thesis: there's no way out. The hero, Yossarian, has flown the requisite number of bombing missions, but must prove his insanity to avoid further duty. Such action would prove his sanity.

The work's virtuosity lies in sustaining this for nearly 600 pages (even though Norman Mailer has claimed that 100 could go without the author noticing). The author's eye for absurd details gives the book its energy: he depicts vain military potentates preening with their cigarette holders, agonising about their prose styles, or desperate to win marching competitions. It is as much a satire on bureaucracy and big business as it is on war, although the figure of Milo Minderbinder combines all three, and the currency of the book's title in English shows that the approach is applicable to any situation.

This triumph was hard to follow. Many years later, *Something Happened* appeared, and disappointed critics. *Good as Gold* places an academic in a current Presidential administration, and *God Knows* has King David tell his story as a Yiddisher wise-guy. *Picture This* is a strange attempt to link ancient and modern ideas of Imperialism starting from Rembrandt's painting of aristotle contemplating a bust of **Homer.** Here as elsewhere, Heller is a wry enough commentator on contemporary America to rival **Gore Vidal**; his success comes from the timelessness of his insights, and a logic worthy of the Talmud.

Hemingway

ERNEST   born Oak Park, Chicago 1899; died Ketchum, Idaho 1961

"Love is a dunghill," said Harry. "And I'm the cock that gets on it to crow."

THE SNOWS OF KILIMANJARO

FEW WRITERS HAVE MADE more use of their individuality than Ernest Hemingway. For not only did he consistently portray a singular kind of heroism and solitude in his characters, but he did so in a style that was inventive, and remains unique. It is now hard to say whether Hemingway provides the very type of manhood, or the model of rivetting yet economical prose.

From an early age he was obsessed with athletic prowess. He received his first fishing rod at the age of three and excelled at sports. His first literary rôle-model was Ring Lardner, the sports journalist, and his non-fiction work deals with bull-fighting (*Death in the Afternoon*) and big game-hunting (*Green Hills of Africa*). The allure of the toreador leads to the crisis point in *The Sun Also Rises*, which many consider his finest novel.

A need to test his heroism to its limits led him to join the Red Cross in 1918. He was badly wounded in Italy, and fell in love with a nurse while in hospital recovering. *A Farewell to Arms* draws on these experiences to depict all-destroying war; but Hemingway did not stop fighting for causes he believed in them. He donated $40,000 to the Republicans during the Spanish civil war, and was with the French Resistance in 1944 when the Allied forces liberated Paris. The political convictions that impelled such stands pervade *For Whom the Bell Tolls* and *Across the River and into the Trees*, with a slight loss of the objectivity Hemingway had acquired as a journalist, and which distinguished his earlier work.

In fact, he told a story very much as a reporter would, succinctly and eschewing emotion. Instead, feeling emerges as a natural consequence of the action, and becomes an action in itself – but the narrator never indulges in it. From this kind of understatement comes the remarkable power of Hemingway's prose. While the style is apparently simple, the variation in rhythm and the development of echoes within paragraphs control the tale's pace and pathos with a true poet's ear.

He was awarded the Nobel Prize for Literature in 1954, but thereafter found his powers failing. He shot himself in a fit of depression seven years later.

Henry

O.

born Greenboro, North Carolina 1862; died New York 1910

Life is made up of sobs, sniffles, and smiles, with sniffles predominating.

THE GIFT OF THE MAGI

O. HENRY'S FIRST BIOGRAPHER described him as the writer who "humanised the short story." Henry's pieces attained a huge readership during his lifetime, and their author could command enormous fees for them. After a spell of disfavour with critics, his work is enjoying reassessments from all angles, and over the years has been cherished as much by Soviet commentators and formalists as by his fellow Americans.

He owes this to his accessible style, his chatty dialogue, his warm, jokey humour, his romantic world and his careful plotting. This last keeps a tale progressing as if naturally, with an ending that is anything but improvised. He is most famous for his concluding twists. As for his world-view, it derives from meticulous observation of people around him, particularly in their urban environments. He would give much of his sudden fortune to people on the street, or leave it in lavish tips: anything for a story. He reckoned this an investment, but soon it became an indulgence, and he died of alcohol abuse.

His stories seem to present a world for which he hankered in his life. His characters are often poor; their curiosity about how richer people live regularly leads them to save and mix with swells. This brief fulfilment of fantasies is enough for them. It was not so simple for Henry himself. He was born into a poor Texan family, and worked at his uncle's pharmacy before becoming a bank clerk. His dreams of literary fortune and helping his wife culminated in embezzlement, and he evaded justice briefly by fleeing to Honduras. He returned when his wife became terminally ill, and he served three years in prison. He had been published before, and began a humorous paper he called *The Rolling Stone* and wrote almost single-handed; but it was in prison that he began producing the three hundred or so stories that brought him fame under a number of pseudonyms. His recurring theme of disguise and assumed identity served him well in his own life.

Herbert

GEORGE   **born Montgomery, Wales 1593; died Bemerton, Wiltshire 1633**

Wit fancies beautie, beautie raiseth wit:

The world is theirs; they two play out the

game,

Thou standing by: and though thy

glorious name

Wrought out deliverance from

th'infernall pit,

Who sings thy praise? onely a skarf or

glove

Doth warm our hands, and make them

write of love.

LOVE

GEORGE HERBERT'S POETRY sounds a genuine note of contrition and humility. When he knew that he would die of consumption, he charged his friend Nicholas Ferrar of Little Gidding with the fate of his poems, collected in *The Temple*, saying that he might burn them unless they might "turn to the advantage of any dejected soul". If this request seems modest, and all the more genuine for the poet seeking an expressly posthumous fame, then it represents a triumph of Herbert's spirituality over his earlier, worldly achievements.

For he was a Fellow at Cambridge, and University Public Orator there. The former post obliged him to take holy orders within seven years, while the latter introduced him to court circles. He did not become a priest when statutes dictated, but rather when he was ready. Throughout his poetry, there is rage, and resistance to the religious life, always yielding to a quiet submission to the will of God; while we recognise the struggle, we know we are reading the work of an Anglican priest.

This shows in his use of the *Book of Common Prayer*, and in his poems on the sacraments (*The H. Communion*), on the church calendar (*Whitsunday*) or specific services (*Mattens*); but more immediately, it shows in his verbal music. He uses anthem forms, with antiphons and hymns, and was a keen musician. This gives his thought a beguiling kind of simplicity, as opposed to **Donne**'s "meaning's press and screw"; Herbert tends to invoke things as well as arguments to convey his message, describing a state of mind, such as in *Sinne* or *Prayer*, in verbless clauses.

Although he draws on rhetoric to convince, as a preacher might, the conviction and repentance remains a personal one, born of self-examination.

Herodotus

born Halicarnassus, c. 484 BC; died Thurii, Southern Italy c. 420 BC

Within a long period of time, anything might happen.

THE HISTORIES

God tends to curb all arrogance.

IBID

HERODOTUS HAS BEEN CALLED the father of History and of Greek prose. The Greek word 'Historia' means enquiry, and like the early philosophers, Herodotus was investigating causes – in this case, of the great war between Greece and Persia. He traced its origins beyond history as we consider it, through reminiscences transmitted orally over generations to myth of the pre-Homeric age, with a sequence of women snatched back and forth across the Bosphorus. Some, from Thucydides onwards, have criticised him for being too credulous of his sources; but generally Herodotus keeps his sense of perspective.

He does so rigorously in his discussion of other cultures. For all the panegyrics on his adopted Athens, he was called a barbarian-lover: the Greeks gave barbarians that name because they were supposed to communicate by saying "bar-bar", although this is not Herodotus' view at all. He starts from the position that "Custom is king of all", and strives to understand other peoples within the context of their traditions. Most of these ethnic groups he discusses in lengthy digressions, notably on Egypt and Scythia. He had travelled as a merchant, but may have undertaken journeys simply for research. His improbable description of Scythian burial customs have recently been validated by archaeological evidence, but when his narrative takes him to what he imagines to be the ends of the earth, we can accuse him of making it up: the race of people with feet so big that they can lie down and use them as a parasol has yet to be discovered.

Herodotus is a born story-teller and his prose has a smoothness unexpected in so early a story-teller. He is as concerned as his contemporaries, the tragedians, with the roots of character, and the problem of motivation. This outweighs his interest in political, economic and military affairs, making him no worse a historian, and a better read.

Herodotus' popularity rose again in 1997 when, for a few brief weeks *The Histories* (in a harshly abridged format) were in the bestsellers listings in the UK following the enormous success of the film of Michael Ondaatje's book *The English Patient,* in which they had a starring rôle.

The Histories

Hesse

HERMANN born Calw, Germany 1877; died Montagnola, Switzerland 1962

Virgil had many lines not half so beautiful, so clearly and yet cunningly wrought, so full of meaning and delight, as this spiral of leaves upon a stalk.

NARZISS AND GOLDMUND

NARZISS AND GOLDMUND tells the story of an unworldly monk charged with the education of a boy who is a beautiful but inattentive student. They commend themselves equally to the reader's attention; but the situation of reading might incline us towards the bookish scholar. That the roving pupil should prove to be (not just physically) more attractive helps to show that Hesse's writings acquired a new type of reader altogether.

He had devoured 18th- and 19th-century novels and his prose was in the fine German tradition; **Thomas Mann** adored his work. But Hesse reached a younger audience. Even before *Narziss and Goldmund*, his autobiographical *Under the Wheel* had spoken for rebellious students everywhere. But his novels of "awakening" became touched by the horror of the First World War.

By then he had left Germany, become a Swiss national and volunteered for the Red Cross. But it was his need for analysis, after the spiritual death he felt he'd suffered as a result of the war, that started him on "the journey within". *Demian* was the first result of this quest, telling a war story similar to Hesse's own. His journey continued to the East, as he sought enlightenment in India. He never arrived, but in *Siddartha* tells the story of a Brahmin seeking salvation. He cannot accept Buddha's example of suffering, nor does he find any comfort in sensualism. Bliss only befalls him as he ferries people back and forth across the river.

Here enlightenment arrives from balance. In *Steppenwolf*, a vision of Mozart prescribes laughter to tame the animal within us. Music is vital to the author, and prevails throughout *The Glass Bead Game*, a world in which a musician is the acknowledged legislator. The choice Hesse's characters face elsewhere challenges the inhabitants of this artistic Utopia: is purity or recklessness better for the soul? If the last book finds for the latter, the message remains that it is a discovery we must make for ourselves.

Hesse was awarded the Nobel Prize for Literature in 1946.

Highsmith

PATRICIA

born Fort Worth, Texas 1921

She knew that the burning had been an action on her part to get rid of a feeling within her, a primitive action, if she thought about. Because, though the basket had been tangible, her thoughts were not tangible. And they proved damned hard to destroy.

THE TERRORS OF BASKET WEAVING

PATRICIA HIGHSMITH IS NOTED for her distinctive handling of the suspense novel. Her treatment of murder plots is rooted less in the tradition of thrillers and action stories than in a more acute approach to the problems of criminal motivation and psychology. She has made clarity her main aesthetic goal, rather than the generation of mystery. For some readers this comes across as a scientific exercise; for others it is more imaginative than that. The actions of her characters can be brutally sadistic, but often shock more for being founded in seemingly rational responses to desperate situations. A natural sympathy for a murderer's suffering, even at the expense of pity for the victim, compounds this horror. She is especially interested in the deeper causes of crime, as if exploring **Auden**'s lines, "Those to whom evil is done/ Do evil in return."

Her first novel remains the most famous: *Strangers on a Train* introduces Highsmith's recurring gambit of presenting two apparently opposite characters who find a sudden kinship in guilt and intrigue. She takes this kind of relationship to a more intense pitch in *The Boy Who Followed Ripley*, the concluding novel in her series about a charming killer whose need to dissemble and make money leads him into farce-like situations which easily turn murderous. But Ripley's strengths as a character come as much from his smoothness as his ability to kill: he aspires to a kind of suavity that he is uniquely able to emulate, while the reader can never forget the roughness beneath.

Later Highsmith books blend grimness with satire to comment on contemporary America (although she has moved to France). She attacks sexism in *Edith's Diary*, and in the short stories contained in *Little Tales of Misogyny* of the same year. Born-again Christians and the effects their strictures on abortion have on a family prompt the violence of *The People Who Knock on the Door*. When Highsmith turns on the law itself, she mocks its dithering with a teasing example: a detective fails to capture a man who kidnaps a woman's poodle and demands $1,000 as ransom.

Hoffman

E.T.A.

born Königsberg 1776; died Berlin 1822

*Can anything else but poesy reveal itself
as the sacred harmony of all beings, as
the deepest secret of nature?*

THE GOLDEN POT

THE 'A' STANDS FOR Amadeus: Hoffman gave himself the same middle name as Mozart. He would have agreed with Pater that all arts should aspire to the condition of music – and few writers have written on music so well, with such a grasp of form. In his stories, he would apply the instincts of a composer to create effects beyond reason, leaving readers reeling.

In music, he preferred bold combinations of different harmonies to delicate counterpoint. His fictions are similar. He introduces science into the world of the imagination. His stories are full of automata that take on human form, and scare children who can never be believed; of clock-makers, indifferent to the powers their creations unleash. In *The Golden Pot*, Hoffman takes us into a dreamscape where eligible snakes haunt an apple-thief. His most daring juxtaposition is his funniest: he gives us his largely autobiographical reflections on a frustrated but promising musical career through the fictionalised figure of Kreisler, whose memoirs are interrupted page after page by the musings of the tomcat Murr. The tone is marvellously captured in Schumann's manic piano pieces in response to it, *Kreisleriana*.

As a critic, he headed straight for the darker side of Mozart, in an essay on *Don Giovanni*, and was Beethoven's earliest apologist. In this, he was Romanticism's champion. He embraced an age when the subjective apprehension of artistic forms was more vital than dry analysis. For Freud, he understood the word 'aesthetics' in its original sense, of feeling. Hoffman's own ability to feel, and to make his readers feel for themselves, make him key to any history of the imagination; **Heine**, **Poe**, **Dostoyevsky** and **Baudelaire** all owe him a great deal.

Hölderlin

FRIEDRICH

born Lauffen, Germany 1770; died Tübingen 1843

I want to celebrate; but what? want to

sing with the others,

But I'm alone, and I feel there's nothing

godly in me.

MENON'S LAMENT FOR DIOTIMA

ONLY LONG AFTER HIS DEATH was Hölderlin considered to be in the first rank of German poets; indeed, in the writings of Heidigger, his importance as a thinker is counted as inestimable. And Heidigger was analysing the work Hölderlin produced in his long, last period of schizophrenia.

If Hölderlin could make a sublime kind of sense even in madness, it was due to his **Coleridge**-like

gift for feeling ideas, and giving them poetic expression. He was often afraid that his thinking would disfigure his verse, and so welded his subject matter to the medium in which he was expressing it. His medium was the Greek metrical patterns adopted by the mystic poet Klopstock: Hölderlin would write in the rhythms of Alcaeus and even Pindar, and elegiac couplets flowed from him. He translated **Sophocles** with a rigid adherence to the quantities of the original.

He was as absorbed by the cultural supremacy of the Greeks as he was by their Pantheism. He studied for the priesthood, but found his beliefs incompatible with orthodox creeds; he chose instead to work as a tutor and his verse spoke of the human yearning for God. It blended classical forms with a hymn-like vocabulary to form a rapturous, love-craving poetry, focusing on the divine figures of Christ and Dionysus (whom Hölderlin saw as one), or Diotima, the woman who taught Socrates how to define love. This last was a manifestation of an employer's wife Hölderlin had adored.

Hölderlin was much troubled by the emergent philosophy (expounded by his classmate Schelling, and derived from Kant) which dwelt on the individual nature of our response to natural phenomena. He was depressed by the loneliness this doctrine entailed, and believed that the only refuge from such solipsism was a love which transcended the senses and which was waiting beyond this world: it is the thesis of his poem *Menon's Lament for Diotima.* It is characteristic of his range – at once ecstatic and despairing – which shows forth in language of singular purity, directness and elegance.

MAJOR WORKS

Best work written between 1798 and 1801, uncollected in his lifetime:

Odes (1797–1798)

Hyperion (epistolary novel, 1797–1799)

Empedokles (unfinished verse drama)

Holtby

WINIFRED

born Rudston, Yorkshire 1898; died London 1935

Councillor Saxon, after 52 years of childless married life, had suddenly lost his heart and virtue to a blonde in a tobacconist's kiosk on Kingsport Station and found himself at 74 the proud but embarrassed father of a son. The whole of South Riding, apart from Mrs Saxon, appeared aware of this achievement. Most of the South Riding, whatever its outward disapproval, was delighted. It enjoyed all feats of procreation.

SOUTH RIDING

WINIFRED HOLTBY IS DUE for a revival. Posterity has treated her with scant regard. During her short life, she was among London's best-known literary journalists and wrote the first critical study of **Virginia Woolf**. Her death from kidney failure came four weeks after she had finished *South Riding*, her most ambitious work, which caused a sensation when it appeared in print the next year. It was filmed, but today only this and her first novel remain in print.

She wrote six novels in all – a remarkable output, even more so given the hectic work-rate which hastened her death. She was director of the journal *Time and Tide*, and wrote frequently for *The Manchester Guardian*. She fought tirelessly for women's rights, and campaigned against racism: indeed, her novel *Mandoa!*

Mandoa! satirises the attempts of a travel agency to market a fictionalised principality in Central Africa. She was a pacifist too, but interrupting her studies at Oxford to work with the Women's Auxiliary Army Corps during the First World War. Here she met Vera Brittain. They became inseparable and lived together even after the latter married: Brittain's *Testament of Friendship* commemorates Holtby.

South Riding shows the understanding Holtby had of local politics: her mother was the first female Alderman in the East Riding of Yorkshire (South Riding is a fictional name). The author was fascinated by the motivations and potentially huge effects at play in administrative decisions. The love-triangles, the feel for local community, and the enormous range of characters presented in most stages between triumph and despair, suggest to the modern reader a mini-series – which would at least have the effect of getting her four remaining books back on the shelves.

Holub

MIROSLAW

born Plezn 1923

You only love

when you love in vain...

Like caryatids

our lifted arms

hold up time's granite load

and defeated

we shall always win.

ODE TO JOY,
TR. IAN MILNER, GEORGE THEINER

MIROSLAV HOLUB IS KEEN that people read his "poems as naturally as they read the papers, or go to a football match". This may seem an ambitious goal for a Czech writer as influenced by the French Surrealists as he is by his work as a Professor of Immunology, but his verse remains remarkably accessible. He avoids using arcane words for their own sake and when he chooses a scientific term, it's as much for its resonance in ordinary language as for its exact interpretation. He has done much to popularise science, both in newspaper columns and in his own magazine *Vesmir*, and sees a poem as something organic, with a life of its own and a capacity for growth. His verse frequently examines microscopic things and finds in them analogies for vaster entities.

The most appealing thing about Holub's poetry is the sense of hope. Although he shares his bleaker visions, such as *Five Minutes After the Air Raid*, there is still, a sense that life – as it evolves – offers the promise that things might improve. He has made an art form out of **Beckett**'s dictum, "Fail again, fail better" – a belief Holub takes from laboratory experiments into the world of emotions.

He has always been modest about his literary achievement. He began writing during his postgraduate research, at the age of 30, and is deferential towards younger Czech poets. His uncomplicated syntax and ear for a conclusive aphorism have maintained his popularity: his books have regularly sold out and, in 1982, his first book to be published in his homeland for 10 years was bought up on the first day of publication. The official reason for issuing no reprint was a paper shortage. Prior to that Holub had been silenced by the Soviet regime since 1968.

MAJOR WORKS

Day Duty (1958)

Achilles and the Tortoise (1960)

Go and Open the Door (1962)

Although (1971)

Sagittal Section (1980)

On the Contrary (1982)

The Dimension of the Present Moment (essays, 1990)

169

Homer

Great Priam slipped by, took

  Achilles' hands,

beseeched him, then he kissed those

  slaughtering hands,

awful, which had cut down a city's sons

ILIAD

He recognised the smooth coat

  on his shoulders,

so like the skin upon an onion dried.

ODYSSEY

WE HAVE TWO TEXTS that are attributed to someone called Homer, the *Iliad* and the *Odyssey*. Seven towns claim to be his birthplace and the writings are in the Ionic dialect: their source was Greek-speaking Asia Minor. They are the finest poems ever written.

Written: it was perhaps as late as the eighth century BC that these perfect compactions of myths and sailor's tales appeared to readers. Research into repeated phrases, rhythmic patterns and recurring structures within structures starts to explain how a bard could have recited line after line, elaborating with each performance. How this way of telling it evolved, we can never know; scholars still argue over which passages might have been appended gradually.

Still, we have two finished works of art. The *Iliad* tells of a brief spell during the war which resulted in the Greeks sacking Troy. The stated theme is the wrath of Achilles. His bitterness and lust for revenge seem to obscure his human sense of compassion; but in conceding the mutilated body of his enemy to the family for burial, he shows the qualities of heroism and dignity the narrative explores. The *Odyssey*, meanwhile, follows Odysseus home from the Trojan War. His 10-year passage, the lies by which he survives, his nakedness and guises, show a search for self-definition. The layers of his personality are like an onion, to be peeled off one by one. The goddess Athene gets to the core – as, finally, does his wife.

These processes have dominated most literature ever since. Imagery describes war and crisis with reference to bees or falling leaves; the subject matter can move to distant places too, as digressions lead to stories within stories. In so controlled a form, each speaker retains a voice of his or her own, from Nestor's rambling to Helen's quiet lament. The poems are composed of many narrative levels, and the *Odyssey* in particular invites us to question which is closest to truth; still, so extraordinary is the work that when "Homer" asks, "Daughter of God, tell us, and start whenever", we believe.

Hopkins

GERARD MANLEY   born Stratford, London 1844; died Dublin 1889

Whatever is fickle, freckled

  (who knows how?)

With swift, slow; sweet, sour;

  adazzle, dim;

He fathers-forth whose beauty

  is past change:

Praise him.

PIED BEAUTY

GERARD MANLEY HOPKINS wrote the most innovative Christian poetry in English since **Milton.** Like Milton, his experiments had a theoretical basis, that was firmly grounded in the classics. He believed that a poet's genius was in originality: just as Milton discarded the tyranny of rhyme, so Hopkins strove to transform rhythms. He wrote a number of sonnets, but in metres of his own devising, with regulated stresses but ample supporting syllables thrown in.

This was an expression of his aesthetic beliefs which, like his religious ones, were formed while at Oxford. Two influences there were the great Walter Pater, and Cardinal John Henry Newman. The former was his tutor, and believed that the artist should take pains to render natural phenomena in purest form; the latter admitted him into the Catholic Church.

Hopkins certainly took pains to express his own spirituality – a fusion of these two creeds. He coined the terms "inscape" and "instress", the former being the perceptible manifestation of the latter, the energy that generates it. This was to dictate his thoughts on poetry, but so was a sense of guilt. He burnt most of his early work and only resumed once he had become a Jesuit priest, encouraged by his colleagues. In this he was much comforted by reading the theologian Duns Scotus, who seemed to have anticipated this kind of thinking.

The result is a poetry in which language becomes that pure form. Internal rhymes, compound words and puns bounce into metres which focus all that neighbouring words have in common, to convey an often ecstatic vision of the world. This comes from the religious symbolism he found in nature (*The Windhover* is a bird representing Christ), or from theological issues (such as how a compassionate God could work His purpose through the nuns who died in *The Wreck of the Deutschland*). In his later years, his loneliness as Professor of Classics at University College, Dublin, drew more despairing verse from him, but he died at peace with the world. His fame as a poet was to be posthumous, when his friend Robert Bridges published the surviving work in 1918.

Horace

born Venusia 65 BC; died Tibur 8 BC

... now the betraying giggle of a girl
hidden in a snug corner happily,
the keep-sake snatched from arms, or
held by a mere finger, pretty limply.

ODES I, 9.

HORACE WAS THE FINEST lyric poet in Latin; and if versatility in tone and metre, absolute grace in form and the knack of surprise in cadence be considered criteria above the spontaneous overflow of powerful feelings, perhaps he is the finest ever. Given so tow-ering a precedent, subsequent practitioners can scarce help but be judged by the standard of what **Petronius** called "Horace's curious felicity".

He had some fine models, too. In an ode, his claim to have "built a monument more lasting than bronze" rests on the introduction of Greek verse techniques to Italy. His chief models were Archilocus of Paros and Alcaeus of Lesbos, both noted for their drinking songs. Horace was from southern Italy, whose Greek colonial past was still evident, and he studied in Athens. In his odes, he eases Greek names into the sturdier Latin, and subverts that language's toughness with his anti-epic stance, referring to Achilles' "stomach" rather than wrath. Even when writing in the standard epic meter, he writes satires and rambling discourses, with conversational rhythms which sound clumsy when compared with **Virgil**. (He called his friend "half his soul", and the two parts complement each other wonderfully.)

This is all part of Horace's celebrated mock mod-esty. In some poems, he is as unexcited about his ambitions as he is elsewhere about his appearance. For all the sophistication of his poetry, the persona most often favours the simple life. If this attitude seems Epicurean, then it is accompanied by Epicurus' belief in restraint and control. This leads some to view Horace as a moral writer. For sure, he was an establishment poet, writing an increasing number of odes to the Emperor Augustus; but even when his patron was Maecenas, effectively Minister of the Interior, his work was allowed its mild naughtiness. He prefigured **Propertius** and **Ovid**, poets who distanced themselves from the Roman rat-race, as a bard in an Imperial culture who preferred love to war — as, perhaps, in private, did his Roman readers.

Housman

A.E.   **born Fockbury, Worcestershire 1859; died Cambridge 1936**

They say my verse is sad: no wonder;

Its narrow measure spans

Tears of eternity, and sorrow,

Not mine, but man's.

FOREWORD TO MORE POEMS

IT IS UNLIKELY THAT someone's reputation as a poet should be rivalled by fame as a classical scholar; but A.E. Housman came close. This has a little to do with the quality of his scholarship. Many of his amendments of corrupt **Propertius** texts have been adopted; in his day he was the only scholar who could translate (or admit to being able to translate, albeit in private memos) the ruder parts of **Juvenal**; and he published a collection of such passages (although only in Germany).

Still, the least characteristic of his poetic works is a skit on **Euripides**, in which he bundles together the most extreme examples of the playwright's pedantry, and translates them as literally as possible. For the rest, his verse is not at all classical. Indeed, in his lecture, *The Name and Nature of Poetry*, his activity as a poet seems to be completely separate from his academic life. It is something that occupies him when relaxing on walks. His approach to the art is physical rather than intellectual: he confessed that he had to be careful when shaving, "because, if a line of poetry strays into my memory, my skin bristles and the razor ceases to act".

A Shropshire Lad is full of this immediacy. The poems are written in an easy, ballad style, focusing on the vulnerability of the rural idyll. There is the shadow of war, and the deaths of fit youths, which became more urgently popular during the First World War than on their publication in 1896. At that time, the work was already nostalgic and its wistfulness and melancholy have earned it affection and mockery in equal measure. **Ezra Pound**'s parody, *Mr. Housman's Message*, lampoons the tone succinctly; but **W.H. Auden**'s poem *A.E. Housman* comes closer to the man's more private misery.

Hugo

VICTOR

born Besançon 1802; died Paris 1885

"Victor in Drama, Victor in Romance,

Cloud-weaver of phantasmal

hopes and fears,

French of the French, and Lord of

human tears..."

TENNYSON

HUGO'S EXTRAORDINARY writing career spanned most of the nineteenth century and, like his life, was always part of French public life. He had incredible energy, and is remembered as much for his plays and poems as for his novels.

He began writing young. At fourteen his literary ambition was to be "**Chateaubriand** or nothing," and his juvenilia accumulated prizes. He was already celebrated for his lyrics when he published his first novel, *Hans of Iceland* (1823) at the age of twenty-one. But his plays earned him a reputation as France's foremost romantic. *Cromwell* was a triumph, although its preface sharply divided the intelligentsia. He further abandoned his youthful classicism in *Hernani*, a drama concerning three men vying for the same woman (echoing Hugo's experience with his two brothers: in life, Victor was the successful one).

All this delayed *Notre Dame of Paris*, a Gothic novel in the truest sense: from the personal tragedies of its characters emerges a public concern for the buildings of medieval Paris. Besides being a literary success, the book spear-headed a campaign which preserved much fine architecture.

Although an establishment figure, as a member both of the Assembly and Academy, he championed "small people against great." His Bonapartist sympa-thies vanished when Napoleon III gained power, and he was exiled in 1851. He returned during the war with Prussia in 1870, and was banished from Belgium for harbouring refugees from the Paris Commune. His concerns about poverty and crime inform *Les Misérables*, a vast social and historical novel which encompassed the gamut of life from Parisian sewers to the Battle of Waterloo. It found an instant public.

Hugo never stopped working; novels and poems poured from him even in old age. Although his compatriots were never unanimous about his genius, his eightieth birthday was a national holiday, and on his death he lay in state beneath l'Arc de Triomphe.

Huxley

ALDOUS

born Godalming 1894; died Los Angeles 1963

You learn by loving – by paying attention and doing what one thereby discovers has to be done.

TIME MUST HAVE A STOP

ALDOUS HUXLEY WROTE in all genres, but is best known for his novels, especially *Brave New World*. His prose presents realms ranging from the refined to the fantastical, often with a rich vein of humour, and always with strong ideas, which he would sometimes express with some cost to plotting and characterisation.

He came from a family which had distinguished itself in the sciences. Aldous himself had wanted a career in medicine, but his eyesight failed him; still, he had inherited the knack of expounding new and advanced thinking from his grandfather Thomas Henry Huxley, one of Darwin's most convincing apologists. Evolutionary theory provides the premise of *Brave New World*. Huxley gives a view of an apparently perfect society, while arguing that it is only in imperfect ones that people can sustain progress: things are too good. The result appears like **Plato's** *Republic* in an industrialised age, in which the names of pioneers and despots are interchangeable, and culture leaves nothing to the imagination; movies have become feelies, and music can be made of smells (a fancy arising in a **Nathanael West** story of the year before).

Huxley had always questioned the effect science could have on the spirit. In his early satirical novels, his characters (scientists, aristocrats and artists) would mull over such problems as if detached from them. Intellectuals would thrash out the problems of the day with inter-disciplinary wit in country houses. Later, he would investigate more practically. His experiments with mescaline and LSD led to the confessional works *The Doors of Perception* and *Heaven and Hell*; seminal as they were, Dr Timothy Leary found them elitist, as though drugs were for intellectuals only. But Huxley's writing continues to reach a wide audience, and his concerns remain globally vital, as long as environmental disaster and social control menace us.

MAJOR WORKS

Limbo (stories, 1920)

Crome Yellow (1921)

Antic Hay (1923)

These Barren Leaves (1925)

Point Counter Point (1928)

Brave New World (1932)

Eyeless in Gaza (1936)

After Many a Summer (1939)

The Doors of Perception (1954)

Heaven and Hell (1956)

Brave New World Revisited (1958)

Island (1962)

Literature and Science (1963)

Ibsen

HENRIK

born Skien 1828; died Oslo 1906

*I am an artist, Irena; and I'm not
ashamed of any weaknesses that
cling to me.*

WHEN WE DEAD AWAKEN

IBSEN'S WRITING NOT ONLY contained ideas well ahead of his time; it also revolutionised drama. His early wish was to be a doctor, but he was drawn to plays, leaving his studies at Kristiania (now Oslo) University to learn about theatre in Copenhagen.

He became stage-manager at Bergen, where he worked on writing, directing, costumes and accounts. His practical experience of the theatre led him away from the contemporary taste for historical verse dramas (though he wrote many); after *Brand* and *Peer Gynt* he abandoned poetry, and plays written more for readers than audiences.

A Doll's House, his second prose play, brought him international attention. He championed women's emancipation in his heroine Nora; and his next play, *Ghosts*, continued to flout conventions, presenting a liberated wife and her son, a victim of hereditary syphilis, to illuminate people's inability to escape their past. The play was rejected everywhere, and the text remaindered. It is his most performed work.

These plays are markedly realistic, and Ibsen insisted on writing as people speak: but increasingly he used symbolism to convey his themes. Disease reoccurs as a cipher for guilt, as in *An Enemy of the People*, where a complacent community attempts to conceal a risk of cholera. Towards the end of his life he would use such devices to describe the artistic process itself:

The Master Builder points to the kind of sin which can lie at the roots of a creator's achievements, just as Ibsen's portrayal of "filth" earned him his own reputation as a moralist.

He claimed that his work was minutely associated with his life; and his early sexual misadventures, as well as his passion, at the age of seventy, for an 18-year-old girl, find expression in his writing (most significantly in *The Master Builder*). But his legacy is at odds with his temperament: the prose dramatist who wrote more in verse; the stern individualist who craved public approval; the quintessential Norwegian who lived most of his life abroad.

Ionesco

EUGENE
born Bucharest 1912; died Paris 1994

Oh you innumerable people who have died before, help me! What did you do to prepare for death – to accept it?

LE ROI SE MEURT

IONESCO WAS A Romanian-born playwright, whose work in French was integral to establishing the "Theatre of the Absurd".

He left Bucharest and settled in Paris in 1940 and much of his work reacts against the rigid social conformity and repression he dreaded in Nazism. The most terrifying vision of this is in *Rhinoceros*, where all but one of the inhabitants become rhinos. The proliferation of beasts on stage is typical of Ionesco's technique: he sets a stage, and thereon sets in motion a process that will transform it. It happens with coffee-cups in *The Victims of Duty*, or the tumescent cadaver in *Amédée or How to Get Rid of it*, while in both *The Chairs* and *The New Tenant*, the stage becomes full of furniture. Ionesco's innovations are often compared to those of **Beckett**; but his practice is the opposite of Beckett's minimalism. Rather than dwindling into nothingness, the drama reaches a point of saturation until it is no longer bearable. If there is change at the end of a play, it is often through a character's death, in one case by suicide, in another (*The Lesson*) by an overflow of words in a way that anticipates the **Pinter** of *The Birthday Party*.

If this view of life is a nightmarish one, it is because Ionesco was very attentive to his dreams. He had no faith in realism whatsoever, finding it lifeless, and found more truth in what his imagination conceived. His plays reflect a universe in which any attempt to impose order will fail. Time itself is doomed: throughout *The Bald Prima Donna* a clock chimes out an increasingly unpredictable number of times. This play remains one of his most successful (it is still the longest-running show in Paris), and presents the ultra-normal (the "typically English Mr and Mrs Smith", straight from the pages of a language primer) going manically awry, as complete strangers turn out to be married and non-conversation is expectorated by characters hurtling around the set.

Isherwood

CHRISTOPHER   **born Disley, Cheshire 1904; died Los Angeles 1986**

I am a camera, with the shutter open, quite passive, recording, not thinking.

GOODBYE TO BERLIN

CHRISTOPHER ISHERWOOD is best known for the autobiographical content of his novels. He gives an account of his schooldays (he was a friend of **Auden**'s since childhood), of his time at Corpus Christi College, Cambridge (with his reminiscences of Stephen Spender and Edward Upward in *Lions and Shadows*) and of his time in Germany in the years leading up to World War Two.

These are usually short works which strive for an objective stance. His love of cinema helps to account for this, and he is always careful to establish his scenes. (*Prater Violet* is a later novel dealing with the film industry). The Berlin stories, *Mr. Norris Changes Trains*, *Sally Bowles* and *Goodbye to Berlin*, show the technique to its most moving effect. The narrator. Mr Issyvoo, tries not to judge the people around him as they yield to the sway of Nazism, instead choosing to report the human consequences.

Indeed, Isherwood tried to avoid espousing political causes. He was a pacifist throughout the war and moved to California in 1940. But he campaigned for the recognition of homosexuality throughout his life and against heterosexual dictatorship of the minority he represented. His own writings never shied away from the issue: he was open about the matter even in the '30s, and gave it his first fictional treatment in *A Single Man* in 1964. He found a summation of these instincts in his adopted Vedanta faith, which does not condemn physical love between men. He collaborated with Swami Prabhavananda on a version of the *Bhagavad-Gita*, and a Hindu spirituality permeates most of his later work.

Isherwood died in 1986, and left critics feeling that his gift for prose and experimental narrative had never quite fulfilled **Virginia Woolf**'s early prediction, that he held "the future of the novel in his hands".

Ishiguro

KAZUO

born Nagasaki 1954

Surely I don't have to tell you that our professional duty is not to our own foibles and sentiments, but to the wishes of our employer.

THE REMAINS OF THE DAY

KAZUO ISHIGURO'S NOVELS display a delicacy and versatility rare in the English of recent years.

He was born in Japan, the setting of his first two books: *A Pale View of Hills* takes place in his native Nagasaki. In his earlier prose he vividly evokes a Japan he left when he was five.

Both *A Pale View of Hills* and *An Artist of the Floating World* have their protagonists confronting Japan's post-war experience. This is necessarily traumatic, and executed with a cinema-goer's instinct for flash-backs. In the former, the housewife Etsuko finds it impossible to ignore the past, even when she moves to England. In the latter, an old painter contemplates his war record and reflects on how the world he had known has been destroyed, both by defeat and Westernisation. Just as the artist has devoted his craft to capturing the ephemeral before it passes, so the task becomes the author's own.

The hero, Masuji Ono, tries to find meaning in his life; when recollecting old colleagues who have committed *hara-kiri*, his thoughts dwell on how his actions were never of sufficient importance to demand such a gesture. The dilemma of what is an honourable action in a situation that demands obedience is one that also plagues Stevens the butler as he tells his story in *The Remains of the Day*. His tone is controlled, punctilious even; it is almost as though Jeeves had assumed the naïvety of Bertie Wooster. While he is always deferential, he must wonder at the human cost of his hitherto unquestioning servility, particularly when his employer emerges as an unabashed apologist for Nazism.

Ishiguro has conceived each book on a more ambitious scale than the last, and *The Unconsoled* introduces a larger range of characters into an unnamed part of Central Europe. He displays the same ear for speech and eye for detail that have made his previous work so accomplished.

Jacobson

DAN

It seemed that in England even the calendar had visible external meanings that I had not fully understood before. And the chief of these meanings was movement; the passage of time made manifest.

TIME AND TIME AGAIN

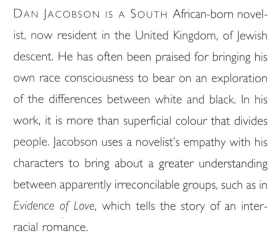

DAN JACOBSON IS A SOUTH African-born novelist, now resident in the United Kingdom, of Jewish descent. He has often been praised for bringing his own race consciousness to bear on an exploration of the differences between white and black. In his work, it is more than superficial colour that divides people. Jacobson uses a novelist's empathy with his characters to bring about a greater understanding between apparently irreconcilable groups, such as in *Evidence of Love*, which tells the story of an interracial romance.

Such compassion is not forced, for his novels frequently reflect his own experiences, which he discusses directly in *Time of Arrival* and later in *The Electronic Elephant*. Again, the perspective is a Jewish one, which he fictionalises most ambitiously in *The Beginners*. The story follows four generations of settlers, to South Africa in the last century and over to London in the 1960s.

Jacobson's own arrival in England seems to lie behind the narrative of *The Trap*, the first novel to bring him acclaim. A book set in California, *No Further West*, sprang from his subsequent experience teaching at Stanford University. For most critics, such personally-felt work has resulted in completely convincing prose with less even structures.

He is Professor of English at University College, London. If anything, he is writing more imaginatively now: his latest work, *The God-Fearer*, presents the history of Europe as though the Jewish faith had prevailed, and not the Christian. As elsewhere, his natural sensitivities demonstrate that the capacity for acting on prejudices can exist in anyone: this inversion of events continues to excoriate it where he finds it.

James

HENRY

born New York 1843; died Rye, Sussex 1916

Her cherished desire had long been to come to Europe and write a series of letters to the Interview from the radical point of view – an enterprise made the less difficult as she knew perfectly in advance what her opinions would be.

THE PORTRAIT OF A LADY

HENRY JAMES WROTE forgotten plays and vivid travel sketches; but his fame rests on some 20 novels and 100 short stories. These are distinguished by their great elegance and delicacy, often dealing with what the author called "the international situation."

He was born an American citizen, but caught the "Europe virus" during his youthful travels, when he had an influential meeting with **Turgenev**. He settled in Europe in 1875, the year of his first novel, *Roderick Hudson*. Its appearance was a triumph, and the plight of its hero presaged the theme that would dominate James's writing: the contrast between the New World and the continent. The former produces characters with an unaffected naïvety of the more sophisticated old world. Like the author himself, they are lured into this atmosphere, often with less happy consequences.

Daisy Miller struggles with this, as does Isabel Archer in *The Portrait of a Lady*. Elsewhere, the dilemmas are personal – between love and political conviction in *The Princess Casamassima*, or feminism and the *status quo* in *The Bostonians*. But James avoided being simply a novelist of ideas, thanks to the subtlety of his technique. As brother of the philosopher William James, who coined the phrase "stream of consciousness," he could describe acutely what was "beneath the surface of things," without taking sides. In *What Maisie Knew*, he portrays a young girl's view of her parents' divorce, while balancing her knowledge with her innocence.

In 1898, James moved to Rye House, Sussex, where he wrote his last three novels. For all his stunning descriptions of the continent (such as the Paris of *The Ambassadors*) he became ever more an Anglophile, adopting British citizenship in 1915. The next year, his last, he received the Order of Merit.

MAJOR WORKS

Roderick Hudson (1875)

Daisy Miller (1879)

The Portrait of a Lady (1881)

The Bostonians (1886)

What Maisie Knew (1897)

The Turn of the Screw (1898)

The Awkward Age (1899)

The Ambassadors (1903)

Jean Paul

born Wunsiedel 1763; died Bayreuth 1825

Creation hangs a veil, woven out of suns and spirits, over the Infinite, and the eternities pass by before the veil, and draw it not away from the splendour which it hides.

HESPERUS

JEAN PAUL'S COLLECTED WRITINGS fill 65 volumes of memoirs, essays, letters, sketches, philosophy, and extraordinary novels. It is hard to know where these last begin, and the rest leave off, for his fictions take in such extensive digressions, with cross-references, personal reflections and arcane citations, that they can appear like rambling tracts of their own. Jean Paul took **Sterne** as his model in this, and he styled his first two names in French in homage to **Rousseau.**

His literary skittishness serves the turn of his thought. The humour throughout belies a disaffection with the surrounding world. This is not to speak of pessimism, although his early sketches born of childhood poverty, and his visionary pieces – arising from deaths around him, including his brother's suicide in 1790 – would seem more than enough to occasion it. Rather, it is a Platonic belief in the purity of things beyond the earth. Albano, the hero of *Titan*, his most read work, can see beyond the clouds, and like Socrates, can look forward to death.

Although Jean Paul's plots are wild and complex, being sometimes delivered by dogs or making random demands of characters (one must become a piano tuner, and then a lawyer), it is the turn of thought and rapturous response to emotion and landscape that most defines his work. Random characters peopling his extraordinary forms can pour forth joyous critiques of the subjective philosophies the author abjured. Unlike **Hölderlin**, he is unswayed by Fichte's and Schelling's arguments that our impression of things is unique, and he recoiled from solipsism. If he introduces dream sequences into his work, it is not to provide insights into the workings of a single mind, but to represent thoughts in their most abstract form. Still, in structure and mood, he is as manic as he is Manichaean, which helps to explain why he was the composer Robert Schumann's favourite writer.

Jhabvala

RUTH PRAWER

born Cologne 1927

There are many ways of loving India, many things to love her for – the scenery, the history, the poetry, the music, and indeed the physical beauty of its men and women – but all, said the Major, are dangerous for the European who allows himself to love too much.

HEAT AND DUST

WHEN WRITING OF INDIA, Ruth Prawer Jhabvala is well placed to bring the international perspective to her subject. Born to Polish Jews, she fled from the Nazis in 1939, settling in England, where she was educated and met her Indian husband, with whom she moved to Delhi in 1951. She now lives in New York. She creates characters with an Indian perspective, but during her time in India felt herself to be neither an insider nor an outsider.

She explores this ambiguity in her novels and short stories. She introduces foreigners to a land she portrays as a harsh one and shows how incompatible the two worlds are. The approach is similar to **Forster**'s; but Jhabvala's concern is the way Westerners entertain sentimental and unobtainable hopes for the country. In *Esmond in India*, a philandering civil servant arrives from England, imagining that he is in love with an Indian woman and all that is mysterious about the subcontinent. Elsewhere in her work, travellers arrive in search of enlightenment, only to encounter crime or *swamis* with a craving for power.

For her delicate handling of the social dilemmas facing the better-off, she has been compared to **Jane Austen**; some critics have thought that this aspect of her work precludes a fuller discussion of India's grinding poverty. But in her first novel, *Amrita*, a listless rich family is contrasted with a poorer one in the Punjab. Their stories cross in Jhabvala's examination of arranged marriages and the caste system and while neither house is free of them, the narrative favours the less privileged and their zestful wedding preparations.

Johnson

SAMUEL   **born Lichfield, Staffordshire 1709; died London 1784**

The chief glory of every people arises from its authors: whether I shall add anything by my own writings to the reputation of English literature, must be left to time.

DICTIONARY, PREFACE

Being in a ship is being in a jail, with the chance of being drowned.

BOSWELL, LIFE OF JOHNSON

DR JOHNSON WAS the complete man of letters and in him, posterity has the picture of a complete man. Thanks to Boswell's memoirs, there are insights into his appearance, habits, mannerisms and, most importantly, his conversation. He appears to have been an unstoppable fount of words.

On paper, he was no less fluent. Although he famously declared, "No man but a blockhead ever wrote except for money", and wrote little on receiving a crown pension in 1762, yet still everything he wrote has passion. *Rasselas*, a romance written in a week to pay for his mother's funeral expenses, brims with purpose. In a framework which would accommodate unrestrained, if poised, discussion of his convictions, his view of poets is not of people waiting for a cheque, while his own translation of **Juvenal** is anything but a workmanlike "version", and carries Johnson's beliefs beyond the choice of poem. He was stern both as a critic and as a moralist – establishing himself as the latter in the twice-weekly essays of his own *Rambler*, the texts which induced Boswell to seek him out.

His mightiest achievement, the *Dictionary*, proves that he was exactly the type of blockhead he claimed to disdain. The Earl of Chesterfield may have received a piece of withering prose when he stopped funding the project, but the master persisted for eight years (three was his original plan) with dwindling recourse to helpers. It contains some 114,000 quotations and while it was neither the first nor the largest work of its kind, it did perhaps more than any other to fix the mutable meanings of words in an ever-developing language.

For all his gargantuan stature and uncompromising bombast, he should be remembered for his humanity, and for the generosity of his friendship. His defences of the poor, his verses on the death of Dr Levett, and his affection for his cat Hodge, show a man whose personal life attained the decency his public writing advocated.

Jonson

BEN

born London 1572; died London 1637

Yet satires, since the most of mankind be

Their unavoided subject, fewest see ...

TO LUCY, COUNTESS OF BEDFORD,
WITH MR DONNE'S SATIRES

IN HIS TIME, Ben Jonson's plays enjoyed a fame almost equal to his contemporary **Shakespeare**'s; critical hindsight has put him in the shadow of the "swan of Avon" (Jonson's coinage), but this normally proud man would be quite happy there, as his fulsome verse praise attests.

It is very much a writer's tribute. Jonson mentions Shakespeare's "small Latin and less Greek", if only because his own knowledge of ancient languages was immense. It shows throughout his lines, many of them translated or adapted from **Catullus** or **Horace**, and he was the first to write in English a full-blown, classically-formed Ode in the style of Pindar, that most demanding of Greek authors.

For all this, his verse is always economical and most moving when simplest. The lament for the death of his son, aged seven, evokes pity with its directness; and his gift for unfussed clarity makes his epigrams particularly forceful. Even when he is complaining that he has wasted his talent, "On such as have no taste", and leaves "things so prostitute" as the stage for "th'Alcaic lute", he does so readably.

But it was accessibility on the stage that brought him fame, as well as trouble: he was imprisoned during James I's reign for anti-Scottish passages in *Eastward Hoe*, and was nearly hanged for killing a fellow actor in a duel. His successes came with Senecan tragedies, and most enduringly with his comedies, *Volpone, The Alchemist* and *Epicene, or the Silent Woman*. Here Jonson's aim is satire, and he sets out to demonstrate that vanity of people's wishes which makes them so susceptible to scams. **Dryden** thought the plot of the last perfect and to this day theatres ask reviewers not to betray the play's fundamental secret, although it is guessable from the title.

In 1616, Jonson became Poet Laureate, and his legacy continued to flourish in the writings of "the sons of Ben".

MAJOR WORKS

Every Man in his Humour
(1598)

Sethe Janus (1603)

Volpone (1606)

Epicene or the Silent Woman (1609)

The Alchemist (1610)

Joyce

JAMES

born Dublin 1882; died Zürich 1941

Tell me, where is fancy bread? At Rourke's the baker's, it is said

ULYSSES

JAMES JOYCE HAS PROVED to be the most influential novelist of the 20th century. Born in Dublin, he was educated by Jesuits and at the Catholic University College, Dublin. Throughout his work,

Joyce struggles with this religious legacy and, like Stephen Dedalus, the hero of two novels, he adopted art as a faith. He was made for it: at eighteen, he had an extraordinary gift for languages (he wrote a letter of admiration to **Ibsen** in Dano-Norwegian) and a fine tenor voice. His musicianship and profound understanding of words' possibilities are evident in all his writing.

Although he was an instinctive nationalist, wanting to send the English tongue "off the face of the Erse," he left Ireland for good in 1912. His last visit was to his dying mother. Earlier publications include **Yeats**-influenced poetry and a play, *Exiles*: but it was in novels that he found his unique voice. The autobiographical *A Portrait of the Artist as a Young Man* brought him attention and patronage in 1915, when he was already at work on *Ulysses*. This was published in 1922, on his fortieth birthday, and is considered his masterpiece.

The book was banned in Britain and America for obscenity. The text follows the most intimate thoughts and actions of many characters, in as many styles. Each chapter takes a different episode from **Homer**'s *Odyssey*, and documents an nour of 16 June 1904, when Joyce first met Nora Barnacle, his future wife. For all the novel's complexity, it offers the simple message of the power of love.

Joyce took language and structure further still in *Finnegans Wake*. This is a vast dream novel, following the nocturnal thoughts of Humphrey Chimpden Earwicker. It is full of vast sentences, lists and multilingual puns, and occupied his last 17 years, a period made more painful by glaucoma and his daughter's schizophrenia. He died in 1941, the acclaimed giant of Modernist literature.

Juvenal

born Aquinum c. 60 AD; died Egypt? c. 136 AD

So give yourself a break. When did you last
stop for a whole day?
No talk of that debtor,
none of your wife giving you silent rage
if she goes out at dawn and comes home late
with dresses drenched and those
suspicious cheeks
and tousled hair and golden face aglow ...

SATIRE 11

JUVENAL'S SATIRES give such a clear and consistent an idea of the poet's personality that we almost think we know him: a middle-aged, bitter man who is no longer ashamed to give his spleen free reign, or to let his more wretched thoughts run away with him. So full of gossip and conviction does he seem that commentators feel tempted to fit him into the picture he paints with such detail — to speak of his hard climb to social rank, his rage at having lost it, exiled for a jibe at his hated emperor Domitian's boyfriend, and his eventual death commanding a military campaign in Egypt at the age of 80.

What of this is not unlikely is uncertain; but Juvenal's genre and technique are so much his own that we can't conclude easily that he was writing to formula. For he blends rhetorical commonplaces with parody to present a world which is completely upside-down, such that "it is hard *not* to write satire". His targets include the moral frailty of the aristocracy, the spitefulness of women, the duplicity of patrons, the habits of homosexuals, and anything else that annoys him at the time. He constantly takes a stern, Stoic attitude — frugality is best, we should learn by example, there's such a thing as decency — while rehearsing often outrageous subject matter.

The result is hilarious. Juvenal has a gift for drawing very economical conclusions from lavish subject matter, many of which remain proverbial: all they want is bread and circuses; pray for a sound mind in a sound body; who guards the guards themselves? In this he displays the knack of timing that enables him to shock as well as titillate and scorn; such that he has left a lurid, unflinching account of his own age and a model for those who have striven to correct with laughter ever since.

MAJOR WORKS

The Satires (110–130 AD)

Kafka

FRANZ   **born Prague 1883; died Kierling Sanatorium, nr. Vienna 1924**

In the battle between you and the world, back the world.

REFLECTIONS ON SIN, SORROW, HOPE AND THE TRUE WAY

GEORGES PEREC WOULD OFTEN try to convince people that he looked like Kafka. It is as though someone lonely, labouring under an intolerable burden of guilt, can find a comfort in sharing anything

with the gaunt figure of the Czech novelist, with his wide eyes staring back at terror. As though someone else had imagined himself in a universe whose powers to crush are exercised uniquely on him. For Franz Kafka, though, there was no such comfort.

For such is Kafka's world. In *The Castle*, it is a village he visits to take up a clerical job which appears not to exist, and where personal destinies are determined by forces always just outside your reach. It is a land organised by a laborious communications system, as in *The Great Wall of China*, where no-one can know who is sending the messages.

Worse still, it is a world whose victims cannot understand why they cannot be understood. Gregor Samsa turns into a giant insect for no good reason in *Metamorphosis*, to be mocked and then ignored. In *The Trial*, Joseph K. is the object of judicial proceedings he cannot witness, when no charge has been made. The more he tries to defend himself, the more hopeless his plight becomes.

It is a world which might seem trivialised by comparison to the Austro-Hungarian bureaucracy which employed Kafka in labyrinthian Prague; but it takes such arbitrary systems to their extreme. Because it is incomprehensible, the storyteller makes no effort to complicate it. All is simple, and events happen apparently in sequence, as if in the tradition of Jewish folk tales. Given such plain, horrifying writing, readers have tried to explain away their own fears from within the sparse material: the totalitarian state, sexual anxiety, the dysfunctional family, social collapse… By doing so it is as though we are avoiding Kafka's own process – looking into ourselves. When we turn instead to find some cause in Kafka, we find a man who felt "accused of life" and died young.

Kästner

ERICH

Born Dresden 1899; died Dresden 1974

Poets have their function again. Their occupation is once more a profession. They are probably not as indispensable as bakers and dentists; but only because rumbling stomachs and toothache more obviously call for relief than non-physical ailments.

NOISE IN THE MIRROR

DRESDEN-BORN NOVELIST and children's writer Erich Kästner found ways of raising his wry, ironic voice in protest at his native Germany's conduct even in its darkest days. Unlike so many other writers and artists, he chose to remain in the country throughout the Second World War. At a public burning of works by 24 authors, he was the only one of those writers who witnessed it. Although the Nazis banned his books, he was still able to publish abroad until 1942, when he sold the script of *Baron Munchhausen* to MGM. He had been placed under surveillance previously, and twice arrested; now he found himself silenced completely.

He had been conscripted into the army during the First World War, and hated militarism of any kind thereafter. His studies might have been hampered by hyperinflation and his parents' poverty, which ren-dered a valuable scholarship virtually worthless at a stroke; but he lived extremely frugally and distinguished himself as a scholar. Shortly afterwards he wrote his best-known work, *Emil and the Detectives*, about a boy who enjoins the children he meets on a visit to the city to help him apprehend a thief. Kästner would continue to write stories with a profound understanding of children, and of the way they speak and think, in books like *Three Men in the Snow* and *The Flying Classroom*.

Throughout his writing life he accumulated a body of poetry, about which he would be unduly modest, and a range of subtly autobiographical work, including the satirical novel *Fabian*. A statue stands to him in Dresden, close to the house where he was born, in tribute to this reserved, often solitary, and always peace-loving writer.

Kawabata

YASUMARI

born Osaka 1899; died Zushi 1972

There were Siberian irises on the girl's obi. Perhaps it was a coincidence. But irises were most ordinary flowers for the season, and perhaps she had planned the combination.

The Japanese irises sent their blossoms and leaves high into the air. One knew that Chikako had arranged them a short time before.

THE GROVE IN THE EVENING SUN, TR.
EDWARD G. SEIDENSTICKER.

IN 1968, THE NOVELIST AND short story writer Kawabata became the first Japanese author to win the Nobel Prize for Literature. The event drew attention to a vein of writing of which he was the purest exponent. Unlike **Mishima**, a younger writer whose work he did much to encourage, his style showed barely any Western influences. Still, the two authors shared a fanatical devotion to their country, to the point of right-wing extremism, and both killed themselves – Kawabata died by gas.

Particularly new to Western readers is the emphasis Kawabata's kind of writing places on images rather than the ideas they embody. While this might have much to do with the physical nature of words as he uses them on the page, it is in keeping with his notions of beauty that our eyes remain on the surface of his texts. He had a great love of Noh theatre, and in *The Sound of the Mountain* writes of an actor's mask,

which is more real than what it covers. The dream-like properties the narrator attaches to it are comparable to those so desired by an old man in Kawabata's most famous story, *The House of the Sleeping Beauties,* included in the collection *The Snow Country*. The protagonist frequents a house of geishas in which the girls have been drugged or enchanted into a sleep that must leave the patrons' desires insatiable.

It is in the world of the imagination that these hankerings for the beautiful must find fulfilment. Kawabata's sparing mode of story-telling leaves the reader with a series of images which the reader must connect just as the characters do – as if by random associations – towards some kind of knowledge, if anything can be certain at all.

Kazantzakis

NIKOS   **born Heraklion, Crete 1883; died Freisburt im Breisgau 1957**

My inspiration and the guiding force throughout my life has been the continuing, merciless battle between the spirit and the flesh; and the soul is the arena where they meet and clash.

THE LAST TEMPTATION OF CHRIST,
INTRODUCTION

THE THEOLOGIAN PELAGIUS was called "the reluctant heretic"; this is even truer of Kazantzakis, who remains modern Greece's most controversial writer. His work was constantly at odds with Orthodox thought, and he died without the full rites of the Church and, in 1997, Greece's chief school inspector sought to have the author taken off the syllabus. However, Kazantzakis was possessed of a profound spirituality which is imbued with the mysticism of the far East (evident in the late play *Buddha*), but finds echoes in the Orthodox liturgy itself. Its view of the Holy Spirit as a giver of life, filling all things, is very much his own: for him, life is not a dynamic cycle of birth and death, but an independent spirit which vivifies existence.

And his most abidingly popular work abounds with life. The exuberant *Zorba the Greek* loves it completely: he is a man "made of rubber". His story is told by a shrinking academic opening a lignite mine in Crete who finds in the hero an earthly corrective to his own remoter stance. The narrative illuminates the dual nature of Greek rural life with its piety, hospitality and extraordinary violence. Even in mourning, Zorba is irrepressible: on his son's death the only way he can ease his pain is by dancing.

The Last Temptation of Christ caused widespread scandal, but is profoundly Orthodox. Christ is still God; but Kazantzakis embraces the human, doubting part of the Messiah as he too chooses life, in a dream sequence. That this life should involve sex was the grounds for shock; but in exploring the alternatives to a hideous martyrdom – one to which Judas is a reluctant party – the author succeeds in rendering the ultimate sacrifice, in fulfilment of the scriptures, as all the more selfless and saving.

MAJOR WORKS

The Odyssey, a Modern Sequel (1938)

Zorba the Greek (1946)

Christ Recrucified (1954)

The Last Temptation of Christ (1955)

191

Keats

JOHN

born London 1795; died Rome 1821

Forgive me if I wander a little this evening, for I have been all day employ'd in a very abstract Poem and I am in deep love with you – two things which must excuse me.

LETTER TO FANNY BRAWNE, JULY 25, 1819

THERE IS NO WAY of getting over Keats. His legend presents the very archetype of a poor, dreaming poet who died tragically early; but we must balance the man whose epitaph is, "Here lies one whose name is writ in water" with the writer who could declare, "I will be among the English poets when I die".

From **Byron** and **Shelley** onwards, there has been the romantic belief that hostile reviews of *Endymion* hastened Keats' death. But he always felt that his days were numbered, and his medical training led him to confront the first symptoms of his consumption immediately. Thus he could face the poor notices with pragmatism, recognising his work's need to develop, as well as the snobbery which animated such savage criticism: it was felt outrageous that a Cockney should attempt classical themes when all his Greek came from the British Museum, or translations.

But he was aware of that too and it is the subject of one of the greatest sonnets in English, *On First Looking Into Chapman's Homer*. His mastery of that form's rigours gave him the control to sustain his argument through the exquisite stanzas of his more luxuriant odes. Even when he seems to be apostrophising, it rolls through the Hellenic odes of *To Psyche* and *On a Grecian Urn*, to the incomparable *Ode to a Nightingale*.

Keats has had many imitators, but most fall for a palpable lushness instead of the rich language so apt for his material. For all his sensual verse, he was less concerned with a subject's outer aspects than with its inner life – which he felt could be more sumptuous still: "Into her dream he melted, as the rose/ Blendeth its odour with the violet." Any notions of the poet's vulnerable fragility might not stand up well to a reading of *On Seeing the Elgin Marbles*, however, which presents a world of the imagination sturdier than our own.

Keneally

THOMAS

born Sydney 1935

*'Don't kill yourself on the fence, Clara,'
the woman urged her. 'If you do that,
you'll never know what happened to
you.'
It has always been the most powerful of
answers to give the intending suicide.
Kill yourself and you'll never know
how the plot ends.*

SCHINDLER'S ARK

THOMAS KENEALLY IS a prolific Australian novelist. He trained for the Catholic priesthood, without becoming a priest; but his books are often concerned with moral dilemmas, and life-or-death decisions. A few of these he has based on fact: *Gossip from the Forest* is about the men chosen to negotiate the Armistice that ended the First World War. Even when not dramatising the actual past, his books are concerned with events real enough to involve Keneally in painstaking research. *Flying Hero Class* intimately observes the psychology of hostage crises in which he depicts the efforts of Palestinian hijackers to win the support of six Aboriginals against their better-off fellow passengers.

Throughout Keneally's writings there is a similar compassion for the poor or dispossessed. The early convicts who arrived in Australia, in a state of exile, are a natural focus for his sympathies, and enable him to invoke the national theme. *The Playmaker* shows illiterate prisoners working on a play in 1787, and restores to them their dignity. This sensitivity is at the core of his best-known work, *Schindler's Ark*, the story of Oskar Schindler's work saving Jewish prisoners from the death camps. The telling involves Keneally's accomplished handling of fact, his eye for the moments when life assumes an art-like quality (the situation is reversed when Schindler himself becomes a prisoner), and his thorough study of heroism. Schindler is a saviour, but no saint; and the author examines moral ambiguities in the face of the ultimate horror. The novel won the Booker Prize in 1982, was filmed in 1994 and has become a vital text in a world that must never forget the Holocaust.

MAJOR WORKS

Bring Larks and Heroes
(1967)

*The Chant of Jimmy
Blacksmith* (1972)

Gossip from the Forest (1975)

Schindler's Ark (1982)

The Playmaker (1987)

Flying Hero Class (1991)

Kerouac

JACK   **born Lowell, Massachusetts 1922; died St. Petersburg, Florida 1969**

"Darling, you know and I know that everything is straight between us at least beyond the furthest abstract definition in metaphysical terms or any terms you want to specify or sweetly impose or harken back ..." and so on, and zoom went the car and we were off again for California.

ON THE ROAD

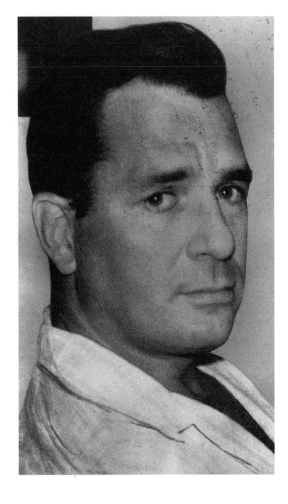

JACK KEROUAC DUBBED HIS circle of writers and adventurers the "beat generation". He meant it to be short for beatific; throughout his writings, he embarks on a quest for all that is holy in his alternative lifestyle, finding benediction in sex, drugs and jazz, as experienced in the light of Neal Cassady's angelic nimbus. Cassady is fictionalised as Dean Moriarty in Kerouac's most cult book, *On the Road*, and as Cody Pomeray in *Big Sur*. **Allen Ginsberg** appears in the former as Carlo Marx; **William Burroughs** as Old Bull Lee.

As in most of Kerouac's work, the journey towards enlightenment in *On the Road* follows tracks truly trodden. It follows his own path, hitching across the States, taking odd jobs and embracing the unpredictable. The prose is faithful to its subject, at times recounting events with **Hemingway's** lack of ornament before losing itself in its own epiphanies. The lengths of paragraphs and the freedom of their direction imitate the course of the narrator's road.

Kerouac's enquiry into the spiritual turned on his upbringing in *Satori in Paris*; he was born into a deeply Catholic family of Breton origins, who were later to repudiate his work publicly. While in France he rhapsodises over candles in empty churches, and elsewhere he explores Buddhism, especially in *The Dharma Bums*.

This last introduces the poet Gary Snyder as Japhy Ryder. Only *Doctor Sax* emerges from Kerouac's writings as pure fiction, but still stands with other works as part of the "Duluoz legend", Kerouac's emulation of **Balzac's** *Comédie Humaine*. He died before he could attempt a further imaginative project, of an abdominal haemorrhage.

Kesey

KEN

> *What the Chronics are – or most of us –*
> *are machines with flaws inside that can't*
> *be repaired, flaws born in, or flaws beat*
> *in over so many years of the guy running*
> *head-on into solid things, that by the*
> *time the hospital found him he was*
> *bleeding rust in some vacant lot.*

ONE FLEW OVER THE CUCKOO'S NEST

KEN KESEY IS A LIVING legend: he has been the subject of **Tom Wolfe**'s book *The Electric Kool-Aid Acid Test*, **Allen Ginsberg**'s poem *First Party at Ken Kesey's with Hell's Angels* and numerous police investigations.

It is hard to know how much of this attention would have been focused on the founder-member of a proselytising pro-drugs group called The Merry Pranksters, had he not created that at once warming and chilling fable of conformity American-style, *One Flew Over the Cuckoo's Nest.* Set in a mental institution, it shows a sane person's bid to awaken the individual spirits within his fellow inmates, and the efforts of the authorities to repress them. For all its allegorical qualities (with the characters embodying human attributes found throughout the supposedly saner world outside) the novel comes with a realism born of its author's own time spent working on a psychiatric ward.

The narrative technique that achieves this is magnificent. Chief Bromden tells the story. A half-native American schizophrenic, he owes his all-seeing, all-knowing position to others' belief that he can hear and say nothing. In spite of the novel's gloom, this device gives its whole execution a faith in patient listening: it is as though we have a story we weren't meant to read.

Kesey was to experiment further with narrative in *Sometimes a Great Notion*, set in a logging town with a peculiarly high suicide rate in his native Oregon. It was a larger project than the first, and he took further pains to make his characters real, conducting extensive interviews with lumberjacks. What writings have appeared since have indicated a kind of disillusion with the aspirations of the '60s, particularly in his piece, *The Day after Superman Died*, written as a memorial for the 'Beat' hero Neal Cassady.

MAJOR WORKS

One Flew Over the Cuckoo's Nest (1962)

Sometimes a Great Notion (1964)

Ken Kesey's Garage Sale (1973)

Demon Box (1986)

195

Kipling

RUDYARD

born Bombay 1865; died London 1936

When 'Omer smote 'is bloomin' lyre,

He 'eard men sing by land an' sea;

An' what he thought 'e might require,

'E went an' took - the same as me!

BARRACK-ROOM BALLADS

KIPLING HAS NEVER BEEN fashionable, but he has always been widely read and loved. Even when regarding his politics with distaste – he called what

he considered the West's duty to bring its civilisation to the world "the white man's burden" – critics acknowledge his great gifts as a story-teller, as a recorder of idiom, as a versifier and a chronicler of British India.

Much of this is evident in *Kim*, in which Kipling shows his admiration both for Empire and Indian mysticism. The book's hero encounters espionage and enlightenment in a backdrop as rich in details of the Raj as we are likely to find in literature. He has a status as variable as that of Mowgli in his *Jungle Books* (anthologised as *The Mowgli Stories*), who is adopted by wolves in the jungle. Although Mowgli rises through the ranks of animals, in a hierarchy strictly controlled by "the law of the jungle", to attain dominion over them, still he does not belong, and eventually must rejoin the world of men.

Kipling's powerful portrayals of animals with human qualities is at its most affecting in the *Just So Stories*, which looks at wildlife's diversity and, taking the premise that it is best "just so", accounts for how it came to be. The tales are aimed at children, and while their cautions against vanity might recall classical myth (including Indian, such as the *Ramayana*) as much as their historical approach does, still they show a complete originality of thought, in a ceremonial language which echoes Indian English. His short stories are often held to be his finest achievements, with their masterful narrative techniques and pacing. His poetry enjoyed a revival when **T.S. Eliot** published a collection in 1941.

Koestler

ARTHUR

born Budapest 1905; died London 1983

Man can leave the earth and land on the moon, but cannot cross from East to West Berlin. Prometheus reaches for the stars with an insane grin on his face and a totem-symbol in his hand.

JANUS, PROLOGUE

AS A JOURNALIST working in Germany in 1932, Arthur Koestler joined the Communist Party. This, his disaffection with the movement, and his training as a scientist, determined the course of his career.

It led him to plunge himself into the heart of international events, reporting on the Spanish Civil War, and fighting with the French Resistance until his incarceration in 1940. Already he was questioning his political beliefs, and his novels continued the process. He had begun *The Gladiators* in 1935, and opened his lifelong debate about whether or not the Marxist belief that the ends justify the means really holds. *The Gladiators* takes Spartacus' revolt as an early expression of Socialism, and portrays the leader's clemency towards dissidents in his force. His best-selling novel, *Darkness at Noon*, applies the same question to Bolshevism: here, however, the protagonist does what Spartacus feels he cannot. *Arrival and Departure* completes the trilogy, placing the emphasis on psychological rather than political motivation, exploring Koestler's academic work as a Behaviourist. The hero undergoes therapy to help him accept the world as it is.

Like Koestler's other novels, it draws on his friends and experiences, including his capture and death sentence under Franco. Much of his work chronicles his political development, from the Zionism that led him from university in Vienna in *Thieves in the Night*, to the rejection of the Soviet dream as he witnessed it in his contribution to *The God that Failed*. *Darkness at Noon* did much to expose the horrors of the Stalinist purges to the West, with its depiction of N.S. Rubashov's arrest, trial and execution. It was his last book to be written in German. Thereafter he used impassioned English to write both his fiction and non-fiction, seeing the two as complementary to each other.

Kundera

MILAN

born Brno 1929

But all the student could see was the butcher's wife slipping out of his hands that whole month, and hard as it was to do, he shook his head. Kristyna meant as much to him at that moment as all his country's poetry.

THE BOOK OF LAUGHTER
AND FORGETTING

MILAN KUNDERA'S WRITING has the intrinsically Czech quality of being immediately readable, while unsettling the reader as he refrains from offering any empirical truths or entrenched attitudes. Like **Kafka**

or **Hašek**, he presents an alternative view of how the world works; and although he guides the reader with a seemingly-tangential commentary, often based on his own experience, the sparing nature of his prose, and the self-conflicting nature of his aphorisms, provide their own refusal to comment.

Still, his analyses are rich in allusions to philosophy, music, poetry and history, which he explains patiently. These take the post-war Czech situation to explore the human condition, and vice versa. He avoids the idealism of his earlier poetry, a forthright defence of Communism, especially for its having prevailed over Fascism; increasingly his work depicted a universal disaffection with the Marxist régime. Until the Prague Spring, he was able to express this quite freely, but in 1967 his first novel *The Joke* worried publishers and was banned on publication in 1969. Kundera was silenced and escaped to France in 1975. He now lives in Paris, in the Montparnasse area.

His work from around the time of his exile onwards has dealt with the effects change has had upon human relations. The totalitarian conditions he describes are dehumanising, and take their toll on people's ability to laugh and love. Seldom in Kundera is even sex free of political significance, and throughout laughter emerges as the only response to a world robbed of meaning – a lightness when things no longer have weight. Even the joke at the expense of Communism becomes a kind of self-mocking on a national scale for ever having espoused it. The recent *Immortality* deals with this more internationally, and makes the point that human beings are more memorable when they are ridiculous; as ever, the quest for meaning finds nothing, and we laugh without knowing why.

Laclos

born Amiens 1741; died Taranto 1803

PIERRE-AMBROISE-FRANÇOIS CHODERLOS DE

I am not surprised that, with a licentiousness that one would be wrong to deny you, you did for once deliberately what you have done a thousand times merely as the occasion offered. Everyone knows that this is simply the way of the world: the way of all you whoever you are, Neros or nobodies. The man who behaves otherwise nowadays is taken for a romantic and that is not, I think, the fault I find in you.

LES LIAISONS DANGEREUSES
TRANSLATED BY P.W.K STONE

LES LIAISONS DANGEREUSES is Laclos' one imaginative work. It spins a web of intrigue around the indolent and rotten circles of aristocratic France on the eve of the Revolution. Two characters turned completely sour have nothing to do, and so create situations over which they can wield their power fully.

The novel is executed entirely in letters. Each is vital dramatically, both as a source of plot and a piece of the plot in itself; letters become challenges, highly-charged objects, and even items of evidence. Their tone varies with violence: exchanges of civil enquiry or maternal advice break up the unrestrained cross-fires of two estranged lovers striving to better each other by any means available to them. They destroy everyone in the process, and mean to, but in doing so they ultimately destroy themselves.

The story reaches us thanks to a diffident editor who annotates the letters, sometimes with trivia, sometimes with crucial information. Laclos' artistry consists in appearing to offer this story for moral reasons, but giving something richer. If we are to learn anything, it is that society demands hypocrisy; that young girls are expected at once to be both innocent and compliant. By the self-revelation of the anti-heroine, the Marquise de Merteuil shows us something beyond such values. Her response to that society transcends revenge. It is a brutality born of lust and boredom: she is a greater study than the lesson.

The book was publicly burned after court action. In presenting a world in which discretion is the only virtue and silence the only sanctity, Laclos told all. The novel sets up boundaries for itself and then blasts through them.

MAJOR WORKS

Les Liaisons Dangereuses
(1782)

La Fayette

COMTESSE DE

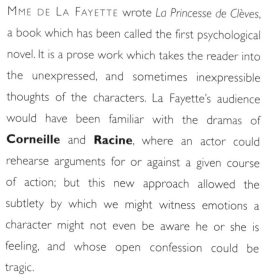

born Paris 1634; died Paris 1693

She could not stop herself from being troubled by what she saw, nor yet from taking pleasure in seeing him; but, when she saw him no longer, and thought that the charm she found in what she saw was the source of passions, she could almost believe that she hated him for all the pain this thought caused her.

LA PRINCESSE DE CLÈVES

MME DE LA FAYETTE wrote *La Princesse de Clèves*, a book which has been called the first psychological novel. It is a prose work which takes the reader into the unexpressed, and sometimes inexpressible thoughts of the characters. La Fayette's audience would have been familiar with the dramas of **Corneille** and **Racine**, where an actor could rehearse arguments for or against a given course of action; but this new approach allowed the subtlety by which we might witness emotions a character might not even be aware he or she is feeling, and whose open confession could be tragic.

The Princess of Clèves is in this dilemma. She is trapped in a loveless marriage (a fate which is suffered by the heroines of other romances by Mme de La Fayette), and falls for a young duke, just as he falls for her. She can never declare her passion to him; instead, as a character in Corneille would do, she opts for the nobler course. She tells her husband, who dies of heartbreak; the Princess herself vows never to see the duke again.

The book appeared at a time when women were not to be acknowledged as authors. At first it was considered to be the work of several hands. It remains possible that the writer collaborated with La Rochefoucauld, but as rumours circulated Paris, those linked with the work admired it sufficiently to be flattered by the association. Only a little more is known about the real author now as was then, although it is possible to find, in the court of Henri II she recreates in her *chef d'oeuvre*, echoes of her own youth in the circle of Louis XIV and Anne of Austria.

La Fontaine

JEAN DE   **born Château Thierry 1621; died Paris 1695**

I had left Aesop so

I'd be Boccaccio

but somebody divine

wanted back in Paradise

some fables just like mine.

FABLES

LA FONTAINE'S OTIOSE reading and thought accounts for the charm of his work. He wrote comedies, verse tales deriving from Ariosto and **Boccaccio**, a version of Apuleius' *Cupid and Psyche*, and translated Terence. But the form best suited to his roving mind was the fable.

Again, his sources were classical, particularly Aesop and **Horace**. The digressive style of the latter is closer to the tone than Aesop's no-nonsense parables. La Fontaine's fables were criticised for the slackness of their morals: if his characters learn anything, it is to accept the world as it is. They should approach kings with sycophancy, try not to stray beyond their natural limitations, and avoid vanity.

But it is not for this that we turn to La Fontaine. His lightness of touch makes the consequences of misguided action seem heavier; the more his animals endear us by their folly and their distinct speech-making, the more we pity them. The frogs who form a kingdom around a log may act like human beings do; but we laugh at them because they are frogs. The author animated creatures in a way that directly confronted Descartes' thesis that animals act as machines, and could boast, "I made the wolf speak, and the lamb reply."

The humour comes as much from the telling; there is no precedent for La Fontaine's style. He does not restrict himself to rigid stanza forms – rather, he weaves in and out of rhyme-schemes with whatever rhythm the pace requires at the time. His timing is so good that it works, and can deliver a punchy cadence after florid reasoning. A rat who complains that he is every bit as worthy as an elephant meets this end: "His utterance was very sage,/ Until a cat came from his cage,/ saw him, and quickly showed him that/ an elephant is not a rat."

MAJOR WORKS

Elegy on the Nymphs of Vaux (1662)

Verse Tales and Novelties (1666)

Psyche and Cupid (1669)

Collection of Christian and other poems (1670)

Fables (1668, 1678–1679, 1694)

Lampedusa

GIUSEPPE TOMASI DI

born Palermo 1896; died Rome 1957

Those days were the preparation for a marriage which, even erotically, was no success; a preparation, however, in a way sufficient to itself, exquisite and brief; like those overtures which outlive the forgotten operas they belong to and hint in delicate veiled gaiety at all the arias which later in the opera are to be developed undeftly, and fail.

THE LEOPARD,
TR. ARCHIBALD COLQUHOUN

LAMPEDUSA'S ONLY NOVEL appeared after his death, to worldwide acclaim. Before he died, he attempted to have it published, with no success. Such stories always sadden but the case of *The Leopard* is especially poignant for the considerable personal investment this book demanded.

Lampedusa wrote it in the last two years of his life. It is a piece that bids farewell to a vanished way of life and, in the act of writing, the author appears to be doing the same. The story of Don Fabrizio, the Sicilian prince presiding over a decaying court when Garibaldi's troops are due any moment to declare the island a part of unified Italy, has points in common with Lampedusa's own. He was also a prince, of Lampedusa, a small island south of Sicily. Like his hero, he had spent his youth in adventure and passion, before withdrawing to become more contemplative. His memoirs share the same regret for a world that is gone: he can empathise with Don Fabrizio's loss with his own recollection of what war and the Fascists had destroyed.

Still, the intellectual Left, especially in Italy, found cause to pan the book. **Louis Aragon** stood almost alone among Marxists in proclaiming its singular excellence, and its vindication of human values above political dogma has appealed to many since. The intrigues and jostlings of the Sicilian court give the novel its movement, while frequent glances back to Sicily's history, from Greek colonisation to medieval Norman settlers, imbue the whole with its nostalgia and fear of change. The Church appears timeless here, with its worldly priests and vulnerable nunneries; but in Lampedusa's hands, these too become symptoms of decay.

Lawrence

D.H.   **born Eastwood, Nottinghamshire 1885; died Vence, France 1930**

The novel is a great discovery: far greater than Galileo's telescope or somebody else's wireless. The novel is the highest form of human expression so far attained. Why? because it is so incapable of the absolute. In a novel, everything is relative to everything else, if that novel is art at all.

PHOENIX

D.H. LAWRENCE HAS WON permanent fame by probing deep into the human psyche, most notably his own, in fiction notable for its tough structure and strong language. His words can attain an ecstatic urgency, and his descriptions are charged with an energy bursting from their symbolic surface. For some, this uneven, passionate novelist is Britain's best.

His work is a realisation of the self-expression and vitality he preached. The childhood depicted in *Sons and Lovers* was very much his own, with a mother doting to the point of claustrophobia, and a relationship with a local farm girl. He grew up in a rural mining area and for him land was always something productive and fertile. This, together with the new social circles to which literary success had brought him, accounts for much in the linked works *The Rainbow* and *Women In Love*. Their appearance caused a scandal for their language and descriptions of sex: neither could be published in Britain. It anticipated the furore

surrounding *Lady Chatterley's Lover*, certainly his most famous novel, though far from his best: it appeared, after a trial, in 1961. For all his convictions, he is even-handed as a novelist, and his repetition of words and phrases suit the stage well (as in *The Widowing of Mrs Holroyd*). Both these aspects make him a potent poet.

He was forced to travel widely, being expelled from Britain for having a German wife; his relationship with Frieda von Richthofen was always turbulent. His search, both in life and art, for the perfect union between man and woman, was hampered by the fear that women absorb male energies, precluding an equitable transference. Frieda nursed Lawrence in the final phases of his tuberculosis, of which he died in a sanatorium in the South of France.

MAJOR WORKS

NOVELS
The White Peacock (1911)
Sons and Lovers (1913)
The Rainbow (1915)
Women In Love (1920)
The Lost Girl (1920)
Aaron's Rod (1922)
Kangaroo (1923)
The Plumed Serpent (1926)
Lady Chatterley's Lover (1928)

SHORT STORIES
The Prussian Officer (1914)
England, My England (1922)
The Woman Who Rode Away (1928)

POETRY
Love Poems (1913)
Amores (1916)
Look! We Have Come Through! (1917)
Birds, Beasts and Flowers (1923)
Pansies (1929)

203

Laxness

HALLDÓR

born Reykjavik 1902

Why are you always trying to rise above things? Wouldn't you rather try to take part in man's folly? But remember, if you do, you must do it with all your heart, and all your heart, and – what was the third thing ...

CHRISTIANITY AT GLACIER,
TR. MAGNUSSON

HALLDÓR LAXNESS IS an Icelandic writer who has worked in all literary genres, but who is most famous for his many novels.

Although he travelled widely around Europe and the United States in the years after the First World War, these books are set almost solely in Iceland. He returned in 1928, having espoused Catholicism in a Luxembourg monastery, and Communism in America. His political concerns feature in his earlier stories, which focus on work and the struggle for survival, and dignify them with a language echoing the ancient sagas known to all his compatriots. They have strong heroes, such as *Salka Valka*, the fish-wife, or the man who spends 18 years trying to buy a sheep farm in *Independent People*.

Although a truly international author, he concentrates on his country's own neglected strengths. In *The Fish Can Sing*, he tells of a singer returning to Iceland, of whose prowess those around him have read but never had any proof. In championing instead the orphan boy who sings at the legend's funeral, Laxness professes his own humility in coming home. *The Atom Station* celebrates simplicity over sophistication too, as Ulga Falsdottír, a girl from the north arrives to learn the organ in Reykjavîk, where she encounters the tolerance of vice and the vanity of public figures.

Later still, in *Christianity at Glacier*, a young bishop's emissary comes from the capital to lose his innocence to an immortal woman in the tundra. On the way he meets her husband, a worldly pastor who is all-but *manqué* and a tycoon eager to patent eternal life. Laxness balances the transcendent with the pragmatic: he presents Iceland with a sense of perspective, but is always alive to its own splendours. He was awarded the Nobel Prize for Literature in 1955.

Lear

EDWARD   **born Holloway, London 1812; died San Remo, Italy 1888**

He weeps by the side of the ocean,

   He weeps on the top of the hill;

He purchases pancakes and lotion,

   And chocolate shrimps from the mill.

HOW PLEASANT TO KNOW MR. LEAR!

And children swarmed to him like

settlers. He became a land.

W.H. AUDEN, EDWARD LEAR

EDWARD LEAR WAS AN ARTIST, poet and story teller who is best known for his inspired nonsense verse. He began writing this for the children of his patron, the Earl of Derby, who had commissioned paintings of his own private zoo at Knowsley Hall. The hospitality, support and contacts Lear found there made it possible for him to travel extensively around Europe, the Middle East, India and Sri Lanka. Before settling in San Remo, Italy, in 1871, he had served as Queen Victoria's drawing instructor.

It was a world far removed from his upbringing. He was the 20th child of a stockbroker, largely ignored by his mother, and educated by his eldest sister. This start left him prey to epilepsy and depression, and this background makes it hard to read his nonsense as merely forced jollity.

Although he is famed for his apparently effortless limericks, they have a brutal edge and he grew tired of the form, once answering a request for one rhymelessly. His brand of nonsense is most often compared to **Carroll**'s; but Lear works less with logic, and his coinages are less punny conflations of other words, than carefully selected noises. These drop into lyrics whose harmony is worthy of **Tennyson**'s ear (the two were great friends, and Lear would ad-lib settings of the Poet Laureate's work at the piano). In the lines, "There was an old person from Grange/ Whose manners were scroobious and strange", the neologism is all the more perfect for its placement drawing so little attention to itself.

Work like this makes an immediate, emotional kind of sense, and it is hard to miss the note of melancholy and resignation in his writing. In an age when so many of Lear's private anxieties were inexpressible, he found a language which didn't ignore them, and in whose silliness there is much comfort.

Lee

HARPER

born Monroeville, Alabama 1926

The one place where a man ought to get a square deal is the court-room, be he any colour of the rainbow, but people have a way of carrying their resentments right into a jury box. As you grow older, you'll see white men cheat black men every day of your life, but let me tell you something and don't you forget it – whenever a white man does that to a black man, no matter who he is, how rich he is, or how fine a family he comes from, that white man is trash.

TO KILL A MOCKINGBIRD

HARPER LEE IS the author of a single novel, *To Kill a Mockingbird*, which is widely read for its social convictions, its account of childhood, its craft, clarity and vivid recreation of life in a small Southern town.

Lee was born in Monroeville, Alabama, and grew up there during the '30s. The action of her novel takes place in "a tired town" in Maycomb county, which "only exists for the sake of government". Jem and Scout (the narrator) grow up here, and with them we see the atmosphere changing from racial tension, as the children rile the reclusive ex-convict Boo Radley, to open hatred, as the crowd prepares to lynch Tom Robinson, accused of raping a white girl. The narrative describes a rigorous caste system: everyone knows everyone else, and each family must be treated differently, but even the least trustworthy white citizens enjoy more respect than their black neighbours.

This plagues the children's father, who must represent Robinson. He knows that he will lose and endure the town's ostracism. But he adheres to the dictates of his conscience, and in a series of conversations with Jem, articulates this as the moral core of the book.

It has become a best-seller, been made into a film, and won lavish praise from **Truman Capote**, an old childhood friend of Lee's, and the model for the character of the wily prankster Dill.

Lehmann

ROSAMOND   **born High Wycombe, Bucks 1901; died London 1990**

"The source, Rebecca! The fount of life - the source, the quick spring that rises in illimitable depths of darkness and flows through every living thing from generation. It is what we feel mounting in us when we say 'I know! I love! I am!'"

THE BALLAD AND THE SOURCE

ROSAMOND LEHMANN'S handful of novels concern girls coming of age in a world they find increasingly complex and sinister. Her youthful debut, *Dusty Answer*, drew on personal experience to present this theme: as it stayed with her, so it continued to dominate her writing.

The novel is set partly at Cambridge, where Lehmann was an undergraduate, and partly at the home of a wealthy family, whose daughter is a fellow student. It won praise for its elegance, its sensitivity, and its delicate portrayal of youth; it continues to attract attention for exploring the varying degrees of innocence at play in a friendship between two growing women. Lehmann's next heroine finds herself in a similar situation: Olivia in *Invitation to the Waltz* is slightly more naïve, at sea in a more aristocratic setting.

In *The Weather in the Streets*, Lehmann follows Olivia's suddenly complicated love-life: the protagonist is seeing a married man. Another love-triangle provides the plot for *The Echoing Grove*. But it is *The Ballad and the Source* which stands as the peak of Lehmann's literary career. Rebecca tries to piece together the life history of another aloof neighbour, the mysterious Sybil Jardin, whose biography emerges without chronological sequence or a strict regard of truth. Throughout, the elder woman exercises a strange power over a girl she would make her protegé, and mixes prophetic insights with a fraudulence from which the narrative must extract whatever truths Rebecca can discern.

Lermontov

MIKHAIL

born Moscow 1814; died Pyatigorsk 1841

And I sat alone

for hours, a king upon a fairy throne –
and while

I live I remember, in spite of storms
and doubt; I keep a tiny island green

in an ocean desert.

JANUARY 1ST, TR. RAFFEL

LERMONTOV WROTE at a time when Europe had started mythologising **Byron**, and when Russia had started to prize its own language. In a country which had always seen the source of culture as France, he followed **Pushkin** in exploring the poetic potential of his native tongue, displaying a love of his country but profound distrust of its rulers. He gave his country its first great novel, *A Hero of Our Times*.

This hero is Pechorin. Lermontov considered him to be typical of a generation, but portrayed him as a solitary figure with no apparent concern for others. Most of this small book is taken from Pechorin's journal, as introduced by his friend Maxim Maximich. The confessions seem sincere from their ability to shock, but the story allows us to doubt even this aspect of the narrator's morality. He dislikes posturing, however, and must fight a duel with the self-absorbed Grushnitsky, who wears his epaulettes too high. Throughout stories within stories, the reader questions whether Pechorin can love, or feel anything, even a fear of death: he even reads **Walter Scott** on the eve of his duel. The concluding tale of these loosely-linked episodes depicts a man never beaten in Russian roulette, who knows exactly when he will die.

The romantic loneliness that Lermontov conveys here finds less dispassionate expression in his verse. The first poem to bring him fame was *The Death of Pushkin*, which pointed to government collusion in Pushkin's death in a duel. For this he was exiled; he too was to die in a duel, which caused others to make similar allegations. His verse is considered more spontaneous than Pushkin's, and is highly rhetorical, especially in his outburst on Napoleon's remains being transferred to France in *The Last House-warming*. His fascination with the misunderstood visionary despot echoes that of Byron's *Childe Harold*, and *personae* of other poems match Byronic mood-swings between rapture and disaffection with love.

Lessing

DORIS

born Kermanshah, Persia (now Iran) 1919

The point is that the function of the novel seems to be changing; it has been an outpost of journalism; we read information about areas of life we don't know – Nigeria, South Africa, the American Army, a coal-mining village, coteries in Chelsea etc. We read to find out what is going on...

THE GOLDEN NOTEBOOK

DORIS LESSING'S FICTION provides a personal account of self-realisation; but it is one which reaches beyond the self, from political to increasingly spiritual concerns. She was born in Persia, but spent most of her childhood in Rhodesia, where she encountered apartheid. Her anger at this injustice animates her first novel, *The Grass is Singing*, in which she shows the tensions inherent in the system erupting into violent murder.

Lessing's own journey through radical politics and the relationships that steered it, is chronicled in the *Children of Violence* sequence, describing Martha Quest's coming of age. Among these books comes her most successful, the apparently unrelated *Golden Notebook*, in which a novelist works on a political novel, *Free Women*, which we receive with excerpts from her notebooks, each a different colour, each bringing a different kind of self-awareness to bear on the process of fiction. The novel has been praised for its experimental structure, and its contribution to feminism (although not universally); it sold nearly a million copies in hardback.

The fourth book of her work in progress, *Landlocked*, is more supernatural than its realist antecedents, involving telepathy and the mystical power of Sufism. A final text, *The Four-Gated City*, takes the story into the year 2000.

This began her career as a visionary. Her subsequent stories of Earth, which she calls "the broken planet" or Shikasta, as reported by emissaries trying to correct its course, are attempts at science fiction whose spiritual and utopian leanings bring the project closer to metaphysics.

In 1983, she submitted a novel to publishers under a different name, aware that her own was big enough to prevent readers from approaching her work objectively. The reviews were mixed, but in itself, her ploy showed a sense of responsibility balanced with a sense of the self which has consistently defined her work.

Levi

PRIMO

born Turin 1919; died Turin 1987

Hurbinek, who was three years old and had perhaps been born in Auschwitz and had never seen a tree, died in the first days of March 1945, free but not redeemed. Nothing is left of him: he bears witness through these words of mine.

THE TRUCE

PRIMO LEVI BEGAN WRITING after his experience of Auschwitz. His life's work was to bear witness to the hell he had seen, and the guilt he felt in surviving it. He compared himself to **Coleridge**'s Ancient Mariner, and had a constant need to tell his story. He was a chemist, and found writing science fiction liberating; but his science was to inform his autobiographical books in a way that denied him any escape. He once collaborated on a paper detailing Nazi methods of extermination as a scientific phenomenon rather than a moral outrage.

His knowledge of chemistry and insight into humanity account for *The Periodic Table*, a series of stories and character studies based on the elements. Each element gains its defining quality from being distinct, and finds a corollary in the way people interreact. Each carries an immediate association which reflects life, until the last, carbon, which becomes it.

The work draws on his experience of growing up with Fascism, and its clinical notions of purity, as well as his time with the anti-Fascist resistance. *If This is a Man* and *The Truce* explore the horror of what followed his capture, from the tattooing of the number 174517 on his arm to the Red Army soldiers discovering him among the handful of survivors. The narrative's increasing awareness of the evil and and its fulfilment echoes **Dante**'s descent into hell.

Levi's testimony became more urgent still when historians began to write articles denying Hitler's crimes, and questioning whether so vast and so rigorously documented a mass slaughter could have taken place at all. This, he said, was to "kill the dead twice". Ultimately, Levi did not survive. The nightmare of guilt and terror would never leave him. He killed himself in April 1987.

Lewis

C.S.

People now all seem to want "a slice of life" (the flaccid, tepid, grey-to-brown shapeless object is a better image than they know) or the "comment on life." To me those who merely comment on experience seem to be far less valuable than those who add to it, who make me experience what I never experienced before.

LETTER TO MERVYN PEAKE

C.S. LEWIS APPLIED HIS immense intellect first to the history of English poetry, and then to a defence of Christianity. He drifted from the faith in his youth, only to return to it after rational enquiry, during which he espoused Pantheism before concluding that, for him, Christianity outshone all other religions.

Still, he described himself as "the most dejected and reluctant convert in the whole of England". His struggle with the faith gave him acute insights into the psychology of believing, and the nature of temptation. *The Screwtape Letters*, in which a senior devil shows a bungling junior how to sway his "patient" from the path of salvation, applies Christian language rather than Freudian to a study of the mind.

The work emerged from suffering: he had made a pact with a fellow soldier in the First World War that, should one of them die, the other would care for the deceased's mother. Lewis fulfilled his pledge for 20 years of what his brother described as "self-imposed slavery". Similarly, *A Grief Observed* confronts the pain of losing the one person he allowed himself to love since the early death of his mother, as he responds to losing his wife to cancer.

His most famous writing can be read as a Christian apology, although it started as a response to what Lewis perceived as the absence of decent children's literature at the time. But the figures that populate the sequence of seven books, starting with *The Lion, the Witch and the Wardrobe*, become increasingly Christianised. Aslan the lion turns Messianic, after being "crucified" and rising from the dead, and by *The Voyage of the Dawn Treader*, Lewis' allegory is made all but explicit as Aslan declares, "In your world you must know me by another name".

Lewis

SINCLAIR

born Sauk Center, 1885; died nr. Rome 1951

Vast is the power of cities to reclaim the wanderer. More than mountains or the shore-devouring sea, a city retains its character, imperturbable, cynical, holding behind apparent changes its essential purpose.

BABBITT

IF SINCLAIR LEWIS was not America's best writer, he was definitely one of its most rebellious. But he managed it in an endearing style that made a rather un-American kind of satire popular all over the States.

He grew up in Sauk Center, a small town in Minnesota – a prosperous, Protestant community. He viewed it with love and hate, but one suspects with more of the latter. It was the starting point of his first major success as a novelist, *Main Street*. The book presents the Kennicotts, who have just arrived in Gopher Prairie, Minnesota. Lewis' depiction of Carol, the frustrated wife, is based partly on his own sense of anger, and partly on caricature. The prospect of her sexual liberation arises, but is ultimately dismissed. Where Lewis does best is with his descriptions: their humour engulfs the narrative.

They work into the bigger town inhabited by George F. Babbitt, who gave his surname not just to Lewis' next novel, but also to fundraisers and loud businessmen with appetites for committee meetings. Its spirit of '20s euphoria is more about gizmos than jazz; but the jazz generation still loved it.

As the seriousness of Lewis' work became harder to ignore, so the quality dwindled. By the time he was writing against racism in 1947, critics had given up hope. But for execution and passion, *Arrowsmith* and *Elmer Gantry* reach a peak, the one following a scientist pursuing his research unswayed by the lure of fame or money, the other lambasting Fundamentalists. Much of this was calculated to upset, and often it did. He was a lifelong Socialist, and disliked the establishment. He refused the Pulitzer Prize, calling it an award for "American wholesomeness" and, in accepting the Nobel Prize in 1930, dismissed all American literature until his own time.

Lewis

WYNDHAM

born near Amehurst, Nova Scotia 1882; died London 1957

A novelist I knew once told me he changed the names of the characters in a book several times in the course of writing it. It freshens them up, according to him; he said that the majority of people were killed by their names.

TARR

THE IMPORTANCE OF Wyndham Lewis' writing lies chiefly in its theoretical content; or at least, in the satire he aims at some theory he opposes. For his aesthetic ideas are best understood, either through his painting, in their affinity to Cubism, or else negatively. With **Ezra Pound** he founded *Blast, the Review of the Great English Vortex*, which ran for two issues (1914, 1915). By 1916, Lewis was on the Western Front.

For such a man of the times, his own timing was often badly awry. He continued to enthuse about the machine age, and rejoice in its impersonality, just when the horror of war had convinced people of the opposite. A burst of novels tried to make a similar point, that artistic creation was an objective process after all; that waywardness, bohemia and vision made for degenerate work. Two artists exemplify this in *Tarr*, his first book; later, he lampoons most of the Bloomsbury set, as well as **Joyce**, and **Proust**, in *The Apes of God*, an outspoken denunciation of aestheticism which also cast a disapproving eye over homosexuals. If this didn't alienate every-

one, his interest in the Fascists did. In 1931, he wrote praising Hitler; in 1939 he recanted in the most biting satire he could muster. Again, his sense of the times failed him.

After the war, he worked tirelessly on what was to be his largest work, an epic in prose set outside Paradise. Called *The Human Age*, it was to run to four volumes, but he only lived to complete three, having already gone blind. With his teaching and criticism, so much of it innovative both in thought and expression, he remained indefatigable to the end.

MAJOR WORKS

Tarr (1918)

The Apes of God (1930)

The Revenge for Love (1937)

The Human Age:
The Childermass (1928)
Monstre Gai (1955)
Malign Fiesta (1955)

213

Lochhead

LIZ

born Motherwell, Lanarkshire 1947

I only have to pause for breath and in he falls, 'yes, dear I'll have the Steak Tartar medium rare, please!' The girl and I just look at each other ... from then on he can't open his mouth without putting his foot in it. Orders a 'cravat of your house white, please!' Then it's 'As you were, as you were, give me a bottle of Chateaubriand'.

GLASGOW'S NO DIFFERENT

LIZ LOCHHEAD IS ONE of a generation of contemporary poets whose work lends itself best to performance. To see her work on the page is already to be hearing it rapped out in a Glaswegian accent with an authority that leaves you unable to answer back. Many of her poems are really sketches or monologues that form part of her revues. She has written extensively for the stage, including musicals and a rhyming version of **Moliére**'s *Tartuffe*. Here she says, "I have been faithful to the original, in my fashion"; the fashion is emphatically Scots. She is also great news for the cause of poetry on TV.

Television can be seen as a theme of her work as well as a medium for it, whether she is attacking the elitism of the arts coverage, or simply leaving it on in the background of her retelling of fairy stories in *The Grimm Sisters*. These versions of **The Brothers Grimm** leave little room for romance: Rumplestiltskin works through every imaginable way to impress a girl before he can get around to saying "I love you", by which time it's too late.

Lochhead can maintain this level of cynicism about a lot of things. The "Glasgow's Miles Better" campaign comes in for special scorn, as does her home town's recent stint as European City of Culture. But while she makes short work of any urban attempts to sound idyllic, she is herself a vital part of that culture, keeping it strong and defiant.

Lodge

DAVID

born London 1935

'So Puss in Boots is equivalent to the Grail?' Persse said facetiously. Miss Maiden was not discomposed. 'Certainly. Boots are phallic, and you are no doubt familiar with the vulgar expression "pussy"?'

SMALL WORLD

DAVID LODGE IS A NOVELIST and a Structuralist literary critic. His work in the former does much to popularise the latter. Although his fiction addresses serious concerns, such as religion and the state of scholarship, it is consistently hilarious.

His first two books were realistic looks at post-war England: *The Picturegoers* tells of a run-down cinema. He wrote it while doing his National Service, which in turn provided material for the next work, *Ginger, You're Barmy*. It was with *The British Museum is Falling Down* that he introduced the themes of Catholicism and academic research. The book's hero must choose the novels on which to base his thesis on the same day that his wife becomes pregnant again. Throughout the text, the post-graduate encounters novels all around him from the butchers who speak like **Hemingway** to the **Kafka**esque encounter at the British Library Reading Room. Finally the two stories are merged as his wife discusses gynaecology in the style of *Ulysses*, ending with a "perhaps" rather than **James Joyce's** resounding yes.

Literature takes over the plots of his two novels on the international lecture circuit, *Changing Places* and *Small World*. The latter exemplifies Barthes' theory that a text can never quite attain closure, and its constant twists and hiccoughs defer any kind of resolution. The academics involved are happy to explain these ideas as they go, but never at the expense of character and belly-laughs.

These novels are set at Rummidge University, which the author is at pains to dissociate from Birmingham, where he teaches. The more recent *Nice Work* again takes place on a campus, but tackles social issues beyond it, as an industrialist and a lecturer explore one another's realms. Lately Lodge has renewed his investigation of how faith manifests itself in the modern world in *Paradise News*, in which a theologian's idea of heaven clashes with that of the travel agents.

MAJOR WORKS

The Picturegoers (1960)

Ginger, You're Barmy (1962)

The British Museum is Falling Down (1965)

Changing Places (1975)

How Far Can You Go? (1980)

Small World (1984)

Nice Work (1988)

Paradise News (1991)

London

JACK

born San Fancisco 1876; died Glen Ellen, California 1916

"Never travel alone" is a precept of the north.

HOW TO BUILD A FIRE

JACK LONDON'S RAPIDLY – produced *oeuvre* presents all aspects of America as he saw it – and he really saw it. His childhood was spent in poverty in San Francisco, and he left home early to work in a cannery before becoming an adventurer. He was also an oyster-poacher-turned-fish-patroller and in the former capacity had his first encounter with alcohol (which was to plague him for years), in an incident that nearly drowned him. Even his immense reading was an adventure, and he enrolled at Berkeley in 1896, studying by day, shovelling coal by night, such that he could barely hold a pen. Later, he would suffer similar blisters from his typewriter, which he said was "informed of an evil spirit".

His experiences and education made him at once a Socialist and a Darwinian. He wrote political tracts and memoirs: of the latter, one volume, *John Barleycorn*, tells of his alcoholism, another, *Martin Eden*, of his rise from rags to riches, and the accompanying guilt. He did not finish his degree at Berkeley, instead joining the Klondike gold rush.

This provides the setting for his most famous story, *Call of the Wild*. It incorporates London's beliefs and insights, and is sustained by a strong survival instinct. Its hero is the dog Buck, once a pet, now hauling cargo across the tundra. His rise through the team of dogs reflects at once a sense of collective responsibility and the ruthlessness staying alive requires. The allegory may be read in many ways, but the story derives most of its strength simply from its telling: the author's admiration for the animals' stamina and loyalty points towards qualities which humans can envy, but never possess.

Longfellow

HENRY WADSWORTH born Portland, Maine 1807; died Cambridge, Mass.1882

Read from some humbler poet
Whose songs gushed from his heart,
As showers from the clouds of summer
Or tears from eyelids start

Who, through long days of labour,
And nights of ease,
Still heard in the soul the music
Of wonderful melodies.

THE DAY IS DONE

LONGFELLOW WROTE SIMPLE unaffected poetry, often of great lyrical charm. He was a New Englander, and went to Bowdoin College with **Nathaniel Hawthorne**. Something of that area's Transcendentalism seems to have touched him, especially in the spirit of **Emerson**, whose view of nature having its own grammar finds fine expression in Longfellow's poem *Snow Flakes*. "This is the poem of the air/ Slowly in silent syllables recorded…"

Like Emerson, too, he campaigned for the abolition of slavery and his humanity is evident in much of his verse. His compassion for the exiled Jew marks his poem *The Jewish Cemetery at Newport*. But most significant is that his attempt at the national epic should be devoted to the native American legend of Hiawatha.

It is in marked contrast to an earlier effort, Joel Barlow's *Columbiad*, preaching simplicity in **Pope**-like rhyming couplets. Longfellow's poem is unrhymed, in short regular lines, that keep the syntax plain. The arguments emerge little by little with lilting echoes mimicking the "rushing of great rivers/ With their frequent repetitions/ And their wild reverberations." The hero's leave-taking has the limpid poignancy of *A Pilgrim's Progress* as it concludes.

But there is still a certain sadness in Longfellow's poetry. He writes as one acquainted with the night, dwelling on scenes of dusk and empty seascapes. He was a man lauded in public life, but one who nursed private unhappiness. His melancholy finds its match in the regretful tone of **Housman**. Both were hugely learned poets who kept their scholarship and verse separate – Longfellow was a Professor of Languages at Harvard. He suffered from outliving two wives, one of whom burned to death with their child in a fire. He won the admiration of Queen Victoria, was awarded honorary degrees from Oxford and Cambridge and is the only American poet to be commemorated in Westminster Abbey.

LOOS

ANITA

born Mt. Shaston, California 1893; died New York 1981

So this English gentleman's name is Mr Gerald Lamson as those who have read his novels would know.

GENTLEMEN PREFER BLONDES

But I really think we ought to do more shopping because shopping really seems to be what Paris is principaly for.

IBID

BESIDES MEMOIRS and film-scripts, Anita Loos wrote *Gentlemen Prefer Blondes*, and the sequel *But Gentlemen Marry Brunettes*. It should be said that these works stand in the American literary tradition, stemming from the **Mark Twain** of *The Innocents Abroad*, or the **Henry James** of *Roderick Hudson*, in which Americans find themselves astray in a Europe that feeds on innocence. But this is no fun; and in any case it is barely true. For sure, the narrator of the two novels is a ditz. Lorelei Lee's diary is a masterpiece only unwittingly, and she expounds her philosophy, "Fate Keeps On Happening", in scantily-punctuated sentences with inconsistent spelling; but unlike her tragic forebears, she has the Old World's number already: French gentlemen only buy you cheap things, London is really nothing, while the museums in Munich are, "full of kunst that I really ought to look at". Men don't fool her either: she finds they talk too much, and she knows what they really mean when they say they're going to Vienna on a top-secret mission of national importance.

But Gentlemen Marry Brunettes can be read as a travesty of all those books reaching for the American dream, where heroes and heroines either marry successfully, or make their own millions, or have the whole process ironised and turn hideous. Lorelei's picaresque narration of her friend Dorothy's journey through life is rich in authorial parentheses, inverted priorities and great gags, the greatest of which is that Dorothy isn't really interested in millionaires after all. An incidental joy is that Loos avoids the loosely-structured story becoming a mere excuse for wise-cracks; Dorothy makes the jokes, and Lorelei fails to get them. But this is for the best because, as Dorothy observes, "no girl wants to laugh all of the time".

Lope de Vega

born Madrid 1562; died Madrid 1635

Love has this one excuse

For all the ills it works, that it is love.

LA VIUDA VALENCIANA

EVEN IN A LIFE SPENT without such diverse activity, a literary output as vast as that of Lope de Vega would be unbelievable. A mere 500 of his plays survive – there have been reckoned to be some 1,800 – although many of these are fragments only, and of those extant, no more than 341 can be attributed to him with much certainty. He wrote these at an amazing speed (he spent just a day composing each of at least a hundred of them); this will have given him more time to be the lover, soldier, priest and poet, in rôles as dramatic as any he wrote for the stage.

His plays are counted as comedies, but he deliberately mixed genres, refusing to distinguish between tragedy and comedy, or noble and vulgar. As with his poetry (which permeates the plays), he combines learning with folky wisdom. The dramas also avoid Aristotle's structures: he settled for a three-act form, and thereafter anything goes so long as it's pacey. They include thrillers, scripted for a wide public, and some for pickier audiences, as well as religious plays, based on Bible stories or lives of the saints. Nowadays most interest centres on his history plays. Many of these pieces are tales of vengeance, and the satisfaction of honour, often with violent conclusions. All display a natural ear for verse, especially for the folk lyric, which was to distinguish him as a poet.

His poetry shows the influence of **Petrarch**,

and the theme of love dominates. He can treat it rapturously and tragically as well as savagely, dwelling on lost romance as readily as he can denounce a dead man he has cuckolded. He shows the same unrestrained energies in verse as in drama, tossing off epics and even mock epics, most notably *La Gatomaquia* – The Battle of the Cats.

In much of his work Lope de Vega's views on life emerge as conventional, and he writes characters who are more "types" than wholly created entities. Still his success as a dramatist overshadowed that of all his contemporaries, and explains why we seldom hear of **Cervantes**' plays. In prose, Lope de Vega was eclipsed; but his romances *La Dorotea*, on an early love, and the classical *La Arcadia*, stand as models of their kind.

Lorca

FEDERICO GARCÍA   **born Fuente Vaqueros 1898; died Granada 1936**

In the living morning

I longed to be myself.

A heart.

And in the late evening

I longed to be my voice.

A nightingale.

Soul,

turn the colour orange!

Soul,

turn the colour of love!

LITTLE SONG OF FIRST DESIRE

LORCA REMAINS ONE of Spain's most cherished poets. His deep social concern, his vivid sense of imagery and his keen ear for music made him the most vital of writers; and yet that vitality owes much to the constant presence of death. Lecturing in Argentina in 1933, he said that great art needs death.

As a child, he would pick up songs immediately, and later in life would forget that he hadn't devised them himself. Recordings of Lorca reciting his own verse, or playing his or his friend Manuel de Falla's music at the piano, help us understand the natural drive of his work. He favoured spontaneity, which gave him sympathies with the Surrealists. He was influenced by Dali, and the movement's impact on him emerges in *Poet in New York*, where an awe of machinery matches his lyrical power; but he never belonged to any school of poetry.

Still, he absorbed a wide range of cultural sounds, from the pulse of **Walt Whitman** (hymned in a famous ode) to the unsentimentalised gypsies of his native Andalusia; *The Divan of the Tamarit* adopts Persian *ghazals*. He was always eager that his poetry struck home, and he reached his widest audiences in the theatre. His late folk tragedies are the best known, and use bold imagery and simple song to lethal effect – in *Yerma*, the heroine wonders why she cannot conceive, to the strains of a lullaby.

In Republican Spain, he directed La Barraca Theatre Company, where his then-illicit passion for the secretary resulted in the incredible *Sonnets of Dark Love*. His prominence as a liberal made him one of the Fascists' first targets in the Spanish Civil War. He was captured, driven into his local countryside, shot and thrown into an unmarked grave at the age of 38.

Lowell

ROBERT

born Boston, Massachusetts 1917; died New York 1977

the corpse of the insect lives embalmed in
honey,
prays that its perishable work live long
enough for the sweet-tooth bear to
desecrate –
this open book ... my open coffin.

READING MYSELF

ROBERT LOWELL'S POETRY seems reserved, remote even. His voice has the controlled tones of the classically-educated New Englander: it rings with mythological echoes and (in the earlier work) polished rhymes, but is always without flashiness. But he

was never the mouthpiece of the Establishment. In private pieces he can be confessional and introspective (but not depressed – depression could stop him from writing altogether); in public ones bitingly critical of authority: "And the Republic summons Ike/ the mausoleum in her heart".

Lowell's public actions included serving a term in prison during the Second World War as a conscientious objector and, in 1965, withdrawing his acceptance of Lyndon Johnson's invitation to the White House. As in the lines quoted above, the strength of his statements comes from his training, particularly with John Crowe Ransom at Kenyon University, in "the high discipline, for putting on the full armour of the past". Much of his finest work, in the later volumes (most notably the slim *Near the Ocean*), is in translating or imitating Latin and Greek. This gives him an acute sense of mortality, especially when contemplating the destiny of his poems; but he makes this borrowed diction his own. It informs his expression of religious crisis, almost as much as his ear for last lines. His cadences can seem throwaway, but never weightless: after describing a civic monument in *For the Union Dead*, he concludes "Everywhere, giant finned cars nose forward like fish;/ a savage servility/ slides by on grease". It is incidental, but damning.

As a worker, Lowell was a perfectionist. He agonised over line-endings, especially when he opted for the free verse of the books from *For the Union Dead* onwards, and achieved his easiest grace in the unrhymed sonnets of *History*. Here, he applies the anecdotal style of the poetry he had written about his family in *Life Studies* to figures of the past – a gesture which makes existence seem all the more fleeting.

Lucretius

born Rome? Campania? 99 BC? 94 BC? died c. 55 BC

Sweet, when the sea swells to the

turbulent winds,

to stand on earth and watch

another's toil;

not through delight in someone

else's struggle –

it's sweet to see the problems

you don't have.

ON THE NATURE OF THINGS, BOOK II

MAJOR WORKS

On the Nature of Things

LUCRETIUS IS NEARLY AS important as a philosopher as he is as a poet. In his extraordinary poem, *On the Nature of Things*, he takes the teachings of his hero Epicurus, and renders them in Latin verse.

He was writing in hexameter, the standard Latin and Greek metre, at a time before **Virgil** had perfected it; and because Latin has fewer words than Greek, he coined new ones himself. This is unsurprising, given the complicated nature of his arguments, many of them scientific, and the rigours of his form: only half the words of his language fit into it.

Like **Callimachus**, he could claim he was attempting a project never yet undertaken, and treading the Muses' untrodden paths. His poetic skills he considered were the drop of honey meant to make medicine less unpleasant. For all the apparent grimness of Lucretius' own dosage – he believed that the soul died with the body, and that the laws of physics preclude love (which he describes sensually

before censuring it) – his purpose was nonetheless to comfort. If the soul will not survive us, we need not worry about it – and worry is the one thing Epicureans want to avoid.

His poem is a verse compression of the arguments about matter taking place in antiquity. He rejects the theories of the Monists, who tried to posit a universe made of some single stuff, and explains instead the activity of atoms, which move around enough to provide a model of mankind's free will. The poem was much admired by Cicero, who was of the opposing, Stoic camp. But Lucretius' own ethical code, which found more comfort in human tolerance than divine compassion, must have appealed to the statesman for its firm rooting in reason.

McCarthy

Every word she writes is a lie, including 'and' and 'the'

OF LILLIAN HELLMAN,
ON NATIONAL TELEVISION.

MARY MCCARTHY'S MOST valued quality has been her honesty, or rather, her bluntness. She made her name more as a critic than a writer of fiction, and became famous for championing unfashionable authors at the expense of fashionable ones. She disliked pretension, and the coteries which would surround experimental dramatists. Her interest in theatre came from an early wish to perform: she was the first to admit that she had no acting talent at all. In self-judgments like this she showed every bit as much candour as she could aim at others. She made many notable enemies, not least Lillian Hellman, the wife of **Dashiell Hammett**: the remark quoted above resulted in a libel action. The injured party died before the case came to court; McCarthy would have preferred vindication to her enemy's demise.

She exercises this in stories and novels with a strong autobiographical line, as well as in actual memoirs. Her first collection was *The Company She Keeps*. It concentrates on Meg and her political ambit, whose involvement in the Trotskyite circles of the thirties resembles McCarthy's; the same is true of the character's sexual intrigues, and a willingness to discuss them openly. This anticipates further appearances of McCarthy figures, notably the Vassar-educated rebel in *The Group*. In *The Oasis* she is taking her progressive friends with a greater pinch of salt. She always comes across as the romantic one, and later remembered pointing out that in a room full of

Communist activists, she was the only one who knew it was Valentine's Day.

While she could be humorous at her own expense, she could be earnest too, recalling the miseries of living with a great aunt after losing her affectionate parents (they died in the 'flu epidemic that followed the First World War) at the same time as satirising her Catholic upbringing. Her plain-speaking humanity found its most serious purpose in criticising American involvement in Vietnam.

McCullers

CARSON **born Columbus, Georgia 1917; died Nyark, New York State 1967**

And somehow every lover ... feels in his soul that his love is a solitary thing. He comes to know a new, strange loneliness and it is this knowledge which makes him suffer. So there is only one thing for the lover to do. He must house his love within himself as best he can; he must create for himself a whole new inward world – a world intense and strange, complete in himself.

THE BALLAD OF THE SAD CAFÉ

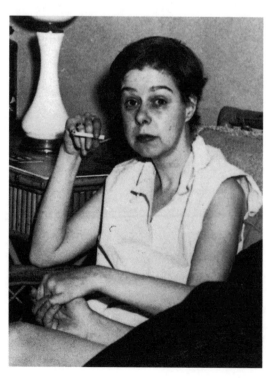

CARSON MCCULLERS NEVER fitted into her home town of Columbus, Georgia. Her unconventional behaviour and relationships with those she loved regardless of gender scandalised the community long after she left it, and even after her death. So as a writer, she can immerse herself in a Southern small town, while retaining a prophet's kind of detachment. In that exemplary work, *The Ballad of the Sad Café*, she plumbs the profundity of her theme, love, while observing the action of her tale as might a curious neighbour, describing the landscape, the food and the surrounding characters with a familiarity that charms.

For McCullers, love is an unlikely force. It is animated more by solitude than desire, as in *The Heart is a Lonely Hunter*, where a deaf-mute awakens the solitary souls around her, or in *Reflections in a Golden Eye*, where military men confront their deepest needs. If this seems a pessimistic view of love, still, in McCullers' writing, it redeems the outcast, in a way she describes with a lyricism to match **Plato**'s treatment of it in the *Phaedrus*. And if people's passions are unpredictable, her narrative remains unshocked. This makes her prose a faithful recounting of surprising events happening around a mysterious, unaccountable core. *The Ballad of the Sad Café* has the story-teller giving the whole a song-like quality, with the last verse echoing the first. Her style is direct and economical, sometimes pointing the meaning of a scene, sometimes just reporting it. We are left with characters who have formed new, unanticipated attachments, supported by a commentary which manages to portray love as an even more all-embracing phenomenon than we might have contemplated before.

Maeterlinck

MAURICE   **born Ghent 1862; died Nice 1949**

Oh Lord, my earthly cravings will

At last expire within my heart!

Lord, let your radiance impart

Light to the hothouses of ill...

TEMPTATIONS

MAURICE MAETERLINCK fell under the spell of Symbolism while studying law at Ghent University, and though his earliest works are books of poems betraying the influence of **Mallarmé** and **Verlaine**, his distinct contribution to the movement was on the stage.

This was an extraordinary step to take. For to attempt the representation of abstract ideas by naming real things is one thing in verse, but to place it in a theatre, where all is to be seen and heard, is quite another. This was Maeterlinck's project, and he undertook it with sonorous dialogue and fairy-tale plots which combine to produce an unreal quality very suggestive of music. His best-known play is still more famous for just that: *Pelléas et Mélisande* has drawn musical responses from Debussy, Schönberg, Fauré and Sibelius.

Maeterlinck conceived his plays as musical wholes. In fact, it was his view that *Macbeth* is not so much a play as a poem and that the unexpected diction it includes is deliberately unlike natural speech. In his dramas, every effect contributes to the symbolic world conceived in a single mind, rather than a world which emerges from the actions of the characters. This extends to the exits and entries on the stage, and even the time-scale of a piece. Developed characters are not what we expect from a Symbolist play, and here the author doesn't shrink from a comparison with puppet shows. If anything, the lifeless movement of those on stage represents the playwright's belief that we have no free will whatsoever, and no guiding spirituality either. Although he has little in common with them in terms of style, still Maeterlinck's experimentation did much to prepare the way for the likes of **Ionesco** and **Pinter**.

MAJOR WORKS

PLAYS

Princess Maleine (1889)

The Blind (1890)

Pélleas et Mélisande (1892)

Monna Vanna (1902)

Mailer

NORMAN

born Long Branch, New Jersey 1923

It had always been the same, love was love, one could find it with anyone, one could find it anywhere. It was just that you could never keep it. Not unless you were ready to die for it, dear friend.

AN AMERICAN DREAM

NORMAN MAILER SEEMS to write with his fists, and he can sting like a bee. His long interest in boxing is a reflection of the combative spirit he brings to his work. He is unafraid of critics, even suggesting that some of them should be "punched out". Such toughness has served him well in the solitary stances he has taken on a wide range of issues, most notably war, sex and politics.

Most of his works are either autobiographical or written out of a deeply-felt personal animus: when he is writing about the Vietnam war (in *Why Are We in Vietnam?*, for example, or *The Armies of the Night*, a memoir of the march on the Pentagon in protest at the war), he is not writing for writing's sake alone, however admirable his prose. And although his writing can contain war heroism and violence, he writes against war – despite seeing violence as inevitable in American society. This is something he exposes in *The Executioner's Song*, a Capote-like study of a man on Death Row who welcomes his own death. In *An American Dream*, the violence is domestic, although a public figure is responsible. The book is notable for containing American literature's first known description of heterosexual anal sex.

Mailer's first success was *The Naked and the Dead*, which drew on his own war experience to find, in the army, a model of his nation's problems. So acclaimed a debut seemed hard to follow, but although he remained his own greatest single theme, he was capable of examining that from a number of different angles, too. He is unembarrassed by his attachment to a wide range of subject matter, from a hagiography of Marilyn Monroe (not alone among works that have riled feminist commentators) to his recent psychological identification with Picasso and first-person telling of the life of Christ. This last especially has proved that Mailer has kept his ability to shock into his seventies.

Mallarmé

STÉPHANE

born Paris 1842; died Valvins 1898

I know that distant from this night, the
  earth
Casts unaccustomed awe with a great flair
under the hideous times, which blot
it less.
Growing or shrinking, space its own
  worth
Spins in this boredom vile fires to profess
The genius of a flaming, festive star.

WINDOWS

MALLARMÉ'S POETRY is a quest for beauty. The poet is aware of the inability of words to express the truly beautiful, which exists beyond things; so what we have in the poems is a yearning for the rose beyond the rose, the light beyond the window, the world beyond worldliness.

This accounts for the extraordinary style of his verse. It strives to go beyond ordinary language, and packs grammatical complexity into only a few syllables. Mallarmé strives to represent the essence of objects; and just as it is impossible to describe a smell without reference to other smells, so he introduces other images to illuminate the things he presents.

This made him, along with **Verlaine**, the founder of the Symbolist style of poetry. Early on he was influenced by **Baudelaire**, to whose strict verse rules he would always conform; but where Baudelaire would evoke disgust to explore the idea of evil, Mallarmé, would use morbid images to throw into relief the poetic qualities that transcend it. For this, he was at once admired by the younger "decadent" poets, while remaining a leading member of the Parnassian school, a group including Verlaine and Gautier, dedicated to classical purity and elegance.

His work is very difficult to interpret, but always gives the impression, in Pater's phrase, of "aspiring to the condition of music". His poem *Saint* speaks of music by describing a painting, so even the music is silent and inexpressible; in his most famous piece, *The Afternoon of a Faun*, a flute solo takes over where words seem to fail. On reading it, one can understand Mallarmé's gratitude for the shimmering Debussy orchestral prelude these lines inspired, even though at first he characteristically doubted that there could be any way to express his insights.

MAJOR WORKS

The Afternoon of a Faun
  (1876)

The Ancient Gods (1880)

Poetries (1887)

Poems in Prose (1891)

Verse and Prose (1893)

Divagations (1897)

The roll of the dice will
  never abolish chance (1897)

Malraux

ANDRÉ

born Paris 1901; died Paris 1976

Art and death are all I hope to rediscover here.

ANTIMEMOIRS

WHEN ANDRÉ MALRAUX WAS WORKING as an archeologist in Cambodia, he was arrested by the colonial service for revolutionary activities. By the end of his career, he would be the Minister for Culture in Charles de Gaulle's cabinet with the specific task of persuading the colonies that they should remain French. Malraux's journey in between, however, was not the normal shift from left to right of the angry young man adopted by the establishment.

Throughout his life he had chronicled uprisings and battles and taken part in many of them: in 1936 he was procuring arms for the Republicans in Spain; in 1939 he joined the French Tank Corps; in 1940 he escaped his German captors and fled to unoccupied France. Throughout, his actions were considered those of a Communist, but despite early Socialist leanings, nothing could have been further from the truth. Malraux was appalled by some of the Left's claims about their activities with the Resistance during the war, by what he considered to be their real ambitions, and most of all by Stalin. For Malraux, one dogma was as bad as another, and to accept unquestioningly was death.

In his books, action takes place in the teeth of such death. The First World War, that marked his adolescence, made him consider God dead. From then on he put his faith in friendships. This is most apparent in *Man's Estate*, Malraux's account of Chiang Kai Shek's battle with the Communists in which feelings preside over politics. Similarly, it is camaraderie which prevails briefly over the Falangists in *Days of Hope*.

This made him seem like an Existentialist, as did his phrase, "A man is what he does". But Malraux went deeper into the brain to confront the trivia that sways people from rational decisions. Ultimately he was concerned with results and permanence. It was this, more than anything, which led him to dig in Cambodia and use his Ministerial brief to preserve buildings in Paris, making him a latter-day Victor Hugo with even more political clout. He found permanence in art, architecture and even in empire; and this makes his art criticism as vital a part of his *oeuvre* as his novels and memoirs. All these works can dart from scene to scene, or subject to subject, as necessity dictates. They sustain life and survive us.

Mandelshtam

OSIP   **born Warsaw, 1891; died Vladivostok 1938**

O indigence at the root of our lives,

how poor is the language of happiness!

Everything's happened before and will

*   happen again,*

but still the moment of each meeting is

*   sweet.*

TRISTIA, TR. BROWN AND MERWIN

FOR MANDELSHTAM, poetry was a matter of life and death. Its pleasure surpasses the praise it accrues; it is as vital as bread. In the end, it would kill him.

For he published a savage denunciation of Stalin in 1934, with the concluding line, "He rolls the executions on his tongue like berries". It led to his arrest. After a second apprehension, he was transported from Moscow to Vladivostok, where he is said to have died, supposedly of heart failure, in a gulag. Only recently have even these details emerged, thanks to his wife Nadia.

For so pure a poet, he was full of a sense of his own times. He had lived through the Revolution, and wrote many poems expressing a change of the ages. If the authorities already had cause to deem him counter-revolutionary, it was because his verse appeared to hark back to an earlier age, and lament its passing. But his work contained this element even before the Revolution, which he had greeted with enthusiasm at the time. His first collection, *Stone*, often talks of twilight, and invokes a lost Classical world. He writes of Caesar's demise, and cites the unfulfilled longings of **Ovid**'s elegies; his reflections on St. Petersburg make it clear that he does not live in a Golden Age.

With **Akhmatova** and Gumilev, he founded the Acmeist school of poetry; its interest in the reality of things, rather than their symbols and ciphers, extends to Mandelshtam's idea of words. In his mouth, they become entities in themselves, and he could ask, "What's meaning but vanity? A word is a sound /one of the handmaidens of the seraphim". This sense of their quiddity, organised in restrained and formal stanzas, makes them so essential.

MAJOR WORKS

Stone (1913)

Tristia (1922)

Poems (1928)

Mann

HEINRICH

born Lübeck 1871; died Los Angeles 1950

Each of us is as nothing, but massed in ranks as neo-Teutons... we taper up like a pyramid to a point at the top where Power itself stands, graven and dazzling...

MAN OF STRAW

HEINRICH MANN'S REPUTATION has long been eclipsed by his brother **Thomas Mann**. It was not always that way, though. Heinrich had once attracted more attention for his fuller treatment of decadence, and Thomas always looked up to him as his big brother figure. They disagreed publicly about Germany's actions during the First World War, and about the use of the novel for political ends. But this was because they shared much of the same subject matter, especially the function of art. Both explore its capacity for good and evil, but Heinrich examined it in more social terms, disdaining bourgeois culture and seeing art as a weapon to combat authoritarianism.

This he did in his two most famous novels, *The Blue Angel* and *The Man of Straw*. The former introduces Professor Unrat, a morbid teacher whose intolerance of class-room disruptions leads him to megalomania, while the latter depicts similar despotism at an imperial level. His hatred of dictators made him one of the first to leave Germany when Hitler became Chancellor in 1933. He headed a group of *émigré* writers in Paris until the city fell to the Nazis in 1940, after which he escaped to California.

Ultimately, apart from the two novels mentioned above, Heinrich Mann is remembered more for his discussion of what a novel should achieve than, say, his characterisation of prose style. His essays on **Flaubert** and **Zola** show him trying to reconcile life with its representation. He practised this most fully in *The Little Town* in which he depicted a theatre company in a small Italian community and showed that while man may be a political animal, he can become more than just that.

Mann

THOMAS

born Lübeck 1875; died Zürich 1955

We can only with difficulty imagine such a thing; and yet it will be, and be the natural thing: an art without anguish, psychologically healthy, not solemn, unsadly confiding, an art perdu with humanity.

DOCTOR FAUSTUS

THOMAS MANN'S IMMENSE GIFT to our times has been his unrelenting, peerless enquiry into the rôle and plight of the artist in a sick age.

He achieved this in books charged with ideas, and a Germanic reverence for all that is pure and noble. But although he was an avowedly patriotic, establishment figure during the First World War, he was already the prophet of decline, in *Buddenbrooks*, his astonishingly precocious study of a family in long-term decay, and in *Death in Venice*, where an esteemed German writer falls for a boy in cholera-stricken Italy.

But the war and the persistence of his brother **Heinrich Mann** shook his conservatism, and altered the course of his work then in progress, *The Magic Mountain*. With its new insights into a diseased Europe, the book assumed a modern wisdom, won its author the Nobel Prize, and has been acclaimed as one of the greatest novels ever.

But soon the Nazis would be burning his books, and destroying everything. Mann found his notions of harmony in art unable to face the terror around him. He turned increasingly to allegory, pleading for tolerance in exile with *Joseph and his Brothers*.

In *Doctor Faustus*, he summoned all his powers to confront evil in its purest form. A diffident classical philologist offers us the biography of his late friend, a composer who yields to the Satanic. All notions of form, and all inclinations towards love, are impotent in the face of the ensuing mental and international chaos which engulf so controlled a work.

Mann's last work, *The Confessions of Felix Krull*, tackles artifice with the hilarious recollections of a charming impostor; but even he must conclude, "The most hopeful situation in life is when things are going so badly for us that they can't possibly go worse". If we cannot avoid sharing such pessimism, at least this joyous book shows us how Mann's art can impart delight as well as despair.

MAJOR WORKS

Stories of a Lifetime (1898)

Buddenbrooks (1901)

Tonio Kröger (1903)

Royal Highness (1909)

Death in Venice (1911)

Master and Hound (1918)

The Magic Mountain (1924)

Mario and the Magician (1930)

Joseph and his Brothers comprising The Tales of Jacob (1934)

The Young Joseph (1935)

Joseph in Egypt (1938)

Joseph the Provider (1943)

Doctor Faustus (1947)

The Confessions of Felix Krull (1954)

Mansfield

KATHERINE   **born New Zealand 1888; died Fontainebleu 1923**

Her dark coat fell open, and her white throat emerged – all her soft, young body in the blue dress – was like a flower that was just emerging from its dark bud.

THE YOUNG GIRL

'The sun's out,' said Josephine, as though it really mattered.

THE DAUGHTERS OF THE LATE COLONEL

KATHERINE MANSFIELD'S OUTPUT was slight. She wrote in sudden bursts towards the end of her life when she knew she was dying of tuberculosis. She stopped altogether in 1922 as she prepared for the end.

Her stories are often slight in themselves. They avoid violence and tragedy – in *Je Ne Parle Pas Français*, for example, a character appears to have shot himself, but turns out to have left more discreetly – and yet like their author, they have scant regard for conventions. Many reflect episodes in her life, or whole phases of it. Her first collection, *In a German Pension*, comes from the time she spent in Bavaria where she had a miscarriage. Critics have found echoes of real-life affairs and domestic dramas throughout her work, which seem to reveal much about her marriage to John Middleton Murray. He strove to publish and publicise her work, but guarded her image jealously and appears to have censored her material.

She was born in New Zealand, but educated in England and after returning home, sought to return to London as soon as possible. She shows a keen ear for the oddities of English upper-class diction, which sometimes reads as caricature; but her sensitivity to what her speakers are actually thinking, and the smoothness with which she combines different idioms for different points of view, redeem all this. A reunion in London with her brother made her long for home again; his death in the First World War made this more intense. She went on to evoke the New Zealand of her childhood in stories concerning a girl called Kezia. As ever, her treatment of girlhood has a delicacy arising from sharp observation and a surprising response to detail; the sudden shifts of focus and mood almost demand that her pieces be read as poetry.

Manzoni

ALESSANDRO

born Milan 1785; died Milan 1873

Poets are the ones who go in search of other documents, of whatever type, in order to enrich or even shape their subject when historical details are lacking. They are well pleased if they succeed in giving a fuller idea of the historical fact being represented; still better if they succeed in offering a new idea, and one different from current opinion.

ON THE HISTORICAL NOVEL

BY FAR THE MOST famous book Manzoni wrote was *The Betrothed*. One might call it the great Italian novel.

It is a historical novel and helped make Italian history itself. It was an immensely powerful text in Italy's resurgent nationalism; but rather than cast the Austrians (who were then occupying the country) as oppressors, Manzoni went back to the Thirty Years' War, when the area around his native Milan was under Spanish control and the Church and the aristocracy appeared to be even more corrupt than they might have seemed in 1827. But faith provides a refuge for the heroes, as it had for Manzoni, who became a devout Catholic in 1810 (to please the wife to whom he would become devoted). It is the Friar in *The Betrothed* who calls divine retribution down upon the novel's villain Don Roderigo, whose crime is his unrelenting lust for the peasant girl Lucia. The story follows her flight with her fiancé Renzo. Historical events part them, as communities fall to war and the plague of 1629-39. In the end, though, their love survives all their trials.

Manzoni gives us the book as though he has rewritten it, replacing a historian's commentary with his own sentiments. The ploy gives the project a sense of the author's commitment to his subject, but also leaves him once removed from the action. This brings his characters more completely to life: he makes them speak colloquially, in contrast to the epic language his model **Scott** gives the Highlanders in the Waverley novels. He wanted the work to remain vital to a wide audience, and for years worked painstakingly on a version in the increasingly dominant Tuscan dialect, with even greater success than the original had enjoyed.

MAJOR WORKS

Sacred Hymns (1815)

Observations on Catholic Morality (1819)

Ode on the Death of Napoleon (1821)

Adelchi (1822)

The Betrothed (1827)

233

Marivaux

PIERRE

born Paris 1688; died Paris 1763

I begged reason to help me, but in vain;

Her distant cure made love a greater strain.

She showed me my mad passion, and
*   I saw,*

Blushing with love, I only loved
*   it more.*

ANNIBAL

MARIVAUX HAD BEEN a law student and endured financial ruin. His early attempts at making a living in literature met with little success: in parodies of **Homer**, prose fiction, and classical tragedies, he failed to find his own style. But as he frequented the theatres and salons of a Paris still obsessed with **Molière**, he found himself caught up in the debates between the Ancients and Moderns – those who clung to the classics and those who found them outmoded. Marivaux sided with the latter. He declared that he preferred to "sit on the back benches with that small band of original authors than in pride of place with the numerous stock of literary apes."

He was an innovator. His language was more conversational, his co-operation with actors more extensive and the troupe itself refreshing. He worked with Italians, whose return to France after banishment by Louis XIV did much to revive the flagging French comedy. He was never afraid to put philosophical ideas on the stage, using remote locations to reverse social conventions: in his plays, slaves change places with masters, and men with women. While his largely autobiographical prose fictions would aim to record their times, his drama would disparage reason as a force in a way less possible in Molière's time. In Marivaux's comedies, love holds sway; as in **La Fayette's** work, it happens at first sight, and poses problems as if from nowhere. His most distinct plot feature came from the obstacles those around lovers strew in their path - again, these could be social concerns, like the problem of rich marrying poor in *False Confidences*, perhaps his most famous piece.

Markandaya

KAMALA   **born South India 1924**

Fear, constant companion of the peasant. Despair, ready to engulf him should he falter.

NECTAR IN A SIEVE

KAMALA MARKANDAYA'S NOVELS offer the Indian perspective on the contrasts between the new and the old, the East and the West, the urban and the rural. Her sensitivities are such that she tries to understand characters for whom readers might naturally have less sympathy, from the British

behaving desperately in the last days of the Raj, to the National Front activists who menace the hero of *Nowhere Man* in South London.

But it is India itself which commands the real compassion. Her first novel, *Nectar in a Sieve*, takes its title from **Coleridge**. Here, Markandaya's narrator reflects on her life as a starving peasant woman having lived all her life in a small village; but with the natural cycle of harshness and promise the land offers. The devastating effects of Western industrialisation on India appear in *Shalimar*, the story of a remote fishing community which becomes the site of an international holiday resort.

The uneasy relationship between India and the West (especially Britain) informs Markandaya's accounts of personal contact too; in *Some Inner Fury* a Brahmin woman falls for an Englishman in 1942, when allegiances between the Hindustani and British causes in the war were at their most complex. The story is reworked in *Possession*, in which a fashionable London woman romanticises of an Indian goatherd's creativity.

Markandaya's most ambitious project so far has been *The Golden Honeycomb*, a dynastic tale spanning from 1870 to the outbreak of the First World War. Its short episodes, swings of angle, and large range of characters all seem to anticipate **Vikram Seth**'s attempt to write the great Indian novel in English, and to continue demonstrating that the subcontinent provides some of the finest handlings of the English language today.

Marlowe

CHRISTOPHER

born Canterbury 1564; died Deptford 1593

Stand still, you ever-moving

   stars of heaven,

That time may cease and midnight

   never come.

Fair nature's eye, rise, rise again,

   and make

Perpetual day; or let this hour be but

A year, a month, a week, a natural day,

That Faustus may repent and

   save his soul.

DOCTOR FAUSTUS

CHEAT, LIBERTINE, possible murderer and definite spy, Marlowe was the finest composer of blank verse until **Shakespeare**, one of the greatest English dramatists ever and, as a translator of **Ovid**, will never be equalled.

His stagecraft relies as much on characterisation as on language. Although his creations are often seen as fulfilling unimaginable ambitions, Marlowe can set them up merely to shrink them to size in a way that anticipates **Brecht**. His first play, *Tamburlaine the Great*, written when the author was 18, presents a ruthless world-conqueror in the final stages of an illness induced by blasphemy, fulminating against his unrealised conquests, moments before his doctors reveal what the hero's urine sample portends. But this humiliation is little compared to the king's horrifying death in *Edward II*: even the hero's weaknesses

serve to expose his rivals as less patriotic than heartless, and the text indicates that the manner of his destruction would be faithful to Marlowe's historical sources, and apparent to the audience.

The Jew of Malta, which provided **Shakespeare** with a model for Shylock, is similarly paradoxical. For Barrabas appears with all the traits one would expect from an anti-semitic age, and yet the hypocritical Christians surrounding him outstrip his vices, while the Jewish daughter emerges as the only decent character. But vanity receives its ultimate damnation in *Doctor Faustus*, Marlowe's masterpiece, which provided the basis for **Goethe**'s mighty work. The hero sells his soul for knowledge and power, but uses it to play pranks on the Pope and dies as little more than a prosperous court conjurer. But this serves Marlowe's genius for evoking pity and terror further, as he makes this non-entity's descent into hell, with his last-minute pleas for salvation, all the more human and harrowing.

Márquez

GABRIEL GARCÍA

born Aracataca 1927

The name [Arcade of the Scribes] dated from colonial times, when the taciturn scribes in the vests and false cuffs first began to sit there, waiting for a poor man's fee to write all kinds of documents: memoranda of complaints of petition, legal testimony, cards of congratulation or condolence, love letters appropriate to any stage of the affair.

LOVE IN THE TIME OF CHOLERA

HOW DID GARCÍA MÁRQUEZ acquire his unique and spell-binding way of writing? There are several possible answers. One is from his grandmother, who would tell him fantastic stories as a boy as if they were true – a later reading of **Kafka**'s *Metamorphoses* apparently surprised him less than it has most read-ers. Another might be his work as a journalist, giving him real authority when he describes impossible events.

But these cannot account completely for his wild imagination, his controlled style, or the atmosphere he conveys. Story-tellers have allowed nature to comment on or influence their tales, but here, nature acts *contra naturam*. His technique is known as 'Magical Realism', and has become widely imitated.

One Hundred Years of Solitude brought this to technique to its widest, most rapt audience. The book narrates the foundation myth of a South American community called Macondo, and plots the town's decline through the intermingled histories of characters and situations which seem to arrive from nowhere. The setting may owe much of its remote-ness to the author's home town of Aracataca, and its plot to public life in his native Colombia; but its river-like structure, its introduction of fabulous episodes which have no further impact on the story once over, and (consequently) its view of memory, open these themes to the whole of human experience.

He is one of the great writers on the nature of love: its durability over ages, taboos, nations, and death. *Love in the Time of Cholera* renders this at the highest pitch of pathos, as a man returns to woo the woman he loves, on the death of her husband, after a lifetime of self-imposed banishment. The author's work has a passionate concern with the public busi-ness of South American politics and history, especial-ly in the story of Bolívar's last journey, *The General in His Labyrinth*, which he refused to publish so long as Colonel Pinochet still held office in Chile. He consid-ers writing of love a "duty": it is as hard to fault his priorities as his prose.

Marvell

ANDREW   born Winestead, Yorkshire 1621; died London 1678

Ye glowworms, whose officious flame

To wandering mowers shows the way,

That in the night have lost their aim,

And after foolish fires do stray;

Your courteous lights in vain you waste,

Since Juliana here is come,

For she my mind hath so displaced

That I shall never find my home.

THE MOWER TO THE GLOWWORMS

IN HIS TIME, ANDREW MARVELL was more highly regarded as a satirist, pamphleteer and public servant than the lyric poet we have come to know. After flirting with Catholicism in his youth, he worked enthusiastically in Cromwell's administration after the English Civil War. **Milton's** recommendation that Marvell become his assistant as Latin Secretary raises the prospect that the two might have shared an office with **Dryden** during what must have been the Civil Service's Golden Age. On Cromwell's death, however, which he lamented in verse, Marvell grew disaffected with the regime, welcomed the Restoration, and served as MP for Hull until his death.

His verse shows a similar ability to move with the times. *An Horatian Ode upon Cromwell's Return from Ireland* is typical: it is a piece of propaganda invoking the Protector's conquests, while allowing dignity to the vanquished Charles I in death. Like almost everything that Marvell wrote, it is in the classical mode. His facility for writing in Latin and Greek shows in his English verse, where his word-order and forms resemble ancient ones. His idylls show the influence of Theocritus, especially in the excellent Mower poems, while his totally memorable *To His Coy Mistress* extemporises on themes found in **Catullus** for one.

His material may be antique, but he preserves its original freshness. He can make tight rhyme schemes sound like naturally-rendered speech, seldom better than when presenting a Nymph lamenting her pet faun, breaking her tripping eight-syllable lines into sob-like units. His versatility is everywhere, and this poem is far removed from his state odes, his epigrams written as ambassador to Sweden, Denmark and Russia, or his lines *The Character of Holland*, full of war-time jibes at the resurgent United Provinces, which proved useful to Dutch campaigns under both Cromwell (in 1651) and Charles II (1665).

Maugham

SOMERSET   **born Paris 1874; died Nice 1965**

I have an idea that some men are born out of their due place. Accident has cast them amid certain surroundings, but they have always a nostalgia for a home they know not. They are strangers in their birthplace, and the leafy lanes they have known from childhood or the populous streets in which they have played, remain but a place of passage.

THE MOON AND SIXPENCE

AS A WRITER, MAUGHAM hoped to consider himself one of the best of the second-rate writers of his day. If this makes his ambition sound limited, he was committed enough to his craft. In fact, his modesty enabled him to create the sort of narrator who could tell the stories of fictionalised first-raters, geniuses like the painter Strickland in *The Moon and Sixpence*, whose story is based on the career of Paul Gauguin and is told by an often uncomprehending friend. Likewise, *Cakes and Ale* is a literary biography within a novel, which Maugham denied was inspired by **Thomas Hardy**'s life. Both examine the private sin that can lie behind an artist's public success; in Strickland's case, there is no remorse.

But an earlier book first brought Maugham acclaim. This time the artist he was discussing more resembled himself. *Of Human Bondage* has a hero whose education is the same as the author's (public school in Kent, Heidelberg University and then medical school in London), and who shares Maugham's experiences of artistic awakening in Paris. The account of Philip's formative experiences alarmed early readers with its open handling of sexual obsession and its macabre consequences.

He is praised for his understanding of human relationships, which emerges more clearly in his short stories. They have a Saki-like bleakness, and present a range of manipulating, vengeful characters, often operating in remote areas of a decaying British Empire. In his time, his capacity for offering audiences 'well-made' works of art was best evident in his plays.

Maupassant

GUY DE **born Miromesnil, Normandy 1850; died Passy 1893**

But yes, she had failed him in her tenderness, failed in pious respect. To him, she had become irreproachable, as all mothers must be to their children. If the fury it had raised almost reached hatred, it was because she had wronged him more criminally even than she had wronged his father.

A LIFE

MAUPASSANT WROTE SIX NOVELS, but is better known for his short stories, of which he wrote some 300. His work in this genre was adopted by **Zola** as representing the aims of the Naturalist movement, and Maupassant contributed one of his earliest, most famous stories, *Boule de Suif,* to the collection Zola edited under the title *Les Soirées de Médan* and and presented to **Flaubert** as a homage to the latter and the influence of Realism.

In fact, Maupassant owed more to Flaubert. They had become related by Maupassant's marriage, which their friendship outlasted. In both their works, they show a strong attachment to their native Normandy. Many of Maupassant's tales depict Norman peasant life, as well as drawing on his own experiences as an administrator during the Franco-Prussian War of 1870-1 and his subsequent work as a civil servant. He avoids sentimentality, and prefers detail. His craft demands that he be economical, and lengthy psychological accounts of a character's motivations do not suit his technique. Instead we see people's actions, and the consequences, which are the more pathetic for being understated. Events lead to tragedy, rather than human attempts to influence them. *A Piece of String* offers a fine example: a peasant dies in disgrace after his neighbours accuse him of finding and keeping someone else's wallet, when he was merely picking up a piece of string. Here the author compresses the passage of time, and the peasant's decline, as effectively as he would record his heroine's boredom in his novel *A Life,* without being boring himself.

His work is considered less finished than Flaubert's. He wrote at a much faster pace throughout an even shorter life – he died insane, capitulating to a form of syphilis which caused him to hallucinate and made him suicidal. He claimed that when he wrote he could sometimes see himself watching himself work. Only when he finished writing did his *alter ego* disappear.

Mauriac

FRANÇOIS

born Bordeaux 1885; died Paris 1950

Maria Cross yielded not so much to drink deep of the branch-encumbered air as to a temptation to lose herself in it, to feel herself dissolved and atomised, till the inner desert of her heart should become one with the emptiness of space, till the silence within her should in no way differ from the silence of the spheres.

THE DESERT OF LOVE

FRANÇOIS MAURIAC'S NOVELS brought him widespread respect and many honours. The conflict in them arises from the clash of spirit with flesh and from the individual with conventional Catholic morality, as played out in the close family units of the rural areas surrounding Bordeaux.

Mauriac empathises with the loneliness of his characters. He places them in a world that God makes miserable by His absence. Instead, nature is present throughout the novels, sometimes oppressively so. Once-benign and desirable features of the landscape can turn menacing when a character's security in the world vanishes. Much of Mauriac's narrative can happen inside someone's head, distorting the timescale with recollected episodes. Thus a story's outer tensions cause inner fury, which his passionate prose captures over lengthy paragraphs. In this way *Thérèse Desqueyroux*, which remains his most widely read and admired work, is made more real to us: we meet a heroine who enjoys an immediate sympathy for nature, but whose instinctive reaction to those around her leads her to feel the universe turn against her, even before she tries to kill her way out of a loveless marriage. The narrative leaves her at the mercy of her vengeful new family.

Love becomes a more potent force in Mauriac's later work. The criticism of colleagues like **André Gide** led him to re-examine his attitudes towards religion and the possibilty of redemption with a degree of humility. As a result, he made his subsequent writing more optimistic, taking Thérèse beyond her spiritual isolation in a sequel and introducing more effective religious figures into other novels. But his realm remained a bleak one, in which sin is still a strong presence and families are ever-ready to turn on individuals to protect their names.

Mauriac was awarded the Nobel Prize for Literature in 1952.

241

Maurois

ANDRÉ

born Elbeuf 1885; died Paris 1967

I think that laughter is produced just when a state of alarm is followed by a state of relief. A young monkey who has the highest regard for the old chief of the tribe sees him slip on a banana skin; he fears an accident and his breast swells with terror, before discovering that it's nothing and all his muscles unclench pleasantly. That was the first joke. And that explains the convulsive movement of laughter.

DR O'GRADY IN
THE SILENCE OF COLONEL BRAMBLE

ANDRÉ MAUROIS WAS a French novelist and belletrist who brought a Gallic refinement to his subject matter. His chief interest was the English-speaking world. During the First World War, he worked as a liaison officer between the British and French armies and launched his literary career with two volumes that shared his insights into the British character. *The Silence of Colonel Bramble* and *The Speeches of Dr O'Grady* remain his most popular works.

Although Maurois can be identified with the novels' French character, Aurelle, the writing is detached from the action, which is realised mostly through speech. The pictures of the phlegmatic Scotsman and the loquacious Irishman take precedence over any account of the fighting: we are firmly in the officers' mess, not the trenches. Here we encounter the British male as he is represented in all classes, and the conflict seems to bring out the best in him – not least the Briton's perceived sense of "fair play". One soldier even goes so far as to propose a toast to the Germans, for providing such excellent sport: he now commands respect on his return home. The images of war are more sentimental than in his later work, such as when the soldier who once toasted the war as a marvellous adventure receives his fatal wound gallantly. Still, the conversations are droll and reveal a French view of the British that remains largely unchanged.

Maurois was drawn to this sporting spirit and lived in England before taking a teaching post at Princeton and settling in the US. He strove to explain both cultures to his compatriots, in his *History of England* and *History of the United States* from Wilson to Kennedy.

Mayakovsky

VLADIMIR

born Mayakovsky, Georgia 1893; died Moscow 1930

On earth,

my love I could never fulfil.

I was seven foot tall.

To me what's a foot or two?

For such works even a

plant-louse can do.

I scratched with a pen, eyeglasslike

squeezed into

the spectacle case of a little room.

ABOUT THIS, TR. HERBERT MARSHALL

VLADIMIR MAYAKOVSKY is the poet of the Russian Revolution, a man who thoroughly embraced the events of 1917. Although only 12 during the 1905 uprising, he busied himself writing propaganda for his classmates. By the time he and the revolutionary movement had matured 12 years later, he was writing such material for the entire nation, as well as producing films and lyrical advertising slogans.

Despite this, his relationship with the new rulers was never easy. Lenin openly disliked his poetry, wrongly linking it to the less social Futurist movement; Stalin publicly praised him, then had him followed by the secret police when he travelled the world to recite his lament for Lenin.

Mayakovsky's artistic problem was reconciling his leanings towards the love lyric with his passionate social concerns. In the former, he is never sentimental, adopting staccato-like lines and modernist images to express the pain of the beloved's failure to "phone" in the most global terms. In the latter he is the prophet of a **Whitman**esque, unselfish and universal love. This balance in his work won him admirers, including **Pasternak** and some in the Soviet establishment, and kept him as deeply in the hearts of his people as any Russian poet.

He shot himself in 1930 – no-one has been able to explain why. His suicide draws attention to his complex private life and the grudges against him, and these are as likely causes as the political climate. A gambler and drinker, he had a morbid turn of mind and had contemplated suicide for many years before he pulled the trigger. The demands he made of himself as a public poet are likely to have led to a sense of failure – Roman Jakobson wrote of Mayakovsky's inability to write epics without making them intimate and episodical. Few people were more alarmed by the author's interest in the human heart and his desire to be loved than he was himself.

Melville

HERMAN

born New York 1819; died New York 1891

Very often do the captains of such ships take those absent-minded young philosophers to task... half-hinting that they are so hopelessly lost to all honourable ambition, as that in their secret souls they would rather not see whales than otherwise. But all in vain; those young Platonists have a notion that their vision is imperfect; they are short-sighted; what use, then, to strain the visual nerve? They have left their opera-glasses at home.

MOBY-DICK

AS WITH OTHER TRULY great American writers, it is deceptively easy to categorise Melville. Although born in New York, his association with **Hawthorne** links him with New England and he lived on Hawthorne's estate for a time. Melville shared his landlord's forebodings of darkness and sin, while having much in common with the transcendentalists living nearby. He embraced the same wildness, if anything more fully; and **Emerson**'s pantheism has its counterpart in Melville's capacity to see the whole of humanity compacted into single things. To Captain Ahab, the great white whale Moby-Dick is such, and it is this vision that rings in our ears as we put down the short story *Bartleby* – "Ah, Bartleby! Ah, humanity!"

Unlike his fellow authors, he died unknown. He wrote incessantly, until it drove him insane. He produced poetry, some in a lyric form, some with **Whitman**'s charge, some endless and rhyming, much of it bleak. This range seems like versatility, but his prose work shows that his method of fitting ideas into language could barely be controlled. In *Moby-Dick*, a description of the slightest thing can become the theme for a discourse on mankind's destiny. Ahab's inner thoughts assume the metre of a **Shakespearean** monologue and characters' interactions can require a staging worthy of **Goethe**'s *Faust*. Melville's utter commitment to his theme dispenses with mere artistry.

Moby-Dick was published in London. It was the culmination of his writings about the sea, which he had known through abandoned adventure, including imprisonment, mutiny and whaling.

Meredith

GEORGE   born Portsmouth 1828; died Box Hill, Surrey 1909

The strangeness of men, young and old, the little things (she regarded a grand wine as a little thing) twisting and changing them, amazed her. And these are they by whom women are abused for variability! Only the most imperious reasons, never mean trifles, move women, thought she. Would women do an injury to one they loved for oceans of that – ah! pah!

THE EGOIST

GEORGE MEREDITH CONSIDERED himself primarily a poet, but he is better known for his novels. Even these have never reached the wide audience he craved, but his ambition did not outweigh his artistic integrity and after a few attempts to address fashionable literary concerns, he decided to write more according to his instincts. Meredith's admirers included **Henry James**, George Gissing and **Thomas Hardy**, whose early works he encouraged when he read them for a publisher.

Like them, Meredith was a progressive. He was a strong advocate of equality for women and is remembered for his particularly sympathetic female characters. In writing, his leanings were towards the poetic. This became exaggerated in later years, when he worried less about attracting new readers; but his earlier work displays a similar richness. His apparently detached narrative technique can suddenly become passionately engaged with a character's thoughts, before leaving them to discuss some idea of his.

His masterpiece is considered to be *The Egoist*. It is the study of an aristocratic figure who cannot understand how his actions can harm other people and so treats them negligently. He displays a callousness towards women and a yen for self-fulfilment, while the narrative concentrates more on those around him. They set off the protagonist, Sir Willoughby Patterne, and reveal aspects of the author's personality – in Vernon's learning and Laetitia's ambition to make a living by writing. Although the love triangles and social dilemmas tend towards a happy conclusion, they oppress the characters throughout, especially the women, who must overcome convention to express themselves.

Metastasio

PIETRO

born Rome 1698; died Vienna 1782

Not only do the things I sing and write

prove to be false, but in

my hopes and fears

I live deliriously, and all's deceit.

My life has been nothing but fantasies.

But Lord, when I have woken

from this night

Then at the heart of truth

may I find peace.

WHILE WRITING THE OLYMPIAD

METASTASIO'S NAME comes from the Greek for change, or passing. He chose it himself, changing it from Pietro Trapassi when he was 20. In fact, he was a poet of the establishment, writing courtly poems for the aristocrats of Naples and serving in Vienna as Caesarean poet under two Holy Roman Emperors (Charles V and VI). His innovations were in dramatic theory rather than in drama – his study of Aristotle's *Poetics* challenged the stage conventions of his time more than his plays did. They were not noted for their characters or plots (enlightened despots become embroiled in affairs of the heart – he was writing tragedy with a strong love interest at 14), but were noted for their poetry.

Even when he was not writing it expressly to be sung, it was always musical. He wrote many melodramas, "lyric scenes" and the libretti for some 27 operas. What his characters lacked in psychological interest, Handel or Mozart provided musically: the latter set Metastasio's *La Clemenza di Tito* sublimely, though only after major structural changes.

Still, Metastasio had extensive practical knowledge of the theatre: he had formed a troupe to perform his plays while working as a lawyer in Naples (financial and amatory problems compelled him to leave his native Rome) and had formative liaisons with actresses. For all his experience of life, he seems to have learned as much from books. He grew up with access to the library of his adoptive father, the poet Gravina: he called it his Arcadia. Henceforth, he immersed himself deeply in the classical temperament of his times and furnished Italian letters with his translations of **Horace** and **Homer**'s *Iliad*. Pope Pius VI is reported to have wept at the news of Metastasio's death.

Miller

ARTHUR

born New York 1915

A man is not a piece of fruit

DEATH OF A SALESMAN

I refuse to believe that man's only way to demonstrate his love for God is to refuse to eat some fruit

LUCIFER IN THE CREATION OF
THE WORLD AND OTHER BUSINESS

ARTHUR MILLER IS a playwright whose works have always been carefully structured, even at their most experimental. In this way he has made palatable the major concerns of post-war America.

He made his name with *All My Sons*. Its representation of a man plagued by guilt at his negligence as an industrialist during the war owes much to **Ibsen**'s *The Master Builder*.

Death of a Salesman tackled more exclusively American dilemmas – Willy Loman's sense of dignity in a modest profession tarnishes with time. He comes to feel disposable, first to society, then his family. Subsequently, Miller's work lost Ibsen's realism, allowing flashbacks and looser time-scales. But he retained his mentor's interest in psychology and the problem of the individual versus society.

He produced his own version of *An Enemy of the People* in 1951. His experience of the play's maxim, "The minority is always right," came during the McCarthy era. *The Crucible* drew on the 17th-century witch-hunts in Salem, which lent their name to McCarthy's hounding of suspected Communists out of public life, often driving them to suicide.

Miller chronicles his refusal to name names in *After the Fall*, which also tackles his marriage to Marilyn Monroe.

Like some of his other plays, it draws on allegory and confronts an issue that recurred, unbidden and unmentionable – the Holocaust. It is a harrowing focus for Miller's abiding preoccupation with guilt and *After the Fall* must face it rather than exorcise it. Miller's plays do not offer us the catharsis we have come to expect from tragedy, but show us a world in which we must remember the past before we can redeem it.

MAJOR WORKS

All My Sons (1947)

Death of a Salesman (1949)

The Crucible (1953)

A View from the Bridge (1955)

The Misfits (screenplay, 1960)

Incident at Vichy (1965)

The Archbishop's Ceiling (1977)

Miller

HENRY  **born New York 1891; died Pacific Palisades 1980**

The books he read – at 18! Not only Homer, Dante, Goethe, not only Aristotle, Plato, Epictetus… but all the small fry in between. Alors, on page 232 he breaks down and confesses. I know nothing, he admits. I know the titles, I have compiled bibliographies… I can talk for five minutes or five days, but then I give out, I am squeezed dry.

TROPIC OF CANCER

HENRY MILLER WAS a wanderer and sexual adventurer who achieved literary fame for his frank books, which would read more like confessions if they were accompanied by a greater sense of guilt. His work has striven to liberate readers from the taboos he found so constraining throughout his upbringing, and which were the reason he left America.

This is what gives his most famous book its joy and freedom. *Tropic of Cancer* celebrates Miller's early years as a writer in France. It broke ground with its expletives and **Lawrence**-influenced rhapsodising of genitalia. But the author's hunger is for food as much as sex and the whole is more interesting for its treatment of Paris than of passion. The latter is urgent, but the former is permanent and Miller finds the city much as **Hemingway** left it in *The Sun Also Rises*.

It is very much a writer's journey – and a solitary one. In an epiphanic passage, he claims to recognise the "absolute". He never tells us what this is, but it gives him an authority that empowers his later books when he rails against American materialism and sexual anxiety, especially in *Tropic of Capricorn*. In the autobiographical trilogy, *Sexus*, *Plexus* and *Nexus*, he describes his odd jobs in prohibition New York, his two marriages, their complications, and ultimately the "Rosy Crucifixion" that gives the books their collective title – it is Miller's "resurrection as a writer".

His generous and seminal output affects readers very differently. **Orwell** welcomed his rendering of real life as that of a proper writer, while for others the apparent sexism is a major obstacle to embracing Miller's profoundly personal vision.

Milne

A.A.   **born St. John's Wood, London 1882; died Hartfield, Sussex 1956**

this   take
If   is   shall   really   to
flying   I   never   it.

WINNIE-THE-POOH

'It isn't their necks I mind,' said Piglet earnestly. 'It's their teeth. But if Christopher Robin is coming I don't mind anything.'

WINNIE-THE-POOH

A.A. MILNE'S CAREER as a light poet and sketch-writer led to his assistant editorship of *Punch* magazine. This was interrupted by the First World War, during which he began writing stage comedies, which are barely performed today, although he did dramatise Kenneth Grahame's *The Wind in the Willows*.

He began writing verse for his son Christopher Robin, anthologised in *When We Were Very Young* and *Now We Are Six*. The work displays a neatness and fluency that his great creations Pooh and Eeyore did not share in their lyric efforts. But their bumbling metres and mad lunges for rhymes are truer to the poetic process than the apparent effortlessness that Milne brought to it They consistently defy **Yeats**' dictum that, "a line will take us hours maybe;/ Yet if it does not seem a moment's thought,/ Our stitching and unstitching has been naught".

And yes, it is easy to be smart about Pooh and his friends, who people (or teddy) Christopher Robin's half-imaginary world in the two gems *Winnie-the-Pooh* and *The House at Pooh Corner*. Their utterances have been taken to support any number of philosophies, including Taoism and most schools of literary theory (Frederick Crews' spoof readings are as handy an introduction to F.R. Leavis, Freud and deconstruction as any), and have even been translated into Latin.

But he could be smarter at our expense. "Every age is a Canterbury Pilgrimage", wrote **Blake**, "we all pass on, each sustaining one of these characters..." and it is a lasting comfort to think the same is true of the Milne toy-box. For if we can recognise in ourselves anything of Pooh's driftiness, Piglet's trepidation, Wol's deluded sense of order, Tigger's bounce or Eeyore's resignation to it all, then even in a world that can knock out all our stuffing, there might remain for us something eternally fluffy.

Milosz

CZESLAW

born Wilno, on the Polish/Lithuanian border 1911

At the entrance, my bare

* feet on the dirt floor,*

Here, gusts of heat; at my

* back, white clouds.*

I stare and stare. It seems

* I was called for this:*

To glorify things just because they are.

BLACKSMITH SHOP, IN PROVINCES

THE POET CZESLAW MILOSZ has spent much of his life outside his Polish homeland (he was born in Lithuania); although he had edited a left-wing journal as a student in Warsaw, he left in 1951 to escape the increasingly totalitarian Communist régime. He settled first in France, then in California. His work was banned in Poland until 1981, when he won the Nobel Prize. His presence in the West has done much to promote the work of other Polish poets, and to draw attention to the circumstances under which they have been working. Some of his most read work comes from the Warsaw he knew during the war. With his underground poetry, he supported the Polish Resistance.

War, and the knowledge of its devastation, might have been the source for much poetry, but he takes this further. The constant presence of death can lead his poems to explore the difference between states of being and non-being. A moment may be part of a developing process, or else be frozen in time. His poetry seizes on minute details, which become dis-tinct from a tide of impressions impossible to capture in words: for example, he decides how the eye might fix upon two blades of grass and a stone during an air-raid. It is this kind of memory snatched from moments of historical crisis that have led critics to call him a "witness" – a label he rejects as characterisation of Western triteness. He has become well-known for poems which occupy imaginary territories: here his influence is particularly marked on **Heaney**. The impact seems to be reciprocated in later Milosz poems, which show a delight in actual things. The two poets have shared reading platforms in the States.

Milosz has translated **T.S. Eliot** and **Walt Whitman** into Polish, and his own poetry into English. His English verse-writing is innovative and extremely accomplished; his expression is direct, and he experiments with line-lengths in a way which a different translator, striving for fidelity to the original, might be reluctant to attempt.

Milton

JOHN   **born London 1608; died Chalfont St. Giles, Bucks 1674**

And all amid them stood the tree of life,

High eminent, blooming ambrosial fruit

Of vegetable gold; and next to life

Our death the tree of knowledge grew
    fast by,

Knowledge of good bought dear by
    knowing ill.

PARADISE LOST, BOOK IV

MILTON'S WRITING HAS had so huge an effect on the language of English poetry that it has often seemed hard to respond to it. One contemporary poet has called him "the great closing down sale of English literature", describing his complete mastery of previous poetical forms – the masque (*Comus*), the pastoral (the lament *Lycidas*), the tragedy (*Samson Agonistes*) and the epic (*Paradise Lost*) – and the vision that led him to transform them for his own ends.

These aims are often the same as those of his pamphlets and public campaigning. He was a Puritan and felt the Reformation had not gone far enough in England. He wrote passionately in favour of divorce, then for freedom of speech when these views encountered censorship.

In politics and religion, he fought against oppression. His faith embraced companionship and sex in marriage (the early relationship between Adam and Eve was his ideal) and after the Restoration he was imprisoned for attacking the new regime. **Andrew Marvell** saved his life.

Milton's masterpiece, *Paradise Lost*, threw off "the tyranny of rhyme". Composed in blank verse, it expounds mankind's history from creation to the fall, then forwards to our redemption through Christ. His knowledge of all previous epics and his verse, which is worthy of the best of them, has made any subsequent attempt at the form seem futile. His complete vision of human history and his power to express it make it hard to imagine that he considered any other theme, although King Arthur had been a likely subject. But by going for the more cosmic option, he still enriched his country's poetry to the point of satiety. His Latinate syntax, his ability to make the abstract vivid, his capacity for making "the worse appear/the better reason" in Satanic speech before persuading us of holier truths, and his sheer conviction, have left English poets stammering in admiration.

MAJOR WORKS

Lycidas (1637)

Areopagitica (1644)

Paradise Lost (1667, 1674)

Paradise Regained (1671)

Samson Agonistes (1671)

Mishima

YUKIO

born Tokyo 1925; died Tokyo 1970

*Death does not go beyond truth. Suicide
might be called death through action. A
man cannot be born of his own will, but
he can will to die.*

FORBIDDEN COLOURS

HOWEVER HARD ONE TRIES to separate art from life, it is almost impossible to consider Mishima's literary career apart from its bloody end. When he had finished the fourth and final book of his masterpiece, he appeared before an assembly of soldiers to harangue them about the Japanese constitution's assaults on the glories of the Emperor and warriordom, before disembowelling himself with unbelievable deftness, assisted by one of his hand-picked troops, who beheaded him.

His work and life over, he had attained *Bunbu-Ryodo* (the union of cultural and warlike excellence) or, in his own phrase, the harmony of pen and sword. Readers asking why often pick through his corpus for clues. His last work, *The Sea of Fertility*, invites the conclusion that Mishima might have anticipated his return to the earth. *The Decay of the Angels* shows a preoccupation with the early, violent death of young men at their most beautiful. This last gesture seems to strive toward the kind of beauty he cherished most.

It was a physical beauty, such as he had desired in other men from youth and which his first novel, *Confessions of a Mask*, explores. And it was a terrible beauty: the novice of *The Temple of the Golden Pavilion* is so drawn yet repelled by the wonder of a building, he must destroy it, then himself.

Mishima's end seems to fulfil aesthetic goals rather than logical ones. He railed against Western materialism, but left a plush flat with Greek statues and foreign novels; he advocated severity, while displaying a merry wit and sociability. In his writing, he can treat what allures him with disgust and his tetralogy shows the appeal of his method of death (called *seppuku*) embraced, only to be dismissed elsewhere. In life, he was a fanatic; in art, an artist.

Mitchell

MARGARET

born Atlanta, Georgia 1900; died Atlanta 1949

Gone With the Wind (1936)

He drew a short breath and said lightly but softly: 'My dear, I don't give a damn.'

GONE WITH THE WIND

MARGARET MITCHELL'S ONLY BOOK broke all sales records and, as a historical epic and a sustained romance, it reached wider audiences than any earlier work conceived on the same scale. Readers of *Gone With the Wind* devoured the tale of the American South set around the Civil War, without being daunted by its thousand-odd pages.

Mitchell was born in Georgia and from her youth had absorbed stories passed down through generations of people with long memories of the war. Her novel is written from the Southern point of view, showing sympathy for the Confederates, if not for slavery. The narrative treats black and white characters equally. The scope of the book is immense, beginning with the seeds of the conflict and following the fate of a family plantation, Tara, to the end and beyond into the Reconstruction period. Mitchell introduces the vastness of the battle scenes, but maintains a female perspective on them, tackling the theme of domestic tragedy through her heroine, Scarlett O'Hara.

Scarlett is an intriguing figure, capable of acting without morals in everything, motivated by self-interest and a need to protect her family's fortune. We follow her through three marriages and her progress from loving a childhood sweetheart to her later relationship with the mysterious outcast Rhett Butler. Whether or not she finds true love in the end is left to the reader to decide; he or she will have

turned page after page only to be as beguiled by Scarlett as her suitors are. She plays games with everyone.

Margaret Mitchell took 10 years over the work, revising it for years after the first draft before offering it to a publisher. She conceived it while recovering from an injury to her ankle and proposed to call it *Tomorrow is Another Day*. Before that, she had worked on the *Atlanta Journal*. Her achievement with the novel was honoured with a Pulitzer Prize in 1936 – remarkably she was chosen over **Faulkner**, whose literary landscape is very similar, but whose technique could not contrast more strongly with Mitchell's. The classic film version was made in 1939.

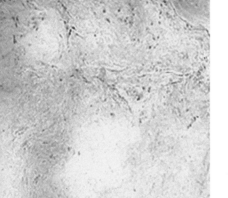

Mitford

NANCY   **born London 1904; died Versailles 1973**

I have long regarded you as an agitator – agitatrix, agitateuse? of genius. You have only to publish a few cool reflections on 18th-Century furniture to set gangs on the prowl through the Faubourg St Germain splashing the walls with 'Nancy, go home'.

EVELYN WAUGH, AN OPEN LETTER TO THE HON MRS PETER RODD (NANCY MITFORD) ON A VERY SERIOUS SUBJECT, IN NOBLESSE OBLIGE

NANCY MITFORD WAS BORN into an aristocratic family in which eccentricities were not just tolerated, but cultivated. The Mitford sisters' activities were more than just quirks, but were surprising nonetheless. One, Jessica, was a Marxist, as her memoir *Hons and Rebels* recalls; another, Diana, married the Fascist Sir Oswald Mosely and was all but in love with Hitler.

Nancy Mitford's remarkable achievement as a belletriste was to avoid coming down on one side or the other, at least on paper. Her novels present families with intricate histories similar to her own, with youthful English girls at sea in Paris. These comedies of manners look at the English upper class (she would never call it British, nor the Scottish "Scots") with an uncritical eye; her narratives would sooner laugh with her characters than at them.

She comes closer to expressing personal opinions in her most frequently consulted work, *Noblesse Oblige: An Enquiry into the Identifiable Characteristics of the English Aristocracy*, a collection of essays by a number of hands which takes its lead from a lecture on linguistics defining the differences between non-upper-class and upper-class speech. In her work popularising this method of class distinction (which she denies has anything to do with wealth or education), she reveals that her concerns hinge on niceties more than politics. Although she is a keen observer of social change, she perceives it so much in particulars that her tone can become camp. This can turn into self-parody; while she avoided expressing her own feelings, stifling her own cries with a pillow even during a painful death from Hodgkin's Disease, she left as faithful an account of the declining aristocracy as we are likely to have.

Molière

JEAN BAPTISTE POQUELIN   born Paris 1622; died Paris 1673

Madam, it is such a great honour for me to have the fortune to be so glad about being so happy that you might have the goodness to accord me the grace of doing me the honour of honouring me with the pleasure of your presence; and if I have deserved to deserve such deserts as yours, and the sky... envying my well-being... would have accorded... the good luck of rendering me worthy... of...

THE BOURGEOIS GENTLEMAN

FEW PLAYWRIGHTS have been more attuned to the needs of an actor and the requirements of staging than Molière. He was set to follow his father into the textile business, but joined a theatre company when he was 21. He trained in the tradition of the Italian *Commedia dell'Arte* – that is, he learned to improvise set scenes in one of the genre's characters. His role was Sganarelle, the two-faced, embittered steward and this was how he first appeared at Court, following a performance of **Corneille**.

He was soon to become the main attraction of his troupe and he wrote prolifically in his early years. In keeping with this "type"-based theatre, he would build plays around characters who displayed a specific weakness and portray their flawed interactions with the rest of the world. The heroes of Molière's plays are often deluded and accomplish little; rather, they become the butt of everyone else's jokes. The exercise is not merely humorous: in their monomania, people can cause others real pain without realising it, such as the *Misanthrope*; or else they can command our pity, like the *Bourgeois Gentleman*, whose naïve insistence on social rules enables everyone to make him behave according to new ones they've just invented.

His last play presents a character whose weakness was craving that weakness: it is a fitting epitaph that Molière died after a coughing fit that began while he was on stage in the title role of *The Hypochondriac*. Legend has it that as he tried to stifle the cough with mock hilarity he so delighted his audience that he had to beg them to stop laughing at him!

Montaigne

MICHEL DE   **born Château Montaigne, Périgord 1533; died there 1592**

That day is the master, that day is the judge of all others: it is the day, says an ancient (Seneca), that must judge all my years past. I leave it to death to essay the fruits of my studies. Then we shall see if my discourses come from my mouth, or from my heart.

WE MUST NOT JUDGE OUR TIME EXCEPT
AFTER DEATH

MONTAIGNE INVENTED the essay. It was a form he could adapt to his qualities: he had a mind that was curious, liberal and encyclopedic. This meant he would base his enquiries on his vast range of reading – sometimes endorsing the views he cited to the point of assimilating them – as often as he would his own personal experience. His interest in the latter make his essays read like explorations of his own character, but he never allows his readers to think they are getting to know him too well. He is fond of introducing a passage with the words "I have seen...", or of sounding subjective – "I'm not what you'd call a naturalist but" – before expounding well-rehearsed opinions on human nature.

The joy of Montaigne lies in the way he organises these works. His essays went through four different editions, each acquiring new essays, with none appearing in the order in which he wrote them. This leads commentators to look in vain for the shifts in his thinking. He is capable of contradicting himself from one essay to another, one moment praising the simple life, the next promoting scholarship.

Montaigne shopped around the various schools of classical philosophy, finding **Lucretius** as apt for his own brand of humanism as was Cicero for his more authoritarian stances. In life, he combined both attributes, campaigning in pamphlets and parliament for religious tolerance and serving two terms as Mayor of Bordeaux.

Whether his insights derive from public duties, private friendships (notably his devoted attachment to the younger, less talented writer La Boëtie), or the seclusion of his own vast library in a secluded castle, he expresses them in a French whose elegance owes as much to Latinate grace as to his own measured humanism – for he was a true child of the Renaissance.

Moravia

ALBERTO

born Rome 1907; died Rome 1990

I answer frankly: 'I want you to stop mixing up literature and life. Maybe you're thinking that I go for little girls because I like a poem where a woman has sex with a little girl. But you're wrong, I like the poem, not little girls.'

THE VOYEUR, TR. TIM PARKS

ALBERTO MORAVIA COMBINED a modernist readiness to experiment and surprise with a romantic mission. His books can take on existential angst (especially in his many adolescent characters), can be sexually explicit or just plain ribald and ultimately contemplate nuclear Armageddon. If people are saved from these terrors, it is through the mysteries of a personal relationship rather than simpler creature comforts or fleeting sexual congress. The latter has its consolations, but they are mostly negative ones: someone having sex with a person is seen to have a kind of implicit sympathy with everyone else who has had sex withthe same person.

His early works appeared in Mussolini's Italy. He did everything he could to rile the regime and still get into print. This included the use of pseudonyms: his real name was Alberto Pincherle. His first novel was wilfully out of tune with Fascist aesthetic dictates and those that followed used allegory to lampoon *Il Duce*. Once Mussolini realised that a series of manic authoritarian leaders were thinly disguised versions of himself, he insisted on censoring Moravia's work personally. Until the end of the war, the author had to live in hiding in the Italian hills or America.

In peacetime, his earlier disdain for middle-class apathy and concern for working-class dignity gave his work a specifically Marxist agenda. He continued to champion humanity and spiritual love over materialism and sex, encapsulating both in *The Woman of Rome*, about a prostitute who finds salvation in her suffering.

Sense continues to struggle with spirit in *The Voyeur*, a dialogue between the hero and his penis. It is in a late work that we find the real and the imaginary at their most confused: *1934* offers a nexus of confused identities and faked suicides between Italian and German characters: did the hero fall in love with twins? Their roles are implicitly political: to the end, Moravia's allegory, complex plots and the thirst for love remained as sure as ever.

Morrison

TONI

born Lorain, Ohio 1931

That I love the way you hold me, how close you let me be to you... I have watched your face for a long time now, and missed your eyes when you went away from me. Talking to you and hearing you answer – that's the kick.

But I can't say that aloud; I can't tell anyone that I have been waiting for this all my life and that being chosen to wait is the reason I can.

JAZZ

TONI MORRISON'S NOVELS examine the black community in Ohio, the state she has known since youth, at various stages of its history. Her passionate and poetic writing particularly addresses the impact that slavery had and continues to have on people who struggle to retain their dignity.

Her characters can never escape their pasts. In *Sula*, the eponymous heroine reappears in her childhood community to find herself stigmatised and accused of all crimes, as those around her try to evade their guilt. The nightmare is intensified in *The Beloved*, in which a woman is haunted by the ghost of her own child, who remains nameless, commemorated only by the word "Beloved" on a tombstone. In tragic error, the mother kills her daughter to avoid her falling into the hands of whites. For her, white people are irrevocably associated with slavery and its repercussions are ineluctable, affecting the victims' lives, even after Abolition.

The telling is strongly rhythmical, evoking the jungle and the characters' African roots. Morrison's lyrical energy takes full flight in *Jazz*, portraying an alternative jazz age to the one chronicled by **F. Scott Fitzgerald**. The inner thoughts of the leading figure roll a poet's eye over all of New York, compacting representatives of its hugely varied population into sustained, incantatory paragraphs. The heroine here tastes the freedoms of women in other novels, in an adulterous romance. Elsewhere, the liberties female characters take can attain extremes of violence – an almost inevitable outcome when other forms of expression are denied.

In 1993, Toni Morrison became the first black woman to win the Nobel Prize for Literature.

Murdoch

IRIS

For an instant she apprehended him there, pale, awkward, strong, with his two large palms seeming to enclose her body. In that instant she saw him close, mysterious, other than herself, full to the brim of his own particular history.

THE SANDCASTLE

IRIS MURDOCH IS AN astonishingly prolific writer of novels, short stories and philosophy – enjoying a long academic career at Oxford, where she has written on **Jean-Paul Sartre** and **Plato**. This intellectual material has informed her fiction, but has not diminished its popularity.

Like Plato, she is concerned with absolutes: absolute Good and Evil. These ideas can be played out by characters susceptibility to human frailty. A typical plot structure can centre on a conventional, happy marriage disrupted by an amoral, Mephistophelean third party. In the ructions this can produce, the evil recedes, but not without its victims discovering their own spiritual weaknesses first. For example, Pim in *The Sacred and Profane Love Machine*, arrives as a dark, magical figure, but administers a sort of justice to the all-too-smug couple he encounters. These interlopers bring a sensuality which the narrative heightens in its avoidance of the explicit. London's National Gallery or the British Museum serve as backdrops which can help bring latent desires to the surface.

She adds force to her stories by her use of myth, in which water often emerges as an image of cleansing. Her themes are Christian, but have been described as "the search for goodness without God." She is seldom drawn to comment on her own work, but has said in a rare interview, "I write because I like it". For all the wealth of ideas at stake in her novels, it is telling the story that counts. She is as concerned about actual human relationships as about the philosophical contrasts they can represent, and she narrates their fortunes with a directness that puts her in the same tradition as **Dickens**, **Hardy** and **George Eliot**.

MAJOR WORKS

Under the Net (1954)

The Sandcastle (1957)

The Bell (1958)

A Severed Head (1961)

An Unofficial Rose (1962)

The Red and the Green (1965)

The Time of the Angels (1968)

The Nice and the Good (1968)

Bruno's Dream (1969)

The Black Prince (1972)

A Word Child (1975)

The Sea, The Sea (1978)

Nuns and Soldiers (1980)

The Philosopher's Pupil (1983)

The Good Apprentice (1985)

The Book and the Brotherhood (1987)

The Message to the Planet (1989)

Musil

ROBERT  **born Klagenfurt 1880; died Geneva 1942**

For the awakening boy's first passion is not love for the one, but hatred for all. The feeling of not being understood and of not understanding the world is no mere accompaniment of first passion, but its sole non-accidental cause. And the passion itself is a panic-stricken flight in which being together with the other means only a doubled solitude.

YOUNG TÖRLESS, TR. WILKINS AND KAISER

ROBERT MUSIL WROTE *The Man Without Qualities*, the unfinished, multi-volumed novel that has been called the Austrian masterpiece.

It is the culmination of a lifetime's work on the problems of morality and the apparent inconsequence of a person's actions. As he does throughout his work, he raises the question, how do we know things exist? Here the decaying Austro-Hungarian Empire of before the First World War is made real enough for the reader, but not for the hero Ulrich, who seems detached from it. His bid to find a purpose in life within a year cannot be confined by conventional morals: in his search for the perfect balance of erotic and selfless love (the theme of the earlier *Three Women*), he opts for his twin sister, and when he wonders if killing can ever be justified, his working model is a psychopath.

The novel's incomplete state means these issues are never resolved, but as elsewhere in Musil's work, the inner, emotional life takes precedence over the outer world of action. In this he resembles **Proust**: what plots his short stories have are often recurring ones and his analysis of developing feelings maintains a drama of its own. He owes this to expressionism as much as to the philosophical rigours he had pursued in his academic life.

His youthful story *Young Törless* shows this. It is more than a story about brutal retribution at a military school (one attended both by Musil and **Rilke**) and more than an account of a youth's character-building. The work reads as a psychological sketchbook, with a different mental state on each page, often without incident to prompt it. Such clashes always dominated Musil's thinking and twice led to breakdown.

Musset

ALFRED DE

born Paris 1810; died Paris 1857

Thank God that authors now have

> *different ways,*

And we prefer the drama that's the craze

Where intrigue, wrapped up in a pretty

> *roll,*

Turns like a rebus round a rigmarole.

A WASTED EVENING

ALFRED DE MUSSET gave the French the line in which many find an encapsulation of the national temperament: "My glass is little, but I drink from mine." As well as describing the French sense of balance and perspective, it expresses Musset's image as a poet. He uses it to justify his restricted subject matter – mostly the pleasures and pains of love.

It is very much his own glass. What bitterness is in it, he shares with the world. His one gift, he says, is to have cried. His most famous poem, *May Night*, takes the Christian image of what Richard Crashaw calls, "the soft, self-wounding pelican" and reworks it in aesthetic terms: the poet, implicitly Christ-like, lacerates himself for those around him.

Much of this public unhappiness stemmed from his on-off romance with **George Sand**. His fondness for women and wine drove him to despair a situation exacerbated by Sand falling in love with Musset's doctor. Yet for all the sensual and lofty lamentations the poet offers us, he remains as self-contained as his glass. He knew himself too well to keep up such a pitch of pathos. In *Tales of Italy and Spain*, a work that brought him fame at the age of 20, he was already mocking the circle of romantics who

had encouraged him (especially **Hugo**). He was as well-known for his writerly comedies as for his verse, most notably the cautionary *Don't Mess With Love*. He also shared his insights by dramatising well-known proverbs. This unwillingness to be original, together with a certain triteness and reckless versification, earned him the scorn of **Baudelaire** and **Rimbaud**. Had he lived long enough to have heard such criticism, one imagines he would have been ready for it.

Nabokov

VLADIMIR   **born St. Petersburg 1899; died Montreux, Switzerland 1977**

I am trying to describe these things not to relive them in my present boundless misery, but to sort out the portion of hell and the portion of heaven in that strange, awful, maddening world – nymphet love.

LOLITA

NABOKOV'S WRITING contains unashamed displays of style and sophistication. He was a scholar, of lepidoptery as much as literature, and his knowledge of the latter spanned many languages. His brand of wit enabled him to play with words' meanings in varied tongues, and to mock the fussiness of Europeans as well as the bewildered response they elicit in his adopted America.

His life took him through a range of cultures. He was born into a privileged Russian family and was forced to flee his homeland during the Revolution. He studied at Cambridge, before living in Berlin and Paris, ultimately settling in the United States as an academic. By then he had written a number of novels in Russian, introducing the brilliant but deluded characters who would descend into madness (such as the chess genius in *The Luzhin Defence*, or the schizophrenic murderer, fraudster and would-be writer of *Despair*) and anticipate later creations in the English books, most strikingly Humbert Humbert in Nabokov's *succès de scandale*, *Lolita*.

This account of a European scholar's passion for a 12-year old girl appears as a confessional memoir written in prison – its introduction, signed by a fictional psychiatrist to lend the narrative authenticity, must have surprised those who encountered the book in its first, pulp pornography incarnation. Nabokov's use of frame devices had already adorned *The Real Life of Sebastian Knight*, in which a man writes a biography of someone who turns out not to be his brother. It reached extreme proportions in *Pale Fire*, a novel in a commentary on a poem by an author who proves impossible to trace.

Nabokov's translation of **Pushkin**'s *Eugene Onegin* also ballooned into proportions that dwarf the text under examination. For him, scholarship and flights of creativity were joyously entangled.

Naipaul

V.S.

So step by step, book by book, though seeking each time only to write another book, I eased myself into knowledge. To write was to learn. Beginning a book, I always felt I was in possession of all the facts about myself; at the end I was always surprised.

FINDING THE CENTRE

V.S. NAIPAUL WAS BORN into Trinidad's East Indian community. His novels and travel books use a journalist's instincts to describe the lives and aspirations of people struggling to survive in the world's poorest areas. His enquiries have taken him to India, Africa and through a range of Islamic countries.

But he begins at home, wondering even if he can call it that. His first four books are novels set in Trinidad. *Miguel Street* presents the buoyant characters of his youth, as well as describing the education that distanced him from his homeland: Naipaul left Trinidad for good, to study in London. *A House for Mr Biswas* tells of a man's dream of possessing his own piece of land, with a house. His ambitions are limited and regularly thwarted and his literary goals don't go far beyond scoop reporting.

It was the start of Naipaul's career in showing the developing world as one he wished could develop faster. His view of India shows this. His experiences of the country were not what he expected (he claimed only to know it from the community around him in the West Indies and the works of R.K. Narayan) and he witnessed its least democratic days since Independence – Indira Gandhi's State of Emergency in 1975. He blamed the poverty and chaos on entrenched attitudes and a refusal to break from tradition. He brought the same criticisms to his study of Islam world-wide, *Among the Believers*. This brought further controversy around him: Edward Said accused him of generalisation and of finding only what he expected to find – ultimately of being too pro-West.

These charges were not new to him and his world view has never been optimistic. But his impatience with people's inability to change is balanced by a faith in individuals, treating them with dignity and humanity through the most extreme struggles.

Narayan

R.K.

"What is the meaning of Tim?" asked Gupta irrelevantly.

"Deity in our village temple," replied Nagaraj on an inspiration.

"What God is that?" asked Gupta with curiosity. Nagaraj gave some answer describing the image as possessing four arms and three eyes.

THE WORLD OF NAGARAJ

India will go on

REMARK TO V.S. NAIPAUL, QUOTED IN
INDIA: A WOUNDED CIVILISATION

R.K. NARAYAN'S long storytelling career has charted the vast transformations India has undergone this century. His first novels appeared under the Raj and have covered shifts in thinking and society through to today.

But national trends never dominate. Rather, he portrays them in the more intimate setting of Malgudi, a small town in Mysore (now Karnataka). There, change is a family affair: different attitudes are evident in different generations, with younger characters more willing to embrace the West. Narayan's narrative leaves no-one free from his undermining irony, although he is gentle enough to treat most of his characters with tenderness. In *The Guide*, an amiable con-man attains status as a guru, talking us through all levels of Indian society without taking the holiest of cows too seriously. A more honest protagonist is *The Painter of Signs*, who falls in love with a woman popularising family planning during the 70s. Although this meeting of an accepting man and a progressive woman seems to encapsulate India in transition, it is a love story and the novelist keeps it personal.

Narayan writes in English and is as at home with **Shakespeare** and the Bible as he is with the Indian myths. Still, he has written re-tellings of the *Mahabharata* and the *Ramayana*. He avoids taking either side too dogmatically and is able to satirise the Anglophile lecturers of *The English Teacher* as well as anti-British fanaticism. In the short story *Lawley Road* a crowd bays for the removal of an Englishman's statue only to discover that he was more benefactor than brute. As one of India's finest writers, Narayan combines a love of his country with a reluctance to mysticise it out of existence.

Nash

OGDEN   **born Rye, New York State 1902; died Baltimore 1971**

Croesus was turned to gold by Minos,

And Thomas À Kempis was Thomas

  Aquinas.

Two Irish Saints were Patti and Micah,

The Light Brigade rode at Balalaika,

If you seek a roué to irk your aunt,

Kubla-Kahn but Immanuel Kant.

WHO DID WHICH? OR WHO INDEED?

OGDEN NASH'S ASTONISHING vocabulary and pertinent humour was a regular feature of the *New Yorker* magazine, of which he was editor. He gave the world a unique brand of nonsense verse. Like that of **Lewis Carroll** and **Edward Lear**, it owed much to the verse of his time. But where other parodists could be biting, Nash could really gnash. Terrible puns were key to his technique, redeemed chiefly by the amazing words he invented expressly to play on them. His lengthy, often deliberately non-metrical lines use form and content to wonder what poetry is in any case. *The Strange Case of Mr Fortague's Disappointment* takes **Yeats**' sublime *The Lake Isle of Innisfree* to make its dreamy yearning sound impractical and ridiculous.

His targets could be easier. He had writers of well-meaning doggerel clearly in his sights. *First Child … Second Child* dashes a bubbly apostrophe of a new-born babe to the ground with the response to a second: "Is it a boy, or quite the reverse?/You can call in the morning and ask the nurse." Sometimes the nonsense can seem like pure sound effects, as if

to parody other studiedly noisy poets such as Vachall Lindsey or Edith Sitwell, but often Nash's purpose is higher. *In The Private Dining Room* four lines about two genteel women become garbled beyond sense until we realise that Miss Rafferty and Miss Cavendish are becoming as drunk as the verse. If this is art for art's sake, he could also be satirically relevant, writing during the Cuban Missile Crisis: "Maybe I couldn't be dafter./But I keep wondering if this time we couldn't settle our differences before a war instead of after."

Neruda

PABLO

born Parral, Chile 1904; died Santiago 1973

I'm nothing but a poet: I love you all,

I've wandered the world that I love:

in my homeland they imprison miners

and soldiers command the judges.

But I love even the roots

of my cold country.

LET THE WOODCUTTER AWAKEN, FROM
CANTO GENERAL, TR. JACK SCHMITT

NERUDA'S POETRY is deeply loved in the Spanish-speaking world and increasingly beyond there. This was true even of his earliest work, which appeared when he was 20. Then, his theme was love, but events were to make his poetry more public.

He joined the Chilean diplomatic service to see Europe, but in 1927 he was dispatched to Rangoon. His experiences in the Far East began to politicise him, although his poetry from this time dwelled mostly on death and he is often called "the poet of death". When he did reach Europe, he was happiest in Spain, among **Lorca**'s circle. There, the triumph of Fascism ensured his eventual conversion to Communism.

He arrived back in Chile after a series of posts in other parts of Latin America. The poetry that shows his greatest pain at the country's plight followed the trauma he experienced when he managed Gonzalez Videla's election campaign in 1945, only to see the pledges he had promulgated come to nothing: the new president abandoned his cause under pressure from America. This betrayal fills the vast *Canto General*, in which the poet aligns himself with victims all over the Americas, recounting their myths and the formation of the lands. The title points to the work's inclusiveness and Neruda wanted his poetry to help everyone, especially those least likely to read it.

The work was published in Mexico, during his time on the run from the Chilean police. He surfaced in Paris and continued to travel, and his poems from this period deal more with love. It wasn't until 1971 that he was able to return to public life, when his friend Salvador Allende became president. But the new democratic government was brutally overthrown: Allende was killed in a coup and Neruda died shortly afterwards.

Nietzsche

FRIEDRICH

born Röcken, Saxony 1844; died Weimar 1900

Of all writings I love only that which is written with blood. Write with blood: and you will discover that blood is spirit.

It is not an easy thing to understand unfamiliar blood: I hate the reading idler.

He who knows the reader, does nothing further for the reader. Another century of readers – and spirit itself will stink.

THUS SPAKE ZARATHUSTRA,
TR. OLLINGDALE

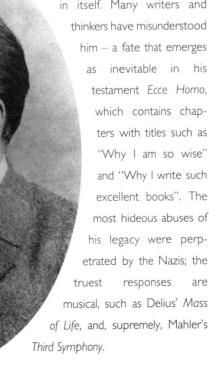

FRIEDRICH NIETZSCHE'S WRITINGS have the quality of a Biblical prophet. He wrote and thought in the purest abstractions and his extraordinary prose made these ideas as real as language could render them.

He was a brilliant and extremely precocious classical scholar – the University of Basel elected him Professor of Philology at 24. A Chair in Philosophy eluded him and illness forced him to retire in 1879, when the migraines that presaged his ultimate breakdown from syphilis became intolerable. His intimate knowledge of Greek never prevented him from positing that culture's vaster patterns: his *Birth of Tragedy* dates from this period and distinguishes Apollonian control from the frenzied Dionysus. His praise for the Athenian tragedians stopped at **Euripides**, whom he found too willing to put the mob on stage.

Nietzsche's writings disdain the masses and herald the age of a Superman – a figure to arise in the universe now that God is dead. This is to simplify his views of a single, entire cosmos with nothing beyond it, wherein events must recur eternally. In *Thus Spake Zarathustra* he represents this idea in aphorisms and poetry too bold and sharp to be paraphrased.

The influence of his work on so much subsequent art has been all the more enormous for being such great art in itself. Many writers and thinkers have misunderstood him – a fate that emerges as inevitable in his testament *Ecce Homo*, which contains chapters with titles such as "Why I am so wise" and "Why I write such excellent books". The most hideous abuses of his legacy were perpetrated by the Nazis; the truest responses are musical, such as Delius' *Mass of Life*, and, supremely, Mahler's *Third Symphony*.

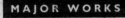

MAJOR WORKS

The Birth of Tragedy (1872)

Human, All Too Human (1878–1879)

The Gay Science (1882–1887)

Thus Spake Zarathustra (1883–1892)

Ecce Homo (1888)

The Antichrist (1888)

The Will to Power (published posthumously in fragments)

Novalis

born Wiederstadt 1772; died Weissenfels 1801

Already the vibrancy

flickers through us, the mystery

of an echo in the sky,

resonating in the gulf.

Those we miss are signalling

with their breath; it's time to go.

HYMNS TO THE NIGHT, VI,
TR. JEREMY REED

NOVALIS WAS THE ADOPTED name of the German poet Friedrich von Hardenberg. He was writing in the purest vein of European poetry. He had the same preoccupation with light as did **Goethe** and **Dante**. For him too it had a divine source: like the former, he could approach light with a scientific interest, and like the latter, it was something to be attained through love.

In fact, Novalis' progress towards the light had a beginning similar to Dante's. He too fell in love with a young girl, in this case a 13-year-old, Sophie von Kühn, who was 10 years his junior. The couple became engaged, but she died two years later, in 1797. The story is told in Penelope Fitzgerald's novel, *The Blue Flower*. Novalis' craving for the light, while still rooted in Christianity (he had written hymns for church use), then took an alternative form of expression. He wanted to die and looked to death as his salvation. Five years later his prayers were answered when he died of tuberculosis. He felt death's presence most strongly at night, which he came to see as a seductive, mysterious entity.

Novalis rhapsodises night in six hymns, mixing prose-poems with verse. He vividly describes the colours he discerns in darkness, and addresses night with the imagination, the inner vision, in which he had such a firm romantic faith. His regard is Platonic: he presents himself as having existed before night, but able to recognise inner truths as signified by the outer signs night provides. He expounded these ideas in essays, published beside those by Schlegel, and in unfinished novels: it is in his poetry that he expresses it most purely.

Oates

JOYCE CAROL

born Millersport, New York State 1938

He said aloud, staring at his reflection in the bathroom mirror, the ruddy skin, the quizzical eyes, turning his head from side to side, slowly, pondering, admiring, 'This is the way it was meant to be.'

'SURF CITY', IN RAVEN'S WING

JOYCE CAROL OATES is an incredibly prolific novelist, as well as the author of poems, plays and short stories. The speed at which her work appears has led critics to assume there must be more faults to find than actually exist. But Oates has mastered a large range of techniques, maintaining great diversity, even within the same genre, and brings this variety to bear upon the contemporary American situation.

There she finds much violent crime and domestic brutality. Often this has a family setting, as in the book that secured her reputation, *them*, which centres on the inhabitants of Detroit's rougher areas over three generations. Although the work's realism highlights modem problems, elsewhere the causes are shown to have deeper roots. In a series of Gothic-style novels – *Bellefleur*, *A Bloodsmoor Romance* and *The Mysteries of Winterthum* – she uses a more traditional form to renew discussion of timeless issues, such as good and evil.

Another family chronicle, *You Must Remember This*, takes pains to recreate the atmosphere in 50s America, invoking nostalgia in order to shock with an unsentimental view of post-war society.

Her gifts of characterisation take her as deep into the male psyche as into the female. She has made an

intimate study of boxing, which she can present as a codified, disciplined manifestation of force far removed from crimes outside the ring. Boxers reappear throughout her stories, as do other masculine characters whose conventional interests emerge without narrative comment. In fact, Oates is so adept at darting in and out of her creations' thoughts and feelings that we can begin to forget that we are in the hands of a detached, third-person storyteller.

O'Brien

EDNA   **born Tuamgraney, County Clare 1932**

It was all about roots, values, not losing one's identity, and so forth... He was mad for roots. Even got books on genealogy, trying to prove he went back to Brian Boru, on his mother's side. Most nights when he got spiflicated he'd put his arms around me and say we'd go home one day, home to Innisfree. It was a prospect I dreaded.

**EPILOGUE TO THE COUNTRY GIRLS
TRILOGY**

EDNA O'BRIEN is an Irish novelist and short story-writer who made her name in the 1960s with her trilogy *The Country Girls*. The books follow Kate Brady and Baba Brennan from their childhoods in rural western Ireland to London via Dublin. The journey is one of self-discovery, in a world made increasingly complex by bigger cities.

It introduces themes that continued to dominate O'Brien's writing. Women strive for emotional and sexual freedom, but must confront both male hypocrisy and Catholic guilt. In a characteristic short story, *A Scandalous Woman*, she evokes a gossipy farming community and describes events that lead the involved narrator to reflect, "I thought that ours indeed was a land of shame, a land of murder, and a land of strange, throttled, sacrificial women."

This darkness is sometimes relieved by flashes of sparkling humour: characters who tend to mythologise their homeland meet others ready to deflate their romanticism. In O'Brien's work, Ireland is not a land of lost innocence, distinct from a corrupt modern world, but a place where harm and temptation exist as much as anywhere else. Her women awaken to this world in a rich variety of veins: their streams of consciousness range from the effortlessly lyrical to the brutally frank. Recently her writing has turned its attention to the political troubles of her country: *A House of Splendid Isolation* follows a woman's responses to a wanted terrorist who is hiding in her house.

O'Brien

FLANN   **born Strabane, County Tyrone 1911; died Dublin 1966**

You recall The Man with the Watch, The Man with the Razor Blade? Would you like me to record some more pests? How about, for example, The Man Who Knows That Hitler/ Hirohito/ Roosevelt/ Churchill/ de Valera Is Really Dead and What You And I See Is Only A Double? Did you ever meet that dreadful spook? (Or have I said the wrong thing – how could you meet yourself?)

COLUMN IN THE IRISH TIMES

MAJOR WORKS

At Swim-Two-Birds (1939)

The Hard Life; The Dalkey Archive (1965)

The Third Policeman (1967)

The Poor Mouth (in Irish as An Béal Bocht) (1973)

WHEN JOYCE LEFT DUBLIN for good, he became a more disciplined writer and was at last able to write *Ulysses* rather than talk it out of himself in a pub. On the other hand, Brian O Nuillain stayed and worked as a civil servant at a level high enough to necessitate his work appearing under pseudonyms.

Some aspects of his work show what might have happened had **Joyce** stayed. The books are shorter, they lost their way toward the end, clouded by alcohol and borrowing too heavily from earlier books. His real problem lay in combining his advanced Catholic education, his wit and oblique storytelling manner without sounding too much like his mentor. Indeed, many critics thought his first novel, *At Swim-Two-Birds*, took on wholesale Joyce's blend of classical myth and exaggerated realism. Joyce loved it. It displays an **O'Casey**-like love of verbal fancy and circumlocution, which tends to emphasise the author's reluctance to write anything rude.

Although his language was the model of propriety, he wanted his subject matter to shock and wrote a book he hoped would be banned by the Irish clergy. *The Third Policeman* contains a boorish priest called Fahrt, but it still expresses much of the author's profoundly Catholic thinking. He researched a final novel by cornering people in pubs and asking them if they thought St Augustine of Hippo might be black: it is not considered his finest work. Many readers rediscovering his novels will have come to him through his collected newspaper pieces, which demand a lot from his audience: in-jokes are even more "in" when they appear sometimes in Irish, or even in rampant medieval Latin.

O'Casey

SEAN

born Dublin 1884; died Torquay, Devon 1964

It's me's the sorry soul for listening to you. You promised a quiet hour of poetry, but we were hardly here when you began to move. Yeats's poems soon flew out of your head and hand. You got as far as 'I will arise and go now, and go to Innisfree'; then before the echo of the line was hushed, you had me clapped down on your knee.

BEDTIME STORY

SEAN O'CASEY BELONGS to a tradition of Irish writers and artists who felt misunderstood in their own country. Like **Wilde**, he moved to England, embracing not so much his adopted home as his status as an exile – he declined a CBE. Like J.M. Synge's work some 15 years before, his plays were capable of causing riots in Dublin and **W.B. Yeats** vigorously defended both to the crowds.

But Yeats was also to feud with O'Casey when he rejected *The Silver Tassie* at the Abbey Theatre in Dublin because it departed from the realism of earlier plays. Although the two men were later reconciled, this dispute, and his love for the London-based actress Eileen Carey, kept O'Casey out of Ireland permanently. In the end, he discouraged performance of his plays there.

What disturbed his audiences were his open Marxism, attacks on the clergy and particularly the appearance of an Irish Tricolour in an on-stage pub scene. These issues called his patriotism into question, but for all his pacifism, he played his own part in the Irish Revolution. His plays are strong on dialect and his spelling reflects pronunciation more than orthography. He writes dialogue with great musicality, with characters building up patterns of rhetoric and echoes between one another; this dignifies O'Casey's world of suffering workers and strong women. If he tends to idolise the latter, he still has much fun at the expense of repressed men and their panic-stricken sexuality.

O'Hara

FRANK

born Baltimore 1926; died New York 1966

an invitation to lunch

HOW DO YOU LIKE THAT?

when I only have 16 cents and 2

packages of yogurt

there's a lesson in that, isn't there

like in Chinese poetry when a leaf falls?

hold off on the yogurt till the very

last, when everything may improve

FROM FIVE POEMS, IN LUNCH POEMS

FRANK O'HARA WROTE many of his poems during his lunch breaks, while working as an assistant curator at the Museum of Modern Art in New York. His descriptions of street scenes fix on the ephemeral, block by block, as he walks to and from his midday meal. In these contexts, he can divulge his thoughts. Although these seldom lie far beneath the level of stimulus response, sometimes the fugitive nature of that response works its own poetry.

His most famous poem is an exception that demonstrates this. It is *The Day Lady Died*, with the poem dithering over a literary present and pausing at a tobacconist's: his poem commemorates where he was when he discovered Billie Holiday had died. He concludes "…and I stopped breathing".

This kind of cadence leaps out of his work. Other epiphanies glint more briefly from the same laid-back verse style. When the sun wakes him up in the morning, it is for a chat about poetry – nothing heavy. O'Hara's description of the technique is best: a poem called *Poetry* begins, "The only way to be

quiet/is to be quick, so I scare/you clumsily, or surprise/you with a stab." He could write at length, as in his pamphlet-sized opus *Second Avenue*, and in a number of plays he wrote for Off-Off Broadway; but his pieces tend to be short. Whether his lines are luxuriant or staccato, crammed with metaphor or just taking in the scene, his tone is always talky, even when he's hectoring.

Ever the art critic, the poet relied on his eye as much as his ear and must account for it in *Why I Am Not a Painter*. His eyes are at their widest when he's at the cinema: like his own poetry, it has an immediate effect, but repays frequent revisits.

'Omar Khayyám

born Nishapur c. 1048; died Nishapur c. 1122

You rising Moon that looks for us again –
How oft hereafter will she wax and
  wane;
How oft hereafter rising look for us
Through this same Garden – and for
  one in vain!

THE RUBÁIYÁT OF 'OMAR KHAYYÁM, TR
EDWARD FITZGERALD

'OMAR KHAYYÁM WAS a Persian astronomer, mathematician and poet, who was summoned to Court in 1074, where he helped enquire into time-keeping. He also published works on algebra, but is best known in the West for his *Rubáiyát*.

This is the collective name for the distinctive form of quatrain called the *rubái*, imitated in the famous translation of Edward Fitzgerald. It is through this version that the work attributed to 'Omar Khayyám is best known (much of the work's authorship has been disputed). The translator admitted to taking liberties with the original and later attempts strove to capture a grittier quality in the original where Fitzgerald favours lyricism. Still, Fitzgerald's offering is still treasured as a miraculous achievement of what Salman Rushdie has called in his novel *Shame*, whose hero is named after the poet, "carrying across".

The original poet drew on the mystical Sufi traditions flourishing around his native Nishapur and shares their theme of intoxication. But whereas in Sufism this invokes heady spirituality, for 'Omar Khayyám, wine is a defence against the brevity of life and the austerity of religion. The poet asks why God has allowed the vine to exist, if it is so forbidden. Drink becomes a metaphor for the human condition. In one sequence, jugs in a shed talk to one another, wondering why they have been made in so many different ways. God is cast as the potter, Time as a crusher of grapes, people as vessels and the wine-cup as bearing the soul.

Throughout, the poetry perfectly evokes the evanescence of life. Even the stanza form suggests it: one rhyme will always slip away uncapped. In expressing an Eastern mistrust of reality, such verse advocates wine "to drug the memory" while facing a future in which the only certainty is death.

O'Neill

EUGENE　　　　　　　　　　**born New York 1888; died Boston 1953**

The makings of a poet. No, I'm afraid I'm like the guy who is always panhandling for a smoke... I couldn't touch what I tried to tell you just now. I just stammered. That's the best I'll ever do. I mean, if I live. Well, it will be faithful to realism, at least. Stammering is the native eloquence of us fog people.

LONG DAY'S JOURNEY
INTO NIGHT

EUGENE O'NEILL IS the first great name in American theatre. His interest in the stage must have been fired in boyhood – his father was an actor – but survived his professions as sailor and journalist, just as he survived tuberculosis. He pored over plays on his sick bed and when he recovered joined a theatre workshop in Harvard. He began as he would end (in *Long Day's Journey Into Night*), with writing strongly reflective of his own experience, especially of his family, and his early plays recall his times at sea.

His early work absorbed many of the current European trends in drama. Many of his pieces would draw on symbolism or expressionism to make his points, which were often profoundly psychological. His plays were regularly on Broadway, although he refused to allow any of his work to be performed between 1934 and 1946. He was awarded the Pulitzer Prize four times, the last time posthumously, and won the Nobel Prize for Literature in 1936.

His writing shows breathtaking ambition. His dramas are reliably lengthy and make enormous demands of the performers, almost to the point of stifling interpretation. Still, there are very different ways of staging O'Neill: directors can treat him with **Shakespeare**an reverence, or else be less daunted by his rhetoric, which can provide some magnificent speeches poeticising a heart-felt, Freudian view of human relationships. His trilogy *Mourning Becomes Electra* does this with **Aeschylus**' *Oresteia*, dispensing with deities and a chorus to give a more realistic view of guilt. It is set in the American South immediately after the Civil War.

Orwell

GEORGE

born Montihari, Bengal 1903; died London 1950

In the public wards of a hospital you see horrors that you don't seem to meet with among people who manage to die in their own homes, as though certain diseases only attacked people at the lower income levels.

HOW THE POOR DIE

GEORGE ORWELL DECLARED that he wrote every word toward the establishment of democratic socialism.

He won a scholarship to Eton, where the difference between his background and those of his fee-paying classmates provided him with an early understanding of social disparities. When he left, he saw the situation in a starker, more global light: he joined the Imperial Police Force in Burma, taught English in France, experienced great poverty there and in England, and encountered politics more formal than guilt alone could have given him when fighting with the Republicans in the Spanish Civil War. From these experiences came the memoirs *Down and Out in Paris and London*, chronicling his struggle to survive down to the last centimes, and *Homage to Catalonia*, which contains glimpses of the widely divergent factions of left-wing thought and action, through which he tried to find his own personal vision.

Further evils abroad made this harder still. The threat of Fascism convinced him that Britain could only confront it by reforming itself totally and Stalinism drove him to explore what form socialism could take without the threat of totalitarianism. To this end he wrote his two most famous books, *Animal Farm* and *Nineteen Eighty-Four*.

The former is an allegory of the Russian Revolution and its failures in the most pathetic and human terms (all the more so because its characters are animals), while the latter shows a society in which the state's power extends to its subjects' innermost thoughts. Orwell's examination of those thoughts as they range from defiance to submission show him to be a writer of great psychological subtlety, able to demonstrate the motivations behind apparently evil acts as much as instinctively human ones. With Newspeak, a jargon-ridden tongue that rehashes ideas into pellet-like form for the "proles" to swallow, he exposes power's abuse of language. His own plain English did much to counter it.

Ossian

Perhaps thou art like me, at times strong, feeble at times; our years descending from the sky, and hastening together towards their end. Rejoice, O sun! as thou advancest in the vigour of thy youth.

OSSIAN'S ADDRESS TO THE RISING SUN

A poet, in his closet, could no more compose like Ossian, than he could act like him in the field or in the mountain.

HUGH AND JOHN MCCALLUM, IN THEIR 1816 EDITION OF OSSIAN'S POEMS

OISIN IS THE GAELIC name for this bard and warrior from the Highlands, who might have lived in the second or third century AD. In 1760, James Macpherson claimed to have recorded poems often about him and usually attributed to him and produced a modest sample of Gaelic to lend his translation authority. **Dr Johnson** expressed doubts as to the work's authenticity in his *Journey to the Western Isles of Scotland* and Macpherson proved unable to procure the sources of his *Fragments of Ancient Poetry Collected in the Highlands of Scotland, and Translated from the Gaelic or Erse Language*. After his death, an enquiry decided Macpherson had found ancient poems, but extemporised so freely on their themes that it was almost a different work.

The English could now dismiss these productions as forgeries, comforted that the Scots had no **Homer** after all. But by 1816, the Highland Society had collected enough material to publish *Ossian's Poems*. The editors' ability to cite their originals and their damning ripostes to Johnson make the neglect of this volume bizarre. Much of it is fragmentary, with less of the plot Macpherson tried to impose, and perhaps transcribed from what the remaining clan-like bards could recite.

What England could ignore now had Europe aflame. Ossian had captured the romantic spirit. **Goethe** and Napoleon were enchanted. Earthier epic had emerged to rival Homer and the refined **Virgil**. The high-pitched rhetoric, the epithets and translationese of the work delivered just what readers wanted. The neat match of supply and demand still seems to many more than a coincidence, but the similarity between the Scottish and Greek oral traditions provides a revealing study of how stories get told, in whatever culture.

Ovid

born Sulmo, the Abruzzi 43 BC; died Tomis, on the Black Sea c.17 AD

We, yield, and take this passion with a fight?

We yield: a burden gladly borne is light.

LOVES

OVID WROTE THAT to produce good poetry, you need "ars" and "ingenium" – knack and luck. Ovid's poetry is so clever and sharp that it seems all artistry. Even in exile by the Black Sea, he never sounds like the tortured genius we meet in **Propertius** – which is not to deny that he was genuinely miserable. For Ovid, everything looks too easy: in the very first lines of his corpus, he demonstrates how Cupid rigged his metre, and then makes it his own. He wrote elegy according to stricter rules than anyone had attempted before and yet made it more immediate: his jokes are still funny and quite rude.

But he was a unique figure, not happy simply to perfect the work of others. He was the author of some completely original poems. Other poets had written wondering why women spent so long on their make-up: it took Ovid to begin it as a treatise in mock-epic language. Even in jest, he wants to enlighten as well as enliven. When guiding the reader through the mysteries of love, he is a more hands-on instructor than other elegists, especially in *The Art of Love*. He suggests you take your date to the circus, where sand gets in awkward places, and obliges you to brush it off.

Other poems aim to provide less erotic information. His work on Roman feast days provides the most complete view we have of contemporary religion, and intrigued the anthropologist James Fraser. Ovid's masterpiece, *Metamorphoses*, is more ambitious still. It is an encyclopedic presentation of myths in which people turn into things. The subject matter is no limit to his imagination and his only attempt at epic shows him varying his material with the same consummate balance of his love poems, introducing contrasting episodes and pacing their narration with a care that never seems precious. As ever, it is as though the theme found him, rather than the other way round – he had as much luck as knack after all.

Owen

WILFRED   **born Oswestry 1893; died on the Western Front, France 1918**

...Behold,

A ram, caught in a thicket by its horns;

Offer the Ram of Pride instead of him.

But the old man would not so, but slew

his son –

And half the seed of Europe, one by one.

THE PARABLE OF THE OLD MEN
AND THE YOUNG

MAJOR WORKS

Poems, edited by Siegfried Sassoon (1920)

"MY SUBJECT IS War, and the pity of War", wrote Wilfred Owen, and except for a few early poems, it was to be his only subject. These first works show a young teacher in France trying out new metres and rhyme-schemes in verses showing facility, but which read as exercises. This is partly because his experiments with poetry were daring enough to need some practice. His style and themes at the time showed his deep love of **Keats**. It was not the language of horror.

He joined the army in 1915. Although less seduced by events than Rupert Brooke, he began the war in a similar spirit, feeling something like heroism. Throughout the hostilities, he showed immense courage and was awarded the Military Cross. But in 1917 his nerves failed and he was sent to recover at Craiglockhart psychiatric hospital.

There he met Siegfried Sassoon, a poet and soldier who was by then actively campaigning against the war. Owen showed him his poems in all humility and received some encouragement. The technical effects he had nearly mastered before the war had now become a successful way of imitating the sheer noise of the trenches and his sudden changes of pace within potentially static sonnets and quatrains could suggest life-or-death panics. He wrote, "I don't want to write anything to which a soldier would say No Compris!" From Sassoon, he learned to adopt a more direct, speech-like voice. Sassoon sometimes used this for brusque and brutal satire, while in Owen's hands this conversational approach let him animate a ghost-world: in *Strange Meeting*, the chilling exchange takes place between dead soldiers.

Here characters reflect on what might have been, if it hadn't been for the war. We know Owen could be given to happiness, but that he would never be able to forget this pity. Today, poets are still indebted to his innovations in rhyme, but we cannot know what he might have done. He was killed one week before the war ended.

Parker

DOROTHY · born West End, New York State 1893; died New York 1967

Razors pain you;

Rivers are damp;

Acids stain you;

And drugs cause cramp.

Guns aren't lawful;

Nooses give;

Gas smells awful;

You might as well live.

RÉSUMÉ

DOROTHY PARKER IS remembered for her wit. Wit can be put to any number of uses – for her, it was peculiarly functional. She was a member of a circle (a Round Table, in fact, which would convene sporadically at the Algonquin Hotel in New York) whose members made a living from their wits. The cheques for Parker's came first from *Vogue*, then from *Vanity Fair*, where, often under the pseudonym of Constant Reader, she became renowned for her damning reviews of plays and books – **Sinclair Lewis**, in particular, came in for brutal drubbings.

But money was not the only object. She had to survive mentally as well. She was the only woman of this circle (**Edna Ferber** would pop in, but even she was too gushy for Parker) and was often stigmatised for wanting to be a man. She later confessed that if the age had demanded cuteness, she would have been cute. But she was the harshest of them all. It is hard to smile at a Parker quip without simultaneously pitying its victim.

Ultimately Parker has a strong claim on our sympathies. Even in her comic verse (which she refused to call poems), she addresses the issue of suicide and the fallibility of relationships. The latter theme came to characterise her short stories. If the public manifestation of failed romances and a disturbed childhood was well-worded impatience, their private expressions were worse amorous entanglements, alcoholism, drug abuse and several suicide attempts. She survived these, too, but remained constantly aware that some things are not proper subjects for humour.

Pasternak

BORIS

born Moscow 1890; died Peredelkino 1960

He both feared and loved that future and was secretly proud of it, and, as though for the last time, as if saying goodbye, was avidly aware of the trees and clouds and of the people walking in the streets of the great Russian city struggling through misfortune – and he was ready to sacrifice himself to make things better but was powerless to do anything.

DOCTOR ZHIVAGO,
TR. MAX HAYWARD AND MANYA HARAI

BORIS PASTERNAK LOVED his country. He was a poet sensitive enough to understand at once its need for change and the suffering much of that change inflicted. From World War One onwards, he was in trouble with the authorities and unable to publish anything for 10 years. When the Stalin era ended, the "thaw" under Khrushchev, which benefitted so many other writers, did nothing for Pasternak. It was then that he wrote his masterpiece, *Doctor Zhivago*. He had worked on it since 1946 and it appeared in print 11 years later in Italy. The book was banned in the Soviet Union and the author's rulers forbade him to accept the Nobel Prize it was awarded.

He had not meant to criticise the regime. He had welcomed the Bolshevik Revolution with modernist poems written in the same vein as his friend **Mayakovsky**, but his sensitivity to the more perennial truths he divined in nature dominated subsequent work. His apparent disregard for historical movements attracted the authorities' attention, particularly with the line, "What century is it out there?" in *About These Poems*.

The poet-hero Doctor Zhivago cannot remain so indifferent. By then Pasternak had suffered his own griefs in the Soviet Union and no longer felt able to address human concerns: his mistress had been sent to a labour camp. His prose shows a lyric poet's leaning toward short episodes, contrasting voices and word music. The hero's own poems are appended to the text, showing the author's continued faith in Christian imagery and complete identification with his central character.

Pavese

CESARE

born San Stefano Belbo 1908; died Turin 1950

I could understand if they talked about brushes, colours, turpentine – the things they use – but no, these people talk obscurely because they like to and sometimes no-one knows what certain words mean and there's always somebody else who suddenly begins to argue, says no, that it means such and such and everything's upside down. They are words like those in the newspapers when they talk about paintings.

AMONG WOMEN ONLY

CESARE PAVESE WAS A POET and novelist who brought to Italian letters a passion for American and English writers, as well as an interest in modernism. His writing is in some ways exemplary of the realism prevalent in the Italy of his day, but there is the strong influence of **Joyce** and **Melville** – Pavese translated *Moby-Dick* into Italian in 1932.

His own prose is more accessible than that of his masters. He avoids rhetorical flourishes, but the construction of scenes and chapters show him to be a natural poet. *Among Women Only* has a narrator who tunes in and out of the socialite babble of surrounding Turin. The whole effect shows Pavese's ear for cadence (the book's last line is stunning), while only a few of his characters are of any consequence to the story.

This quest for a meaning in life occupies characters elsewhere in his work. They typically seek it in their history or sexuality. Failure in the search can bring out their suicidal tendencies, or extreme violence. For all the realism of a work like his last, *The Moon and the Bonfires*, the farmer who murders his incestuous lover does so after so little provocation that his motives can barely exist outside him.

Pavese seems to have shared this extreme form of loneliness. Like several of his characters, facing the choice of accepting life or refusing to take part in it, he chose death. After producing a flurry of instantly-acclaimed work and prizes, he committed suicide.

Paz

OCTAVIO

born Mexico City 1914

Between what I see and what I say,

between what I say and what

   I keep silent,

between what I keep silent and what

   I dream,

between what I dream and what

   I forget, poetry.

SHEAF, TR. ELIOT WEINBERGER

OCTAVIO PAZ IS the leading poet working in Spanish today. His public life has extended well beyond poetry – he has worked as a diplomat and teacher – but his commitment to poetry is particularly single-minded. He has always avoided dogmatism: when **Neruda** made it possible for him to witness the Spanish Civil War, the left-leaning Paz found much the same mess of political objectives that **Orwell** encountered and he was not completely convinced by the Republican cause. Still more upsetting for many on the left was his insistence on speaking up about the atrocities of Stalin and the Soviet labour camps. His continued refusal to represent beliefs that are not his own culminated in his resignation in 1968 from the post of Mexican ambassador to India, when his government's troops fired on student demonstrators during the Olympic Games.

His poetry is avowedly free of political creeds and celebrates the purity of the form. "Every poem is time, and burns," he has written; his lines show care over each syllable that composes them. His haiku prove this most succinctly: "The whole world fits in-/to seventeen syllables,/and you in this hut." His verse, meanwhile, found a kind of freedom through the surrealism of **Breton**, but his sensitivity to his language's unique way of evoking the erotic properties of sun and landscape fills *Sun Stone*.

His memories of that sun and of Mexico illumine his subsequent work. His poetry from India notes a similar dryness: in fact, the poems in *East Slope* balance reflections on the gardens of Delhi with recollections of his own country in a time of trouble. The result is an insight into the poet's sense of isolation: "The writer should be a sniper, he should endure solitude, he should know himself to be a marginal being."

283

Peake

MERVYN   **born Kuling, Kiangsi Province, China 1911; died Burcot, Oxon 1968**

> '*What have you brought with you?*' *she said. Mr Pye turned his gaze upon her. 'Love,' he said. 'Just... Love...' and then he transferred the fruit-drop from one cheek to the other with a flick of his experienced tongue.*
>
> MR PYE

MERVYN PEAKE WAS a writer of alarming imaginative powers. He was as much a visual artist as a verbal one and would draw his characters before describing them. He illustrated his own books, such as *Mr Pye*, his volumes of verse and he provided images for other texts. **C.S. Lewis** praised those that accompany *The Rime of the Ancient Mariner* for their rendering of terror in purely formal designs and his pictures for *Bleak House* are stunning.

The atmosphere and characterisation (including the names) in the *Gormenghast Trilogy* show the continuing importance of **Dickens** to Peake. He has the same propensity for bursting into blank verse (at which he excelled) and while Gormenghast seems like a fantastical creation, its absurdities are grounded in a Dickensian kind of realism. There events advance slowly, with a formal precision. In this dilapidated family seat, everything happens strictly according to order and precedent long-established: Titus Groan is the 77th Earl. The pile itself is skirted by slums: so apparently remote and changeless a world is vulnerable to the charismatic boy-rebel Steerpike, who provides a peerlessly plotted portrait of moral collapse as he menaces the place with destruction.

Peake worked on the book during World War Two while recovering from the nervous breakdown he suffered in 1943. He remained active in wartime as an artist and was one of the first to witness the death camps at Belsen. What he depicted there moved him to extraordinary poetry, which strove to express the horror of trying to represent a consumptive woman there: "If such can be a painter's ecstasy... Then where is mercy?" His words and lines always contrived to make his bleak vision real, but at the last he concluded, "To live at all is miracle enough", and left it as his epitaph.

Perec

GEORGES

born Paris 1936; died Paris 1982

Let us imagine... a man of exceptional arrogance who wishes to fix, to describe, and to exhaust not the whole world... but a constituted fragment of the world: in the face of the inextricable incoherence of things, he will set out to execute a (necessarily limited) programme right the way through, in all its irreducible, intact entirety.

LIFE: A USER'S MANUAL, TR. DAVID BELLOS

PEREC WROTE a 300-page novel without the letter "e"; a shorter book (*Les Revenentes*) without "a", "i", "o", or "u"; a palindrome 500 words long; an inventory of everything he ate in 1974; works in autobiography with deliberately misremembered facts; symmetrical texts which negate themselves; and the unbelievable *Life: A User's Manual*.

These might seem like arid exercises with no point and no soul, but work so moving can never be pointless. Even his driest lists can be dreamy or hilarious, poems even, full of soul. His first book, *Things*, presents a young couple in the 1960s who want material proof that they've "arrived", attain it, but start craving "things" simply for their own sake. Their lives become "frankly insipid". Other Perec characters can anticipate this realisation; in *Life: A User's Manual*, they dedicate themselves to projects they often know will come to nothing. Even the "e-less" *A Void* shows a world in which first a vowel vanishes,

then the hero Anton Vowl, then anyone who looks for him. And the Paris block housing the apartments of *Life...* will hardly survive its inhabitants.

This can reflect the author's tragedy. His father died in battle, moments before Paris fell in 1940, while his mother "disappeared" at Auschwitz. Much of Perec's writing points towards guilt and loss. But what he has achieved in *Life...* , in glimpses of often empty flats at a moment fixed in time, where artefacts occasion stories leading to other stories, with jokes, teasers, tearful histories, parodies, hidden quotes, all fitting – jigsaw-like – into a purposely-flawed system, is the most perfect, most joyous account of the novel, and of life, imaginable.

Perelman

S.J.

born New York 1904; died New York 1979

There aren't any humorists any more, except for Perelman... Perelman must be very lonely.

DOROTHY PARKER

Love flies out the door when money comes innuendo.

MONKEY BUSINESS

WHEN GROUCHO MARX said, "From the moment I picked up your book to the moment I laid it down, I was convulsed with laughter. Some day I intend reading it," he was talking about S.J. Perelman's first collection of sketches. This was meant to commend the book rather than condemn it, and appeared as blurb. Still, Perelman felt that he was remembered only as the co-writer of the Marx Brothers' films *Monkey Business* and *Horse Feathers*. In turn, Groucho felt Perelman's brand of joke could be too literary to reach a wider audience.

Perelman worked as a cartoonist and sketch-writer, appearing regularly in *The New Yorker*. There he pioneered his parodic and punning prose: the most regular butt of his wit was himself. These pieces are considered to be his best writing. He had a technique that seemed impromptu, similar to the best Marx Brothers moments, when sheer pace let his verbal schtick lead to more without us having to spot the connections. But this gift did not transfer well to the stage: however fine the lines were, they did not cohere as whole shows. As with his film work, he wrote for the theatre collaboratively, both with his wife, (the sister of **Nathanael West**), and with **Ogden Nash**. His pace dialogue, balanced by Nash's comic verse skills, went into the musical *One Touch of Venus*, with a score by Kurt Weill.

His acute eye for the absurd focussed on his compatriots, though few could take offence: if he was describing human folly, he involved himself in it fully. Still, few of his fellow fools had so reliable a knack with language.

Petrarch

FRANCESCO

born Arezzo 1304; died Arquà 1374

And cowarde Love, then, to the hart apace

Taketh his flight, wher he doth lurke

and playne

His purpose lost, and dare not

shew his face.

For my lordes gilt thus fawtles

byde I payine;

Yet from my lorde shall not my

foote remove:

Sweete is the death that taketh end by love.

RIME 140, TR HENRY HOWARD,
THE EARL OF SURREY

PETRARCH'S GREAT LEARNING and poetic skill anticipated the literary concerns of the Renaissance and contributed enormously to the later interest in expressing classical themes in new, lyrical forms. His scholarship began with legal studies and then a training for the priesthood, although he never took full orders. He distinguished himself at the court of Robert of Naples, whose clothes he wore when becoming poet laureate at Rome in 1341 and through whom he became a friend of **Boccaccio**.

It was Petrarch who advised Boccaccio not to renounce his life's work and become a priest; yet the poet's own work displays qualms about the same issues. He repudiated his famous lyric poetry later in life and would have preferred recognition of his contemplative Latin writings, most notably the *Secretum Meum*, an imaginary conversation with St Augustine on this dilemma.

Although his poetry is remarkably pure, celebrating his unrequited love for a married woman many think to be Laure (Laura) de Noves, it has the same paradoxical spirit. His theme of freedom in servitude is as classical as it is Christian; his imagery and rhetoric are straight from the Roman erotic elegists (he owned a now-famous manuscript of **Propertius**) and echoes **Catullus**'s sentiment, 'I love, I hate – perhaps you wonder why…' He refined his expression of these ideas in sonnets and provided the model of that verse form. His methods of listing symptoms or states of mind throughout a poem, to subvert them at the end and of using 14 lines to explore an image only to point out how ill it fits his own case, established a genre that dominated the Renaissance and that **Shakespeare** later perfected, in adapted form, in English.

Petronius

Roman, 1st Century AD

*'And no-one taught him. I refined him
myself by sending him to the tramps. So
he has no equal in imitating muleteers or
tramps. He's madly clever: he's as much a
cobbler, cook and fisherman as property
of all the muses. He has two weaknesses,
without which he'd be all there: he's
circumcised and snores. As for his
squiffey eyes, incurable: that's how Venus
sees.'*

TRIMALCHIO'S FEAST

The Satyricon, including
Trimalchio's Feast

PETRONIUS MAY HAVE been the "Judge of Taste" in Nero's court – a stoic whose suicide was made famous in the film *Quo Vadis?* – or he may have been someone else who just happened to be called Judge (*Arbiter*). The work attributed to him is an equally unknown quantity. Only fragments survive of what might have been a long work called the *Satyricon*. The name derives from satyrs – half-men and half-goats, whose lewdness would round off the Dionysian play festivals (see **Harrison**), but might be punning on the Latin *satura*, meaning a ragout or hotchpotch. The work is just that, incorporating snatches of verse and parodies of epic in slangy and immediate Latin prose. It is appropriate that the surviving excerpt gives an account of a lavish feast, with delicacies from all over the world served in relentless mixtures by Trimalchio, a loud-mouthed host eager to display his wealth. Even faced with this plenitude, his guests don't mind talking exhaustively about other meals they've eaten recently and telling stories that spin off from those.

We see it all from the point of view of two slaves who have gate-crashed. They are on the run and the banquet is just one adventure on the way. There is much satire: Petronius shares **Juvenal**'s target of the *gauche parvenu* and makes fun of Trimalchio's much-vaunted love of his slaves. The slaves themselves are silent witnesses to the extravagance around them, but do not emerge sympathetically from other fragments. In showing us the extremes of Roman decadence (especially if he was writing during Nero's reign), Petronius leaves us to contemplate a society in which these abundant depravities are even imaginable, let alone likely. Fellini's film embraces this chaos and takes it further still.

Pinter

HAROLD

born London 1930

In Düsseldorf about two years ago I took, as is the Continental custom, a bow with the German cast of The Caretaker at the end of the play on the first night... we took 34 curtain calls, all to boos. By the 34th there were only two people left in the house, still booing. I was strangely warmed by all this, and now, whenever I sense a tremor of the old apprehension or expectation, I remember Düsseldorf, and am cured.

WRITING FOR THE THEATRE

IT WOULD BE EASY to call Harold Pinter's plays experimental – his method of composition involves putting characters in a room and seeing what happens – but through all his innovation, he seems to know exactly what he's doing. From the age of 20, he acted in many plays and occasionally performs in his own; his stagecraft is matched by an ear honed by writing a lot of poetry, only a little of which he has published.

His subject matter and language is prosaic, but as his characters interact, they attain the rhythms of verse. They play with words and transform their registers: in Pinter "succulent" can become taboo, or "Sidcup" talismanic. In *The Birthday Party* two men in suits who come from nowhere harass a jobbing pianist as much with clichés as with violence. We don't always discover why characters find certain phrases so threatening, but during a good performance, we come to share their sense of dread. The relationships that form between them can be more convincing than those in plays with fuller plots.

Pinter avoids writing plays with a moral purpose, although human dignity emerges as a major concern. He campaigns for human rights and has written a play for Amnesty International, *Mountain Language*. He keeps his own passions for offstage, including his love of cricket and dislike of America.

MAJOR WORKS

The Birthday Party (1958)

A Slight Ache (1959)

The Dumb Waiter (1960)

The Caretaker (1960)

The Homecoming (1964)

No Man's Land (1974)

Mountain Language (1988)

Pirandello

LUIGI

born Agrigento, Sicily 1867; died Rome 1936

I persist in giving audience every Sunday morning to the characters of my future short stories.

Three hours, from seven to 10.

I almost always find myself in bad company.

A CHARACTER'S TRAGEDY,
TR. STANLEY APPLEBAUM

PIRANDELLO TRANSFORMED theatre to express an extraordinary state of mind: the feeling that we are not in control of our actions. In his work, this is not so much because we are puppets of fate or the gods; we just feel like puppets. There is no philosophical accounting for this sensation. Its roots lie in rootlessness, or an inner madness.

Pirandello knew about both of these first-hand, from his efforts to raise a family in his native Sicily. His wife became dangerously insane, accusing him of sleeping with their daughter; when she was institutionalised, he felt free but homeless. He began reworking his stories into what became his 40 or so plays. The most famous of these shows a family incapable of acting out its own story. That the memories of their tragedy are too painful is not their only problem. *Six Characters in Search of an Author* is a play within a play, whose actors protest that they aren't proper actors; if anything, they are ghosts of an author's ideas, much like **Ibsen**'s ghosts. The two plays are comparable as landmarks in the development of drama.

The idea that the self is a composite of how we interact with others, rather than something fixed within us like a personality, continues in Pirandello's most admired play, *Henry IV*, which takes the idea into the realms of madness. This kind of expression eventually brought him into conflict with the Fascist regime with which he had previously enjoyed good relations: he wanted social change and Mussolini wanted progressive art. His country was naturally proud of his Nobel Prize in 1934, but by then he no longer wished to be buried in Italian soil. He wanted to be cremated, and his ashes scattered to the air around his childhood home.

Plath

SYLVIA

born Boston, Massachusetts 1932; died London 1963

Love set you going like a fat gold watch.

The midwife slapped your footsoles, and

> *your cry*

Took its place among the elements.

MORNING SONG

SYLVIA PLATH'S SUICIDE cut short a career that produced forceful and immediate poetry. Much of it is hard to read without thinking of her early death, but this tends to obscure the range of her work, which can be ecstatic as well as bleak. Throughout her life she suffered from manic depression, which may account for the violent swings in mood. Towards the end she was writing at speed – sometimes up to two or three poems a day – a rate that would seem to indicate extreme emotional activity. This contrasts with her earlier output, which she wrote methodically, often with a thesaurus, and includes sonnets and several villanelles, a form requiring the discipline that served her well.

This part of her poetic training was complemented by classes with **Robert Lowell**, whose confessional style suited Plath's mode of self-expression. But both before and after, Plath's emotional pitch remained high and her themes constant. In early work she used classical myths to explore herself – Persephone's dual personality reflects her own experience – and later poems are just as subjective. They dwell increasingly on the clinical institutions she had come to know through mental illness and childbirth: her short, sparing lines and quickly captured images convey a terrifying cleanliness, sterility even.

Her only novel, *The Bell Jar*, explores this sense autobiographically, telling of her education both in the US and at Cambridge, and ultimately of her breakdowns and an early attempt at suicide. It examines the protagonist's youth in well-to-do America, and expresses anger at the strictures and the demands made of women. These do not disappear in England, although she is happier there for a time. Plath settled in London and married Ted Hughes. She was becoming increasingly established as a leading poet, especially through radio broadcasts, when she took her own life. Posthumous publications of her work have confirmed this reputation, won by the vivid representation of otherwise unimaginable terror in verse that seldom loses control.

MAJOR WORKS

A Winter Ship (published anonymously)

The Colossus (1960)

Ariel (1965)

Crossing the Water (1971)

Winter Trees (1971)

The Bell Jar (novel, 1963)

Plato

born Athens c. 429 BC; died Athens c. 347 BC

But my point is that what they call love isn't love of a half, or of a whole, my friend, so much as of whatever strikes them as being good, since men really want to cut off their own feet and hands if they reckon there's disease in them. You see, I don't think people embrace what is theirs, unless one can call something that seems good one's own, and something bad someone else's.

DIOTIMA, IN THE SYMPOSIUM

PLATO WROTE the finest prose in Greek. All the peculiarities of the language serve his turn, down to the tiny words that can spring a sentence's rhythm or swing an argument completely.

But he preferred interaction and speech to writing, which he felt could not stand up for itself. This is why his writing is so conversational. His dialogues present his teacher Socrates hailing people in the street and teasing out of them definitions of words he would query through compelling dialectic. To some, such as **Aristophanes**, this seemed like sophistry. Plato defended Socrates' reputation, losing his faith in a political system that sentenced his hero to death.

Plato's ideal state would have been ruled by philosophers; but even the severe constitution he proposes emerges from another attempt to define one word: justice. The whole *Republic* aims to show it in action. Other works follow such enquiries to less definite conclusions and a discourse leads typically to a state of *aporia*, or cluelessness. This might seem like a sophist's technique; but in Plato's thinking, we cannot understand real truths with language, or the senses. They existed before we were born and await our contemplation when we die.

Plato is his own best critic, even of this most dearly cherished belief: his dialogue *The Sophist* attacks it directly. Throughout his career, he recreated this *aporia*. The most sublime single example of this is *The Symposium*, in which party guests try to describe Eros. Even when Socrates argues that the exercise is misguided and convinces us with another view, his drunken admirer Alcibiades crashes in to subvert the whole process. Elusive as ever, Plato never tells us what love really is. But then, whoever did?

Plautus

born Sarsina, Umbria c. 250 BC; died Rome 184 BC

*From what I hear this writing to be
    saying,*

unless it makes you cry out silver coins,

*you'll no more get the thing you want
    with tears*

than you could catch a rainfall in a sieve.

*I won't leave you, now you're in love;
    don't worry.*

PSEUDOLUS

PLAUTUS DID MORE than anyone to bring comic drama to Rome. Of some 130 plays, 20 survive complete. These are usually taken from earlier Greek sources, which he acknowledges, without indicating how much he has adapted or simply lifted from his originals. These originals were most notably Menander and Diphilus, who represented the "new" Athenian comedy, as opposed to the older style of **Aristophanes**. It was from there that Plautus drew the character types that were to dominate the theatre for centuries afterwards: the braggart soldier, the love-sick youth (a figure who influenced lyric poetry as much as drama) and the slave who knows more than his employers about life and the plot.

Plautus' achievement was to translate these tales for an audience he knew well. The presentation was always in Greek dress, but the language was distinctly Latin. Not only did this accommodate more word-play; it also allowed fun at the expense of Greek names, which could become ludicrously long. He was a practical man of the theatre and only took to writing after spells as a stage-hand and actor. He learned how to take a Greek scene as a starting point for his own comic invention, or dispense with the original plots according to his own dramatic requirements. His scenes advance in pace verse styles and songs can break up the action. His own plays have become the model for later dramatists, especially **Molière** and **Shakespeare**: the latter turns the plot of *The Brothers*, with its two sets of identical twins, into *A Comedy of Errors*. Three Plautus plays were conflated to produce the musical *A Funny Thing Happened on the Way to the Forum*.

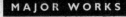

Po

LI

Her robe is a cloud, her face a flower;

Her balcony, glimmering with the bright

spring dew,

Is either the tip of the earth's Jade

mountain

Or a moon-edged roof of paradise.

A SONG OF PURE HAPPINESS,
TR. WITTER BYNNER

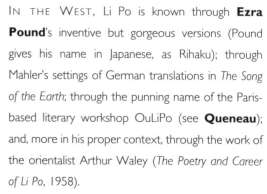

IN THE WEST, Li Po is known through **Ezra Pound**'s inventive but gorgeous versions (Pound gives his name in Japanese, as Rihaku); through Mahler's settings of German translations in *The Song of the Earth*; through the punning name of the Paris-based literary workshop OuLiPo (see **Queneau**); and, more in his proper context, through the work of the orientalist Arthur Waley (*The Poetry and Career of Li Po*, 1958).

In China he is better known as the reckless, drunken counterpart to the language's other best-loved poet, Tu Fu. While Tu Fu shows restraint and observes the constraints Chinese tones impose on its poetry, Li Po is more spontaneous and famed for producing eloquent formal verse for the emperor at a moment's notice and in an alcoholic stupor. Legends about him abound, as if they are measures of his popularity: he is said to have died either drunk in a boat, trying to grasp the moon's reflection, or else by being carried to heaven on the back of a dolphin. The idea that he was divine and immortal was one that Li Po was only too pleased to confirm.

He grew up in exile, in what is now Sinkiang province (then outside the empire). As a young man, he travelled around performing good deeds. In his dealings with the establishment, he showed scant regard for Confucian precepts, as did his early poetry, whose promise led the authorities to indulge him, without ever giving him any official position. In *The Bridge at Ten-Shin* he casts a dispassionate eye over court jostling. His skills won him a pleasant enough existence – he had four wives. His work celebrates wine and women in song, while in his treatment of youth and beauty, death is ever absent: even in his cups, he was contemplating the moon.

Poe

EDGAR ALLEN **born Boston, Mass. 1809; died Maryland 1849**

We stand upon the brink of a precipice. We peer into the abyss. We grow sick and dizzy. Our first impulse is to shrink from the danger, and yet, unaccountably, we remain.

THE IMP OF THE PERVERSE

POE WROTE OF POETRY'S PURITY in his criticism, while writing theatre reviews that would shift copies for their ruthlessness. He began his literary career with verse that would charm readers with its musicality, and became famous for later stories of imponderable bleakness.

In his short, turbulent life, he had known such bleakness. He was orphaned at the age of three. He gambled as a student, and was expelled from military academy; he became an alcoholic, and was regularly fired from periodicals. When he was 24, he secretly married a 13-year-old girl, who died when she was 25. He died in circumstances that have never been explained, his memory was vilified by his agent and friend, and true details of a life-story he had largely invented for himself were long in emerging.

In his fiction, he would explore apparently motiveless crimes, with the recurring theme of entombment. The horror is intensified by Poe's presentation of apparently sane people, who chronicle their own mania coolly, until the hypersensitivity induced by intolerable guilt takes over. But this is not the usual structure of cause and effect; it is as though crimes are waiting to happen. In his criticism, Poe would explore how elements in a story should contribute equally to one another, rather than that one should be of primary significance, to create a unified work of art. It is the same with the coherent sound-world his poems summon; he would consciously produce work that could be read whole in one sitting.

He can obsess readers, while some English-speaking critics have shrugged him off. His influence on the literature of other languages has been colossal: **Baudelaire** produced definitive French translations, **Mallarmé** would emulate his awareness of the inexpressible in decadent themes, and **Dostoyevsky** acknowledged his own debt to Poe.

Pope

ALEXANDER

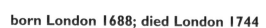

born London 1688; died London 1744

The vulgar thus through imitation err;

As oft the learn'd by being singular;

So much they scorn the crowd, that if the throng

By chance go right, they purposely go wrong.

AN ESSAY ON CRITICISM

AS A CATHOLIC, Pope could not receive a school education, hold a public office, or even live in London for part of his childhood. Physically, he was a peculiar figure in an awkward age, but his poetry had a robustness that the age demanded. When his critics became personal about his faith or frailty, he trounced them in *The Dunciad*, a lengthy skit that he updated as his rivals varied.

The best introduction to Pope is his *Essay on Criticism*, more for its technique than its precepts. He writes in rhyming, "heroic" couplets and shares with us the dos and don'ts of composing them. He not only parodies bad poetry, but shows the reader how to achieve the best effects – as if his imitators could produce lines as harmonious.

He used the form to translate **Homer**, as **Dryden** had done with **Virgil**: his *Iliad* and *Odyssey* did as much for English verse as his original works. One commentator remarked of his efforts, "It is a pretty poem, Mr. Pope, but it is not Homer…" For all Pope's luxuriance, his version, where every line has a strong finish and repeated phrases echo for longer with the rhymes, comes as close to Homer's tone as English has yet managed.

This work was crucial to his own poetry. He was the master of an epic style he could now parody better than his rivals and he used it in his most polished poem, *The Rape of the Lock*. Figures that in Homer would have been agents of the gods are now skulking in boudoirs, waiting for some heroic action to sway: but the stakes are no higher than a lock of hair (although this reaches the heavens) and the work's climactic event is a sneeze.

Pound

EZRA

born Hailey, Idaho 1885; died Venice 1972

There is no end of things in the heart.

I call in the boy,

Have him sit on his knees here

  To seal this,

And send it a thousand miles, thinking.

EXILE'S LETTER

IT IS TOO EASY to pass over Ezra Pound's poetry. To open *The Cantos* is to confront a text decorated by Chinese ideographs, Greek script and transcriptions of French or German texts, sitting beside banking letters from Renaissance Italy. The work of his beneficiaries is less intimidating: He encouraged writers as diverse as **Robert Frost**, **T.S. Eliot**, **H D** and **Ford Madox Ford**. Even **W.B. Yeats** was indebted to him. He could recognise others' talents and weaknesses without imposing his own artistic agendas. His extensive and often unacknowledged advice on *The Waste Land* shows Pound's expert ear for the types of verse Eliot could and couldn't write.

He was more dominant in organising the Imagist group of poets and persuading a large number of authors to share his faith in poems with an oriental economy, presenting images rather then expounding ideas. Again, all of these poets pursued their own artistic goals afterwards, but were nonetheless involved in his prophetic vision of literature, which he described as "news that stays news".

His own work followed this vision further than his contemporaries. His poetry is always at least one step ahead of cultural developments, seeking to rebuild what he calls in *Hugh Selwyn Mauberley* "a botched civilisation", most doggedly in *The Cantos*. This huge assembly of verse attempts to tell "the tale of the tribe" from *The Odyssey* onwards. His idiosyncratic understanding of history nearly cost him his life, when his anti-semitic, pro-Mussolini broadcasts brought him accusations of treason from the advancing Americans during the war. He was not executed; instead he spent a third of his working life in a mental institution. He recanted his Fascistic rantings, but not the questionable Cantos, which he claimed were misunderstood: he continued revising his masterpiece until the end. For the richer passages, Hugh Kenner has credited Pound with an ear to rival **Shakespeare**'s in *Twelfth Night*.

Powell

ANTHONY

born London 1905

'Seeing the world broadens the outlook. You can learn a lot abroad. They're a funny lot, foreigners. I always go abroad for my holidays. I like it over there.'

VENUSBERG

ANTHONY POWELL IS AN English novelist best known for the 12 novels which make up the series called *A Dance to the Music of Time*. The title comes from a painting by Poussin, and refers to the unpredictable rhythms of life. The source of these rhythms becomes less identifiable the more characters crowd the drama and interact, and ultimately it is time itself which determines the action.

There is a Powell-like novelist figure throughout the work, called Nicholas Jenkins. His story spans from his childhood before the War to his situation in the early 1970s. This is the period of Powell's own development, from his school-days at Eton, his time as a student at Oxford, through his service in the Second World War (in the Intelligence Corps) to his life among fellow aesthetes. The lushness of the books' language, and their focus on the plights of the privileged, make it seem like the product of a **Proust**ian age rather than British post-war austerity, particularly with its introspection. But it follows the social fragmentation of the times, and responds to the age's new-found pragmatism with the manipulative new man, Kenneth Widmerpool. He makes the narrator long for a lost age with the wistfulness of **Evelyn Waugh**'s *Brideshead Revisited*.

Like Evelyn Waugh, Powell began his career with satirical novels, and retains the humour throughout his *magnum opus*. Readers have tried to find the identities of his friends depicted within, and have found clues in Powell's similarly cyclical memoirs beguiling, as if the fictionalised account is more informative than what passes for autobiography.

Priestley

J.B.   **born Bradford 1894; died Alveston, Warwickshire 1984**

We can find many excuses, however, for those foreign visitors, and especially the Frenchmen, who have come so quickly to the conclusion that we are forever morose and melancholy. England is the land of privacy, and therefore, the stranger who comes here is at a disadvantage. He sees the high walls, but not the gardens they enclose.

ENGLISH HUMOUR

J.B. PRIESTLEY WAS an extremely prolific writer, whose work is imbued at once with a love of England and a strong social commitment. This meant, as Winston Churchill said, that the government found him useful in World War Two (he had fought in the Great War), but his social criticism was always able to rile the establishment. Between the wars he wrote long and gritty novels. The first of these, *The Good Companions*, drew on his theatrical experience, which was also invaluable for the lucrative playwriting career he pursued later.

In his plays he displayed the journalist's instinct for what people wanted, but remained faithful to his own purpose. *An Inspector Calls* combines the metaphysical elements of his earlier pieces (he was interested in the tricks time can play on the mind) with the slippery detective story, to take a direct aim at his audience's conscience. *Three Men in New Suits* address the vexed issue of rebuilding the country after the war and was written for the 1951 Festival of Britain.

In his essays and memoirs, he displays himself as a dour Yorkshireman, full of good advice and canniness. He once said a writer should be a rebel, not a revolutionary. He was certainly a gadfly, but also a connoisseur of traditional Englishness. He declined a knighthood but accepted the Order of Merit, with its less imperial connotations.

299

Pritchett

V.S.

born Ipswich 1900; died London 1997

Human beings are simply archaic, ivy-covered ruins, preserved by the connoisseur, and they stand out oddly in the new world of the masses.

THE FUTURE OF FICTION

SIR VICTOR PRITCHETT – known familiarly as VSP – was primarily a story-teller who became as highly regarded for his criticism. He would never over-complicate or intellectualise writing, relying instead on wide reading and breadth of vision; he never regretted not attending university, while finding books and life vital to each other: "books have always seemed to me a form of life, and not a distraction from it."

He was born in a toy shop in Ipswich, gaining from his father an insight into personalities that can become unhinged by minutiae, and from his mother an ear for the way natural speech can carry narrative. These combined to make his short stories have something of the air of **Dickens**; for Pritchett, the oddities of speech could convey a whole world lying hidden behind them.

He considered his novels less successful. They often draw on his travels. He left his family for Paris when he was 20, and travelled as a journalist to Ireland and Spain. His natural gift for languages (he was fluent in French, German and Spanish) gave him a feel for cultural differences, which his fiction would explore. His more home-grown products would focus on undistinguished but quietly extraordinary figures. He would write by pretending to be them, seeking to "unself" himself.

In his critical writing, he discusses his influences, and his preferences reveal much about his own literary

ambitions. He wrote biographies of **Balzac** and **Chekhov**, and has drawn comparisons with the latter. In turn he has influenced younger writers, including **Raymond Carver.** He lectured in American and British universities, which came to honour him; students and readers have cherished him for his great humanity untrammelled by any kind of dogma or nonsense.

Propertius

SEXTUS   **born Assisi c. 48 BC; died Rome shortly after 16 BC**

Let well-read girls praise me because I
*   please,*
and tolerate their frequent raileries;
henceforth let the neglected lover read me,
and my known problems help him should
*   he need me.*

ELEGIES, I. 7.

NO POET HAS SUFFERED as much from misprints as Propertius. Early scholars tried correcting what they thought to be mistakes, to be corrected in turn by later scholars… now there is confusion about whether he wrote four books of verse or five, even about where one poem ends and another begins.

He wrote Latin elegy. Propertius was its first real master, bringing to his verse form such conventional discussions of love as a state of servitude, or a state of warfare. He describes the rapture of first love, the sadism of sustained love and the pain of parting: ultimately not even death separates the poet from his beloved Cynthia. After Propertius, the language of elegy froze. This has led scholars who have asked what he actually wrote to assume he is more boring than he is.

In fact, his treatment of his themes and sources is strikingly individual. His most important influence is **Callimachus**, whom most of his earlier commentators cannot have read. His later work is often dated by how much of **Horace**'s poetry he appears to have absorbed: Horace had no time for him, although they both had the same patron (Maecenas), as did **Virgil**. Propertius provides a link between Horace and **Ovid**, an obvious admirer, but Propertius' handling of elegiac couplets is more flexible and his material more prone to a lover's waywardness.

He introduced to Latin verse questions such as "Is poetry the proper activity for a young man?" and "Does it impress girls?" He is unembarrassed by his immense knowledge of mythology, which he parades when looking for a conceit or when explaining how a town acquired its name. But even then, he shows heroes at their frailest, as when he describes Hercules confessing that he dressed as a slave-girl ("a gentle girdle bound my shaggy chest") before being turned away from a women-only drinking fountain.

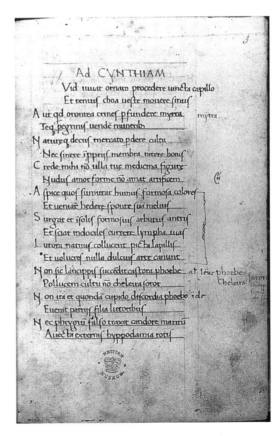

Proulx

E. ANNIE

born Vermont 1935

Dear Sirs: I recently saw your advertisement in The Globe and Mail for a research assistant. Although I do not speak Japanese I am willing to learn...

Dear Sirs: I recently saw your advertisement in The Globe and Mail for a position in brokerage operations. Although my training is in marine traffic control I am willing to learn...

THE SHIPPING NEWS

E ANNIE PROULX'S WRITING embraces the sense of alienation central to her view of America, which she perceives beneath a façade of instant remedies. But rather than leave her characters stranded in the urban soullessness of, say, **Saul Bellow**'s world, she lets them explore their loneliness in matching terrain. Her first novel, *Postcards*, introduces Lloyd Blood, whose feelings of guilt force him to live as a wanderer. It shares with her earlier stories an emphasis on the need to survive – a theme dear to the heart of the American novel with its frequent evocation of the pioneering spirit.

The book that secured Proulx's international reputation takes an isolated soul back to his roots beyond the United States, to Newfoundland. The achievement of *The Shipping News* is in its painstaking account of life there, recording its dialects and remoteness with such faith and warmth that it makes those who have never visited the area want to, and those who have want to return. It describes small communities whose over-fishing has created aching unemployment and that try patiently to adopt new industries. But at heart the story is a personal one, telling of an individual's battles with the elements and ultimately his search for love.

She had already been hailed as the author of something like the Great American Novel before the publication of *Accordion Crimes*, which seems a more direct attempt at it. Generations of immigrant life are made real to us through the presence of a green accordion, which changes hands many times throughout the book: its varying strains summon traditions and memories of the cultures that have formed the United States, recalling and reviving the nation's claim to be built as One from Many.

Proust

MARCEL

Moreover, pained to reflect, at the moment [the phrase of Vintueil's sonata] passed at once so near and so linked to the infinite, that as long as it was directed at them, it did not know them, he almost regretted that it had any meaning, any fixed and intrinsic beauty, foreign to them, as in jewels that are gifts, or even in letters written by a beloved woman, where we find the water of the gem, or the words of language, wanting, because they are not formed uniquely by the essence of a fleeting liaison and a particular being.

SWANN'S WAY

MARCEL PROUST IS A colossal figure in literature, remembered as the author of the mighty, multi-volumed work, *In Search of Lost Time*. He wrote it in bed, in a pollen-proof room, over the last 10 years of his life.

It is a testament both to the times and to the individual genius. Proust spent his youth in Paris during the early Third Republic, and so moved in circles more concerned with aesthetics than anything else. The account he gives of his impressions of the world shows a profound subjectivity displaying his deep admiration of figures such as John Ruskin.

While his prose examines these sensibilities in his unique style (for Proust style bore the stamp of personality and so was everything to a work of art), it analyses sensations such as love and loneliness as though they were scientific phenomena, striving to find objective ways of describing them.

This is what makes the project an attempt at the complete novel, a book that might somehow account for the whole of a life's experience. It seeks its wholeness by trying to chart inner realities rather than external ones, and attempts this through memory. The narrator's inability to remember and recapture everything right up until the work's end begins to explain the work's shape. Sections the length of whole novels can appear only as digressions within still larger enquiries; but themes and characters recur and develop in ways that reveal an almost perfectly constructed piece of art.

Pushkin

ALEKSANDER born Moscow 1799; died St. Petersburg 1837

Love passed, the Muse appeared, the weather

of mind got clarity new-found;

now free, I once more weave together

emotion, thought, and magic sound...

EUGENE ONEGIN, TR. JOHNSTON

BEFORE PUSHKIN, Russians considered French a better language than their own for their literature: what writing there was in Russian was earnest and worthy. Pushkin read European literature widely – he was especially fond of **Byron** and in fact had Byron's range. He made a more liberated treatment of almost every genre possible in Russian, making even tragedy and heroic epic less daunting to his audiences.

In his masterpiece, the verse novel *Eugene Onegin*, he lets all his talents loose at once. He displays his gift for love lyric, with insights culled from strings of his own romances, as well as the descriptive powers of his folk poetry. He adds to this a dramatist's ear for speech, especially pace dialogue, and a novelist's sensitivity to a character's inner feelings, when novel-writing was still a relatively new craft. It is at this form that he excels. Critics since (notably Bakhtin) have marvelled at the way the poet is present at every stage of the story, sounding like his characters or having his characters sound like him. They must all talk in a strict but addictive sonnet form: this never stifles Pushkin's vitality. He is constantly commenting on his own technique and his knack for parody leaves us wondering how seriously we should be taking even his most moving passages.

But *Onegin* is more than just an entertainment. The hero has a kind of world-weariness that was the poet's own. Pushkin had been exiled for his friendships with revolutionaries and finished up writing under the patronage and surveillance of Tsar Nicholas I. The death of the posturing bard Lensky in the poem prefigures his own death: he was shot in a duel that may have been orchestrated by the authorities. **Lermontov** was exiled for writing a poem publicising this theory.

Pynchon

THOMAS

born Glen Cove, New York State 1937

If they can get you asking the wrong questions, they don't have to worry about the answers.

PROVERBS FOR PARANOIDS,
GRAVITY'S RAINBOW

THOMAS PYNCHON is a famously reclusive writer. His novels appear after varying periods of total silence. In the absence of biographical information about him, readers have scoured his texts for personal references.

There seem to be so many clues. The work is so hugely inventive that any character's name could be concealing something: Oedipa Maas, Dr. Hilarius, Isaiah Two Four (named by hippies after Biblical chapter and verse) and Genghis Cohen might be leading anywhere. Such figures can appear anywhere in Pynchon's multi-layered narratives, and disappear without warning. They are experts on the minutiae of life, often at the expense of a bigger picture. An ability to date any film exactly, or to discuss anything from plastics to plastering, can lead to a jumbled world-view, abounding with international conspiracies. The result is a modern mythology: in a book like *Gravity's Rainbow* (his most famous work, which scandalised the Pulitzer Prize committee), this can include the ever-lasting light bulb, the Schwarzkommando (a crack troop of African Nazis), and a hero whose penis can predict air-raids.

The style devours all other styles, and has become distinctively Pynchon's own. Fairy-tales, songs, science fiction, hysterical rants and all-too-plausible bands or B-movies pile into narratives that have abandoned any traditional ideas of structure. If he inherited this freedom from the Beats, he owes an unstoppable sense of adventure to John Buchan, with whom he shares an addiction to chase sequences. The element of political thriller. introduces forces of darkness sometimes absurd enough to make the characters susceptible to them seem merely paranoid; but Pynchon's feat is to present a world which makes such warped sense on its own terms that the readers feel paranoid too.

Recently he has published his largest book yet, *Mason & Dixon*, a novel about the creators of the eponymous line dividing North and South. It seems to have occupied him for many years, during work on other projects. Again, it follows a spell of silence; as with his other books, it seems to have come from nowhere.

MAJOR WORKS

V (1963)

The Crying of Lot 49 (1966)

Gravity's Rainbow (1973)

Slow Learner (1985 collected short stories)

Vineland (1990)

Mason & Dixon (1997)

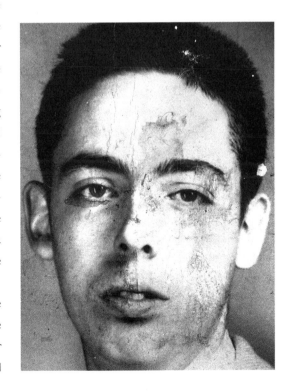

Queneau

RAYMOND

born Le Havre 1903; died Paris 1976

'I'm telling you, my husband, the other day, had this idea about... (details). How did he come up with this craving, that's what I want to know.'

'Maybe he read a dodgy book,' someone suggested.

ZAZIE ON THE METRO

RAYMOND QUENEAU COMBINED an enormous intellect with a perverse sense of humour. When parodying, he had no end of sources and unlimited techniques. When thinking, he was able to draw on any number of disciplines and was as at home with science and mathematics as he was with imaginative literature.

After some bad experiences with the Surrealists, whose journal he had edited, he formed the group OuLiPo (Workshop for Potential Literature). Rather than unleashing possibilities from the unconscious mind, he sought to generate texts by more arbitrary, often mathematical, systems. His hilarious *Exercises in Style* relates an incident on a bus in 99 different ways, sometimes working encyclopedically through rhetorical devices and word-games, sometimes just improvising. *One Hundred Billion Poems* lets the reader loose on further strategies, with any number of possible results.

He was a serious scholar: he edited the Pléiade encyclopedia, wrote on the relationship between literature and science and analysed his own psychoanalysis. Although his scholarship is evident throughout his creative work, he was eager to keep it accessible, and was impatient with French that was too precious in literature. *Zazie on the Metro* is the most famous example, in which Queneau transliterates exactly the ripe argot of a nine-year-old girl let loose on an unsuspecting Paris. It was filmed by Louis Malle. Queneau's knack of reproducing vocal French served him well in his screenplays. He also wrote the French subtitles for *Some Like It Hot.* After him, Parisian buses and trains could never be the same and there is a metro stop named in his honour, on the Bobigny line.

Rabelais

FRANÇOIS

born Chinon? c. 1494; died c. 1553

Pish, said the monk, that is not the reason (that Friar John hath such a fair nose), but, according to the true monastical philosophy, it is because my nurse had soft teats, by virtue whereof, whilst she gave suck, my nose did sink in as in so much butter. The hard breasts of nurses make children short-nosed.

GARGANTUA, TR. SIR THOMAS URQUHART.

RABELAIS WAS A Franciscan friar, Benedictine monk, surgeon, intimate of the king and (for a while) the papal authorities. He travelled extensively in Europe, knew Greek and Hebrew, performed one of the first human dissections in France, wrote Latin treatises on archaeology and medicine and in fecund French wrote *Gargantua* and *Pantagruel*.

Both giants, Gargantua is Pantagruel's father. Like Rabelais, the former is born and educated in the spiritual tradition of the Middle Ages and is cramped by a ponderous clericalism that he must undermine however he can. His son and successor comes to a more amicable arrangement with the mother church, whose representative, Father Thélème, advocates doing what one wishes.

The narrative takes place in Rabelais' home town of Chinon, Paris, Utopia, even China. There is no plot as such – the work is more a series of brilliant, rampantly conceived interludes in which the sacred is balanced by the profane: characters can pass through Hell unscathed (after decapitation) or meet the Cumaean Sybil – a belching crone whom Michelangelo would never recognise, she has no qualms about showing Panurge her "hole". Even the author's more deeply-felt points are made scurrilously. Rather than advocating pacifism, Pantagruel proposes codpieces as the best weapon. The whole, with its joyous invocation of wine, food, and more wine, is a celebration of joyous excess: Rabelais insists that the best authors wrote while drinking and wants to be read by bibbers, too.

As **Chaucer** did for English, Rabelais enriched his language with a teeming vocabulary, rich in verbs and ripe insults. The translation by Sir Thomas Urquhart in the 17th century expands the original, with the larger vocabulary English affords, but does so with complete fidelity to the Rabelaisian spirit.

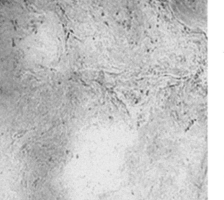

Racine

JEAN   **born La Ferté-Milon 1639; died Paris 1699**

Don't ever doubt that my redoubled fire
could be discomforted by some risk higher.
Fighting's in vain after a struggle so great –
I yield blindly unto my dragging fate.
I love; I seek Hermione in this place
to woo her, take her, die before her face.

ANDROMACHE

RACINE WROTE INTENSE tragedies for the court of King Louis XIV of France. His achievement was to express such uncontrollable passions in very controlled French verse, while adhering to the most classical understandings of drama.

He could take his themes from **Euripides**, as with *Phaedra*, from **Virgil**, as with the story of *Andromache*, with a heroine captured by the Greeks, or the histories of Tacitus, as in *Britannicus*, which follows Nero's accession as Emperor. In an art form that strove for perfection, there was intense competition. Comparison between Racine and the established **Corneille** was inevitable: public and critical opinion since has most often found for Racine.

Commentators have found explanations for Racine's psychological acuteness in his vacillations between spiritual and earthly devotion (he was brought up in the strict Jansenist faith, but had many mistresses); or in his being orphaned early and his subsequent survival instinct – manifested at court and in writings about his rivals. He might also be supposed to have gained his innate sense of theatre from court. He witnessed one of the few monarchs who could rival his regal creations for absolute power; to public life, Racine added the dimension of the all-consuming passion rulers might have had over subjects – they could control but not compel to love.

In expressing this, Racine outdid his predecessors in imaginative twists and vengeful instincts. Love can swiftly turn into murderous hatred, whose consequences are unstoppable. The greatness of his heroes is emphasised by the incomprehension of their minions, barely loftier than slaves: they are like us, shuddering at the characters' extremes. But he establishes tragedies whose outcomes are so inevitable that often, by the time the curtain is up, it is already too late for us to intervene.

Ratushinskaya

IRINA
born 1954

Granny Tonia weeps again. After blowing her nose, she fishes out a wrinkled apple from somewhere. 'Here, daughter, you have it, you're young. I'm not going to come out of the camp alive, anyway, but you'll live. You keep writing!'

I accept the apple, my first honorarium, still warm from her hands. I'll keep writing, Granny Tonia. If I survive, I'll write.

GREY IS THE COLOUR OF HOPE,
TR. ALYONA KOJEVNIKOV

IRINA RATUSHINSKAYA was a youthful atheist, but then embraced religion; she trained as a scientist, and became a poet. These two decisions put her at odds with the Soviet authorities, who became aware of her poetry when it was being circulated among underground movements. By similar means, she had managed to read the poems of **Mandelshtam**, **Akhmatova**, **Pasternak** and **Tsetayeva**. Her own work included love lyrics and poems pointing to the regime's guilt in stifling human rights. This, and her political activity with Igor Geraschenko, who became her husband, led to her arrest several times. In 1983, she was sentenced to seven years in a labour camp.

She had always felt compelled to write: a poem would announce itself to her, either by its emerging rhythm, or by a feverish sensation. Even in prison, she wrote by any means necessary – on tiny slips of paper the warders would not find. In 1986, a collection, *No, I'm Not Afraid* appeared in the West, drawing at once admiration for the work and anger at Ratushinskaya's detention. International lobbying and Gorbachev's reforms led to her release.

Her memoirs chronicle her years in prison and the indignities through which the mind can still preserve a hope of freedom. She turns to her youth in *In the Beginning*, describing her childhood in Odessa, her religious crises and her trial. The last, especially, reveals an unshakable courage, borne with a writerly estrangement from events (she finds the day of her trial, when no defence appears, "entertaining"). Her poetry helped, too: "If I were to break, and in the calling of a poet, at that, it would be a disgrace beyond words!"

Rhys

JEAN   **born Roseau, Dominica, West Indies 1894; died Exeter 1979**

There were two children under the big mango tree, a boy and a little girl, and she waved to them and called 'Hello' but they didn't answer her or turn their heads. Very fair children, as Europeans born in the West Indies so often are: as if the white blood is asserting itself against all odds.

I USED TO LIVE HERE ONCE

JEAN RHYS WAS BORN in Dominica, the daughter of a Welsh doctor and a Creole woman. Some of her short stories recall the landscape of her childhood and the tone of an outsider pervades her work. Much of it drew on her experiences of wandering in and out of jobs in Paris and London: she worked as an artist's model, a film extra, a mannequin and a chorus girl, just like the heroine of *A Voyage in the Dark*. Her first book, *The Left Bank*, was a collection of short stories published with an introduction by **Ford Madox Ford**, who did much to promote her work. In this work she began her examination of superficial coteries and the vulnerable existence of women in the arts world, where they are prey to exploitation.

In spite of her early promise, she published nothing for 37 years. In 1958 she was discovered living reclusively in Cornwall and in 1966 she produced her most famous work, *Wide Sargasso Sea*. The narrative takes up the few leads **Charlotte Brontë** gives us about Mr Rochester's first wife (in *Jane Eyre*), who had been brought over from the West Indies. In a markedly different style, Rhys begins with Antoinette Cosway relating her plight as a mulatto, looking after a wayward mother, before being given in marriage to Mr Rochester to redeem a debt. The narrative continues from Rochester's point of view: Rhys' even-handedness lets us feel some sympathy for him even when he is behaving irresponsibly. The principal characters feel the loneliness and alienation that Rhys would study in her later work.

Richardson

SAMUEL   born Mackworth, Derbyshire 1689; died Parson's Green, nr. London 1761

Will you, good Sir, allow me to mention, that I could wish that the Air of Genuineness had been kept up, tho' I want not the letters to be thought genuine; only so far kept up, I mean, as that they should not prefatically be owned not to be genuine...

LETTER TO WILLIAM WARBURTON,
ON THE PREFACE OF CLARISSA

MAJOR WORKS

Pamela: or, Virtue Rewarded (1740)

Pamela in Her Exalted Condition (1742)

Clarissa: or, the History of a Young Lady (1747–1748)

The History of Sir Charles Grandison (1754)

RICHARDSON WROTE SOME of the earliest novels and in *Clarissa* one of the longest (it is considerably longer than the Bible). If his work's dimensions were not ambitious enough, the form was extremely adventurous. His books are called "epistolary novels", being composed entirely from exchanges of letters. The chief advantage of this narrative technique is that the length of time between action and reaction (action often happens almost while a character is writing about it) is long enough to ensure suspense and keep the reader turning the page.

Richardson had developed the idea after producing a book of model letters on a variety of "common concerns in human life": it occurred to him to shape a story he remembered in the same form. His purpose was to teach: for many readers, he seemed to provide too ideally moral a world-view. **Fielding** was quick to parody *Pamela*, but considered *Clarissa* a work of great genius, as did **Dr Johnson**. Nowadays, Richardson seems odder for his presentation than his precepts. The letter form demands that we suspend disbelief and it has been suggested that Clarissa must have spent up to eight hours a day writing – leaving precious little time for anything to happen to her. One cannot deny the genre's potential, however, especially as perfected by **Laclos**, and by Woody Allen in *The Gossage-Vardebedian Papers*.

Rilke

RAINER MARIA   **born Prague 1875; died Montreux, Switzerland 1926**

...let what we are by liberal increasing of
that be exceeded;
let but the small bird's liberal flight
gift us with heart-space, making a future
unneeded!

MEANINGFUL WORD, 'INCLINATION'!,
TR. J.B. LEISHMAN

ROSE, OH THE PURE CONTRADICTION,

DELIGHT, OF BEING NO-ONE'S SLEEP

UNDER SO MANY LIDS.

EPITAPH

RILKE CONSECRATED his life to poetry. He escaped from a military academy in Austria near the Polish border (also attended by **Musil**: unlike Musil, however, Rilke could never bring himself to discuss it) and travelled Europe with a wide inner-eye. He met **Tolstoy** in Russia and settled in Paris as secretary to the sculptor Rodin. He took up his master's belief in artistic labour as the only joy.

Although relations between them cooled later, Rilke persisted in this faith. Inasmuch as art was life to him, he began to see objects as though he, the Poet-Creator, could imagine becoming them. In this way, they would become part of his inwardness, rather than the outwardness of the world: ultimately, he could feel ideas within him in much the same way as **Hölderlin**. Rilke was under his spell for a time and wrote of him with Hölderlin-like power, displaying the same mastery of elegiac metre. But his vision was more attached to things and his vocabulary richer.

Rilke expresses the artist's befuddlement with the world of things, especially when writing as a Danish visitor to Paris in *The Notebook of Malte Laurids Brigge*. Increasingly, poems became things to Rilke – particularly sacred ones, no matter what the subject matter. Magnificently, his verse attained a purity to match his vision, most notably in his series, *Sonnets to Orpheus*. In this he expounds on love while hymning music with extreme lyricism: for Rilke, love occurs when two solitudes become united. It is a notion so idealised that he seems only to have realised it in poetry – and that is real enough.

Rimbaud

ARTHUR   **born Charleville 1854; died Marseilles 1891**

*Boredom is no longer my love. The
rages, the debaucheries, the madness I
have known in all their dash and disaster
– the burden is cast aside. Let us
appreciate the height of my innocence
without vertigo.*

A SEASON IN HELL

MAJOR WORKS

POEMS
New Poems (1872)
A Season in Hell (1873)
Illuminations (1886)

RIMBAUD'S APPEARANCE and disappearance as a boy visionary and "cursed poet" is barely believable. He lived only 37 years. Although he may have written more poetry after *A Season in Hell*, it is likely that he had said all he had to say by the time he was 19.

The first poems we have of his were written when he was only 15. Very few, if any, read like exercises. Some seem at first glance like testaments to youthful rebellion, even if technically beyond the reach of most poets, let alone teenagers. But Rimbaud is further ahead still: he reveals everywhere an awareness of his youth and can portray it with a wisdom quite detached from the subject matter.

At 17, this had already become his aesthetic project: to ignore morals, to explore the limits of personality, but to observe the effects and record them faithfully. When Rimbaud ran away to Paris, he wrote to **Verlaine**, who joined him in this quest, as fellow-poet and lover. But they parted violently (Verlaine shot Rimbaud in the wrist), Verlaine was imprisoned, and Rimbaud continued alone.

A Season in Hell is the summation of his findings. But it is the work in which he says he will divulge no more. He had broken enough poetic rules before and denied even his self-imposed obligation as a poet's obligation itself: "I'll shut up. Poets and visionaries would be jealous." He still takes us through his terrifying fairy-world with a clamour worthy of **Nietzsche**, before assuring us that he is in possession of truth, in soul and body. At the opening of *Illuminations* the poet assures us, "I have the key to this savage parade.".

For the rest of his life, he wandered around Africa and the Middle East, trading and dealing in arms and coffee: what we have left is not so much a biography of Rimbaud as a series of sightings (although one has recently been published, dealing with these years). He only returned to France in the year of his death, which was brought on by gangrene.

Rostand

EDMOND

born Marseilles 1868; died Paris 1918

I'm in a garden when a perfume blows,

Inhaling with my devil of a nose

April – and then I notice by the moon

A girl embrace her horseman. In a swoon

I dream that, step by little step, I might

Also find love beneath the silver light,

I thrill, forget… then suddenly recall

My profile's shadow on the garden wall!

CYRANO DE BERGERAC

EDMOND ROSTAND WAS the author of a work that must have seemed a most unlikely triumph in *fin de siècle* Paris. It was miles away from the prevalent, **Ibsen**-influenced realism, or Alfred Jarry's surreal *Ubu Roi*. *Cyrano de Bergerac* looked back to other times, which in themselves were nostalgic, invoking the spirit of **Dumas'** *The Three Musketeers*. It was a verse drama. In fact, all that was experimental about it was its sheer scope – it was conceived on an operatic scale, in length and in cast.

So doomed did the project seem that Rostand sobbed to the actor Coquelin, "Forgive me, my friend, for having dragged you through this disastrous venture!" But Coquelin had noticed the success Sarah Bernhardt had enjoyed with Rostand's *The Distant Princess* and asked for a piece with a good part for him. *Cyrano* was perfect material for both of them: it suited Rostand's non-realist poetic bent and Coquelin's technique – he had not appeared on stage without a false nose for 40 years and Rostand had scripted the most famous *conque* in the repertoire.

Other plays by Rostand failed because the poetry took precedence over the demands of theatre. His earlier successes owed much to their fancy, their performers and costumes. Later plays attempted more singly tragic or comic themes (as with *L'Aiglon* and *Chantecler* respectively). Perhaps *Cyrano* also works better on page than on stage, but the hero is a poet, in whose mouth the verse is as much a part of the action as is his swordsmanship and ill-fated, chivalric love for Roxane. The blend of virtuosic badinage, farce and pathos has proved endlessly popular. Rostand became an overnight hero and won the *Légion d'Honneur*.

Roth

PHILIP

born Newark, New Jersey 1933

Monstrous that all the world's suffering is grist to my mill – that all I can do, when confronted by anyone's story, is to wish to turn it into material, but if that's the way one is possessed, that is the way one is possessed. There's a demonic side to this business that the Nobel Prize committee doesn't talk much about.

THE ANATOMY LESSON

PHILIP ROTH WRITES confessional stories. His characters confess so much that one might accuse them of indulgence, if what they had to tell us were less hilarious, intriguingly sick, or psychologically acute.

His protagonists are typically male, well-educated (if not academics), seldom from prosperous backgrounds and almost always Jewish. The hero of the Zuckerman trilogy is a writer whose journey through Jewish literature resembles Roth's own. Nathan Zuckerman begins by meeting an eminent writer, whose work he compares to **Babel**'s, and in an epilogue finishes up in **Kafka**'s Prague.

In the trilogy we learn of a shocking "1969 bestseller", which causes Zuckerman's father to have a heart attack.. It is hard to distinguish this fictional guilt from the effect on Roth of writing his most celebrated work, *Portnoy's Complaint*. Portnoy is a chronic masturbator, whose imagined, sustained plea to his doctor constitutes a search for a cure. But from the first descriptions of his mother, who dotes on him more than on his sister, we are aware that the "complaint" finds a peculiarly Jewish expression. The narrator craves freedom and a release from guilt, with such cries as "Let my peter go!" and "LET'S PUT THE ID BACK IN YID!" His quest for shameless pleasure is ultimately frustrated – women tend not to understand him – but can be more liberating for the reader, who might well need recourse to Leo Rosten's *The Joys of Yiddish* as a guide to this addictive brand of humour.

Rousseau

JEAN-JACQUES

born Geneva 1712; died Ermenonville 1778

Henceforth everything outside me is foreign to me. In this world I no longer have companions, nor fellows, nor brothers. I am on the earth as on a foreign planet, to which I have fallen from the one I used to inhabit.

REVERIES OF A SOLITARY RAMBLER

ROUSSEAU'S WRITING AND THINKING come from the Age of Enlightenment, but anticipate an age of social upheaval and romanticism. In his various works he discusses political philosophy, education and the development of the personality.

Fundamental to his arguments is a belief in the power the environment has in shaping people. He saw people's surroundings as a corrupting force, whereas nature was liberating. His very moral views on society led him to view those removed from it as "noble savages" and in *Émile* he advocates a solitary education, with a natural sense of God providing a better conscience than more formal Christianity.

The dictates that such a conscience would offer would actually be freedoms and in society, these freedoms would become "the will of the people" – an idea Robespierre took to bloody extremes some 30 years after the *Social Contract* was written.

Rousseau had tasted pains and freedoms, although if they gave him the moral sense he sought, it arrived late. His *Confessions* look back over his life. His childhood environment in a succession of homes, his formative romances – notably with the older Mme Warens, for whose sake he adopted

Catholicism – and his subsequent wanderings on being rejected, might have provided him with enough excuses: still, the value of *The Confessions* lies in their honesty in confronting his misdeeds, even if he misremembers the exact details. Ever the philosopher, he draws general truths from his self-reflections, but as in *The New Héloïse*, he reveals still more strongly his gifts as a storyteller. **Joyce** found more psychological interest in Rousseau's true account of stealing tablespoons than in **Dostoyevsky**'s description of a man confessing to an imagined murder, while **Lermontov** concluded, "The trouble with Rousseau's confessions is that he read them to his friends."

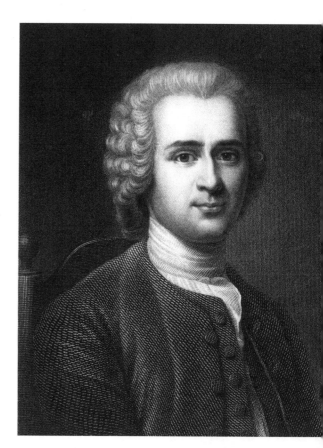

Roussel

RAYMOND

born Paris 1877; died Palermo 1933

I will swamp their minds in radical moisture.

THE CABINET OF DOCTOR CALIGARI

RAYMOND ROUSSEL was a French writer commonly considered an eccentric, who had a yacht and enough money to fund productions of his own plays, and publish what he wanted. He was convinced of his own genius, and anticipated huge literary celebrity.

His works seem like the product of a wild imagination, but in fact Roussel's method (which he called "procedure") was extremely systematic. He would create whole plots by playing small but painstaking word-games, for example, taking two very similar words, then fitting them into sentences in which each word would be ambiguous, giving the whole several different possible interpretations, before spinning out those words in turn to form compound nouns, or go where his associations would take him. The finished product would seem like a loose assembly of randomly selected elements, so far had it come from the germ of the original idea; the large number of steps Roussel had taken would blot out the source.

For a while, the results impressed no-one so much as the Surrealists, who figured, only a little correctly, that the unconscious was at work. But Roussel's real impact was on the OuLiPo group of writers, especially **Georges Perec.** The idea of working with tight linguistic restraints proved as fertile to the imagination as abandoning them altogether: once Roussel has forced his action, or the composition of his poems, into a particular direction, the words assume an unexpected kind of rightness. But only later admirers of Roussel would learn of "procedure", and its potential. He made his system known posthumously, sending the manuscript of *How I Wrote Some of My Books* to be published after his death – which he timed by increasing his dosages of barbiturates until they killed him. Even his end was part of a plan whose author never seemed eager to let it be understood.

Runyon

DAMON

born Manhattan, Kansas 1884; died New York 1946

'Do you remember Johnny Blues?
The one they call Big Boy Blues?'
'Why, certainly,' I say. 'I remember him
as well as if he is my own big brother
only I am thankful such is not the
case.'
'Do you know Big Boy Blues has a son?'
Willie says.
'Yes,' I say, 'I know it. They call him
Little Boy Blues.'

BIG BOY BLUES

DAMON RUNYON USED a hardened reporter's knowledge of New York and a humourist's fine ear to produce amazingly sophisticated and still-accessible stories about the gangster types with whom his narrator associates.

This narrator is nameless, although his name would doubtless rival High-C Homer or The Seldom Seen Kid for a suggestive sobriquet. He reports the tales he hears in a voice that maintains an unsurprised tone by using understatement and the present tense. The result is a cool, hilarious account of the characters who meet at Mindy's to bet on ludicrous "propositions" at odds that the narrator can always recall.

The pieces are celebrated in the Broadway musical *Guys and Dolls*, making famous Runyon's use of slang. His ear for dialect is obvious in his other stories, where mariners and pioneers speak with distinct voices. In all his work, these sanguine characters make us laugh, but are seldom too remote from the consequences of their violence.

There is a darkness in Runyon, which leads him to confront death, notably his own, which he faced bravely over a year of suffering. He even feels sorry for Death when it arrives, because so pallid a figure can have no social life. He also addresses execution, the prison system, and, magnificently, the plight of the soul, which can be wagered in a crap game with the mission worker Sarah Brown, whose "eyes are like I do not know what, except that they are one-hundred-per-cent eyes in every respect". In his insights into what goes on in the minds of such people, we are lucky the narrator tells the reader more than he tells the other characters, or, for a moment, the police.

Salinger

J.D.   **born New York 1919**

'I'll exquisite day you, buddy, if you don't get down off that bag this minute. And I mean it.'

'TEDDY', FROM FOR ESMÉ WITH LOVE AND SQUALOR

Could you try not aiming so much?

THE ZEN WAY OF PLAYING MARBLES, IN SEYMOUR, AN INTRODUCTION

MAJOR WORKS

The Catcher in the Rye (1951)

For Esmé, With Love and Squalor (1953)

Franny and Zooey (1961)

Raise High the Roof-beam, Carpenters and Seymour: an Introduction (1963)

J.D. SALINGER'S LITERARY fame is over-shadowed by the fact that he refuses to be famous, living as a recluse in New Hampshire. This should leave commentators free to discuss his small, marvellous body of work. But since newspapers are full of people on the trail of J.D. Salinger, and people on the trail of people trailing him, there is little hope of this happening.

He has published stories of various lengths and one short novel. *The Catcher in the Rye* is a first-person narrative that shares some qualities with his other work: an ear for colloquial speech, which conveys situations and states of mind with great economy, and a sympathy for precocious youths. Holden Caulfield's story, starting with his suspension from school and finishing in an institution, is crammed with hypersensitive observations on everything he notices around New York City, the capital of that "phoniness" that so unnerves him.

The young people who figure in Salinger's stories can have Caulfield's confusions, his acuity, or the regenerating affection of his little sister Phoebe. The later published works focus on the Glass family, full of child prodigies, all of them disturbed by the suicide of the eldest son, Seymour. The narrator, Buddy, fails to find motives for it, but the very act of writing about his brother becomes a manic process. The prose bursts at moments with a sheer, barely communicable elation. Some who speculate on what any unpublished Salinger texts might be like anticipate increasingly incoherent, indulgent work. But if *Seymour, an Introduction* is a guide, then writing for its own sake, with its infectious joys and traumas, deserves our attention. Salinger has given enough people the right to be misunderstood to be able to exercise it himself.

Sand

GEORGE

born Paris 1804; died Nohant 1876

I'm setting sail on the stormy sea of literature. I must live. I am not rich at the moment.

LETTER TO JULES BEUCOIRAN

LIKE **George Eliot**, George Sand was a woman. She freed herself from an aristocratic marriage to Baron Casimir Dudevant in 1831, rebelling against the social strictures that confined her. She would spend a lifetime as a prolific novelist railing against social *mores*, and would live out her precepts of freedom too. She had a trail of distinguished lovers, including Jules Sandeau (with whom she collaborated, and from whom she derived her pseudonym), the obsessive **Alfred de Musset**, and the composer Chopin. This last liaison lasted nine years; in a painting of Sand's coterie, he is depicted as the colourful budgerigar on her wrist.

Her sympathies were completely Romantic. She rushed to Paris in 1848 to support the revolutionaries, but condemned the bloodshed as an outrage in the name of fraternity and equality. These were profoundly her own goals – she proclaimed herself a friend of the people. The spirit of the age is evident throughout her writings, strongly championing the passions of the individual in the face of society's constraints, to which suicide can be a just response: in *Mauprat*, Edmée famously declares: "We cannot tear a single page out of our lives, but we can throw the book into the fire."

As **Mme de Staël** before her, she found conventions especially repressive towards women, since "men make the rules and apply them." Her early work found marriage to be the instrument of this humiliation, and although her attitude towards marriage mellowed later in her career, she never relented in a call for freedom that echoed **Rousseau**'s. Although her late, pastoral novels are less read now, they were much loved by **Proust** and **Flaubert**, who was desolated by Sand's death and wrote *A Simple Heart* in his friend's memory.

Sappho

born Lesbos c. 612 BC; died Mytilene

MAJOR WORKS

Fragments from nine books of poetry

To me, that man, whoever he is sitting

　opposite you seems equal to the gods who

　listening near responsively to your sweet

　utterances, your

laughter so lovely that it makes my heart go

　fluttering in my ribs, for when I see you

　all ablur, then there's nothing left of any

　utterance in me,

rather my tongue solidifies, a subtle

　undercurrent of flame upon my skin comes,

　to the eyes, nothing, everything I hear is

　out of proportion,

and a sweat comes in patters, and a shivering

　over me whole, I'm pallider than grass and

　faltering I appear to be approaching

　dying a little.

TO A GIRL

WHEN THE THEMES and images of lyric poetry start seeming tired, as they might in the duller moments of Latin love elegy, it does us good to recall how they got there. **Gertrude Stein** talks about a time when a poet "could say "O moon", "O sea", "O love", and the moon and the sea and love were really there." Something of this feeling comes with reading Sappho.

This is partly because we have her work in fragments only: just one poem, to Aphrodite, seems intact. Later ancients, especially **Catullus**, who translated her sublimely, would have known more poems and complete ones. For them, she would have belonged more firmly within a tradition and her themes of marriage, hopeless love and the night skies would have seemed as much their territory as hers.

This territory existed before Sappho. But we still have the sense that she found it. When she names things or actions, she can do so in long, compounded Greek words that seem (and often are) invented for her metre. That metre was hers, too: lines end with a distinctive "tum-ti tum-ti tum tum" made smoother by flowing into the next line.

Senses run into other senses as well and can dissolve into non-sense. Where previous poets praise the stature of a bride-groom, Sappho wonders how so grand a man will fit into the hall – "Raise high the roof-beam, carpenters!" Where **Homer**'s sunrise has rosy fingers, in Sappho it is the moon.

Sarraute

NATHALIE

born Ivanovno-Voznesenk, Russia 1902

And the word is there, completely ready, the word 'love', open, blessing... and what was drifting everywhere, whirling, engulfs itself stronger and stronger, immediately condenses, fills it wholly, founds, confounds itself with it, inseparable from it, they are just one thing.

'THE WORD LOVE' IN THE USAGE OF SPEECH

NATHALIE SARRAUTE was born in Russia but writes in French. Her parents settled in France, where she trained as a lawyer at the Sorbonne. she continued her studies at Oxford.

There is something forensic about her writing. She analyses a character's inner motivations thoroughly, even clinically, before turning the narrative's attention to actions or dialogue. Her first novel best exemplifies this technique. It takes its name, *Tropisms* , from the unseen shifts of auxin from cells on one side of a plant to the other, causing the organism to incline towards the sun. What makes people behave as they do is thus depicted here as invisible and barely explicable, while anything they say is incapable of justifying it. In Sarraute, the narrator can address the reader in an immediate style, sharing vivid images in a conversational-enough way – while actual conversation itself must remain stifled by clichés.

She examines this beautifully in her pieces on language, *The Usage of Speech*. She takes phrases and strives to name the impossibilities they invoke; at one point she points out that words, in all their lightness, are incapable of describing their source.

Still, much of Sarraute's narrative takes place nearer that source than most writing comes. She uses interior monologues, and can shift from the thoughts of one character to another without warning the reader. In the 1950s, she was a chief exponent of the *nouveau roman*, the new novel, a genre seeking to unite such diversely-collected impressions in a single work of art. Like **Simone de Beauvoir**, the substance of her novels often deals with educated characters, whose involvement with literature enables them to discuss the kinds of texts which include them (as in *The Fruits of Gold*).

Sartre

JEAN-PAUL   **born Paris 1905; died Paris 1980**

I have understood the autodidact's method: he is teaching himself in alphabetical order... Today he has reached 'L'. 'K' after 'J', 'L' after 'K'. He has passed abruptly from the study of coleopterae to that of quantum theory, from a work on Tamerlane to a Catholic pamphlet against Darwinism... Behind him, before him, there is a universe. And the day approaches when, closing the last book on the last shelf on the far left, he will say to himself: 'And now what?'

NAUSEA, TR. ROBERT BALDICK

SARTRE WAS A PHILOSOPHER for whom people could only be justified by their actions, rather than their personalities (for example, being a coward should not prevent you from doing something brave). He embodied this principle when he joined the army in 1939, was imprisoned, then fought for the Resistance on his release in 1941.

But his writings were actions too, and the characters of his plays and novels had to act on his philosophy. This is why the books can be read autobiographically: *Nausea* is the diary of an academic who frequents cafés. He begins with an inability to doubt and is prone to the kind of malaise that gives Sartre's philosophical work its subjectivity; he finishes intending to write a novel.

Sartre wrote more novels: the *Roads to Freedom* trilogy has a young man facing domestic and political crises as World War Two begins. The second volume, *The Reprieve,* becomes as fragmented as Europe during the "appeasement" period, before it finds a note of deluded hope. Here, as in his treatment of tragedy (*Les Mouches* takes on **Euripides**' *Electra*), events that seem to have no immediate consequence reveal themselves as meaningful by the conclusion, as if to question the effects an existential way of life can have on the surroundings of the person living that life.

Sartre's reflection on what the times demanded led him and his partner **Simone de Beauvoir** to support Communism, Chairman Mao and the Paris student uprising of May 1968. He declined the Nobel Prize for Literature in 1964.

Schiller

FRIEDRICH VON born Marbach a. Neckar 1759; died Weimar 1805

> *Give him the nectar!*
> *Pour out for the poet,*
> *Hebe! Pour free!*
> *Quicken his eyes with celestial dew,*
> *That Styx the detested no more may he view,*
> *And like one of us Gods may conceit him to be!*
> *Thanks, Hebe! I quaff it! Io Paean, I cry!*
> *The wine of the Immortals*
> *Forbids me to die!*

THE VISIT OF THE GODS, TR. COLERIDGE

SCHILLER WAS PROFOUNDLY influenced by the spirit of **Rousseau**, and a strong zeal for freedom emerges from his plays and poems. He was one of the leading figures of the *Sturm und Drang* movement (storm and stress, a robust expression of Romanticism), and as such, drew inevitable comparisons with **Goethe.** They were friends, especially when Schiller was Professor of History at Jena, and when Goethe was asked to judge between them, he said, "Germany is lucky to have two such boys."

In both drama and historical texts, Schiller portrayed free spirits at odds with their rulers. In *Don Carlos* and *William Tell*, he presented oppression in Spain and Switzerland respectively, in pieces which, as operas, would serve Italy in its own struggle. In *Mary Stuart*, the freedom is more spiritual: the hero-ine's joy at being even briefly out of prison, and on the ultimate liberation of her soul, finds lyrical expression worthy of *Faust.* Such a work shows the influence of the hugely Graecophile spirit pervading Germany at the time; although Schiller's drama is not as classical as **Racine** thought it, the way characters can put their cases, as if disputing in court, certainly echoes **Euripides.**

His poetry too can emulate Greek lyric, both in subject matter and in form, as his *Ode to Joy*, so famous from Beethoven's Choral Symphony. But its influence depends more on its heady response to an age of revolution. While much of this might seem overblown to readers in English these days, Schiller can convey his passion with a persuasive urgency, just as his characters do onstage.

Schnitzler

ARTHUR

born Vienna 1862; died Vienna 1931

The human ear is so formed that it can sleep at the sound but wake at the echo.

BOOK OF SAYINGS AND REFLECTIONS

ARTHUR SCHNITZLER MADE his name principally as a dramatist. He worked in *fin-de-siècle* Vienna, that great moment in cultural history when Jewish artists and thinkers secured such freedoms of expression in the face of intolerance. It was a city under the grip of the mayor Karl Luger, who managed to maintain the support of the intellectual classes while relying on anti-semitic journalism and propaganda. Schnitzler was keenly aware of these apparent disparities, feeling that of all people, liberals treated Jews the worst. He would approach anti-semitism in his work, dramatically in the hospital politics of *Doctor Bernardi*. (He lost his own job as a medical orderly for publishing the novella *Lieutenant Gustl*, ridiculing the military figures around him.) He suffered the same persecution as Freud, Mahler, Schoënberg and his friend Hugo von Hofmannsthal. He stayed in Vienna throughout his life.

He trained as a physician, and followed keenly the development of psychiatry. As with **Robert Musil**, his work is so contemporaneous with Freud's that it becomes hard to say who anticipated whom. They all share an interest in the unconscious. Schnitzler's plays particularly raise the question of what we are really thinking: mostly about decadent forms of sexual pleasure. In *Paracelsus* we are told that life is a dream, and that nothing is certain; throughout Schnitzler's dramas, characters enact their dreams, providing manifesta-

tions of aristocratic fantasies in an age of decadence.

He presents these often in one-act plays consisting of short, sketch-like themes. *Anatol* is the most famous example, and introduces character-types much like those found in **Plautus** and New Comedy, notably the lovelorn rich boy and his wilier factotum. Scenes are linked, with characters reappearing; in *Merry-go-round,* this is systematic, with one partner in each duet surviving into the next one, until the ensemble forms five couplings in a tight circle.

MAJOR WORKS

PLAYS
Anatol (1893)

Playing With Love (1895)

Paracelsus (1897)

The Green Cockatoo (1899)

Merry-go-round (1900)

Intermezzo (1905)

Professor Bernardi (1912)

NOVELLAS
Lieutenant Gustl (1901)

Flight into Darkness (1926).

The Road to the Open
  (novel, 1908)

Scott

SIR WALTER

born Edinburgh 1771; died Abbotsford 1832

To aching eyes each landscape lowers,

To feverish pulse each gale blows chill;

And Araby's and Eden's bowers

Were barren as this moorland hill.

THE DREARY CHANGE

FOR MANY PEOPLE, Walter Scott *is* Scotland. He would have liked it that way. He invented clan tartans, as though they were ancient, for the moment when George IV visited Edinburgh, and Scott took

him round the town as representative of all things Scottish. In his Romantic age, when Europe was already in a swoon over the discovery of **Ossian**, his poetry and prose evoked a lost world of Celtic gallantry.

Scott worked hard to restore some idea of that world. It had been destroyed systematically by the English after Culloden, who banned clans from assembling, and sent their leaders into internal exile. Scott has been accused of pandering too much to his neighbours, not least by glamourising the English in *Ivanhoe*, but he was as concerned to reconcile England with Scotland as the Lowlands with the Highlands.

The success he won with his poems enabled him to build a castle at Abbotsford, near the border, where he became a self-styled laird. His poetry was enormously successful – he was offered the post of Poet Laureate in 1813, but recommended Southey. His fame was eclipsed by **Byron**; feeling the need to build an extension to his pile, he turned, anonymously, to prose fiction.

In this, he is credited with the invention of the historical romance. He produced them with an astonishing fluency, making few plans for his first, *Waverley*, and dictating *Ivanhoe* in two weeks. This kind of speed served him well when he fell into immense debt, which he worked ceaselessly to earn the equivalent of £5 million during the last seven years of his life. Such work might seem mass-produced for the tourists it began attracting in his life-time; but his poetry shows that his epic feel for tales of honour were motivated as much by Romanticism as by a benign Scottish Nationalism.

Seth

VIKRAM

born Calcutta 1942

She lies asleep, unswiftly breathing;
Her thoughts are not with him, her
*   dreams*
Traverse the solitary streams
Of inward lands, yet her hair, wreathing
The pillow in a mesh of light,
Returns him to the fugitive night.

THE GOLDEN GATE

VIKRAM SETH IS A POET and novelist who delivers breathtaking virtuosity in every form he attempts. He has published several volumes of lyric verse and versions of Chinese poetry, all of which reveal a vast range of interest (he trained as an economist, but his knowledge does not seem to stop anywhere convenient). Still, this did not prepare anyone for *The Golden Gate*.

In Chapter Five, Seth describes the surprise that greeted his decision to write a verse novel, before pointing to the model of **Pushkin**'s *Eugene Onegin*, which was made accessible to English readers by Charles Johnston's miraculous translation. Seth's tale plays the same games with a strict but addictive verse form, to tell the stories of educated young San Franciscans. He crams in their responses to everything from love and death to nuclear war, art, sex, viticulture and pet iguanas; the work is studiedly complete, but completely refreshing.

He is more famous still for *A Suitable Boy*, perhaps the longest novel ever published in English. However, only its size is intimidating. Literary great Salman Rushdie is falsely alleged to have called it a "soap opera": it is nonetheless a symptom of how the adventurous spirit of Seth's enterprises can blind critics to his works' deeper merits. The book is set in India in 1951 (shortly after Partition), in an imaginary town, conceived in the spirit of **R.K. Narayan**'s Malgudi. Narayan's delicate handling of local intrigue also informs the work, especially on faculty politics. But in its romantic theme (the burgeoning relationship between a Hindu girl and a Muslim boy) and the huge cast of characters, it also takes on the 19th-century English novel. It is hard to know what to expect next from Seth: if hints that he is attempting drama prove correct, theatre might never be the same again.

Shakespeare

WILLIAM   **born Stratford-on-Avon 1564; died Stratford-on-Avon 1616**

Enter a Messenger, with two heads and a hand.

TITUS ANDRONICUS

The voice of the Lord answered from a whirlwind: 'Neither am I anyone; I have dreamt the world as you dreamt your work, my Shakespeare, and among the forms in my dream are you, who like myself are many and no-one.'

JORGE LUIS BORGES

SHAKESPEARE COULD HAVE been anybody. Claims that his plays were written by Bacon or the Earl of Oxford (since Shakespeare could not have been educated enough to create such plays himself), or even by **Marlowe** (whose death may have been faked for security reasons and for whom Shakespeare may have acted as a front) show how eager factions are to control at source what few people deny is the finest literature in any language. He has been discounted as a reactionary apparatchik and heralded as a radical thinker; held at once as a champion and detractor of women as sentient beings; portrayed as bellicose and peace-loving; summoned to render service to the British Empire, as well as troubled housing projects.

Bids to pin him down only elevate him higher. Few facts are known about him. He worked most often with a collaborator: in *Macbeth*, an interpolator has been blamed for parts that are doggerel or rude. The longest stage run he had in his lifetime was 11 days (which constituted a hit). He was universally popular then: his ribald banter accompanied peerless poetry in a way that has been called crowd-pleasing, but that shows an unparalleled understanding of how to represent all humanity in five acts on a stage shaped like a wooden O. We know he was married and had two children: attempts to deduce his sexuality from the *Sonnets* are as deluded as efforts to learn what he thought and felt on any subject anywhere in his corpus. What documents we have of his reveal that he spelled his own name at least 13 different ways. This is as revealing about his personality as anything we know about him.

Shaw

GEORGE BERNARD **born Dublin 1856; died Ayot St. Lawrence, Herts 1950**

It is impossible for an Englishman to open his mouth without making some other Englishman despise him.

PYGMALION

You see things; and you say, 'Why?' But I dream things that never were; and I say, 'Why not?'

BACK TO METHUSELAH

SHAW'S LONG LIFE was spent campaigning against the indignities of capitalism, the degradation of women, the crime of poverty, the evils of war, the ravages of disease and any kind of hypocrisy. He did it in pamphlets, in letters to the Press, in the endless oratory he painfully taught himself to perform and, most enduringly, in his plays.

He wrote some 50 pieces for the theatre: few dramatists have put their social messages on stage with such urgency, or conveyed them so starkly. His characters argue out ideas and although Shaw took great pains to indicate how his dialogue should be delivered, actors are made to discuss the pros and cons of Shavian thinking. If the meaning of a work is not clear enough in the performance, Shaw appends prefaces, often longer than the plays they explain. Ultimately, his creations owe much to his mastery of rhetoric, his Wildean wit, his admiration of **Ibsen** and his reading of **Nietzsche** and Marx. Again like

Wilde, he was a fine satirist, especially of the English (he arrived from Dublin when he was 20), but like **Brecht**, his hope was that audiences would think for themselves and look to individual consciences.

His prose argues his case more directly. As a youthful critic, he defended independent artistic spirits like Ibsen and Wagner to the English – his own work prospered more on the Continent in his lifetime than it did in Britain – and his papers defended socialism to the end. He practised what he preached, living frugally, declining honours (including a peerage), using the money from his 1925 Nobel Prize to found an Anglo-Swedish literary society, working for the Fabian Society and abstaining from alcohol, tea, coffee and meat, pointing out that things that were bad for him did not tempt him.

MAJOR WORKS

Widowers' Houses (1893)

Arms and the Man (1894)

Mrs Warren's Profession (1898)

Man and Superman (1903)

Major Barbara (1905)

Getting Married (1908)

Androcles and the Lion (1912)

Pygmalion (1916)

Back to Methuselah (1921)

Saint Joan (1924)

Shelley

MARY

born London 1797; died London 1851

And now, once again, I bid my hideous progeny go forth and prosper. I have an affection for it, for it was the offspring of happy days, when death and grief were but words which found no true echo in my heart.

FRANKENSTEIN,
INTRODUCTION TO THE 1831 EDITION

MARY SHELLEY'S NIGHTMARISH imagination was awakened early in her life. Her youth was spent at the very heart of the romantic movement. Her mother was Mary Wollstonecraft, author of *A Vindication of the Rights of Women*, and her father was William Godwin – whose rational but anarchistic philosophy attracted the attention of the young **Shelley**, whom Mary married.

After Shelley's early death, she edited and published his poetry, wrote travel memoirs and fiction set in the future. In this she was always careful to maintain a realistic view of human nature, however fantastical her stories became. *The Last Man*, for example, tells of a plague-ridden British republic in the year 2100, where only one human survives.

Her most famous work is *Frankenstein*. It shares with the later *Lodore* the **Rousseau**-inspired theme: can a creature grow up in a state of innocence? The creature that looms out of the novel cannot: he has been made by a man, who has stolen the vital spark, imparted by a bolt of lightning, that is only God's to impart. The creation is necessarily flawed and evil. This aspect of the tale shares her husband's attraction to the figure of Prometheus, while drawing on his other verse (quoting *Mutability* and invoking Mont Blanc, a view of which inspired one of Percy's most awesome poems). The supernatural theme was suggested by conversations with Shelley, **Byron** and Byron's doctor (with each of them agreeing to undertake the writing of a ghost story): subsequent nightmares helped. Whatever she owed to the latter, she left a profoundly personal vision that expressed her age's tendency to distinguish individual genius from the agencies of God.

Shelley

PERCY BYSSHE

born Horsham, Sussex 1792; died Livorno 1822

Strangers have wept to hear his
*   passionate notes,*
And virgins, as unknown he past, have
*   pined*
And wasted for fond love of his wild
*   eyes.*
The fire of those soft orbs has ceased to
*   burn,*
And Silence, too enamoured of that
*   voice,*
Locks its mute music in her rugged cell.

ALASTOR

SHELLEY FAMOUSLY CALLED poets "the unacknowledged legislators of the world". He was profoundly unhappy with the acknowledged legislation and his remedies for society's ills involved love and a sensibility to the natural forces of the universe.

In his identification with animals and the elements, he voices his most urgent social theme: his call for freedom. When he was 20, he was distributing pamphlets in Dublin towards the emancipation of Irish Catholics; at the end of his short life, he found in the Greek uprising against the Turks a model for all servitude, by which he felt the English were also bound. For himself, he legislated as he went. At 18 he eloped with Harriet Westbrook, two years his junior, then invited her to live with his new lover and soon-to-be wife **Mary**. In this he denied divine authority (he had been expelled from Oxford for avowed atheism) and railed against the courts, finding morality in love alone.

When he writes against tyranny and inhumanity, love accounts for his abiding optimism. His *Ode to the West Wind* has the wind vivifying the poet; the *Sky-Lark*, too, is made to share the poet's vision of a better world. In all this, he saves himself from the curse of being "morally dead". As nature frees the poet from this fate in the blank verse *Alastor*, so in *Prometheus Unbound* the elements rally round the mythical saviour of humanity in a poem that emulates **Aeschylus** in form and **Milton** in language. Often this **Platonic** notion of the soul's freedom leads Shelley to hope for a better existence after death; his drowning seemed to fulfil the craving his richly wrought verse frequently captured; but his personal generosity and gift of friendship (with **Keats** and **Byron**) bound him as closely to the living.

MAJOR WORKS

Prometheus Unbound (1820)

Epipsychidion (1821)

Adonais (1821)

other works collected and published posthumously

Sholokov

MIKHAIL   **born Veshenskaya 1905; died there 1984**

The pages in Russian history written in '37 and '38 contain lyrical as well as tragic lines, and the handwriting of those lines is rather musical.

COMMITTEES FOR THE POOR
TR. JOHN GLAD

CONTROVERSY WILL SURROUND Mikhail Sholokov for a long time. His career can seem to have prospered from his close involvement with the Communist Party. He joined the Party in 1932, and the Writers' Union in 1934.

By then, his four-volume masterpiece had started appearing. *And Quiet Flows the Don* and *The Don Flows to the Sea* chronicle the effects the Revolution had on his native area in the 10 years after 1917. If the works are seen as having purely a social purpose, it is to depict the acceptance of change, and the benefits it can bring to an initially reluctant Cossack community. It celebrates local vigour as well as Soviet ideology: Sholokov felt (or was) obliged to expand his narrative to include Collectivisation, the often violent process of bringing farms under state control that began in the late 1920s. His work endorsed Stalin's economic policies; he could update his agricultural novel *Virgin Soil Upturned* in 1960 to demonstrate the continued success of five-year plans.

Bitter debate ensued about the books' authorship. Rumours circulated that they were not the work of Sholokov, but of a dead White Russian, a Cossack needing to find a front to express his views. Sholokov seemed too young, and too briefly educated, to produce such a masterpiece. **Solzhenitsyn** made the same accusations loudly in the West, pointing at inconsistencies to show where Sholokov might have taken over from the original manuscript. While other critics agree there are faults, there is also consensus that the work shows greatness, at least in parts. Sholokov won the Nobel Prize in 1965. By then, he had huge power within the Writers' Union, and courted fresh controversy by calling for the State's retribution on dissidents **Sinyavsky** and Yuri Daniel.

Sidney

SIR PHILIP   born Penshurst 1554; died Zutphen, nr. Arnhem 1586

Biting my truant pen, beating myself for

spite –

'Fool,' said my muse to me; 'look in thy

heart, and write.'

ASTROPHEL AND STELLA

SIDNEY WAS ALREADY known during his lifetime all over Europe as the ideal courtier, poet and soldier. After his early death and the subsequent publication of his works, his legend only increased. He was knighted in 1583, rather as a courtesy than as a reward for service, and when he finally received a royal appointment in 1585 it was to a minor post in the Low Countries. It was there that, in an otherwise unimportant skirmish at Zutphen in 1586, Sidney was wounded in the thigh. He died three weeks later. The manner of his death – a wound in the thigh being a powerful symbol in European folklore (as with Adonis, or the Fisher King) – added to his already legendary status and all Europe publicly mourned his death.

Sidney's writings, which reveal his mastery of prose, verse and criticism, had circulated in courtly circles during his lifetime, but were published only posthumously. *Astrophel and Stella*, the first sonnet-sequence in English, was written 10 years before its publication, when Sidney was in love with Penelope Devereux (Stella in the sonnets), who married Lord Rich. The 108 sonnets, interspersed with songs, show a breathtaking variety and they launched a fad for sonnet sequence in the 1590s – perhaps the most glorious fad in the history of English letters.

In 1595 two different printers published his great critical treatise, which one called *The Defence of Poesie* and the other *An Apologie for Poetrie*. Today it is known by both names. Although it contains many observations that were well known from classical and neo-classical treatments of the topic, Sidney's work is distinguished by its elegance and courtly wit. Sidney's longest and greatest work is the *Arcadia*, a prose romance sprinkled with pastoral poems and metrical experiments. It was first published in two versions called the *Old* and the *New* and then conflated into *The Countess of Pembroke's Arcadia* (after Sidney's sister). In whatever form, the *Arcadia* was unmatched as a piece of English prose fiction until the rise of the novel in the early 18th century.

Simenon

GEORGES

born Liège, 1903; died Lausanne 1989

'So, you're concentrating your thoughts?' said someone who prided himself on his psychological acuity.

And Maigret had replied with comic sincerity:

'I never think.'

MAIGRET'S RIVAL

THE STATISTICS ON Georges Simenon raise some alarming questions: how did a man who could claim to have had liaisons with some 10,000 women find time to write 500 novels, under 16 different pseudonyms, including "Bobette" and "Plick et Plock"? He lived long, and started young: by the time he was 28, when he began the Maigret series, he had already produced about 100 titles. He wrote a book a week, sometimes needing only four days.

They are usually short, and extremely accomplished. Far from speed diminishing his quality, it seems that a huge amount of practice made him all but perfect. His mysteries (usually of murder) are apt to contain clues that lead nowhere especially; but if anything, this makes the drama more real. Simenon's detective Maigret sometimes seems like he's improvising; and if those in control of the narrative don't know what's coming next, how can the reader guess?

But Simenon's books are better than whodunits. They are famed for their atmosphere: things are generally soggy and foggy. This intensity points to where the real action is: in the characters' minds. Crimes are committed through passion, and are treated with remorse. Maigret's methods of detection may be psychological, depending on soaking up the most intimate details about everyone around him (a colleague compares him to a sponge); but he relies so much on intuition that sometimes, as in *Maigret in Vichy*, he can be involved in an investigation even when no crime has taken place yet. As **Dostoyevsky** has written, "The evil existed before men." Like **Chandler**'s hero, Maigret is too jaded to be caught in it. As a sleuth, he is brilliant, but not invincible; still, "if they *had* got the better of him, they hadn't done so with money or fine words."

Sinclair

UPTON   **born Baltimore 1878; died Bound Brook, New Jersey 1968**

So long as we are without heart, so long as we are without conscience, so long as we are without even a mind – pray, in the name of heaven, why should anyone think it worthwhile to be troubled because we are without a literature?

ON BOURGEOIS LITERATURE

UPTON SINCLAIR WAS a committed American Socialist writer, whose 100 or so books relied on journalistic research into the plight of his country's poor. He militated against poverty, working condi-

tions, and employees' lack of rights. Ultimately, his characters could turn to Socialism for a hope of improvement. For this reason, Sinclair has seldom been fashionable in the United States.

He began his career writing pulp fiction, first to fund his education, which was eventually at Princeton, and then to support his wife and child. When he was 22, he produced sentimental novels, including one empathising with **Goethe**'s Werther; but he found his voice addressing injustices past and present. He researched *Manassas* meticulously, telling the story of a Southern Abolitionist during the Civil War, and for *The Jungle* investigated meat-packers in Chicago for seven weeks. As in other work, this book aimed to establish an equal dignity for women and men; it led to an enquiry into meat-packing (more because of allegations that the meat was bad rather than the hours) and remains his best-known work.

With the proceeds, Sinclair founded Helicon Hall, a commune which attracted **Sinclair Lewis**, who changed his name in Upton's honour. The building was destroyed by fire. Subsequently Sinclair sought election as Governor of California, explaining in his memoir *How I Got Licked* that MGM studios screened devastating smear campaigns against him for proposing a tax on films.

His writing is passionate about his cause. He argued strongly for the social use of literature, as opposed to seeking profit through it. His writing has a purity of purpose, especially his journalism: his use of fact in fictional form anticipates **Capote's** techniques, notably in *Boston*. Although he is seen as dry and humourless, his tireless lobbying has the oratorical conviction of Cicero.

Singer

ISAAC BASHEVIS born Radzymin, Poland 1904; died New York 1991

When the writer becomes the center of his attention, he becomes a nudnik. And a nudnik who believes he's profound is even worse than just a plain nudnik.

INTERVIEW WITH RICHARD BURGIN

ISAAC BASHEVIS SINGER IS a demon in a gaberdine. He wrote in Yiddish, which he said "has minerals other languages lack", and was steeped in its tradition: he was born in Poland, the son of a rabbi. His stories range from the Hassidic communities of his youth, with their Messianic mentality, to the esoteric circles of Manhattan. He settled in New York in 1935, to escape European anti-semitism.

He is chiefly remembered for his tales set in the villages of Kreshev, Frampol and Goray, where his first novel is set. *Satan in Goray* is just one of many appearances the devil would make in Singer's work – a figure who might fulfil his role as malignant tempter, but more often is heard complaining and making jokes. In Singer's work, the Devil can present himself as a reject and an outcast and so provides a disturbing analogy with the Jewish experience of exile and persecution. The presence of evil can be felt in more human forms: "The Gentleman of Cracow", for example, offers a starving village a wedding banquet, only to incite an orgy and leave the children charred in their cradles.

But this fantastical and unsentimental world provides Singer with his richest moments of absurd humour. In "The Dead Fiddler", a venerable elder fears an extra-marital pregnancy only to discover that a dead fiddler has taken abode in his daughter's stomach, soon to be joined by a simple girl who died several hundred years before.

Singer was a great admirer of Aesop's Fables; like Aesop's, his writing shows an interest in character types, such as *Gimpel the Fool*, optimistic and lanky, well versed in the Torah and little else. Singer would always avoid over-intellectualising, and he made a natural story-teller for children. He won the Nobel Prize in 1978.

Sinyavsky

ANDREI

born Moscow 1925; died Paris 1997

[I advocate a] phantasmagoric art with hypotheses instead of a Purpose, an art in which the grotesque will replace realistic descriptions of ordinary life.

ON SOCIALIST REALISM

IN 1966 THE KGB discovered it was Sinyavsky who, under the name of Abram Tertz, had been publishing work in the West that the authorities thought slandered the Soviet Union and provided propaganda for reactionaries overseas. There was a sort of trial. Sinyavsky pleaded that he loved Russia and that he had published abroad for stylistic reasons rather than political ones: he was told he was attending criminal proceedings, not a literary seminar.

His claim was justified, up to a point. As a budding historian of Russian literature, he had aligned himself with the fantastical work of **Gogol** and **Dostoyevsky**, rather than the socialist realism of **Gorky**. To have claimed this was brave enough even during Khrushchev's thaw. However, as a close friend of **Pasternak** (he was his pall-bearer, and wrote an introduction to his poems), he knew the new leniency was superficial and that his Symbolist, richly imaginative novels based on the Stalinist terrors – during which his father was arrested, but of whose horrors he was only just learning – could not be published in his own country. He had become a political writer in spite of himself.

The Trial Begins described the sense of fear that was everywhere during the Stalin years. The *Makepeace Experiment* criticised Soviet ideals more generally. In subsequent volumes, Sinyavsky followed his own victimisation. The court sentenced him to seven years' hard labour. During his term, he wrote a book in the guise of letters to his wife, *A Voice from the Choir*. He was released in 1971 and in 1973 began teaching Russian literature at the Sorbonne, in Paris. He then wrote autobiography, journalism and criticism, leaving at his death the first completed draft of a new novel.

MAJOR WORKS

On Socialist Realism (1960)

The Trial Begins (1960)

Fantastic Stories (1961)

The Makepeace Experiment (1965)

Thoughts Unawares (1965)

A Voice from the Choir (1973)

In Gogol's Shadow (1975)

Walks With Pushkin (1976)

Goodnight (1989)

Ivan the Simple: Paganism, Magic and Religion of the Russian People (1990)

Snow

C.P.

born Leicester 1905; died London 1980

We talked about personal politics, of which, not only in the college, we had now seen a good deal. One point had struck us both: will, sheer stubborn will, was more effective than cunning or finesse or subtlety. Those could be a help; but the more one saw, the more one was forced to the conclusion that the man you wanted on your side was the man who believed without a shade of doubt that you were right.

THE MASTERS

C.P. SNOW'S REFINED NOVELS document his own distinguished public life, from the varied perspectives of academic, scientist and civil servant. His first works of fiction included a detective story, *Death Under Sail,* and *The Search,* on scientific research. All his novels after 1940 come under the collective title of *Strangers and Brothers.*

The brothers are Lewis and Martin Eliot, the one an academic lawyer, the other a scientist. The former is the narrator, sometimes telling his brother's story, sometimes those of strangers. His knowledge of law gives him an understanding of the corridors of power (Snow's title introduced the phrase into the language), which the author culled from his own time in Whitehall. Snow's own administrative work drew on his scientific knowledge – he was Under-Secretary in the Ministry of Technology, the source of Harold Wilson's "white heat." Consequently his work casts a rare view on the ethical dilemmas at stake when political and scientific power combine. He discussed these themes, and his own treatment of them, in his controversial Rede Lecture of 1959.

His best-known work remains *The Masters,* set in a Cambridge college much like the Christ's of which Snow had been a fellow. In his handling of disparate personalities seeking to succeed a dying Head of House, he displayed a wryness and reverence towards the subject; however, after Tom Sharpe's *Porterhouse Blue,* the former seems more appropriate nowadays.

Solzhenitsyn

ALEKSANDR

born Kislovodsk 1918

Literature is the memory of peoples; it transmits from one generation to the next the irrefutable experiences of men. It preserves and enlivens the flame of a history immune to all deformation, far from every lie.

NOBEL PRIZE LECTURE, 1970

IN HIS NOW CELEBRATED speech on accepting the Nobel Prize for Literature in 1970, Solzhenitsyn spoke of the writer's obligation to bear witness to the truth; for what he called "the lie" allowed violence to flourish.

Solzhenitsyn's courage appears all the greater for the evil he witnessed himself. In 1945, he was arrested for remarks he was supposed to have made against Stalin. He had been fighting in the war, had been twice decorated and attained the rank of captain: now he would be imprisoned for eight years in a labour camp. On his release, he was kept in exile until 1956, when he was rehabilitated under the increased tolerance of the Khruschev régime. But his writings would soon suffer the same backlash as Sinyavsky experienced under Brezhnev. His work was banned in Russia, and he was expelled from the Writers' Union.

His courage had to endure disbelief in the west too. Communists internationally considered Solzhenitsyn's testament a betrayal, especially his three-volume account of Russian history from the implementation of the Soviet Terror in 1918 to 1956, *The Gulag Archipelago*. Commentators scrabbled around for explanations as to why the Gulag system was somehow "not as bad" as the Nazi death camps, and so missed the author's treatment of inhumanity and evil on its own terms.

For all the specific documentation of Stalin's crimes in his work, Solzhenitsyn recognised these injustices as being far from unique to the Soviet Union. Once in the West, he spoke of the cowardice displayed by the United Nations, and campaigned against what he saw as the imperial conflict in Vietnam. By now he had embraced Christianity, and demanded of political systems only that they be founded on love, compassion and the humility of its governors. Literature remains for Solzhenitsyn the means of reflecting "the growing spiritual unity of mankind."

Sophocles

born Colonus c. 496 BC; died Athens 405 BC

All that is mine will go today, and you

will need take no more onerous

  care of me;

it's harsh, children, I know:

  and yet one word

alleviates this kind of suffering.

There is no man than he from

  whom you part

to live out your remaining life, from

  whom

you could have had more love.

OEDIPUS AT COLONUS

SOPHOCLES WAS THE DEFINITIVE author of Greek tragedy. In *Oedipus Rex*, he provided what Aristotle considered the model of what a tragedy should be. The judges of the Dionysian theatre festival thought him the best, too: he wrote some 30 cycles of plays (123 pieces in all), won first prize with 24 of them and second prize with the rest. He stands between **Aeschylus** and **Euripides** chronologically and in the history of drama's development he added a third actor to Aeschylus' format, hugely increasing the possibilities of staging. He also anticipated Euripides' less lyrical, more psychologically economical representation of action.

Sophocles' timing and poetry can make the drama agonisingly tense, even in the one example of weak structure (*Women of Trachis*). His lyric odes, which involve the chorus very emotionally, can praise mankind, or love, or the poet's birthplace. Although he is known to have written non-dramatic verse, it is his ear for the inevitable cadence in the mouth of an actor (and he had been one) that can move us as much as the terrible crisis a character may face.

He gave words their fullest value. Oedipus puns on his name to invoke the theme of self-knowledge (it can sound like the Greek for "I know where…" in this plot of detection), and yet can descend into panicked or alliterative stuttering. The hero in *Philoctetes* must also howl his pain in strict Greek iambics: "Papapapai papai papai papapapai!" This visceral incoherence bursts into a play whose language elsewhere is marked by subtle persuasion and vivid scene-setting. Sophocles was always in control of his effects and the text of his last play is said to have been used as evidence when his relatives thought him of unsound mind.

Soyinka

WOLE

born Abeokuta, Western Nigeria 1934

Who does not seek to be remembered?

Memory is the Master of Death, the

  chink

In his armour of conceit. I shall leave

That which makes my going the sheerest

Dream of an afternoon. Should voyagers

Not travel light? Let the considerate

  traveller

Shed, of his excessive load, all

That may benefit the living.

DEATH AND THE KING'S HORSEMAN

WOLE SOYINKA IS a Nigerian writer who has published poems and prose (the latter largely autobiographical), but he remains better known for his theatrical work.

To some extent this shows the influence of **Brecht** and Greek tragedy – he has adapted *The Threepenny Opera* and **Euripides**' *Bacchae*. He studied at Leeds University, then worked reading plays for the Royal Court Theatre in London, but his voice is distinctly African, whatever his detractors there might say. His Brecht treatment attacks dictators such as Idi Amin, Bokassa and Nguema; his version of the *Bacchae* introduces African songs and dances as choric episodes and casts the story, with the death of the king, Pentheus, as an event whose ritual implications can rejuvenate the earth.

This is the theme of *Death and the King's Horseman*, in which a chief must follow his king to the grave, to complete the burial rites. Colonial attempts to intervene can only pervert the natural order as presented in the play, which the drama makes lyrical and real in the face of Western incomprehension. Still, the chief's tragedy is more to do with the human condition than Empire. Soyinka's earlier depictions of a society under the spell of a sham prophet in *The Trials of Brother Jero* and *Jero's Metamorphosis* are as telling about corruption as they are about the potential disaster Christianity can bring to a community with very different traditions.

Soyinka's relationship with Nigeria has always been difficult. He was imprisoned there for two years during the Biafran War, has left in self-imposed exile and has protested loudly against the barbaric actions of General Abacha's present régime. He won the Nobel Prize for Literature in 1986.

Spark

MURIEL

born Edinburgh 1918

'Love,' says Felicity as they all take up their work again, 'and love-making are very liberating experiences, very. If I were the Abbess of Crewe, we should have a love-Abbey. I would destroy that ungodly electronics laboratory and install a love-nest right in the heart of this Abbey, right in the heart of England.' Her busy little fingers fly with the tiny needle in and out of the stuff she is sewing.

THE ABBESS OF CREWE

DAME MURIEL SPARK is a novelist distinguished by her humour and by her deeply imaginative treatment of large and sometimes alarming themes in small, hitherto stable settings. She was born in Edinburgh to Scots and Jewish parents and she became a Catholic in 1954. With *The Comforters,* this conversion began to make an impact on Spark's work, which first attracted attention with her short stories.

The novel *Memento Mori* brings an overbearing sense of mortality to the London elderly of all classes. The action of *The Ballad of Peckham Rye* introduces a similar feeling of disquiet to working-class south London with the arrival of Dougal Douglas to the area around the park where, we learn, Boadicea committed suicide. *The Abbess of Crewe*, newly elected, takes this kind of transformation to farcical lengths when she bugs her nuns. But the most famous and troubling example of such upheaval in Spark's work must be *The Prime of Miss Jean Brodie*.

This tells of the following a teacher cultivates among pupils at a school much like the Edinburgh one Spark attended – James Gillespie's School for Girls. Miss Brodie's stated intention to encourage girls to think for themselves rather than spoon-feeding them with knowledge yields to her predilections for the other teachers and European Fascism. She provides Spark's definitive portrayal of the power-crazed woman and her "betrayer's" treatise, *The Transfiguration of the Commonplace,* points to the author's own achievement.

She has recently been awarded the British Literature Prize, half of which the recipient must share to help promote the artistic cause of his or her choice: it is fitting that she opted for the school which inspired *The Prime of Miss Jean Brodie.*

Spenser

EDMUND

born London c. 1552; died London 1599

That jolly shepheard, which there piped,
was
Poore Colin Clout (who knows not Colin
Clout?)
He pypt apace, whilest they him daunst
about.

THE FAERIE QUEENE

EDMUND SPENSER WAS the great epic poet of the reign of Elizabeth I, holding the same relation to 16th-century poetry that **Milton** holds to that of the 17th century. In 1580 he became secretary to the Lord Deputy of Ireland, where he lived most of his remaining years and his prose work, *A View of the Present State of Ireland*, was a result of this residence. There is some speculation that he died in poverty, even in hunger, but his reputation was great during his lifetime and by the 17th century he was an acknowledged classic.

Spenser consciously modelled his career on **Virgil**'s, moving from pastoral poetry to national epic. His first major work, *The Shepheardes Calender*, a series of 12 eclogues, made great claims for itself: it was published with all the annotations of a classical text, with extensive commentaries by a certain 'E K', widely assumed to be Spenser. But these claims were recognised by contemporaries, notably **Sidney**, who praised the anonymous poems in his *Defence of Poesie*.

Sidney in return exerted an influence on Spenser, whose *Amoretti* was one of the numerous sonnet sequences that followed the publication of Sidney's *Astrophel and Stella*. The *Amoretti* are distinguished by their use of a single, interlocking rhyme scheme (now referred to as the Spenserian sonnet), by their highly refined religious and numerical symbolism and by their narrative. For they are addressed to the poet's wife Elizabeth and the sequence is perhaps the first ever in which the poet is represented as winning the girl. They stand with Sidney's and **Shakespeare**'s sonnets as one of the three great sequences of the English Renaissance.

Spenser's greatest work is the allegorical epic-romance, *The Faerie Queene*. Drawing on classical epic, on chivalric romance and on traditional English lore, while introducing its own stanza form and allegorical system, it is at once the longest, most complex, most sensuous and most spirited poem in the language.

MAJOR WORKS

The Shepheardes Calender (1579)

Amoretti (1595)

The Faerie Queene (1590, 1596, with fragments published posthumously)

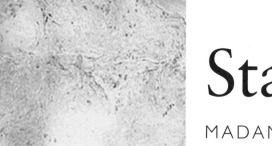

Staël

MADAME DE

born Paris 1766; died Paris 1817

A man must know how to brave public opinion, a woman how to submit to it.

PREFACE TO DELPHINE

Her château is a real arsenal against me; you have to go there armed as a knight.

NAPOLEON

MME. DE STAËL was a French woman of letters, whose wanderings, social position and convictions made her on the one hand extraordinary, and on the other a true child of her times.

Her father was Jacques Necker, the finance minister at odds with the doomed régime of Louis XVI. From him, she gained a liberal tolerance and access to the finest minds of her generation. Politically she had been sympathetic to the Revolution, but disgusted by its bloodshed: during Robespierre's terror, she saved many from the guillotine. She was almost as appalled by the rise of Napoleon, who banished her from Paris in 1802 for the novel *Delphine*, and then from France altogether in 1807 for her all-too respectful treatise on Germany. It is a mark of her literary clout that she managed to upset the Emperor so often, even with the most mindless attacks of the "he couldn't run a whelk-stall" kind. He badly needed her support during his return from Elba, and even hinted that the treasury might repay debts owing to her father.

In her criticism, her achievement was to combine vast reading with a first-hand knowledge of the cultures that produced them. This led her to glorify the traits of other nations innocent of nationalism's uglier manifestations. She would contrast the writing of northern Europe favourably with that of the south, and she had an especial love of **Ossian**. Her tastes inform her fiction, notably *Corinne*, about a love-triangle centering on the heroine (an Italian poet), and a Scots aristocrat. Here, as elsewhere, her incipient romanticism and her distaste for social conventions (especially as applied to women and suicide) anticipated **George Sand**.

Stead

CHRISTINA

born Rockdale, Australia 1902; died Sydney 1983

There next came in THE POET. He was tall, spare and ill, with hollow cheeks and eyes. He liked to rake through muck for a jewel: he exalted things like himself, useless and attenuated in form.

THE SALZBURG TALES; THE PERSONAGES

STEAD'S WRITING IS AS hard to place as its author. It takes in as many parts of the world as she did. She was born in Sydney and came to London in 1928. She then worked in Paris for five years before moving to Spain, only to move back to London when Franco took over, before settling in America. Her stories follow many of these wanderings. All her heroines are similar — searching for freedom and experience of love, often in the face of an oppression that can manifest itself in a quietly political way. The problems Louise faces with her father in the middle-class American family unit of *The Man Who Loved Children* are like those Teresa experiences with her husband in *For Love Alone*. The plots of these narratives are as wandering as her characters: Stead agreed that for her the latter were more important.

But for Stead, story-telling was completely natural. She found the perfect medium for her talent at the very beginning of her career. In *The Salzburg Tales*, she used the form of **Boccaccio**'s *Decameron* and **Chaucer**'s *The Canterbury Tales* to present a number of characters, brilliantly described in her introduction, telling stories over a week. As ever, the tellers come first, but it is a wonderful outlet for Stead's own richness of style and fund of imagination.

Stories emerge sometimes as jokes, sometimes as fairy-tales from her childhood, but as with characters who tell stories in other books, the recounting serves some deeper purpose, whether it be a response to love, or hate, or a way of passing the time.

Stein

GERTRUDE

born Allegheny, Pennsylvania 1874; died Paris 1946

I am I not any longer when I see. This sentence is at the bottom of all creative activity. It is just the exact opposite of I am I because my little dog knows me.

HENRY JAMES, DUET

GERTRUDE STEIN WAS a writer whose importance to modern literature is immense. She is more often remembered for her influence on younger writers such as **Fitzgerald** and

Hemingway than for her own work, which is often barely comprehensible.

But she was a great experimenter and this inscrutability is part of her adventure with words. As a student at Radcliffe, she was the star pupil of William (brother of **Henry**) **James**, gaining top marks even when she walked out of the exam room. She embraced his notions of the stream of consciousness and of the value of words. Although she did not produce "automatic" writing, she played with parts of speech. Her special concern was with nouns. Sometimes she tried to restore to them their full value (her famous "rose is a rose is a rose" is an attempt to take the word out of the context of its commonplace connotations) and sometimes she tried to do without them altogether.

In Paris (where she lived for 40 years), she was a great collector of paintings and a friend of Picasso. Her writing sometimes aims for a kind of cubism, where her perversely-punctuated sentences can throw up ambiguities that invite reading from different angles. This makes her narratives deceptively simple, and sometimes unstoppable, as she chases up possibilities: *The Making of Americans*, a telling of national history through that of her own family, runs to 900 pages.

During her lifetime, her following was at best cult, with publishers feeling able to send her rejection letters in her own imitable, studiedly repetitive style. The almost besotted **Thornton Wilder** did much to bring her work academic and popular respect, although she barely needed him to remind her of what a great writer she was. Still, although she ranked herself with **Whitman**, **Poe** and James, she had a fine sense of humour.

Steinbeck

JOHN   **born Salinas, California 1902; died New York 1968**

Tell you what – I use to get the people jumpin' and talkin' in tongues an' glory shoutin' till they just fell down an' passed out. An' some I'd baptise to bring 'em to. An' then – you know what I'd do? I'd take one of them girls out in the grass an' I'd lay with her… Come the nex' time, them an' me was full of the spirit, I'd do it again.

THE PREACHER, IN THE GRAPES OF WRATH

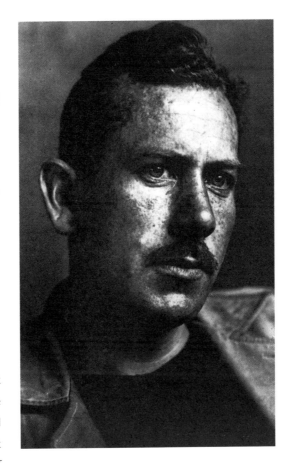

JOHN STEINBECK WROTE with real commitment and experimental style, largely about his native California. In *The Grapes of Wrath*, a family is uprooted from a plot they have always farmed. They head west in the dream-like hope of fruit-picking in a land of plenty, only to become disillusioned and to lose innocence in a politicised world. The trek west, always an epic motif in the US, provides the action of *The Wayward Bus*, in which a disparate group of travellers are thrown together on a journey they eventually share.

Steinbeck's is an arid landscape, with characters typically waiting for rain. They live by the land, but this has become corrupted: in *In Dubious Battle*, fruit is left to rot. *Tortilla Flat* again focusses on fruit-pickers and looks beyond immediate economic problems to tell the story of Danny, a libertine who nonetheless attracts a Christ-like following in his community. The recurrent idea of original sin in Steinbeck has attracted criticism that he is too fond of his intellectual premises for his stories' good. *East of Eden* has him tackling this problem insistently: the Salinas Valley is the setting for his re-telling of the conflict between Cain and Abel and introduces a range of characters in the Old Testament manner. The collected letters he wrote to his editor show what a professional he was: "Today I wrote 3,000 words and built a coffee table."

However difficult his subjects, his language is markedly straightforward, experimental in its juxtapositions perhaps (like his contemporary **Dos Passos**), but direct in its narrative and persuasive in its poetry.

He was awarded the Nobel Prize in 1962.

MAJOR WORKS

The Pastures of Heaven (1932)

Tortilla Flat (1935)

In Dubious Battle (1935)

Of Mice and Men (1937)

The Long Valley (1938)

The Grapes of Wrath (1939)

The Moon is Down (play and film, 1942)

The Wayward Bus (1942)

Cannery Row (1945)

East of Eden (1952)

The Short Reign of Pippin IV (1957)

Winter of our Discontent (1961)

HISTORY

The Sea of Cortez (1941)

The Log from the Sea of Cortez (1951)

Once There Was a War (1958)

Stendhal

born Grenoble 1783; died Paris 1842

He was afraid of terrible remorse and eternal ridicule if he deviated from the ideal model he had set himself to follow. In short, what made Julien a superior being was precisely what prevented him from savouring the happiness which came his way. Every inch the young girl of 16 who has delightful colouring, and is foolish enough to put on rouge to go to a ball.

THE RED AND THE BLACK,
TR. CATHERINE SLATER

STENDHAL RECALLED THAT when he was five, he saw a hatter shot in the back on the street outside his home in Grenoble. He considered it the first bloodshed in the Revolution. Even then, he could respond immediately to his times. Later, his career was very public: he was a diplomat in Italy during Napoleon's reign and had been part of the Emperor's military administration. In fact, when he was awarded the *Légion d'Honneur* in 1835, he would have rather had it for statesmanship than literature.

Like Napoleon, he combined a revolutionary spirit with an innate understanding of social niceties. He was an artist working in an atmosphere at once classical and romantic. The aristocratic hero in *Armance*, his first completed novel, was a means of satirising the effusive excesses of **Chateaubriand** and **Hugo**, although Stendhal acknowledged his debt to both. Elsewhere, his heroes consider themselves "superior beings" on the Napoleonic model, before becoming bound up with intrigues that recall an earlier age; but they regularly lack the *sang-froid* to cope with it.

This calls on the irony at the disposal of Stendhal's narrators, as well as pacy narration. He designedly wrote page-turners, which won over **Balzac**, who wrote fulsome praise of *The Charterhouse of Parma*. That book had been written in 53 days – the author is as eager to get on with the story as is the reader. His masterpiece, *The Red and the Black*, often uses the present tense and even shifts in characters' psychology can come across as action.

Sterne

LAURENCE   born Clonmel, County Tipperary 1713; died London 1768

The fifteenth chapter is come at last; and brings nothing with it but a sad signature of "How our pleasures slip from under us in this world." For in talking of my digression – I declare before heaven I have made it! What a strange creature is mortal man! said she.

This is very true, said I – but 'twere better to get all these things out of our heads, and return to my uncle Toby.

TRISTRAM SHANDY,
VOL IX, CHAPTER 15 (COMPLETE)

MAJOR WORKS

The Abuses of Conscience
(1750)

A Political Romance (1759)

*The Life and Opinions
of Tristram Shandy,
Gentleman*
(nine vols, 1760–1767)

The Journal to Eliza
(1767, abandoned)

A Sentimental Journey (1768)

LAURENCE STERNE WAS a sickly parish priest with one of the wildest imaginations in literature. His 18th-century readers scarcely knew how to greet his work: clerics' wives were bitterly offended, urbanites were hugely admiring and **Dr Johnson** wrote the author off as an oddball.

Although his triumphant *Tristram Shandy* glosses the rising novel genre just as *A Sentimental Journey* mocked Smollett's splenetic brand of travel-writing, still the work transcends its place in history. Wayne Booth has compared it to the passage of an hourglass, through which everything before it passes and that fills everything after it.

It is cast as an autobiography, but its narrator isn't born until the end of Volume IV: first we must learn of his conception, his shameful name and why his nose is mis-shapen. Shandy is in no hurry; his digressions are "incontestably the sunshine of the work" and any reader caught skipping is sent back to re-read sections. As if to make the point that such a book is too strange to be bound, we are invited to rip out pages that don't exist, or provide illustrations for blank ones. Sterne is happy to fill other lacunae with marbling or black pages. Even without the in-jokes, the reconstruction of Uncle Toby's part in the Siege of Namur and the inconclusive anecdotes (one of which takes most of the narrative even to begin to emerge), the prose provides a magnificent adventure of its own.

Stevens

WALLACE   born Pennsylvania 1879; died Hartford, Connecticut 1955

The leaves cry. It is not a cry of divine

attention,

Nor the smoke-drift of puffed out heroes,

nor human cry.

It is the cry of leaves that do not

transcend themselves,

In the absence of fantasia, without

meaning more

Than they are in the final finding of the

ear, in the thing

Itself, until, at last, the cry concerns no

one at all.

THE COURSE OF A PARTICULAR

WHEN WE HEAR the quiet, assured poetic voice of Wallace Stevens, we begin to forget that he worked in insurance. When a critic came to ask him about his achievements, Stevens walked him around town pointing out the buildings he had insured, before bidding him good day. He never gave up his day job and wrote at nights, but one colleague joked that if they hadn't known he was a poet, the firm would have fired him long before.

And what a poet. He had a modern angle on **Emerson**'s theory that language has a counterpart in the natural order: "words of the world are the life of the world". Stevens would have agreed with his friend **William Carlos Williams**' dictum, "no ideas but in things", and he found these things beautiful on their own terms: "The pears are not seen/ As the observer wills." He drew a **Rilke**-like distinction between the world outside and inside the poet: but the poet offers his productions as things in themselves, which can make their way into other apprehensions.

This means the beauty of his poetry can come from simply naming more things in his restrained and elegant diction and making us feel them. Nothing appears to happen except in the mind. *Sunday Morning* takes place during a church service, but removed from it: it collects the images a woman summons as bearers of a non-religious joy, to preserve them. Elsewhere he writes, "Beauty is momentary in the mind.../ But in the flesh it is immortal./ The body dies; the body's beauty lives."

So Stevens' poetry can be calm, even static in diction, but still celebrate the life force, especially as manifested in music-making, and rejuvenated by the sun and beaches which he so loved.

Stevenson

ROBERT LOUIS   **born Edinburgh 1850; died Vailima, Samoa 1894**

All the brothers were hurrying to the chapel; the dead in life, at this untimely hour, were already beginning the uncomforted labours of their day... And I blessed God that I was free to wander, free to hope, and free to love.

TRAVELS WITH A DONKEY
IN THE CEVENNES

ROBERT LOUIS STEVENSON was a Scottish novelist and poet, who trained first as a civil engineer and lawyer. His decision to become a writer estranged him from his parents until he was 30. He was always given to wandering. His earliest published work includes travel-writing, of which he was a master. *Travels with a Donkey* provides beautiful examples of sensitive but detached observation and it is impossible to be unmoved by the ultimate parting of man and beast.

Travel-writing (particularly Kingsley's *At Last*) inspired his most widely-read work, *Treasure Island*. It contains the intrigue and buccaneering that characterise much of his work. This guaranteed him eager audiences in his own time and critical respect later for his efficient and compelling technique as a storyteller. He wrote with deep feeling of 18th-century Scotland, scarred by the aftermath of the Battle of Culloden in 1746. This is the spirit that informs *Kidnapped* and *Weir of Hermiston*, an unfinished tale, which many agree to contain his most accomplished work.

Many of his wanderings were prompted by a search for the climate best-suited to his sickly disposition. Eventually, he settled with his family in Samoa, where his grasp of local affairs provided material for *The Beach of Falesa*; but his quest had previously taken him to the US, where he married, and to Bournemouth, where he befriended **Henry James.** By the end, he was as famous for his travels as his writings, although he considered books "a mighty bloodless substitute for life".

Stoppard

TOM

born Zlin, Czechoslovakia 1937

DOCTOR: *Keep saying to yourself, 'I have no orchestra. I have never had an orchestra. I do not want an orchestra.'*

IVANOV: *Absolutely...*

DOCTOR: *Good.*

IVANOV: *There is one thing you can do for me.*

DOCTOR: *Yes?*

IVANOV: *Stop them playing.*

EVERY GOOD BOY DESERVES FAVOUR

TOM STOPPARD'S PLAYS share **Beckett**'s bleakness and humour and they are similarly concerned with the loneliness of being alive. But they have a parodic wit and a sparkle all of their own.

The content can often be densely philosophical, but themes emerge through word-play and teasing paradoxes. This would not make fine theatre on its own and Stoppard's stagecraft is especially evident in *Rosencrantz and Guildenstern Are Dead*, a student production of which on the Edinburgh Fringe brought him rapid fame. The two nobodies are disposable to the greater characters of *Hamlet*. They while away their numbered days by tossing a coin, at once speculating on probability and pacing their own tragedy.

Stoppard's play takes place behind the scenes of **Shakespeare**'s; elsewhere he extrapolates the lives of historical characters, such as **Byron** in *Arcadia*, or the meeting of Lenin, Tristan Tzara and **Joyce** in Zürich, where they will be involved in staging *The Importance of Being Earnest*. This calls for several layers of parody. In *The Real Inspector Hound*, the humour is at the expense of blatant stage mysteries of the *Ladies in Retirement* kind.

Stoppard asks many questions, many about theatre itself, but he is committed to answers, too. In *Jumpers*, a relativist thinker expresses satisfaction that not as many people suffer these days as used to. Elsewhere the drama's purpose is idealistic and there is a belief in absolute values such as universal human rights. Stoppard's work has campaigned for freedoms in his birthplace, Czechoslovakia, and he has worked hard to draw attention to **Václav Havel**'s plight. He has translated Havel's work, adapted farce from German and collaborated with Terry Gilliam on the marvellous screenplay for *Brazil*.

Stowe

HARRIET BEECHER   **born Connecticut 1811; died Connecticut 1896**

His idea of a fugitive was only an idea of the letters that spell the word; or at the most, the image of a little newspaper picture of a man with a stick and bundle, with 'Ran away from the subscriber' under it. The magic of the real presence of distress, the imploring human eye, the frail, trembling human hand, the despairing appeal of helpless agony; these he had never tried.

UNCLE TOM'S CABIN

HARRIET BEECHER STOWE'S family left New England to take their Christian mission to the frontier town of Cincinnati. It was there that her values were first affronted by the inhumanity of the slave trade. She was in a position to help runaway slaves and was in on the secret of an "underground railway" that conveyed people to Canada.

When the anti-fugitive laws were tightened, Stowe reacted with *Uncle Tom's Cabin*, which chronicles the slave Tom's plight at the hands of a series of owners. Throughout, the hero is called "property", which seems like irony now, but at the time this reminded readers that they were discussing sentient beings. The author has been criticised for her melodramatic style, but when she takes us aside and preaches, we can feel that she addresses us with little more than the conviction required by the age.

The success of the book can be judged by its sales (300,000 in the first six months) and by the feelings it inspired in the build-up to the American Civil War. **Emerson**, who was campaigning for the same cause, wrote that it was read "in the parlour, in the kitchen, and in the nursery of every house".

Stowe later wrote on other subjects – her native Connecticut and Lady Byron, whom she met on one of several trips to Britain. She created a scandal by publishing Lady Byron's account of the incestuous relationship her husband had had with Augusta Leigh, only to be vindicated as further evidence appeared. Still, **Byron** had been an early influence, as had **Shakespeare** and **Chateaubriand**'s *Atala*, with its similar sense of the American landscape. She also wrote more anti-slavery fiction and danced in the streets when Lincoln declared slaves free in 1863.

Strindberg

AUGUST   **born Stockholm 1849; died Stockholm 1912**

We are bastards all.

COMRADES

Strindberg began with naturalistic plays such as *Miss Julie* and *The Father* and ended his career with lyrical "chamber" pieces such as *The Ghost Sonata* and *A Dream Play*. Also unlike Ibsen, his treatment of women is markedly reactionary, notably in *Comrades*, ending with Axel's casual eviction of his wife; or *The Father*, in which a woman manipulates her husband into madness. Strindberg's autobiographical works and the short stories in *Married* are full of the traumatised misogyny his three marriages left him with. But his heroes' quest for superiority owes as much to **Nietzsche** (with whom Strindberg corresponded) as it does to the sex wars. Even a remark such as "women have no existence outside men" might point to the sexes' interdependence and towards a deeper misanthropy.

Strindberg was able to express such malevolence in pamphlets against his detractors – one was so vehement he fled to France to escape its consequences. Back in Sweden, a late novel's thinly-veiled attack on his critics divided the literary establishment. In this, he found support from **Shaw**, one of his earliest apologists, and from modernists, who came to owe much to his particularly subjective method. His approach anticipated 20th-century expressionism: just as the painter Edvard Munch gave his viewers snap-shots of the soul's tormented inner life, so Strindberg presents us with rapidly-shifting cameos of man's bestial impulses.

IT IS PERHAPS TOO EASY to see Strindberg in contrast to **Ibsen**. The Swedish dramatist, story-writer and poet often wrote plays in response to Ibsen's and the Norwegian had a picture of Strindberg in his study: "He's my arch enemy. He's going to hang there and guard what I write."

While Ibsen abandoned verse drama for realism,

Styron

WILLIAM

born Newport News, Virginia 1925

And once in my strange journey I thought I heard again her whispery voice, thought I saw her rise from the blazing field with arms outstretched as if to a legion of invisible onlookers... But then she vanished before my eyes – melted instantly like an image carved of air and light – and I turned away at last and went back to join my men.

THE CONFESSIONS OF NAT TURNER

WILLIAM STYRON'S WRITINGS confront depression. His novels deal with the loss of innocence in the face of the horror of the world. In his first, *Lie Down in Darkness*, a patriarch commits suicide at the exact moment that the atomic bomb falls on Hiroshima. Only in this death is there any kind of atonement. The work is an ambitious epic set in the American South, with a technique and scope reminiscent of **Faulkner**.

Styron's own loss of innocence came during World War Two. He served in the Marines when he was 18 – an experience that eradicated what little religious faith he had. He was called up again to fight in the Korean War, which provided material for his novella, *The Long March*. His play, *In the Clap Shack*, presents a ward of diseased soldiers. Styron explores the guilty aftermath of war further in *Set This House on Fire* (which did better in Europe than in the US) and *Sophie's Choice*. The latter shows the grimmest

manifestations of guilt felt by survivors of the Holocaust. Sophie lost both her children in the *shoah* and must face the stigma inflicted on her by a tormented lover. This will scar her teenage friend Stingo forever.

His concern with the suffering of the oppressed accounts for *The Confessions of Nat Turner*, narrated by the leader of a murderous slave revolt. This would arouse concern among some black critics, as if the book were portraying extremes of racial rather than human behaviour.

Styron has recently told of his own agonising, inescapable depression in *Darkness Visible*.

355

Swift

JONATHAN

born Dublin 1667; died Dublin 1745

> *As for his works in verse and prose,*
>
> *I own myself no judge of those;*
>
> *Nor can I tell what critics thought 'em:*
>
> *But this I know, all people bought 'em,*
>
> *As with a moral view designed*
>
> *To cure the vices of mankind.*

VERSES ON THE DEATH OF DR SWIFT

SWIFT THOUGHT SATIRE had its limits and famously called it a "glass, wherein beholders do generally discover everybody's face but their own" But he believed that through it humans could be brought to see sense and so set about achieving this by all the means at his disposal.

He was born to English parents in Dublin, became a Protestant priest and, after seeking the favour of Whig grandees in England, became disillusioned and co-founded the Tory-sympathetic Scriblerus Club. His political shift reflects his anger at the Whigs' refusal to tolerate Catholics, as well as his more conservative mode of thinking. He returned to Ireland on the death of Queen Anne, where he eventually became Dean of St Patrick's Cathedral in Dublin. There, his pamphlets argued for religious understanding and defended the Irish poor. He always published anonymously. The English Parliament and Irish Senate offered rewards to any who would betray his identity, but no-one did.

A Modest Proposal... demonstrates the savagery of his "satiric touch:/ No nation wanted it so much."

Drapier's Letters, meanwhile, showed it worked, preventing a corrupt minter's coins from entering Ireland. A bleak view of mankind emerges from his poems, which transmogrify classical idylls with contemporary slants (squirm at *A Beautiful Young Nymph Going to Bed*). His prose works allow a more comprehensive view of humanity. *A Tale of a Tub* shows with astonishing psychological acuity how one person's devotion is another's delusion, while *Gulliver's Travels* blends topical references and playfulness with a profounder regard for our fallibility.

He was a fount of wit and the soul of generosity, giving away two-thirds of his earnings to good causes. The brilliance of his writing earned him £200 in his lifetime and, for all his bitterness, a conscience without blemish.

Tagore

RABINDRANATH

born Calcutta 1861; died Calcutta 1941

Only when waves fall on the shore do

they make a harmonious sound;

Only when breezes shake the woods do

we hear a rustling in the leaves.

Only from a marriage of two forces does

music arise in the world.

Where there is no love, where listeners

are dumb, there can never be song.

BROKEN SONG, TR. WILLIAM RADICE

RABINDRANATH TAGORE LIVED a life of breathtaking achievement. He wrote some 1,000 poems, 24 plays, eight novels (besides shorter fiction), composed 2,000 songs (including the Indian National Anthem) and from his late 60s executed 3,000 paintings. He founded his own pioneering educational institution at Santiniketan; he campaigned for Indian self-rule and against the partition of Bengal, while repudiating nationalism; he was often at odds with Gandhi, a dear friend with whom he was ultimately reconciled.

He is India's most revered poet of modern times. His work became known in the West through the efforts of **Yeats** and **Pound** (the former helped touch up Rabindranath's English versions) and he won the Nobel Prize for Literature in 1913. His work has a musician's love of rhythm and enjoys Bengali's capacity for sound effects. His poetic range is enormous, from love lyrics heart-rending in their oratory, to powerful hymns in the manner of the *Upanishads*. His verse has a strong urge to tell stories It shares with his fiction a concern for India's poor: the poem *A Half-Acre of Land* is bitterly ironic about a tenant's eviction and the story *Four Acres of Land* documents similar exploitation and was made into an acclaimed film by Balraj Sahni.

Rabindranath travelled extensively around the world and was at first allured by the West. He admired the British temperament, but deplored its Raj. He returned his knighthood in 1919, after General Dyer's atrocity against the unarmed citizens of Amritsar. In speeches everywhere he championed Asia as the mother culture. His work combines a Hindu awareness of all-pervading spirituality with the playfulness of that tradition's myths.

MAJOR WORKS

POETRY

Morning Songs (1883)

The Lady of the Mind (1890)

The Golden Boat (1894)

The Multi-Coloured (1896)

Imagination (1900)

The Child (1903)

Gitanjali (1912)

The Message of the Forest (1931)

Recovery (1941)

PLAYS

Chitra (1913)

The King of the Dark Chamber (1914)

NOVELS

The Home and the World (1919)

Gora (1924)

Broken Ties (1925)

The Housewarming (1965)

Tennyson

ALFRED, LORD

born Lincolnshire 1809; died Surrey 1892

Behold, ye speak an idle thing;

Ye never knew the sacred dust.

I do but sing because I must,

And pipe but as the linnets sing:

And one is glad; her note is gay,

For now her little ones have ranged;

And one is sad; her note is changed,

Because her brood is stolen away.

IN MEMORIAM

TENNYSON WAS THE BEST-LOVED poet of his day. He succeeded **Wordsworth** as Poet Laureate in 1850 and to this day remains one of the most

quoted writers in English. Rather than stifling him, the large readership Tennyson enjoyed during his lifetime gave him the authority to say whatever he wanted. Although much of this was undoubtedly public, he remained able to explore personal ideas. *The Idylls of the King*, for example, is an epic on the theme of King Arthur, a subject **Milton** had wanted to undertake. Like Milton, Tennyson found in the story a way of expressing his own view of human destiny.

Still, poems such as *The Charge of the Light Brigade* have done much to overshadow his more intimate work, even while displaying his work's virtue. **Eliot** and **Auden** both praised his ear for rhythm, although many have thought this led Tennyson to write lines for their sound effects alone. Although we can see his virtuosity everywhere, with words or phrases echoing as they disappear, or lengthening to lull us (as with *The Lotos-Eaters*), his word music (which has suggested song to many composers) is often so suited to his subject that we can allow its wizardry to work on us unconsciously: *Maud* provides a showcase for metre matching mood. But Tennyson is able to draw attention to his devices, as in a poem where he explains that he is using a metre of **Catullus**, or, in *Northern Farmer*, where the language is more emphatically suggestive for the broad Yorkshire accent.

His best work remains *In Memoriam*, written over 17 years to lament his dear friend Arthur Hallam. Although fairly long, it has economical episodes in a tight stanza form, chronicling grief that we start to share. At its more hopeful close, Tennyson finds plain language that profoundly reflects the aesthetic thinking of his age while reaching a conclusion echoing **Dante**'s.

Thackeray

WILLIAM MAKEPEACE   born Calcutta 1811; died London 1863

Fifty years ago, and when the present writer, being an interesting little boy, was ordered out of the room with the ladies after dinner, I remember quite well that their talk was chiefly about their ailments; and putting this question directly to two or three since, I have always got from them the acknowledgement that times are not changed. Let my fair readers remark for themselves this very evening when they quit the dessert-table, and assemble to celebrate the drawing-room mysteries.

VANITY FAIR

LIKE **DICKENS**, THACKERAY developed his fiction from sketches he had been producing as a journalist. He wrote for *Punch* and *The Times* and became known for satire that systematically skewered bombast wherever he found it.

His contemporary writers were not safe from his mocking either – writers such as Bulwer-Lytton, producing sensational novels based on prison records, were outdone by *Catherine*, in which Thackeray takes the lurid to parodic extremes. Here we see society at its worst and although she can meet saintly characters (Thackeray's purest creations were based on his wife, Isabella who went mad after the death of their second child), the heroine is at the heart of the darkness.

His most famous work, *Vanity Fair*, has a similarly calculating heroine in Becky Sharp, who manipulates her way around the London of the Napoleonic Wars in a way that provided a model for Scarlett O'Hara in *Gone With the Wind*.

We begin to see how Thackeray gained his intimate knowledge of society from top to bottom in his novel *The History of Pendennis*, which charts "a Rake's Progress". Through the book's eponymous hero, Arthur Pendennis, who – as Thackeray did – gambles away his education and time at Cambridge, the author sought to present a realistic picture of the complete man.

More often than not, Thackeray's humour found historical settings, as in *Henry Esmond* and its sequel *The Virginians*, both set in the 17th century. But he still created worlds that were unsettlingly familiar to his readers.

Thomas

DYLAN

born Swansea 1914; died New York 1953

My one and noble heart has witnesses
In all love's countries, that will grope
awake;
And when blind sleep drops on the
spying senses,
The heart is sensual, though five eyes
break.

WHEN ALL MY FIVE AND COUNTRY SENSES

DYLAN THOMAS DIED SUDDENLY in New York, thanks to the ruinous lifestyle that had become as famous as his public readings. His reputation has wavered between the poles of tormented prophet and obscene drunkard. In productions of *Under Milk Wood*, the former can lead to a preciousness that makes one wonder if performers have noticed how the name of the play's fictional Welsh village, Llareggub, reads backwards.

As recordings attest, he was an inspiring lecturer and reader of others' verse. He was particularly fond of **Hardy**, with whom he shared a great inventiveness in stanza form and refrains. In **Hopkins** he saw the possibilities of sprung lines bouncing with internal rhymes.

But it is possible to over-emphasise Thomas' reliance on devices. His phrase "dogs in the wet-nosed yards" is much-quoted as an example of "transferred epithet", but elsewhere it becomes clear that his perceptions can become jumbled to induce a more total experience. This gives his work that robust sense of life that makes the poet respect death all the more. Even death becomes inextricable from the knowledge of death: this fills the poems with a resonance that Thomas' own early end can make deafening. Such work is obviously passionate, but in a poem such as *A Refusal to Mourn the Death, by Fire, of a Child in London*, there is an acceptance of the inescapable life cycle, and an awareness of what a poet can and cannot say by way of comfort, that is worthy of **Yeats.**

Thoreau

HENRY DAVID

born Concord, Mass. 1817; Concord Mass. 1862

Poet. See those clouds; how they hang! That's the greatest thing I have seen today. There's nothing like it in old paintings, nothing like it in foreign lands – unless when we were off the coast of Spain... I thought, as I have my living to get, and have not eaten today, that I might go a-fishing. That's the true industry for poets. It is the only trade I have learned. Come, let's along.

WALDEN

IT WAS **EMERSON** who made Concord, Massachusetts, the home of transcendentalism, but of all the movement's prophets, only Thoreau was born there. He also lived the philosophy more completely than any of his fellows. He campaigned against war and slavery; he went to prison in 1845 for refusing to pay taxes towards the war with Mexico; he advocated civil disobedience in an essay that later had an impact on Gandhi and Martin Luther King; he helped runaway slaves escape; and by championing John Brown, backed violent intervention against slavery.

He embodied the individual at odds with society. He said he could be sociable, but coined phrases such as "the majority of one" and "different drummer" to indicate that truth often resides in those who stand alone. In his masterpiece, *Walden*, he does just that. He built a cabin beside Walden Pond, on Emerson's land, where he lived self-sufficiently for two years. Like his earlier book, *A Week on the Concord and Merrimack Rivers* it is written in the journal form that Emerson encouraged him to pursue (Thoreau's journals proper have been published posthumously), offering us a detailed description of the forest with wisdom-studded essays alongside. The work abounds with his intimate knowledge of botany and wildlife and with the calls of birds, in which he found literary echoes.

He also had a taste for puns and felt etymology and word-play revealed language's deeper meanings. Thus Walden becomes "Walled-in", although throughout that great book, the author finds everything but confinement there. Sharing Emerson's pantheism, Thoreau sensed the presence of the divine as much in the soil as he did in the sky.

Thurber

JAMES   **born Columbus, Ohio 1894; died New York 1961**

Ophelia Oliver, who had vanished from the haunts of men, returned, wearing both her Os again. Otto Ott could say his name without a stammer, and dignity returned to human speech and English grammar. Once more a man could say boo to a goose, and tell the difference between to lose and too loose.

THE WONDERFUL O

JAMES THURBER WAS a humourist who gained prominence in *The New Yorker*, where he was as cherished for his sparing, faultless cartoons (especially of dogs) as for his writing.

These are sparing, too, at least in technique, even if he did not spare psychoanalysts or his family from his normally mild-mannered brand of satire. The latter appear throughout his work, with all their peculiarities. He often sees the family from the viewpoint of a child, particularly in *My World and Welcome to It*. The inabilities of husbands and wives to understand one another is a constant theme and he produced a series of cartoons entitled *The War Between Men and Women*. In one story, *The Unicorn in the Garden*, a man causes his wife to tell the police that there is a unicorn in the garden and she is put in a straitjacket. As elsewhere, Thurber uses the fable form and depicts a quiet kind of lunacy.

His style achieves this brilliantly in *The Secret Life of Walter Mitty*, where heroic fantasies invade the narrative of a man waiting for his wife to have her hair done. It is this story which introduced "Walter Mitty" as a linguistic trope. In *There's an Owl in My Room*, he criticises **Gertrude Stein** for saying "alas" about pigeons, (pigeons are pigeons after all), while absorbing her style and showing a deeper understanding of her work than appears at first. His own verbal trickery draws attention to language, and more: just as **Georges Perec** made the letter "e" vanish from a whole novel, so Thurber wonders what the world would be like without the letter "o". Where Perec expresses loss, Thurber leaves us with a sense of joy in possible words and their unforeseen combinations, making him closer to Stein as an artist than he'd have us think.

Tolkien

J.R.R.   **born Bloemfontein 1892; died Bournemouth 1973**

Though the hobbits ate, as only famished hobbits can eat, there was a lack. The drink in their drinking-bowls seemed to be clear cold water, yet it went to their hearts like wine and set free their voices. The guests became suddenly aware that they were singing merrily, as if it was easier and more natural than talking.

THE FELLOWSHIP OF THE RING

MAJOR WORKS

The Hobbit (1937)

The Lord of the Rings:
    The Fellowship of the Ring
    The Two Towers
    The Return of the King
(1954–1955)

The Adventure of Tom Bombadil (1963)

The Silmarillion (1977)

TOLKIEN WAS A DISTINGUISHED scholar — an Oxford professor whose interests were Celtic and Teutonic myths and Anglo-Saxon literature (when lecturing on *Beowulf* he knew the work so well that he could recite it word for word when he had mislaid his text). This learning went into his imaginative works.

The plot of *The Lord of the Rings* has much in common with the 13th-century *Nibelungenlied*, but its mood is altogether different. The setting is Middle Earth, a land where elves, "the first-born", are dwindling, and magic, as a power for good, is falling under the sinister forces of Sauron. Instead of glorifying the virtuous knight, Tolkien concentrates on the infinitely engaging hobbits (his only original contribution to folklore) and the little land of the Shire.

They provide Tolkien with a means of expressing his sadness at the passing of a familiar English landscape in a time of simplicity and rustic vigour. His imagery of industrialisation, with machines, wheels and cogs of death, is as foreboding as that of **H.G. Wells**. But he hated allegory and denied that his creations had much in common with the real world. In a foreword, he explained how differently his books would have turned out if based on World War Two. Both wars presented Tolkien with a moral crisis since he loved Germanic culture, but recoiled from the emerging horror. If there is a message in his work, it is one at odds with his times: the forces of goodness must remain pure and separate from each other (the Dark Lord's crime, after all, is to mix and mock) and, above all, that we must not pollute the earth.

Tolstoy

LEO

born Yasnaya Polyana 1828; died Astapovo 1910

If he had any feeling for his brother at that moment, it was rather one of envy for the knowledge the dying man now possessed that was denied him.

ANNA KARENINA

COMMENTATORS OFTEN REMARK on how much Tolstoy had in common with Levin, the hero of *Anna Karenina*. They were alike in details – both were land-owners, deeply concerned by the plight of their serfs, and both compelled their future wives to read diaries of their sexual exploits. They were also alike in spirit: they approached everything in life with a painstaking enthusiasm, bringing insight and huge knowledge to bear on whatever issue they discussed.

But Tolstoy's strength lies in identifying completely with all his characters, women as much as men (and even dogs) and not just those he resembles. He began his career with memoirs and his observations of war from the Crimean campaign, before producing the two novels which, for many readers, vie to be the best ever written. *War and Peace* is a chronological account of Napoleon's invasion of Russia and an attempt at a completeness that the author admits, in a lengthy postscript, to be impossible. *Anna Karenina*, meanwhile, applies the same absorption of detail to the plight of its unhappily-married heroine, with numerous interior monologues documenting psychological minutiae.

Shortly after its publication, Tolstoy turned increasingly to the spiritual. He denounced private property (while maintaining his) and declared that the public owned his work after 1881. He wrote to the Tsar warning of imminent social upheaval and urging him to yield power to the people. But his pacifism led him to argue against violent revolution. His political legacy was acknowledged by Lenin and Gandhi.

Ultimately he repudiated his luxurious texts, preferring a simpler, more moral tone, but everywhere in his work the veneer of sophistication cannot stifle his characters' real passions for long (*The Kreutzer Sonata* is an extreme example). His oeuvre, which fills 90 large volumes, includes tragedies and comedies for the stage, as well as stories that vary widely in length and subject.

Trollope

ANTHONY

born London 1815; died London 1882

He loved to sit silent in a corner of his club and listen to the loud chattering of politicians, and to think how they all were in his power; how he could smite the loudest of them, were it worth his while to raise his pen for such a purpose.

THE WARDEN

ANTHONY TROLLOPE WROTE 47 books – 21 of them as a man of letters when he was still working for the Post Office, where, as a valued employee, he devised the red pillar box. He unashamedly wrote for money (his mother Frances had raised him by doing the same, nursing his dying father and scribbling frantically in the next room) and in his autobiography he documents his industry, explaining how he trained himself to produce, reliably, a fixed number of words an hour, usually between 5.30 am and breakfast every day. He also tells us how much he earned for his work and that he wishes it were more.

His methods make his novels through – composed and there is a stronger sense of time passing in his work than there is of a plot developing. Consequently, he is best known for his characters, who reappear throughout series of novels. He began his Barsetshire books with *The Warden*, introducing early on his gently – stated theme, progress versus tradition, the town of Barsetshire, an intimately – realised conflation of Salisbury (where *The Warden* suggested itself to him) and Winchester, of which he harboured miserable memories as a schoolboy flogged (or "tunded") by everyone, including his brother.

Later came his "Palliser" novels, which replaced Barsetshire's high-church/low-church intrigues with affairs of state. Trollope stood for Parliament in 1868 and used his books to air his political views (which were far from radical). The recently – ousted Conservative Premier John Major was an admirer, even before the dilemma at the heart of *The Prime Minister* – in which a politician leads a vulnerable minority government longer than anyone expected – became so like his own.

Tsvetayeva

MARINA

born Moscow 1892; died Yelabuga 1941

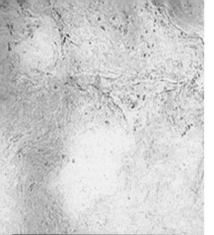

> for the path of comets
>
> is the path of poets: they burn without
>
> > warming,
>
> pick without cultivating. They are: an
>
> > explosion, a breaking in –
>
> and the mane of their path makes the
>
> > curve of a graph
>
> cannot be foretold by the calendar.

THE POET, TR. ELAINE FEINSTEIN

TSVETAYEVA'S WORK has an immediate appeal to Western readers, thanks to Elaine Feinstein's universally acclaimed translations. These present us with a fresh, almost epigrammatic compactness on the subjects about which it is hardest to be concise: love, loss, poetry, displacement and death.

For a Russian poet of her time, these are inextricable. To explore personal feelings at the expense of public commitment was to be at odds with the Bolshevik agenda, which she thought "satanic". She left Russia in 1922 and her husband fought as a counter-revolutionary. In Europe she had a number of intense love affairs, which contributed greatly to her work: in her poetry, the end of love and the end of life are barely distinguishable from one another.

Poetry proved to be equally vital. She was able to endure poverty while creating and would sublimate all other concerns to it. This absolute integrity led to her being outcast by the Paris literati after she refused to join other Russian émigrés and sign a document belittling **Mayakovsky**'s achievement. She eventually returned to Russia in 1939. The war forced her to leave her beloved Moscow (she offered the city paeans as classical as **Mandelshtam** reserved for St Petersburg) and she hanged herself in 1941.

It is hard to avoid sharing something of this great sorrow when reading *A Poem of the End*. It picks up on the tiniest details of lovers' meeting and parting, to deduce the profoundest truths. The things the poet sees, even in passing, are so much a part of her experience that they seem like symbols. She also looks at words as though they must represent her point of view simply by being there, notably the one that appears as "sep   arating". But even this points to a pain the verse can scarcely bear to acknowledge: "In what language is it, when the meaning itself doesn't exist?"

Tucholsky

KURT   **born Berlin 1890; died Hindäs, Sweden 1935**

From time to time women don't have it easy either. But we men have to shave.

SCRAPS

KURT TUCHOLSKY WAS a novelist, satirist, journalist, critic, poet and songwriter. He worked in Germany from just before World War One and then during the Weimar Republic. He became known for his cabaret pieces, being part of a tradition that had included Joachim Ringelnatz before him and that Kurt Weill and **Bertolt Brecht** made world-famous. Tucholsky was one of the first critics to bring Brecht and **Kafka** to prominence.

Of the two, he identified more with Kafka. His material obliged him to write under a number of pseudonyms, such as Theobald Tiger, Peter Panter, and Kaspar Hauser. Kafka declared he felt more lonely than Kaspar Hauser, the guilt-ridden wanderer whose appearance in **Verlaine** is revealing about Tucholsky: "Although I had no king and country/ And am hardly brave/ I wanted to die at war/ But death did not want me."

Although Tucholsky survived World War One, the experience left him feeling stateless and he lived in Paris from 1924 and Sweden from 1929. The horrors of the war gave his work focus and his writing is full of attacks on innate German militarism, while his satire aimed to promote the fragile democracy of the Weimar Republic. With the rise of the Nazis, his statelessness was officially endorsed, while in the land he had once called home, his books were either banned or burned. He wrote little or nothing from 1932 and killed himself in 1935.

His work includes love stories (one of which may derive from a real liaison in Sweden) and verse. But he is best remembered for his epigrammatic wit, in pieces that explore the differences between the nations (particularly German and French) and the sexes. His irony shows he had more sympathy for non-Germans and non-men.

MAJOR WORKS

Rheinsberg. Ein Bilderbuch für Verliebte (1912)

Deutschland Deutschland über Alles (1929)

Schloss Gripsholm (1931)

The World is a Comedy (1957 Journalism collected posthumously in)

What If? – Satirical Writings (1967)

Scraps (1973)

Collected Works (3 volumes, in German, 1960–1961)

Turgenev

IVAN

born Oryol 1818; died Bougival, nr. Paris 1883

First love is like a revolution; the uniformly correct ordering of life is smashed and destroyed in an instant, youth takes to the barricades, its bright banner raised on high, and no matter what awaits it in the future – death or a new life – it sends to all things its ecstatic greeting.

THE TORRENTS OF SPRING,
TR. RICHARD FREEBORN

IVAN TURGENEV WAS a Russian writer who began to attract attention in the late 1840s. Some of this was from the police, who arrested him in 1852, after an obituary of **Gogol**.

At that time in Russia, opinion was divided between "Slavophiles", who felt the world spirit (as described by Hegel) would pass to the East, and those who saw themselves as a marginal people. Turgenev had sympathy with the Slavophiles but, as he had studied in Berlin, considered himself a Westernised writer. Consequently, he has perhaps enjoyed more success in Europe than in his own country.

He left Russia in 1856 and made for Baden-Baden, where **Dostoyevsky** later visited him. Despite their friendship – Turgenev helped Dostoyevsky's with his gambling debts – Dostoyevsky attacked him as a traitor, considering *Smoke* the work of someone who barely knew or cared about Russia.

Still, Dostoyevsky recognised the perfection in Turgenev's work and his elegantly-structured tales of love. Not that Turgenev was a writer given to lyrical tenderness. He had a life-long wish to see the abolition of serfdom and had firm political convictions that were radical at first. When *Fathers and Sons* first appeared, the Senate summoned him to justify the book. In the end, the police realised its critique of nihilists favoured the *status quo*. What he faults in a character such as Bazarov is the unwillingness to recognise the power of love, a force from which no wanderer can flee.

Twain

MARK   **born Florida, Missouri 1835; died Redding, Connecticut 1910**

Very often, of course, the rambling and disjointed humorous story finishes with a nub, point, snapper, or whatever you like to call it. Then the listener must be alert, for in many cases the teller will divert attention from that nub by dropping it in a casual and indifferent way, in the pretence that he does not know it is a nub.

HOW TO TELL A STORY

MARK TWAIN'S OFTEN FUNNY, often compassionate writing does much to preserve the innocence of the American South. However, it is not a naïve project; his work is always aware of the evils that threaten the South – as when *The Gilded Age* shows it being industrialised.

His hope was to restore the unheroic charm of **Cervantes**, as eroded by the romantic myth-making of **Sir Walter Scott**. He went so far as blaming Scott for the Civil War, in which Twain briefly took part.

In much of his fiction, he tries to imagine an American South in which the conflict never happened but is already disfigured by the evils of slavery. Huck Finn grows up with it, but he is marginalised enough in his society to use his conscience and so appeal to ours.

The Eden of this lost world is the Mississippi. Twain lamented the decline of its slang, whose rhythms and cadences he froze in time with his masterpieces, *Tom Sawyer* and *Huckleberry Finn*. He was apprenticed to a printer and became a pilot on the Mississippi, where he gained the nickname Mark Twain (an expression meaning literally "mark twice", calling on the sailor to measure the draught of water with a plumbline). His real name was Samuel Langhorne Clemens.

A humorous style had always characterised his narrative structures, right from his first success, *The Celebrated Jumping Frog*. But in later years, as Twain's fortunes declined and he suffered a series of family bereavements, his work, particularly his aphorisms, developed an unaccustomed gravity. Despite this, he never lost his ability to tell a joke.

MAJOR WORKS

The Celebrated Jumping Frog of Calaveras County (1865)

The Innocents Abroad (1869)

Roughing It (1872)

The Gilded Age (1873)

The Adventures of Tom Sawyer (1875)

The Adventures of Huckleberry Finn (1885)

A Connecticut Yankee in King Arthur's Court (1889)

Undset

SIGRID   **born Kalundborg, Denmark 1882; died Oslo 1949**

I haven't time to receive you. I am studying scholastic philosophy.

REMARK MADE TO JOURNALISTS
ON WINNING THE 1928 NOBEL
PRIZE FOR LITERATURE

SIGRID UNDSET WAS a Norwegian novelist, chiefly famous for her series of books, *Kristin Lavransdatter* and *The Master of Hestviken*.

She was born in Denmark, the daughter of a famous archaeologist. He had hoped she would follow a scientific career, but she worked as an office clerk before publishing her first books. *The Happy Age*, a tale of young girls coming of age in a time of moral laxity, launched her new career. She commanded attention with the appearance of *Jenny*, a novel whose heroine shares the author's artistic aspirations. It is written in the confessional style that she developed in *Mrs Marta Oulie*, which was written in diary form.

The realism that characterises this work is the hallmark of her historical novels. They are lengthy and full of detail. She had converted to Roman Catholicism in 1924 and successive volumes show her taking an increasingly moral, didactic line with her readers. Her persistent criticism of Protestants aroused some controversy in Norway, but her discussion of the issue was rooted in theology more than prejudice: she had a great interest in St Augustine and Thomas Aquinas. She wrote biographies of saints, calling the works "sagas". Just as she had Christianised the realist novel, she reworked the pagan elements of Nordic mythology. The feel of Icelandic sagas, and *eddas*, informs much of her fiction.

She was considered the best Norwegian writer of her age, next to **Knut Hamsun**. But unlike him, she hated the Nazi occupation of her country. Quisling's government sent her into exile and she settled in the US. Her compatriots welcomed her back after the war with the highest awards the nation could offer.

Updike

JOHN

born Shillington, Pennsylvania 1932

But church was too exciting, too full of light and music, for prayer to take place, and his mind slid from the words being intoned, and skimmed across several pieces of property that concerned him, and grazed the faces and limbs of women he knew, and darted from the image of his daughters to the memory of his parents, so unjustly and so continuingly dead.

COUPLES

JOHN UPDIKE IS A VERSATILE and prolific writer whose terrain is Middle America. His characters are educated and financially comfortable, but there is nothing twee about them. Updike deals with their desires directly, often graphically, and although this might seem sordid, physical congress never ousts psychological interest. Moreover, Updike's warm, tolerant Christianity ensures that hope survives post-coital depression.

He grew up in Shillington, Pennsylvania, a small town that provides the model for Olinger in some of his short stories and Tarbox in *Couples*. He distinguished himself academically at Harvard, before working for *The New Yorker* magazine. His first books were of verse and short stories, but he has become best known for his novels.

The *Rabbit* series is central to these. In each of four books, Updike chronicles the most recent decade in Harry "Rabbit" Angstrom's life. The tone of each varies with the period. As time passes, he mellows from a bored retired athlete to become a replete car sales executive, ultimately meeting a dignified end as the 1980s slip away.

His struggles to reconcile himself to a life that might become all-too predictable are shared by other Updike figures – the sexually-frustrated academic theologian in *Roger's Version*, or the stunning but stultified housewives in *The Witches of Eastwick*, who form a coven and dream up a devil. *Couples* perhaps displays Updike at his most playful and adventurous: his story of partner-swapping in Tarbox has a liberty and eroticism that comes straight from its time – the late 1960s. Over the years, he has kept his ability to feel the pulse of America, and give us a diagnosis.

MAJOR WORKS

POETRY

The Carpenter Hen and Other Tame Creatures (1958)

Telephone Poles (1969)

Midpoint (1969)

Facing Nature (1985)

SHORT STORIES

The Same Door (1959)

Pigeon Feathers (1962)

Olinger Stories (1964)

NOVELS

Rabbit, Run (1960)

Rabbit Redux (1971)

Rabbit is Rich (1982)

Rabbit at Rest (1991)

The Poorhouse Fair (1959)

Centaur (1963)

Couples (1968)

The Coup (1978)

The Witches of Eastwick (1984)

Memoirs of the Ford Administration (1993)

Brazil (1994)

Verlaine

PAUL

May your verse become a splendid spree
Sprinkled on the morning's crispy wind
Flowering as it goes the thyme and
*   mint...*
Everything that's left is literary.

POETIC ART

PAUL VERLAINE WAS associated with the Parnassian movement in French poetry, a group responding to the less-honed romantic effusions of the likes of **de Musset** by saying "Passion is no excuse for writing bad verse." His own verse was always sonorous, experimenting more and more with rhythm. It is harder to be convinced by his own passions.

He seldom seemed to be sure of them himself. In his refined expressions of decadence, he followed **Baudelaire** too slavishly for some. In his quest for a poet's purity and experience, he vacillated between his young wife and the even younger **Rimbaud**, who was less timid in exploring extremes. The two set up together in Camden, advertising a French course in what must have been a revelatory teaching environment. During a two-year prison sentence for shooting Rimbaud in the wrist, he turned briefly to Catholicism. This was still not the answer for Verlaine: out of subsequent confusions came his famous essays on the "cursed poet", as he saw **Mallarmé**, Rimbaud and himself. Tempestuous creators have vied for the epithet ever since.

Still, in Verlaine's best poetry, there is little to shock. Its most unsettling aspect is the metre. Even this works entirely in keeping with its own rules and beats beneath delicately placed internal rhymes and half-rhymes. But his ear was entranced by lines with odd numbers of syllables. His deployment of them meant that in order to be read smoothly to the end, each line starts with a jolt, as if the first syllable were missing. This leads to a disruption of the sense and shifts attention to the verbal music of a poem. His extraordinary achievement is keeping poetry that was so based on sound sensible. Where such instincts led **Apollinaire** into surrealism, in Verlaine's work they sometimes yield exquisite phrases, and in *Poetic Art*, quoted in the metrical translation above, it even begins to account for them.

Verne

JULES

born Nantes 1828; died Amiens 1905

His teaching was what the German philosophers would call 'subjective': that is to say it was for himself and not for others.

JOURNEY TO THE CENTRE
OF THE EARTH

JULES VERNE'S WRITING has so engaging a charm, so playful a use of the intellect, so boundless an energy, so adventurous an imagination and such enduring characters that he has directly influenced the most diverse of subsequent authors.

His way of stretching science to just beyond the possible had an immediate effect on **H.G. Wells**; **Raymond Roussel** met him and confessed to worshipping him (emulating the great man's passion for yachting); **Georges Perec** was as hooked as generations of French schoolboys have been, and has paid the master innumerable tributes in his own work, including the use of puzzles and scholarship; and for sheer adventure, as well as locations, **Edgar Rice Burroughs** is deeply indebted to him. Even to pick up a novel by Michael Crichton is to see his enduring legacy, with computer print-outs where Verne would have shared codes and lists with us.

His reputation suffers in that his career was a commercial one; he speculated on the Paris stock exchange and began his literary life writing opera libretti. He could not remain indifferent to the success of **Dumas**' romances and loved travel. Once he had found his *métier* as a mentor of science fiction and fantasy, he wrote at least one novel a year. His first adventure story, *Five Weeks in a Balloon*, told of a fantastic journey – a motif that recurred throughout his work, most famously in *Around the World in Eighty Days*.

Characters also reappeared, in the manner of **Balzac**'s *Comédie Humaine*: Captain Nemo goes *Twenty Thousand Leagues Under the Sea* and his confessions in *The Children of Captain Grant* resurface in a trunk on *The Mysterious Island*.

His appeal was universal in his lifetime. He was a Companion of the *Légion d'Honneur*, and fêted in society, with a global audience eagerly awaiting new translations.

MAJOR WORKS

Five Weeks in a Balloon (1862)

Journey to the Centre of the Earth (1864)

From the Earth to the Moon (1865)

Twenty Thousand Leagues under the Sea (1869)

Around the World in Eighty Days (1872)

Vidal

GORE

born West Point 1925

MAJOR WORKS

Cynthia is a very serious woman and ceramicist, with a sense of the sacredness of all life. Naturally, she eats only macrobiotic vegetables and tofu and, of course, nothing that has ever had a face except cauliflower.

LIVE FROM GOLGOTHA

GORE VIDAL IS A WRITER so experienced at provoking controversy that he is as much a part of the American landscape as the institutions he attacks. He is a consummate talker, whose life has afforded him extraordinary insights into how his country really works.

He was born at West Point Military Academy, where his father was an aeronautical instructor, and he became the first child to cross the Atlantic in a plane. His early knowledge of the political process came from his grandfather, who was a senator. In 1960 Vidal ran for office as a Democrat, intending to spend more on education and less on defence.

He commands most consistent respect for his fictionalised examinations of American history's turning points – Alexander Hamilton's death in a duel in *Burr*, Lincoln's presidency, or the scandals threatening to emerge during the Constitution's centenary in *1876*. This book appeared during the Constitution's bi-centenary and provided an opportunity to reflect on the recent Watergate affair. Although his stories might seem all too real, he sometimes broaches great "what ifs" – such as, in *Hollywood*, the possibility of **Shaw** or **Maeterlinck** working there in 1917.

He has rewritten much of early Christian history, including *Julian* – the confessional memoirs of the liberal Roman Emperor Julian the Apostate – and *Live From Golgotha*, in which Christ's passion takes place in an age of mass communication. He portrays a modern kind of decadence and an obese Messiah in a prose distinguished by Vidal's tasty brand of camp.

People have claimed his *The City and the Pillar* as America's first gay novel, although Vidal has argued that the distinctions between sexualities are so blurred as to be meaningless. If his characters' speech seems fey elsewhere, this early novel has been praised for refusing to stereotype homosexuals.

Virgil

born Mantua 70 BC; died Brundisium 19 BC

I sang about maintaining flocks and fields

and about trees, while Caesar storms the

   deep

Euphrates in the war, and winning, gives

compliant peoples laws, heads for Olympus.

Then sweet Parthenope sustained me,

   Virgil,

blooming with zeal for genteel scholarship,

who played at shepherds' songs and, bold

   in youth,

sang Tityrus, beneath a beech tree, you.

GEORGICS, LAST LINES

VIRGIL WROTE THE MOST PERFECT poetry in Latin. He wrote three works and in each he introduced different strands of Greek culture, in their most polished forms, to Rome, which was emerging from lengthy civil wars into an empire under Augustus.

His adaptations were always applicable to his native Italy and, some have thought, to himself – many have sought a hidden, anti-imperial agenda in his writing. He grew up in Mantua at a time when Augustus (then Octavian) was responsible for reallocating land – like Meliboeus in *The Eclogues*, Virgil's father was one of the losers. *The Eclogues* present the rural charm of the Greek poet Theocritus, but with some updates, including a piece on an imminent imperial baby so Messianic that many in the Middle Ages took Virgil for a Christian before his time.

The Georgics likewise use the Greek poet Hesiod's technique of versifying practical advice and apply them to Italian farming. Virgil's guide blends praise of hands-on graft with a pious respect for the earth as a living thing and **Dryden** rightly called it "the best poem by the best poet" in Latin. No Latin verse betters the work's concluding myth.

Homer provides the sources for Virgil's epic, *The Aeneid*. In telling the story of how the Trojans founded Rome, Virgil draws on *The Odyssey* to describe how they arrived and *The Iliad* to depict them battling for it. The work echoes, adapts and even translates Homer. It was nearly finished on his death and, because it wasn't sufficiently polished, the poet asked that it be burned. Virgil agonised over the project, thinking he must have been mad to undertake it and certainly there was madness in his obsessiveness. His technique involved working and reworking drafts, settling on about a line a day "licking them into shape" according to his biographer, "as a mother wolf does her cubs" – an appropriate image for a poet whose greatest work anticipates the birth of Romulus.

Voltaire

FRANÇOIS-MARIE AROUET

born Paris 1694; died Paris 1778

I may be suffocated, but it will be under a shower of roses.

ON HIS DEATH-BED, TO WELL-WISHERS

VOLTAIRE EMBODIED the Age of Enlightenment. He was a man of many excellent parts: his *oeuvre* consists of plays (tragedy and comedy), poetry (including the epic), pamphlets, letters, essays on any number of subjects and, most famously, his fable-like stories. He was committed to reason, order and tolerance, using his unfaltering wit to condemn any kind of political or religious tyranny, as well as the uneven distribution of wealth in society. In much of this, he resembled his friend **Rousseau**, although the two fell out. His chief hatred was "infamy", as he called the Church's corruption and hypocrisy – and in turn the Church did all it could to portray him as a demonic figure.

In fact, his was a faith made stronger by his capacity to doubt and to ask questions. He stayed a while in England – he was exiled for lampooning the winner of a poetry prize he had expected to win – where he met **Pope** and **Gay** and became deeply attracted to Newton's way of viewing the world. Back in France, he advocated the British political system and was again exiled, finding refuge with Frederick the Great of Prussia.

His wanderings make him seem like the eponymous hero of his story *Candide*, who travels around Europe during a period of war. Candide's travelling companion is his tutor, Dr Pangloss – a man with such a Utopian view of society that when Candide recoils at the increasing carnage they encounter his teacher reassures him that "All is for the best in the best of all possible worlds."

The work's much-discussed ending, "We must cultivate our garden", is optimistic, but not glibly so. The whole is a bitter attack on complacency and is typical of Voltaire's longing for change. He was considered a hero of the Revolution he did not live to see and in 1791 his body was brought back to Paris to be buried in the Panthéon, where Charles de la Villette proclaimed, "The Glorious Revolution was the fruit of his works."

Vonnegut Jr

KURT

born Indianapolis, Indiana 1922

There's another clear moral to this tale now that I think about it. When you're dead you're dead. And yet another moral occurs to me now. Make love when you can. It's good for you.

MOTHER NIGHT

KURT VONNEGUT IS ONE of the most effective experimental writers working today, not least because of his accessible, chatty style. This apparent simplicity welcomes readers into his complex and often personal view of the world.

He is a satirist with a mission. There is a shock that resounds through his work, deriving from his own experience of war. In 1944, he witnessed the bombing of Dresden, with its unprecedented number of victims. He recalls the event in many of his books, most famously in *Slaughterhouse Five*.

There Vonnegut identifies himself strongly with his hero, Billy Pilgrim. In other books, the author interacts with his characters, advising them on how to bear their "lot" before abandoning them; but we learn that Billy's experience is Vonnegut's. That is, before he is abducted by aliens who enable him to see all of time, including his own future, making him feel powerless to change anything. The narrative is capable of responding to the horrors of the past and the future with nothing more than the shrugging refrain, "So it goes." Its insistence makes the author's voice a surprisingly loud one, railing at our indifference.

Characters travel from book to book, culminating in *Breakfast of Champions*, which Vonnegut wrote as a 50th birthday present to himself. Regular readers again encounter Mr Rosewater, whose philanthropy is so random that its beneficiaries find him deeply suspicious, and Rosewater's favourite writer ever, Kilgore Trout, who seems to have come up with many of Vonnegut's ideas. But Trout can't help being one of those ideas himself. He is stuck in a world where authors vie for a divine kind of omnipotence, and are unhappy to accept it in its present guilty state.

Walcott

DEREK

born St Lucia 1930

This wound I have stitched into
  Plunkett's character.
He has to be wounded, affliction
  is one theme
of this work, this fiction,
  since every 'I' is a

fiction finally. Phantom narrator, resume:
Tumbly. Blue holes for his eyes.
  And Scottie wiser
when the shock passed. Plain men.
  Not striking. Not handsome.

OMEROS

DEREK WALCOTT IS ONE of the greatest poets writing in English at the moment. He won the Nobel Prize for Literature in 1993.

He was born on the Caribbean island of St Lucia and his education had a British imperial slant – he was taught to think of his homeland as a good naval base. Throughout his work, there is a tension between his love of English language and literature and his native culture. He admires **Conrad** and says that when he began writing, he modelled his poems on those of **Yeats** or **Dylan Thomas**. Early on, though, he was crafting stanzas with strong calypso rhythms and Creole *patois*.

Other cultures merge in Walcott's work, which sometimes tries to find a place for voodoo within a Christian framework or a way to accommodate Hindu myths. The experience of empire and displacement leaves the poet with harsh choices between them all and **Homer** begins to show a way to reconcile them. The figure of Odysseus, the island wanderer, is present in his earliest poems. Later, Walcott wrote a play, *The Odyssey*, and approached the epic theme in his greatest work so far, *Omeros*.

Its virtuosity is breathtaking and Walcott's sumptuous sound-world is best appreciated when the author reads it. He takes **Dante**'s stanza form, but slows it down with the metre. Some of the rhymes work best in a Caribbean accent (bars/claws); some are freer still (soundless/sandals). If the text involves Creole, he translates it and makes the translation fit beautifully. But he is being more than just stylish. He sees the process of working towards a rhyme as akin to redemption. Just as his puns reveal much about language, so the harmony his words create can unite the factions that produce them.

Warner

SYLVIA TOWNSEND

born Harrow 1893; died Dorset 1978

'You look very well in black, my child. Most women do, and it is providential since life compels us to mourn so often.'...

SUMMER WILL SHOW

SYLVIA TOWNSEND WARNER'S work combines an intimate knowledge of organised religion and its occult equivalents. She was an expert on witchcraft, but also spent many years of her life co-editing 10 volumes of Tudor church music. The contrast is especially evident in *Mr Fortune's Maggot*, in which a missionary persuades natives to attend church, but can make little impact on their very alternative lives.

Her more sympathetic characters are constrained by conventions and search for their personal freedoms. The heroine of *Lolly Willowes* is a spinster aunt surrounded by pious relatives, whom she scandalises by leaving London for an extraordinary village whose name, Great Mop, attracts her on a map (the book is full of such small but potentially life-changing signs). But even their Black Masses fail to interest her and she can only fully enjoy her liberation in the civilised company of the Devil.

Warner's heroines seek a liberty that some readers find peculiarly feminist, but although she shows society to be dominated by men, above all it is the individual who must be free. She lived her life braving public outrage, notably over her open lesbianism. Her writing shows a hatred of hypocrisy, but when she exposes society's flaws, she does so in an entertaining, compassionate way, with characters more likely to charm than shock.

Waugh

EVELYN

born London 1903; died Combe Florey, Somerset 1966

'The problem of architecture as I see it,' he told a journalist who had come to report on the progress of his surprising creation of ferro-concrete and aluminium, 'is the problem of all art – the elimination of the human element from the consideration of form... All ill comes from man,' he said gloomily; 'please tell your readers that.'

DECLINE AND FALL

EVELYN WAUGH WAS ONE of the funniest English novelists of the 20th century. His trick was to provide a narrative that is essentially dead-pan and to let the characters come up with the absurdities on their own. The result is a completely convincing account of the vapid pretensions he observed among the upper middle class of the 20s and 30s.

In essence, it was the same emptiness **T. S. Eliot** portrayed in *The Waste Land*, as Waugh recognised. *A Handful of Dust* takes its title from that poem. In it a man responds to his marriage crisis by running away to the Amazon, where he must read the complete works of **Dickens** forever to the man who rescued him from near death. Such English eccentricity, located in this heart of darkness, conveys a horror all of its own.

Other novels draw more directly on Waugh's experience, including the depressing time he spent as a schoolmaster (in *Decline and Fall*) and his stint as a journalist for the *Daily Mail*, who posted him to Africa, where his refusal to condemn Mussolini's actions in Abyssinia (now Ethiopia) attracted attention: this work provided material for the farcical *Scoop* and *Black Mischief*. The *Sword of Honour* trilogy derives from his time in the Royal Marines during World War Two.

Waugh became a Catholic in 1930 and this increasingly affected his writing, with religious novels and biographies of saints appearing later in his career. The most famous fruit of this thinking is *Brideshead Revisited*, blending sensuality and guilt to impart a queasy aristocratic nostalgia. The prose's elegance came less naturally to Waugh than the more economical comedy of his earlier books, but stands as a wistful *aubade* to a lost generation.

Wells

H.G.   **born Bromley, Kent 1866; died London 1946**

Fruit, by the by, was all their diet. These people of the remote future were strict vegetarians, and while I was with them, in spite of some carnal cravings, I had to be frugivorous also. Indeed, I found afterwards that horses, cattle, sheep, dogs had followed the Ichthyosaurus into extinction.

THE TIME MACHINE

H.G. WELLS DESCRIBED himself as a first-rate second-rate thinker. He is primarily remembered for his science fiction works, notably *The Time Machine* and *The War of the Worlds*, which relates the story of an alien invasion of Earth. Less popularly recognised are those stories which study contemporary society as acutely as his factual work, such as *Kipps: A Modern Utopia*, whose critique of how wealth is distributed would have alarmed readers at the turn of the century.

His thought was profoundly apocalyptic, on a par with **Aldous Huxley**, whose grandfather had taught him science. In *The Time Machine*, a scientist invents a way to propel himself into the furthest reaches of the future. Far from finding humanity at last at peace with itself, he discovers a world where the "leisured classes" have become charming but brainless, living in grisly symbiosis with the sinister troglodytes that centuries of oppression have made the working classes: they are called Morlocks, and claim their wages in human flesh.

Wells drew on his considerable scientific knowledge to tell his story. **Jules Verne** also had a strong influence on him, but modern science fiction owes its more visionary aspects to Wells. Still, he was an outspoken social reformer above all, strongly (if briefly) identified with the Socialist Fabian Society. He disdained social conventions in life as well as literature, and although he had a charmed marriage, had been reluctant to endure the actual institution. He supported World War One, thinking it would "end all wars", but by the end of the next, he saw no hope for a mankind perpetually at war with itself, concluding that it had lost all power over its cannibalistic impulses.

Welty

EUDORA

born Jackson, Mississippi 1909

There she was! Come for her shampoo an' set. Why, Mrs. Fletcher, in an hour an' twenty minutes she was layin' up there in the Babtist Hospital with a seb'm pound son. It was that close a shave. I declare, if I hadn't been so tired I would of drank up a bottle of gin that night.

PETRIFIED MAN

EUDORA WELTY BELONGS to that tradition of American writers from the South who rejoice in a strong sense of place. Like **Mark Twain**, her place is the Mississippi, notably the imaginary but real enough town of Morgana. Indeed, her writings would have comforted him because they illustrate that the region's distinctive dialect has not died out as he had feared after all.

She writes novels and short stories strongly led by speech. She has noted her admiration for the late **V.S. Pritchett** for this and she can make a chance remark similarly telling or loaded. For her, form is as important as meaning. When she writes about her technique in *The Eye of a Story* she speaks of the relationship her words have to one another and of a beauty that lies waiting for us in a story that is seldom as inevitable in life. This can make her pieces almost musical, with narrative patterns reaching our ears as though they had been there all along.

The words themselves are often snatches of gossip assembled to tell a larger story, such as the example above, overheard amid the noise and cross-purposes of chatter in a hair-dresser's. But overall the effect is more coherent than that. She has been compared to **Faulkner** for her skill at chronicling the South in times of decadence, but unlike other modernist writers, her work does not convey a sense of fragmentation.

In fact, if anything, her stories seek reconciliations and love in a way more reminiscent of **Carson McCullers**, who shares her sense of community. *Losing Battle* aims for this most adventurously: Welty's ear for conversation's harmonies portrays an extended Southern family coming together rather than falling apart.

West

NATHANAEL   **born New York 1903; died Los Angeles 1940**

Some time ago, a publisher asked me to write a biography, and I decided to do one of E.F. Fitzgerald. Fortunately, before commencing my study, I met Samuel Perkins who told me that he had written a biography of Fitzgerald the biographer of Hobson the biographer of Boswell... we will all go rattling down the halls of time, each one in his or her turn a tin can on the tail of Doctor Johnson.

MRS MCGEENEY, IN THE DREAM
LIFE OF BALSO SNELL

NATHANAEL WEST
The Day of the Locust and
The Dream Life of Balso Snell

IN THE 20TH CENTURY, many writers from the US have fictionalised soullessness, alienation, the death of the American dream. Nathanael West was one of the first, the bleakest and the best. He has not been widely read until fairly recently, but in his small body of work (four short novels) he identifies the roots of modern pain more efficiently than most of his successors.

In *The Dream Life of Balso Snell*, the narrator disappears up the Trojan horse's backside, to meet scholars, prodigies and myths and hear their stories. They are all as lonely as he is, in a world where only the misfits are beautiful. West's telling relies on a **Joyce**-like pastiche of styles, all held together with the dream-like fluency of the Surrealists.

His next protagonist encounters the same range of lost voices pleading for his attention: the columnist in *Miss Lonely Hearts* becomes a vessel for the misery of his anonymous correspondents. West's interest in style continues, but the letters in the text seem less like parodies.

When West parodies, he can do it without love, targeting the rags-to-riches novel in *A Cool Million*. Its hero, Lemuel Pitkin, is far from the local boy made good. For all his optimism and letters home, he becomes caught between extremists through an ex-President. He is dismembered throughout the story and dies still hoping for a rise, still trying to send money to his parents.

West spent five years as a script-writer in California before dying in a car crash. His circumstances produced his last and longest work, *The Day of the Locust*, a less sparing, more real glimpse at despair, culminating in scenes from the Napoleonic wars re-enacted on a film set.

383

Wharton

EDITH

born New York c. 1861; died St. Brice-sous-Forêt 1937

One of your great-grandfathers signed the Declaration, and another was a general on Washington's staff... These are things to be proud of, but they have nothing to do with rank or class. New York has always been a commercial community, and there are not more than three families in it who can claim an aristocratic origin in the real sense of the word.

THE AGE OF INNOCENCE

EDITH WHARTON WAS A novelist born into a privileged family, wealthy enough to flee the war-torn American South and return to settle in New York without too much discomfort. Her writing shows she was well-placed to record the city at its most opulent, but her background gives readers cause to be grateful that she wrote at all – to her family it would have seemed too much like working for a living. Still, she narrated the harsher fates of those around her.

The scenery for her drama is much like that of her friend and mentor, **Henry James**. Both have an ear for society's often oppressive niceties and an interest in the contrast between America and Europe. They share themes, too, both writing about an America that is coming of age and its emerging class system. In an atmosphere of new wealth, people become commodities. Wharton's heroines are as collectable art works as Isabel Archer in *The Portrait of a Lady* and in *The House of Mirth*, her first successful novel, Lily Bart is even more trapped by social convention than Daisy Miller. But Wharton suffers from the comparison. While she was fond of her intimate's "elaborate hesitancies", she favoured more direct language, once waiting for him to finish a lengthy sentence excusing some breach of etiquette before asking him, "Where's the Post Office?"

White

PATRICK

born London 1912; died Sydney 1990

It appeared that pure happiness must await the final crumbling, when love would enter into love, becoming an endlessness, blowing at last, indivisible, indistinguishable, over the brown earth.

VOSS

PATRICK WHITE WAS AN Australian novelist, a mysterious figure who seems to have shared the dogged singularity of the heroes he created. He was born in London and was educated in England, finishing his studies at King's College, Cambridge, but spent much of his childhood in Australia, where he worked on the land. His father was a sheep farmer.

The two novels that have brought him greatest acclaim show solitary heroes battling with land in the outback: Stan Parker in *The Tree of Man* is trying to survive, Johann Voss in *Voss* is trying to explore. But they are not simply tales of pioneers from Australia's past. The narrative finds poetic truths as it realises man's relationship with the earth and the earth is vital to the characters' relationships with one another. Before setting out to cross the continent, Voss meets Laura. What begins as an exercise in monomania becomes a labour of love.

The severe German explorer and the ingénue girl exchange letters, but feel themselves sharing new knowledge without needing to write. They find a love as unbounded as the vast spaces of desert that sustain it: Voss writes, "No ordinary House could have contained my feelings, but this great one in which greater longings are ever free to grow."

Among his men, who crack under the extraordinary strain and stage a chaotic mutiny, Voss is alone, driven on only by his vision. It remains incomprehensible to those around him. So it seemed to White himself sometimes. He was awarded the Nobel Prize for Literature in 1973, but aroused controversy by failing to accept it in person, sending

his friend, the painter Sidney Nolan, to receive it on his behalf. He used the money to fund an award for underestimated older Australian writers, all of this was deemed "ungracious" by the literary world: it is hard to imagine the author being too upset by the rebukes.

Whitman

WALT   born West Hills, Long Island 1819; died Camden, New Jersey 1892

Ebb, ocean of life, (the flow will return,)

Cease not your moaning you fierce old
mother,

Endlessly cry for your castaways, but
fear not, deny not me,

Rustle not up so hoarse and angry
against my feet as I touch you or gather
from you.

AS I EBB'D WITH THE OCEAN OF LIFE

WHITMAN IS TO AMERICAN poetry what **Virgil** is to Latin. He stands as a genuinely national poet, who sounds a uniting voice across his country after a time of civil bloodshed. He is aware of his prophetic role and shares Virgil's conviction that a divine spirit permeates everything.

And yet he is the opposite of a classical poet. He parades little learning and pounds out his words in an untaught rhythm. Although **Hopkins** tried analysing his scansion into Greek units, it is easier to feel the poetry's "passion, pulse and power". Whitman may have composed with care and revised like a fidget, but he never sounds fussed or hesitant.

He does not read as a political poet either, but just as Virgil hymned the new order, Whitman's lines venerate democracy. From the epic *Song of Myself* onwards, he establishes his absolute equality with anyone or thing there is. In *Calamus*, this "camerado" feeling becomes effusive enough for some to find it homo-erotic (it disgusted **Dickinson**, and Whitman lost his clerical job for it). In *Drum-Taps*, people die for it. During the Civil War, Whitman worked as a stretcher-bearer, a friend to everyone as ever. When it was over and Lincoln had been assassinated, he mourned a lost leader in *O Captain, My Captain!* and *When Lilacs Last in the Dooryard Bloom'd*.

His generosity of spirit is irresistible. His arrogance in *Song of Myself* (which he was to call Walt Whitman) sits well with his humility: "If you want me again look for me under your boot-soles". His poetry admits any extreme: "I am vast, I contain multiples." For many, he is the voice of liberty: a hero of the Beats and a huge presence in verse in Spanish, notably **Lorca** and **Neruda**.

Wilde

OSCAR

born Dublin 1854; died Paris 1900

And out of the bronze of the image of The Sorrow that endureth for Ever he fashioned an image of The Pleasure that abideth for a Moment.

THE ARTIST

FOR OSCAR WILDE, living was an art. Much of his work is ornate, even precious. Just as he embodied an aesthetic ideal, a beautiful man devoted to beautiful things, so his writing comes to represent the decadent 1890s in which he flourished.

But there was more to him than camp. He recognised it as if from a distance and parodied it in turn. He saw the finest minds of his generation obsessed with manners and sensuality. In their London, he was a cultural and sexual outsider (a gay man born in Dublin) and he needed the manners to play at their game and craved the pleasures with which they toyed.

Both art and life were involved in that parody. He went to America in 1881. Gilbert and Sullivan's operetta *Patience* arrived with its Wildean hero in 1882. In turn, he took their brand of comedy further and in *The Importance of Being Earnest*, travestied not just British institutions, but a whole way of life.

In spite of the aesthetic creeds of the day, work like this was more than "art for art's sake". While his writing may celebrate lushness of language, his stories were told to entertain his own children. A tale such as *The Happy Prince* goes further, urging greater care for the poor. If even that seems sentimental, then we should remember his campaign to end the child labour he witnessed in prison. He was undoubtedly clever, excelling in Latin and Greek verse, composing the sumptuous *Salomé* in French (even though it was first to be performed in London, before the Lord Chamberlain prevented it), but his greatest gift was for simplicity. His compassion for his fellow prisoners in *The Ballad of Reading Gaol* is without ornament and as his Happy Prince shows, the argument, "As he is no longer beautiful, he is no longer useful," is flawed.

MAJOR WORKS

POETRY
Poems (1881)

The Ballad of Reading Gaol (1898)

PROSE
The Happy Prince (1888)

Lord Arthur Savile's Crime (1891)

A House of Pomegranates (1891)

The Picture of Dorian Gray (1891)

PLAYS
The Duchess of Padua (1891)

Lady Windermere's Fan (1892)

A Woman of No Importance (1893)

Salomé (1894)

An Ideal Husband (1895)

The Importance of Being Earnest (1895)

Wilder

THORNTON

born Wisconsin 1897; died Connecticut 1975

The Bible says that God created man on the eighth day and rested, but each of those days was many millions of years long. That day of rest must have been a short one. Man is not an end but a beginning. We are at the beginning of the second week. We are children of the eighth day.

THE EIGHTH DAY

THORNTON WILDER WAS an American novelist and playwright whose popularity has proved enduring, mostly because of its winning blend of modernist techniques with traditional optimism.

He grew up in China and on returning to the United States, became a successful academic. He trained as an archaeologist, working in Rome, which provided material for his first novel, *The Cabala*, in which American students come across secret societies: the classic situation of the new world meeting the mysterious old one. Rome is also the setting for *The Ides of March*, a novel in letters about Julius Caesar. But the traditional view of a more innocent mid-west America prevails elsewhere, as in *Heaven's My Destination*.

He is most famous for the play *Our Town*. At first it seems remarkable that a piece owing so much to the experiments of **Pirandello** should be staged so regularly by younger school children, but its devices, such as the empty set and the stage manager's commentary, act as more than an effective "young person's guide to the theatre". It enables the audience to see an ordinary community from a new angle, so as to look to the little things – here, through the eyes of a dead woman spirited back to her 12th birthday party.

Ultimately, Wilder's work is full of the sense that life is worth living. In both prose and drama, he presents life as a cycle, with love bridging the gap between the living and the dead.

Williams

TENNESSEE   born Columbus, Mississippi 1911; died New York 1983

Don't you just love these long, rainy afternoons in New Orleans when an hour isn't just an hour – but a little piece of eternity dropped into your hands – and who knows what to do with it?

BLANCHE, IN A STREETCAR NAMED DESIRE

TENNESSEE WILLIAMS WROTE extraordinarily powerful and perfectly-formed dramas. They are distinctive in atmosphere: the action takes place in oppressive heat and this serves to bring out tensions that are physical, often sexual. He is most remarkable for his creation of female characters. His heroines are unstable and prone to those who can manipulate them. They are motivated by a desire that can be at odds with their apparent purity or refinement and that can lead them to madness.

Williams' life gives commentators clues about these concerns. He was homosexual – once he had come out, a flamboyant one. As a child he had formed a very close relationship with his sister. An incident of his father's violence traumatised her and she underwent a frontal lobotomy.

This might begin to explain why Williams creates unsympathetic men such as the overbearing father figure in *Cat on a Hot Tin Roof* or the poker players in *A Streetcar Named Desire*. That play's heroine can manifest insatiable lust as well as horror at the sexuality of a late husband whose memory she comes to pity. The secrets in a Williams play are guilty ones that will shock his characters.

But his dramatic influences are as important. He knew he wanted to become a playwright when he saw **Ibsen**'s *Ghosts*, and many of his great strengths as a writer are Ibsen's. They are both natural poets. Williams wrote poetry, even working for a time as a "poet waiter" in Greenwich Village. Although none of his plays is in verse, his ear for the music of dialogue and for the tellingly-repeated phrase can give his plays the form of a poem. His technique has transferred easily to film, with *Baby Doll* written expressly for the screen.

MAJOR WORKS

The Glass Menagerie (1945)

A Streetcar Named Desire (1947)

Summer and Smoke (1948)

The Rose Tattoo (1951)

Cat on a Hot Tin Roof (1955)

Suddenly Last Summer (1958)

Sweet Bird of Youth (1959)

389

Williams

WILLIAM CARLOS

born New Jersey 1883; died New Jersey 1963

The poem

if it reflects the sea

reflects only

its dance

upon that profound depth

where

it seems to triumph.

ASPHODEL, THAT GREENY FLOWER

WILLIAM CARLOS WILLIAMS worked as an obstetrician for most of his life to support himself as a poet. Although he would always "Make It New", as his friend **Ezra Pound** asked of all good Modernists, his work never fitted into a particular school of writing.

Still, his poetry appeared in the Imagist collection Pound published in 1914. Like other poets in the book, he favoured economy of expression and short lines. His chief poetic credo was " – say it – no ideas but in things". Imagist poetry assembled such things for the reader to contemplate and Williams retained a similar interest in the visual, as in *Pictures from Breughel*. Still, it is in Williams that one has the strongest sense of a poem being a thing in itself. By far his most famous poem is not really Imagist: it is a note on a fridge door, apologising for eating some plums. Although the words are delicately placed, we can imagine the person who had been saving the plums for breakfast feeling unappeased.

Although his work is experimental, commentators have tried to intellectualise it out of the reach of the readers Williams would most have wanted. Like **Wordsworth**, he wanted to bring ordinary speech into the rhythms of his poetry. *Paterson* is a long poem attempting to achieve this. He called it "a reply to Greek and Latin with the bare hands". Here poetry sheds its ornament to become a way of communicating. Transcripts of a taped interview appear, as does a quote from a scholar explaining how Greek metres can reflect the way people speak.

The piece is a gift to his town in New Jersey, full of population figures, histories, an idyll here and a letter there. The work's joy is that it is composed of small things, but the whole is greater than its parts. The idea takes off from the things at last.

Wodehouse

P.G.   born Guildford, Surrey 1881; died Southampton, Long Island 1975

Other men love you. Freddie Threepwood loves you. Just add me to the list. That is all I ask. Muse on me from time to time. Reflect that I may be an acquired taste. You probably did not like olives the first time you tasted them. Now you probably do. Give me the same chance you would an olive.

LEAVE IT TO PSMITH

IN AN EXTREMELY LONG writing career, P.G. Wodehouse wrote some 120 novels, besides plays and the words for many successful Broadway musicals. The latter show their age, while the novels have lost nothing of their freshness, even though they are seldom set any later than the 1920s.

Shortly after leaving school, he began writing stories about the schoolboy Psmith, who would grow up in later stories to become a journalist, before being able to put in appearances at Blandings, the home of Lord Emsworth, itself the scene of many stories…

Indeed, Wodehouse's characters are most at home in luxurious country piles, or at the Drones Club; although some venture to the East End of London, they are quite stranded there. If they are bemused by the intrigues that embroil them and greet them with language to match, the author can find himself in the same fix. The formula that distiguishes the Jeeves and Wooster stories provided him with the perfect solution. For Wooster as narrator he invented a language consisting of half-finished sentences, conflated quotations and images plucked from panic through which Wodehouse could share his protagonist's bewilderment.

He sustains several plots at once, all hinging on seemingly insignificant props – flower-pots, policeman's helmets, umbrellas… ultimately, it is only Jeeves, his inscrutable butler, "the gentleman's personal gentleman", who can make any sense of it all. Beneath Jeeves' façade of compliance lies an evil genius for manipulation, excusable only if it prevents our hero from looking the chump he really is.

Wolfe

TOM

born Richmond, Virginia 1931

Had his father ever played around? It wasn't out of the question. He was a handsome man. He had the chin. Yet Sherman couldn't imagine it.
And by the time he saw Brooklyn Bridge, he stopped trying to. In a few minutes he would be on Wall Street.

BONFIRE OF THE VANITIES

TOM WOLFE HAS WORKED as a journalist and commentator on his times, but is now equally acclaimed as a novelist after the huge success of *The Bonfire of the Vanities.*

Its examination of the legal process uses Wolfe's experience as a court reporter. He worked for a number of newspapers, including the *New York Herald Tribune*, after an award-winning piece on Cuba. But he is better known as an observer of fashions and a pop critic, writing in *Esquire* and *Rolling Stone*. Some accuse him of following trends, others think he sets them. If anything, he does society the service of pointing out when modishness has gone too far and telling us when moral crusades stop being holy.

He follows **Ken Kesey**'s drug-preaching bus West in *The Electric Kool-Aid Acid Test*, wondering how its passengers can co-ordinate anything. He saves more scorn for Leonard Bernstein in *Radical Chic*, savouring every last touch of the conductor's party in honour of the Black Panthers: the glitterati on Park Avenue try so hard to seem groovy that they embroil themselves in *faux pas* around the Bronx's toughest black leaders.

In *The Bonfire of the Vanities*, Wolfe points to the deeper human problems. He has a cast as large and riotous as any 19th-century novelist: many of his characters are distinct types. But in a nightmarish New York, whose dangers he depicts so vividly, the unlikely figures genuinely eager to improve the city find their best efforts scuppered by extremists from all communities, while moderate functionaries yield to venality.

Woolf

VIRGINIA

born London 1882; died Rodmell, Sussex 1941

Hunted out of existence, maimed, frozen, the victims of cruelty and injustice (she had heard Richard say so over and over again) – no, she could feel nothing for the Albanians, or was it the Armenians? but she loved her roses (didn't that help the Armenians?) – the only flowers she could bear to see cut.

MRS DALLOWAY

VIRGINIA WOOLF'S UNIQUE STYLE and approach to fiction meant that, with **Joyce**, she had an immense impact on the the modern novel.

She was born into literary circles and was the leading light of the Bloomsbury group, a coterie of leisured intellectuals huddled around the British Museum. In *A Room of One's Own*, she shows how hard society makes it for women to write fiction: this comfortable atmosphere (money and a room of her own) she found invaluable, especially given her persistently frail mental balance, which would eventually lead to her suicide by drowning.

She has been called a feminine modernist. She was unconvinced by **Joyce**'s *Ulysses*, but took many of its innovations in new directions of her own. In *Mrs Dalloway* she employed a similar time-scale, indicated by Big Ben throughout, but chimed at moments more determined by the character's thoughts than the passage of hours.

In Woolf, the state of mind takes over all other realities, rather than respond to them as Joyce's creations might. *To the Lighthouse* explores the difference between men and women further, significantly through the frustrated artist Lily Briscoe. The heroine, Mrs Ramsay, is as anxious a hostess as Mrs Dalloway, with inner thoughts somewhere between fuss and euphoria.

Man and woman merge in the unusually exuberant *Orlando*, the story of an Elizabethan boy soon to be a Victorian girl. The book provides a rare glimpse of Woolf's humour. While her other heroines can prioritise their reflections in a way that betrays a snobbery the author confesses, here, readers looking for Woolf's self-revelation in fiction might seek intimations of her own sexuality.

Wordsworth

WILLIAM   **born Cockermouth 1770; died Grasmere 1850**

Our birth is but a sleep and a forgetting:
The soul that rises with us, our life's Star,
Hath elsewhere had its setting,
And cometh from afar.

INTIMATIONS OF IMMORTALITY

WORDSWORTH LIVED MOST of his life in the Lake District, which provided the setting for much of his poetry. He began to write poetry at Cambridge, but it was only after he left and met **Coleridge** that a revolution took place in his work.

The two jointly published *Lyrical Ballads* and

Wordsworth's contribution was the more substantial – even more so in the second edition, which included a second volume of poems and Wordsworth's famous preface defending his new mode of poetry. In it he argued that the very ornate poetry of the 18th century was flawed and that true poetry consisted in "the spontaneous overflow" of feeling and should be written in the "real language of men" – the rural, marginalised characters of his area and work.

Almost all of his important poetry was written in the decade that followed. His *Intimations* ode is the most perfect statement of one of his central motifs – the loss of spontaneity and inspiration as we grow older, and the need to re-imagine the world in order to compensate for that loss. *Tintern Abbey* is a similar example.

During these years Wordsworth all but completed his greatest work, the autobiographical epic *The Prelude*. He considered it only part of a larger project, which was never completed – *The Prelude* was not published until after Wordsworth's death, when the final title was agreed, and it describes the poet's development from his love of books and nature to sympathy with all mankind. It includes a description of events surrounding the French Revolution as its backdrop, but omits big moments in the poet's personal life, most notably the birth of a daughter to a mistress he never married.

His later achievement was his criticism and a number of impressive sonnet collections. In 1843 he succeeded Southey as Poet Laureate and died seven years later, like **Shakespeare**, on St George's Day. He has been, with **Milton**, the greatest literary influence on all subsequent English poetry.

Yeats

W.B.   **born Sandymount 1865; died Roquebrune 1939**

But naught they heard, for they are ever

listening,

the dewdrops, for the sound of their own

dropping.

MISERRIMUS

YEATS IS ONE OF poetry's towering figures. He was the greatest Irish poet to write in English and perhaps the greatest poet writing in English in his day. His verse seems simple and direct. He wrote that it should be that way: "I said, 'A line will take us hours maybe/ Yet if it does not seem a moment's thought/ Our stitching and unstitching has been naught.'"

It is hard to believe that even those lines occasioned toil. Yeats' expressed poetic goals often seem strange. He was an expert in the occult, on a quest for both Irish and Eastern spirituality, forming "Celtic Dawn" as a student, investigating Noh plays and the poetry of **Tagore**. Throughout his life he balanced pragmatism with dreaminess, quite in command of the Abbey Theatre's day-to-day running, yet easily duped (and doped) into watching for leprechauns; consistently attractive to women, yet allured by what he thought was his beloved Maud Gonne's chastity; avidly wanting to form a new Irish poetry, yet unable to master Irish, and uncomprehending when the experimental plays he produced in Dublin occasioned rioting.

Finally, he believed his writing had the power to change things. Here he was less deluded. He expressed some guilt that a play of his might have sent viewers to their deaths in the Easter Rising of 1916. It was thanks to his poetry that he became a figure of national importance, a senator, charged with the Republic's coinage. For all his life's complexities, his poetry succeeded with a direct simplicity that became clearer still over 50 years of writing. The poet's rages or yearnings are felt immediately. His half-rhymes and slackening metres seem to be buckling under the weight of passion, however often he stitched and unstitched them.

Zola

ÉMILE

born Paris 1840; died Paris 1902

*The mechanic shrugged. He despised
people with the gift of the gab, who take
up politics as others go in for the law, to
make big money out of phraseology.*

GERMINAL, TR. LEONARD TANTOCK

ÉMILE ZOLA DESCRIBED himself as an
experimental novelist. He settled in Paris to lead the
professional life of a writer, which he pursued with
uncommon vigour, producing a number of studiedly
"naturalist" texts. He filled his prose with details so
meticulously researched that he was almost writing
up a laboratory test. A problem with his legacy is that
he anticipated the results. His readers are told they
will enter a world where a character's fate is
determined by his genetic make-up and physiology.

The result is that events seem inevitable and so all
the more tragic. Zola's artistry outdid his social
purpose. When Napoleon III lost power, he was able
to express his socialist views openly, even though his
famous letter beginning "J'accuse!" exposing a military
cover-up in the Dreyfus case, landed him a spell in
prison and on the run.

Most of his novels follow the fortunes of a family
during Napoleon III's reign and were published after
it, so that it was too late to implement the reforms
he advocated, and his claims to absolute naturalism
were impossible to prove. But he remains read for
the sheer scope of his project, covering French life in
all its aspects from bishops to call-girls.

Ibsen charged Zola with going into the sewer to
bathe in it rather than to cleanse it; and although it is
true Zola was unsparing in his ribald dialogue and
textual innuendo, he is left with the defence that he
is portraying people as a dehumanising, industrial
society has made them, rather than concluding that
human beings are necessarily beasts.

Index

Picture credits

The publishers would like to thank the following sources for their kind permission to reproduce the pictures in this book:

AKG London; Archive Photos; Ardis Publishers; Associated Press; Marion Boyars Publishers Ltd.; The British Library; Caledonian Newspapers Ltd.; Camera Press Ltd.; Jonathan Cape/Random House; Jean-Loup Charmet; Corbis-Bettmann /EWO Hoppe /Hulton-Deutsch Collection /Bob Krist /David Lees /Library of Congress /Michel Nicholson /Reuter /UPI /Oscar White; Dorset County Museum; Mary Evans Picture Library; Faber and Faber Publishers Ltd.; Fourth Estate Ltd.; Harper Collins Publishers;

The Harvill Press, London; Hodder and Stoughton; Hulton-Getty Images; Image Select /Ann Ronan Collection; Dan Jacobson; Jaico Publishers; Le Livre de Poche Publishers; Orion Publishing Group Ltd.; Peter Owen Ltd.; Penguin UK; Pictorial Press Limited /Waring Abbott /Rob Verhorst; Rex Features Ltd.; Popperfoto; Frank Spooner Pictures Ltd. /Viollet; Topham Picturepoint.

Every effort has been made to acknowledge correctly and contact the source and copyright holder of each picture, and Carlton Books Limited apologises for any unintentional errors or omissions which will be corrected in future editions of this book.